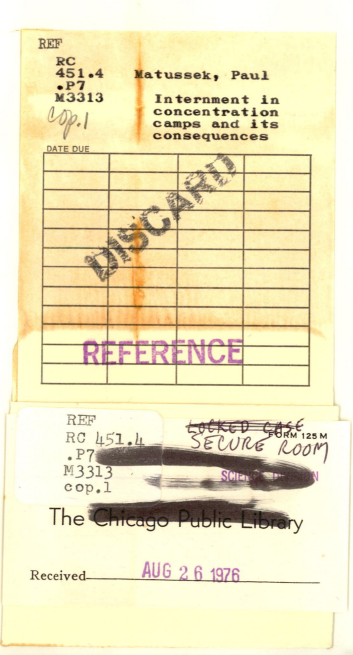

Internment in Concentration Camps and Its Consequences

By

Paul Matussek

With

Rolf Grigat · Hannelore Haiböck · Gert Halbach · Reiner Kemmler
David Mantell · Axel Triebel · Moshe Vardy · Gesine Wedel

Foreword by

Hans H. Strupp

Translated by Derek and Inge Jordan

With 19 Figures and 73 Tables

Springer-Verlag New York · Heidelberg · Berlin 1975

Professor Dr. med. Dr. phil. Paul Matussek, Leiter der Forschungsstelle für Psychopathologie und Psychotherapie in der Max-Planck-Gesellschaft, D-8000 München 40,
Montsalvatstraße 19

Professor Dr. Hans H. Strupp, Vanderbilt University, Nashville, Tennessee 37240, USA

Derek and Inge Jordan, 1495 Fisher Avenue, No. 24, Ottawa, Ontario K2C 3M9,
Canada

German Edition: Published 1971 with the Title "Monographien aus dem Gesamt-
gebiete der Psychiatrie", Psychiatry Series, Band 2 — Die Konzentrationslagerhaft
und ihre Folgen — Springer-Verlag Berlin · Heidelberg · New York

ISBN 0-387-07123-7   Springer-Verlag New York Heidelberg Berlin
ISBN 3-540-07123-7   Springer-Verlag Berlin Heidelberg New York

Foreword

It remained for Nazi Germany to design the most satanic psychological experiment of all time, the independent variables consisting of brutality, bestiality, physical and mental torture on an unprecedented scale. What were the effects of this massive assault on the human spirit, on man's ability to assimilate such experiences, if he survived physically?

While the terror of the Nazi concentration camps has been indelibly engraved in the history of Western civilization as its most shameful chapter, little systematic study has been addressed to the subsequent lives of that minority of inmates who were fortunate enough to escape physical annihilation and lived to tell about their nightmare.

Dr. PAUL MATUSSEK, a respected German psychiatrist, aided by a small group of collaborators, performed the task of identifying a group of victims (mostly Jews but also political prisoners), who, following their liberation, had settled in Germany, Israel, and the United States. By careful interviews, questionnaires, and psychological tests he brought to bear the methods of sensitive clinical inquiry on the experiences of those who dared to reminisce and who were sufficiently trusting to share their feelings and memories with clinical investigators. It is a telling commentary that many people, even after the passage of years, refused to respond. The study deals not only with the former inmates' current adjustment in terms of quality of their interpersonal relations, marriage, vocation, and outlook on life but also casts a searchlight on their developmental history and the extent to which it affected their ability to sustain the onslought of the concentration camp experience.

The analysis of the clinical data is sophisticated and sensitive. The results are brought into stark relief by the case histories and verbatim accounts, and throughout there lurk the memories of the horror to which these unfortunate men and women were exposed for months and years. Consider two vignettes: One man said: "A person who has been a prisoner can only tolerate another former inmate as a marital partner. No one else can understand what happened." A former attorney and judge who attempted to resettle in Berlin after the war but eventually decided to emigrate concluded: "For Jews there is no room in Germany." Like many others he found that the end of World War II had brought only new problems: survivors discovered that they were homeless, their families had been killed or dispersed, and their material possessions had been lost. No longer was there a place for them in their former society: They had become "displaced persons."

Professor MATUSSEK presents evidence that in a substantial majority of survivors the physical and psychological damage of the concentration camp experience was pervasive and lasting, ranging from what he called "psychophysical syndrome" to resignation and despair. In determining eligibility for compensation, physicians regularly underestimated the psychic damage to the victims. He explodes the notion of the "concentration syndrome" as an immutable entity; instead, the data pointed to manifold individual reaction patterns. Of poignant significance in its implications for the psychotherapist, the data underscored the continuity of reaction patterns and attitudes ingrained early in life, particularly the quality of the child's relationship to his mother as a determinant of his ability to relate to others, notably in times of stress.

Dr. MATUSSEK's study, despite formidable methodological and technical difficulties, is research of high quality. It is a fine amalgam of objectivity, clinical penetration, and compassionate understanding. It is rare that a research report becomes a deeply moving document. This book does. After I read it, I wept—not only for the members of my own family and the millions of innocent men, women, and children who perished in the holocaust, but also for the tragedy of man's awesome cruelty to his fellows, a phenomenon that unhappily did not become extinct with the death of Adolf Hitler.

Nashville, February 1975   HANS H. STRUPP

Preface to the English Edition

This book met with such an unexpectedly positive response in the German-speaking world that I wish it a similar success in the larger English-language family. The events I have written about, although they belong to the past, are still very relevant to today.

After World War II many people held the justified belief, or at least hope, that the crimes of the Nazi terror represented the ultimate hell of man's inhumanity to man. In certain respects this hope has been fulfilled: great wars, and above all the systematic extermination of large groups of people, have not been seen again on this scale. Yet cases of torture inflicted by one human being on another have not disappeared since that time. Rather, they continue to propagate, whether in the West or in the East. Wherever an authoritarian regime feels itself threatened by its opponents, or a nation confronted by its enemies, torture, terror and cruelty are part of the method. One way is to put detainees in camps, which creates living conditions resembling those in the Nazi concentration camps.

It is therefore not surprising that doctors and psychiatrists find that those who have survived such camps show symptoms like those recorded in former concentration camp inmates. It is thus customary to speak by analogy with the concentration-camp syndrome of the Vietnam syndrome, or in general of a survival syndrome. Such diagnostic labels now come so naturally to the lips of many physicians that no-one stops to ask what the syndrome actually consists of and — perhaps even more pertinently — what were the conditions during and after the detention period that produced it. Do all detainees have this syndrome? Must the terror have lasted for a certain time? Which of the stress factors are the most destructive as far as they can be measured from the late effects recorded? And finally, the important, much discussed question: Has the development of personality before the detention period any significance for coming to terms with terror in the camps?

Which factors play a part here?

This book is an attempt to answer these and similar questions, on the basis of studies of former concentration camp inmates. Such an investigation cannot, of course, make the infinite suffering of the past as if it had never happened. It can, however, help people to understand the physical and mental health damage that follows camp terror. It provides a corrective to outdated theories as well as to ideological generalizations. In this way it serves both the sufferer and science.

Munich, January 1975   PAUL MATUSSEK

Preface to the First German Edition

Ever since the end of the last war, researchers in various fields have been trying to discover how anybody could have survived the terror of the Nazi concentration camps. For example, doctors were particularly interested in determining the extent of the permanent or temporary health damage suffered by the survivors, but so far the studies made of these problems have failed to produce any coherent results. One important reason for this is that the cases were selected according to purely medical criteria. The doctor examined the patient either in order to treat some particular complaint or, as more frequently happened in the cases described in the literature, to prepare a medical report for pension purposes.

We wished to avoid the sources of error associated with such preselection, and we therefore tried to find a sample of ex-inmates of concentration camps which was as random as possible. It took us years to interview a sufficient number of such people.

Not only is the psychiatric literature on late injuries based on cases which were selected for the purpose of pension appraisal, it is also restricted to clinically relevant findings. This has meant that "peripheral phenomena", which are more difficult to study, have been ignored. But it is precisely such phenomena that are emphatically stressed in the reports some ex-inmates have published on their own experiences. In the course of their long drawn-out pension procedures these people have come to feel misunderstood because psychiatrists have devised a variety of diagnostic labels without coming to grips with the problems currently suffered by the ex-inmate. We have therefore tried to study the effect of incarceration on certain areas of existence, such as interpersonal contact, marriage, occupation, and Weltanschauung, quite independently of any psychiatric diagnosis.

Finally, we wish to drawn attention to the theoretical implications of our study. It was not our intention to add a new and unproven theory to the many others on the character and consequences of extreme stress. Instead, by using statistical methods to analyse the material we wished to establish a series of hypotheses or to test the relevance of certain assumptions and theories.

At this point we would like to thank the ex-inmates without whose cooperation this study would not have been possible. They did more than just sacrifice their time — quite often the old memories which were resurrected by the interviews imposed a severe strain on these people.

I must also thank the many persons who have participated in this project in one way or another over periods of months or years, on either a full-time or part-time basis. Special mention should be made of the persons who between 1958 and 1962 conducted the interviews and collected the data in Bavaria, Israel and New York. In the face of considerable difficulties and repeated refusals by ex-inmates to cooperate they managed to bring together all the material used in the present study

(Dr. RUBEN KOHEN-RAZ, Dr. STEFAN GERÖLY, Dipl.-Psych. AMREI HALBACH, Dipl.-Psych. GERT HALBACH, Dr. MARIE KALAU VOM HOFE, Dr. LISELOTTE KÖHLER, Dr. KARL-HEINZ MANDEL, Dr. VIKTORIA MICKANS, Dr. MOSHE VARDY). I am also grateful to Dr. LUDWIG BARTH, Dipl.-Psych. GISELA BERTULIS, Dipl.-Psych. ROLF GRIGAT, Dipl.-Psych. HANNELORE HAIBÖCK, Dipl.-Psych. GERT HALBACH, Dipl.-Psych. REINER KEMMLER, Dipl.-Psych. DAVID MANTELL, Dipl.-Psych. AXEL TRIEBEL and Dipl.-Psych. GESINE WEDEL for their invaluable and enthusiastic assistance in evaluating the interviews and compiling the manuscript. It is only possible to name a few of these people as co-authors on the title page, but this should not be taken to mean that the work the others performed was in any way less important or necessary. Although the individual contributions are difficult to assess, each person has played a decisive part in shaping the final form of this book, and I am much indebted to them.

Finally, it remains for me to express my thanks to Herr TROBERG, who at the time in question was President of the Regional Indemnification Office (Landesentschädigungsamt Bayern) in Bavaria, and also to his deputy, Herr MEIER. Without their friendly cooperation we would never have obtained the documents needed to put together the random sample which we were after.

Munich, January 1971 PAUL MATUSSEK

Contents

CHAPTER 1

Study Methods

I. Obtaining a Representative Sample of Persecutees

The broad scope of the problems to be studied indicated that the analysis would be a painstaking and long drawn-out process. It was thus necessary to limit the number of former persecutees to be included in the study sample.

In order to obtain an optimum group for study, the following selection criteria were laid down:

a) The sample would include only formerly persecuted individuals now living in Germany (Munich and environs), Israel, or New York.

b) The sample would include only persons persecuted on the grounds of what the regime then in power termed their "racial" origins (Jews), their "political" views (Communists, Socialists, etc.), or their "religious" beliefs (Catholic priests, Jehovah's Witnesses) [1].

c) The sample included only persons born in Germany or in Eastern Europe (mainly Poland) who were not over 65 years of age in 1960.

d) The sample included only persons who had been incarcerated in concentration camps or similar internment camps during the period of persecution and who had submitted claims for indemnification to the Landesentschädigungsamt München (Regional Indemnification Office, Munich).

Claims for indemnification could be based on the following: damage to health, financial loss, loss of freedom, or impairment of career prospects. It was immaterial whether one or more applications for indemnification had been made by persons to be included in our sample group. Thus, persons who had never submitted a claim for damages on account of impaired health could also be included.

In accordance with the above criteria, the group to be studied was put together as follows: The alphabetical index compiled by the Regional Indemnification Office in Munich contains the names of 210,811 former victims of persecution. Every 40th name was selected from these files, giving a total of 5,270 names. This number was further reduced by taking only former victims of persecution now living in Munich and who satisfied the above criteria. This selection procedure reduced the group to 737 persons.

However, when this group was broken down according to the reasons for persecution, it contained subgroups that were quantitatively too dissimilar. All those born in Eastern Europe had been persecuted on racial grounds; therefore every 7th

---

[1] In order to identify these groups succinctly and clearly, the terms "racial persecutees" or "persons persecuted on racial grounds" and similarly "political persecutees" and "religious persecutees" have been used throughout this report to characterize the interviewees on the basis of the persecution suffered.

name was picked out and included in the final list for study; every 3rd of the politically persecuted persons born in Germany was selected and included; and of the
racially persecuted persons born in Germany every 2nd name was included.

The number of former persecutees who had been incarcerated because of their
religious beliefs selected up to this point by the sampling procedure (2 Catholic priests
and 2 Jehovah's Witnesses) was increased to 10 by means of a specifically oriented
sampling procedure. We were able to evaluate the pension assessment documents of
9 of these interviewees. We would very much have liked to analyse the cases of
Protestant pastors to compare their treatment with that of Catholic priests, but there
were none on file at the Regional Indemnification Office in Munich.

This procedure left us with 217 of the 737 persecutees living in Munich and
environs. These were contacted by letter and visited. Sixty-six of them refused to
cooperate with the investigators or gave such fragmentary information that it was
useless for the purposes of our investigation. However, in the case of 26 of the 66
persons who opted out, it was at least possible to evaluate the indemnification claim
documents in order to obtain relevant medical data, and this information was in-
corporated in the Chapter on "Late-Appearing Damage to Health".

We had the addresses of only 47 former persecutees resident in Israel at the time
of the investigation. We could have obtained further addresses of prisoners who had
emigrated to Israel, from the Regional Indemnification Office in Berlin, but we were
refused permission to examine the address files or to study the medical documents.
We thus had to rely on being given more addresses by the persons we interviewed in
Israel. The result was that the final number of cases covered and evaluated in this
group was limited to 42.

The investigators in New York faced similar difficulties. Seventy addresses were
known but in only 26 cases was it possible to conduct viable interviews. The other
persons were away, categorically refused to be interviewed, or did not respond to
attempts to contact them by letter or telephone.

Consequently, the total sample group comprised 245 former victims of persecution. The sociological characteristics of this group are summarized in Table 1.

All the subgroups on which the various study areas are based are included in the
overall group and are adequately representative of this group. Details are given at
the start of the relevant chapters on the selection of persons in each case.

We were unable to investigate systematically why certain people refused to be
interviewed, because the persons in question evaded making any statements at all, not
even wanting to explain their refusal. The arguments most frequently advanced
were:

"I haven't got time";
"I'm afraid that being interviewed will stir up all the old horrors of my concentration-
camp days";
"There's nothing wrong with me. I'm in good health. You won't find anything to study
in my case."

The last argument was put forward by people who had not, in fact, submitted
any claim for indemnification for damaged health. This point is of particular significance to us because we must assume that among those who refused to be interviewed
there were some who were presumably completely healthy, but we cannot say how
many.

Table 1. Sociological characteristics of the whole group (n=245)

Characteristics	Total number
Sex:	
male	175
female	70
Age in 1960:	
up to 40	55
41 to 50	68
51 to 60	87
over 61	35
Grounds for persecution:	
"racial"	
Eastern European Jews	115
German Jews	71
"political"	
Communists	19
Socialists	19
Others	3
"religious"	
Catholic priests	9
Jehovah's Witnesses	9
Country of origin:	
Germany	131
Eastern Europe (Poland)	114
Country of residence:	
Germany	177
Israel	42
USA (New York)	26

It seems important in this context to point out that the group under investigation was not selected on the basis of general medical factors (consultations or medical appraisal in connection with indemnification procedures) or special medical factors (concentration on one particular group of symptoms). It will become clear later on why this fact is so significant.

II. Collecting the Data

It was our aim to achieve a careful and as far as possible an objective reconstruction of the life history of each persecuted person included in the investigation. We tried to obtain comprehensive data on the individual's development during the period of persecution, the precise form taken by the persecution, and the period following release from captivity (up to the time of interview between 1958 and 1962).

We decided to conduct psychoanalytical depth interviews as the main source of our study data. In addition, we also evaluated documents relating to indemnification procedures — where available — to obtain information on medical problems.

As a check on the interviews and to complement the material already available, we compiled a questionnaire for some of the persons investigated and also had them take the Rorschach test. The subject areas covered by these methods are listed in more detail below.

After the persecutees had been contacted by letter or telephone, one or more detailed interviews were conducted with altogether 219 of them. The interviewers were doctors and psychologists trained in psychotherapeutics.

From previous experience with ex-victims of persecution, we knew that particular difficulty could be expected in specific areas of questioning. In order to minimize the sometimes considerable reluctance to make any statements and thus to prevent information being lost, an attempt was made in each individual case

    a) to establish a trust relationship with the interviewees and

    b) to encourage spontaneous communication of information.

For this reason, the questions asked in the interview were not put in any fixed sequence. The aim was to retain the character of a conversation and not to create the impression of a "cross examination". Often the only way for the investigator to overcome the interviewee's reluctance to communicate was to give repeated and emphatic assurances that the interview was being conducted solely for scientific purposes and not at the request of any Indemnification Office. Quite a few of those interviewed hoped or were afraid that, despite our emphatic claim to be pursuing purely scientific goals, we could nonetheless have some positive or negative influence on their pension situation. We had to stress, sometimes over and over again, that none of the observations made and none of the information gathered would under any circumstances be passed on to the assessment authorities in the form of a medical report, whether the person in question wished us to do this or not. For this reason we never prepared medical reports on former inmates of concentration camps. This effectively enabled us to dispel any hopes or fears entertained by those interviewed that we would influence their pension procedure. Apart from this, we also wanted to avoid any compulsion to prepare a "routine" medical appraisal so that we would remain unbiased in assessing the scientific problems.

The most important problem categories covered in the interviews are listed below.

a) Information on parents and relationship with members of family prior to persecution:
    1. Parents' profession.
    2. Parents' standard of living.
    3. Parents' Feeling of belonging in the country of residence.
    4. Parents' interest in the world around them.
    5. Parents' method of bringing up children.
    6. Influence of either parent on the family.
    7. Emotional relationship of interviewee to parents.
    8. Solidarity of family in difficult situations.
    9. Position of interviewee in sequence of siblings.
   10. Sibling constellation.
   11. Relationship with siblings.
   12. General conditions of existence during childhood and adolescence.
   13. Harmony of family life in general.

b) Individual development, interpersonal contact and marriage prior to persecution:
    1. Development of activity in childhood and adolescence.
    2. Mood in childhood and adolescence.
    3. Relationship with partners of the same sex.
    4. Relationship with partners of the opposite sex.
    5. Time of leaving home.

6. General psychic and social development.
7. Marital status prior to start of persecution.
8. Group affiliation of marital partner.
9. Relationship with marital partner.
10. Number of children.

c) Occupational training prior to persecution:

1. Education.
2. Type of occupational training.
3. Occupational qualifications obtained.
4. Occupational achievements.
5. Personal standard of living before the start of persecution.

d) Weltanschauung prior to persecution:

1. Association of parents with political, religious or similar groups.
2. Association of interviewee with political, religious or similar groups.
3. General orientation of interviewee's Weltanschauung.
4. The influence of the interviewee's Weltanschauung on his actions.
5. The way and extent to which an interviewee identified with a particular Weltanschauung.

e) Form of persecution:

1. Age when persecution commenced, age upon incarceration, age upon release, age at time of interview.
2. Total duration of persecution: duration of incarceration in concentration camps, forced labour camps, ghettos, penitentiaries, prisons.
3. Name and type of place where imprisoned.
4. Conditions and type of work to be performed during imprisonment.
5. How many members of the family were lost as a result of persecution.
6. Maltreatment, punishments and illnesses suffered.
7. Worst experiences during concentration-camp imprisonment.
8. Fate of members of family.

f) Personal experiences and attitudes during persecution:

1. Activities pursued during incarceration.
2. Attitude towards fellow prisoners.
3. Interpersonal contact with fellow prisoners.
4. Relationship with guards.
5. Life-threatening experiences suffered during incarceration.
6. Reasons for survival.

g) Mental state following release:

1. Plaintiveness.
2. Depression states.
3. Unstable mood.
4. Hypochondriacal complaints.
5. Guilt feelings.
6. Restlessness.
7. Distractibility.
8. Fatiguability.
9. Irritability.
10. Self-pity.
11. Dissatisfaction.
12. Sleep disturbances.
13. Low drive.
14. Despondency.
15. Eccentricity.
16. Aloofness.
17. Emotionalism.

18. Unequivocalness of the syndrome.
19. Repression tendencies.
20. Sexual disturbances.
21. Anxiety dreams.
22. Present mood.

h) Present problems in interpersonal contact:
    1. Adaptation to environment in first years after release.
    2. Hostility towards fellow humans.
    3. Personal contacts.
    4. Participation in the general life of society.
    5. Attitude towards fellow humans.
    6. Interest in environment.
    7. Ways in which aggression is expressed.
    8. Ability to get on in life outside the family.

i) Family life following release:
    1. Time when marital partner was selected.
    2. Group affinity of marital partner.
    3. Relationship of marital partners with each other.
    4. Degree to which family life is fixed on the past or the future.
    5. Harmony of family life.
    6. Number of children following release.
    7. Relationship with own children.
    8. Approach to bringing up children.
    9. Role played in the family.

k) Occupation following release:
    1. Type of occupational activities.
    2. Occupational rehabilitation.
    3. Occupational history.
    4. Occupational level compared with the pre-persecution period.
    5. Present standard of living.

l) Emigration following release:
    1. Emigration plans.
    2. Motives for emigrating.
    3. Dates of moves.

m) Summary assessment of the reactions to the experiences suffered during persecution:
    1. "Maturation".
    2. "Despair".
    3. "Demonstration".
    4. "Disavowal".
    5. "Forgiveness".
    6. "Indictment".
    7. "Ideological interpretation".

These categories are not all created on the same level of abstraction. Some of them (e.g. certain data relating to childhood, adolescence and period of incarceration) relate to the experience of the interviewee. The validity of these categories derives from the fact that they reflect the psychic reality of the experienced events. Other categories (e.g. the data relating to present mental state, marital problems and problems of interpersonal contact) have been obtained interpretatively from a wealth of detailed information. The final group of categories (e.g. data on occupation, duration of incarceration, place of imprisonment, marriage) is much more objective and unambiguous in character.

We used our discretion in allowing for these differences when interpreting the associations between the categories. In spite of the interview procedure, the interviewees showed differences in willingness to divulge information.

Table 2 shows clearly how willingness to divulge information varied in the interviews.

Table 2. Willingness of former persecuted persons to divulge information during psychological interviews (n=219)

Period	Factor studied	Unwilling-ness to divulge facts %	Willingness to divulge facts %	Need to divulge facts %	No infor-mation %
Pre-persecution period	Individual development	16.4	63	20.6	—
	Family conditions	28.3	62.1	9.6	—
Persecution period	Individual fate	13.2	42.5	44.3	—
	Fate of relatives	34.7	33.8	5.5	21.5
Following release	Physical condition	15.5	68.5	16	—
	Mental condition	11.9	49.3	38.8	—

Table 2 shows that the willingness to divulge facts was not constant but varied depending on the factor under investigation.

One third of the interviewees were unwilling to provide any data on family conditions in the pre-persecution period and on the fate of relatives during the persecution period.

On the other hand, it is apparent that many of those questioned felt a definite need to discuss and provide information on their own fate during persecution and their mental condition following release.

Those evaluating the interviews sometimes found that data given by interviewees in certain areas (interpersonal relationships, partnership, Weltanschauung, mental attitudes) were inadequate. Other methodological procedures were therefore employed in an attempt to enrich the material obtained up to that point.

A questionnaire was drawn up for this purpose: it contained 39 questions and was filled out and evaluated for 116 former victims of persecution (52.9%). These persons are sufficiently representative of the total group of n=219. This questionnaire is reproduced in the Appendix. The results obtained with this procedure and their interpretation are discussed in the chapter on "Contact with Fellow Humans and Society" (p. 120).

The Rorschach test proved to be a very suitable study method for interviewees who had difficulty in providing spontaneous information on their fate and how they came to terms with it. It was administered to 145 former persecutees (59.2%). This group of n=145 persons is also sufficiently representative of the total group. The test results were independently evaluated by two psychologists who were not informed of the purpose of the study or of the composition of the group of individuals tested.

Detailed data on the Rorschach categories used are given in the Appendix. The interpretation of the results obtained with this test is discussed in the chapters on "Basic Forms of Psychic Disturbance" (p. 109) and "Contact with Fellow Humans and Society" (p. 125).

The interviewees were on average visited twice and the total exploration period in each case was approx. 5 hours. The exact breakdown of the interview duration is given in the Table 3.

Table 3. Interview duration (n=219)

Number of interview hours	Number of interviewees
1	3
2–3	77
4–6	87
7 and more	52
Total	219

Table 3 shows that a great deal of time was spent obtaining the data. For this reason, the data-gathering period extended from 1958 to 1962. Since the largest number of interviews were conducted in 1960, we will for simplicity use this year as the cutoff when referring to the date when the survey was conducted.

Medical reports had been prepared for 170 of the total of 245 persons in connection with indemnification procedures. It was possible to conduct and evaluate interviews in only 144 of these 170 cases. In the case of the remaining 26 persons, it was not possible to conduct or evaluate an interview because of death, unavailability, refusal or inadequate information. However, these 26 persons were taken into account in our evaluation of indemnification and pension procedures.

The data in the chapter on "Late-Appearing Damage to Health" are therefore based mainly on the 170 persecutees with medical documentation relating to pension procedures, or on the 144 with similar documentation with whom psychological interviews had been conducted in addition. Both groups are sufficiently representative of the total group under investigation.

A special group of 18 persons was also formed. This group comprised individuals who had made no pension application, i.e. former persecutees who had been interviewed but for whom no medical appraisal documentation existed. These persons had made no claim for indemnification of damage suffered to health and they are considered separately in the chapter on "Late-Appearing Damage to Health" (p. 43).

III. Processing the Data

So much information was obtained and so many factors were to be investigated that systematic processing of the accumulated material was essential.

In order to transpose the qualitative information into quantitative, countable units, we formed a large number of categories that could always be used as alternative characteristics (in the sense of "present — not present" or "strongly pronounced — weakly pronounced"). This formalization of the material had the advantage that all the categories could be included in the statistical analyses. We tried to compensate for the loss of information, which had to be accepted as an unavoidable side-effect of this simplification, by covering as many aspects as possible. We developed 710 categories for processing medical problems and for the psychological problems 423 categories (321 in the interview, 62 in the questionnaire, 40 in the Rorschach test).

The following example will demonstrate how the most important categories were obtained and structured:

Factor: Emotional relationship of interviewee to his mother.

Definition: The emotional attitude of the interviewee to his mother as formed presum-
                ably during childhood and still remembered today as the mother image
                experienced.

Characteristics: (to be borne in mind when assessing this category):
                variety and differentiation of the remembered experiences; the amount of
                time devoted by the mother to the interviewee and his upbringing; common
                interests and activities; influence exerted by the mother on the choice of
                male and female friends; attitude of siblings to the mother and the attitude
                of the interviewee to these siblings; sources of dispute and conflict with the
                mother; attitude of the interviewee in quarrels between mother and father;
                relationship to other mother-figures (e. g. women teachers, aunts, etc.).

Category: A. Good emotional relationship with mother:
                   a) Loving devotion.
                   b) Recognition, respect.
                B. Poor emotional relationship with mother;
                   c) Inconstant relationship.
                   d) Rejection, alienation.

This type of category structure permits both a rough comparison of characteristics (A and B) and a more differentiated comparison (a—d).

On the basis of the categories, all the information (interview results, pension documentation, questionnaires, Rorschach test) was independently evaluated by 3 psychologists (for the psychological factors) and by 2 doctors (for the medical factors).

The mean agreement between the evaluators was $r_{phi} = 0.72$. The scatter in the various fields was between $r_{phi} = 0.61$ and 0.83. Having regard to the complexity of the data, this degree of correlation seemed adequate to us.

The great majority of the characteristics contained in this material represent quantitative variables. As already mentioned, they were used in dichotomous form for the statistical calculations. The relationships between various characteristics or groups of persons were determined by means of chi-square tests and correlation procedures.

For the sake of clarity, when presenting the results of the chiquare tests, only their significance level was given. Statistically significant findings were taken to be those with a level of significance of 0.1% (highly significant), 1% (very significant), 5% (significant) and 10% (trend).

The correlation coefficients have been given for the results calculated by means of correlation procedures. They correspond in form to the Pearson coefficients. The degree of correlation is merely slightly underestimated.

An attempt was made by means of factor analysis procedures (Q and R analyses) to determine whether fundamental dimensions or factors were present in complex associations of characteristics. In each case at least two factors were extracted from the correlation matrix. The extraction, which was conducted in accordance with the main axes procedure, was terminated once the values fell below the intrinsic value 1 of the matrix. All the factor structures which resulted were rotated according to "simple structure" principles (Varimax criterion; HARMANN, 1960). The factor structure which remained most constant throughout all the extractions and which possessed the most plausible content was accepted as valid.

The characteristics included in the R analyses are listed in the Appendix. The Q analyses have not been explicitly described, but they were used in some cases as the basis for compiling groups and for selecting representative individual cases.

The characteristics included in the factor analyses are arranged in accordance with their significance (loading) relevant to a particular dimension. In our procedure, we agreed to regard characteristics with a loading from 0.40 upward as characteristic. In order to determine to what extent each individual person represented a certain factor, factor values were calculated. These factor values are defined as the sum of the characteristics that typify a certain factor and that apply for the various persons. The characteristics were not weighted according to the degree of loading. As a result, a certain loss of information had to be accepted in order to avoid over-differentiation, which would no longer have been appropriate to the material. This solution seemed most practicable to us for the comparisons between groups.

Comparisons of extreme groups and analyses of individual cases were further methods that were employed.

The mathematical operations were carried out with the aid of a computer (Telefunken TR 4, using ALGOL as the programming language) at the Leibniz Computer Centre of the TH München (Technical University of Munich).

CHAPTER 2

Stresses Imposed by Concentration-Camp Incarceration

Outline of Problem

In order to establish the late sequelae of incarceration in concentration camps it is first of all necessary to enquire into the stress situation encountered during actual imprisonment. From reports given by concentration camp inmates on their experiences (UTITZ, 1948; KRAL, 1951; KOGON, 1954; FRANKL, 1959; BETTELHEIM, 1960) and from follow-up examinations (TARGOWLA, 1950; BENSHEIM, 1960; KLIMKOVA-DEUTSCHOVA, 1961; HERMANN and THYGESEN, 1964; v. BAEYER, HÄFNER and KISKER, 1964; EITINGER, 1964, inter alia) one thing is apparent, namely that there is no single, clearly definable form of stress which typifies the experiences of all camp inmates. Different elements acted in different ways on different personalities. Therefore we could not make use of the current model concepts established on the basis of animal experiments (BRADY, 1958), internal medicine (SELYE, 1953) or psychoanalysis (FREUD, 1892; SPITZ, 1960).

To avoid repetitive enumeration of the literature published to date, we concentrate on three questions in this chapter:

1. What did inmates of concentration camps interviewed by us 15 years after their release consider the worst experiences suffered?

2. What general stress characteristics — as distinct from the individual experiences of camp inmates — can be determined?

3. What adaptive behaviour permitted the ex-inmates to survive incarceration?

I. Worst Experiences

Fifteen to twenty years after incarceration it was possible to obtain details on only a few of the stress situations experienced in the camps. Quite often the ex-inmates consciously avoided mentioning tortures and indignities because they were afraid that recalling the experiences and feelings of those times would be too painful. Some people allowed us to conduct our interviews only with the proviso that they would not have to describe what they went through in the camps. Many of the interviewees became extremely worked-up when describing their imprisonment. In quite a few cases, interviewees suffered severe anxiety dreams during the night following the interview. However, despite the fact that they were emotionally affected, their reports on their sufferings were still highly credible. We were more doubtful of the statements made by former camp inmates on their relationships with the concentration-camp guards. Here, one frequently had the impression that certain cooperative attitudes were not mentioned because the interviewee could not square this behaviour with his present understanding of himself. It was also extremely difficult to conduct any reliable investigation into differentiated emotional reactions to the reality of incarceration in a concentration camp. In particular, the interviews yielded practically no information on complex ways of releasing aggression such as identifying with the aggressor (according to BETTELHEIM, 1960) or masochistic attitudes during imprisonment. These particular methods of releasing aggression have been superseded by more recent ones which constitute an adaptation of the former inmates to a situation in which the ex-persecutee has become a potential prosecutor.

Three main sources of suffering or complaint were mentioned by almost all the interviewees:

fear for their lives,
physical attrition, brought on particularly by hunger and beatings,
poisoning of interpersonal contacts.

In the following descriptions, which are intended to illustrate the experiences endured, these three basic types of suffering appear in a wide variety of forms. The descriptions are extracted from replies to the question as to what were the inmates' worst experiences during incarceration.

"The worst thing we suffered there was hunger. We even ate tainted food and as a result were ill all the time. Just as bad as the hunger were the sudden roundups when it was decided who would be taken to Auschwitz and gassed. My husband, who also lived in the ghetto, was transported to Auschwitz and gassed. I myself was sent to Auschwitz a few months later. Life there was paradise compared to the ghetto. We got real barley soup and margarine. Of course, the selection parades were terrifying. We always lived in dread of them. But, at all events, we did get something to eat. In Auschwitz swellings occurred all over my body and I was transferred to the camp hospital at Bergen-Belsen. When I had to parade there for selection, other inmates made me up to look healthy and I stood as straight as possible, using my last reserves of strength, so that I would not be chosen for the gas chambers. I was freed by the advancing Allies."

"The thought of being at the mercy of people who might kill you at any minute was the worst thing. It soon wore me down completely. I thought I would go crazy with fear. They said that every Jew had his death warrant in his pocket. And then they were always selecting people to be gassed ... "

"We were no longer regarded as human beings. To illustrate what I mean, let me cite the following episode: Once, when I was in a work squad, I encountered the owner of a restaurant where I had often had a few beers. In the past he had always welcomed me with great respect. On this occasion, however, he made no attempt to greet me, although I recognized him, but instead beat me with his whip."

"The worst thing for me was the maltreatment. I always had a very bad time in that respect because my size and my Jewish nose made me an easy target for the SS. I was always the first to get beaten up."

"You had to expect a beating at any time. It was possible to bear the hunger. But the kapos * and block leaders were beasts. In Dachau, a Polish, non-Jewish barrack leader tried to asphyxiate me as follows: He rammed a hose pipe into my mouth and connected the other end of the pipe to a water tap. However, I put up a fight and just managed to get away from him before he finished me off."

"I felt the worst thing was having to live in constant fear of being beaten up for trivialities. It was also very painful for me to have to watch others getting beaten. I lived in a constant state of tension and fear that I would be noticed and maltreated. As a result, I had my first frequent attacks of diarrhea in those days, and even today, I still get diarrhea when I am worked up."

---

* kapo = a prisoner employed as an overseer in the camp — Translator.

"The very worst thing in those days was that you didn't know what might happen to you from one minute to the next. Secondly, we were not treated like human beings. We had to watch other people suffering without being able to help. That was sometimes even worse than one's own agonies. With my own eyes I saw in the kitchen how the political prisoners got two lumps of margarine in their soup, the Jehovah's Witnesses got one and the Jews got none at all. Another very bad thing for me while I was imprisoned was that my parents were at home sick without me to look after them. This thought got me down most of all. On the other hand, despite everything, I spent the finest days of my life in the concentration camp because I really felt committed to a cause at that time and the feeling of comradeship was quite incomparable."

"I found the most upsetting and confusing thing was the senselessness of everything that happened in the camp. The behaviour of the SS was paradoxical. On the one hand they demonstratively made a great effort to create perfect order, to make optimum use of man-power and to treat the inmates 'fairly'. On the other hand, thousands of people were daily sent to their deaths in the gas chambers. Beatings did not bother me all that much. I never had the feeling of being shamed or degraded by the blows. I did not consider it was myself that was being abused but just someone else whom the SS wanted to beat, like all the others. I did not go around worrying that I would be killed. I just felt a little uneasy. The only time I experienced true fear was during selection parades because I knew they really were a matter of life or death. Otherwise, I was never afraid. It was possible to get used to the conditions in the camp. After all, there were others around who were suffering the same fate as myself."

Various experiences were thus felt to have been particularly stressful. This depended not only on the varying ability of the individual to withstand stress in different areas but also on his ability to adapt to a constant level of stress:

"I can't say that I was really ever afraid in Auschwitz. The threat of annihilation was so imminent that it was impossible to feel anything more about it. The human limits within which a person can still experience fear had long been exceeded. We just vegetated."

In the light of this very plastic description, it is also understandable that a person's conception of the worst stress situation could change, as is made clear in the following description, given by a woman.

"My worst experiences varied. When I was first imprisoned, they cut off my hair and to me this was a terrible degradation. Later, in Auschwitz, I was particularly humiliated by having to stand naked in the shower room washing myself in full view of SS guards while they chatted about trivialities. As the conditions in the camp grew worse, incidents like that seemed totally unimportant. In the Weissensee camp the worst suffering was due to hunger. The way in which one experienced something varied greatly."

It is remarkable that in a certain situation even apparently peripheral stresses, such as cutting off a person's hair, could assume the character of the worst possible indignity, while in other phases of incarceration these incidents appear harmless as compared with hunger, beatings and the threat of annihilation. This means that even in extreme stress situations the actually experienced degree of stress depends on the needs and reactions of the individual. This is made clear once more by the following statement:

"There was absolutely no sign of human relationships or comradeship in Auschwitz. You were not regarded as a human being or even an animal. You were no more than a number. Fellow-inmates were just as bestial as the Nazi persecutors, with whom there was actually rarely any contact."

In answer to the question what were the worst experiences suffered during in-carceration, we can say in summary that certain stress situations were repeatedly mentioned. However, the way in which these were experienced and the way in which inmates came to terms with them depended very much on individual personality structures.

II. Stress Characteristics

There seems little point to us in attempting a quantitative analysis of the worst suffering experienced by camp inmates. Here, we intend to elucidate certain characteristics of stress situations which can be correlated by group statistics with the ex-inmate's present ways of coping with life. We were unable to take any earlier studies of stress situations as examples. The conventional stress theories mentioned at the outset are not applicable to the situation of the victims of Nazi persecution, nor do the reported approaches seem to be sufficiently differentiated. It is, of course, not enough merely to refer to the horror of concentration camps in general and then to take this as a basis for a scientifically adequate explanation of the health damage suffered. It is also unsatisfactory to pick out just one stress factor, e.g. hunger, and to use this to explain a large number of sequelae of concentration camp imprisonment. This is what happened, for example, in the earlier Scandinavian studies (HELWEG-LARSEN, HOFFMEYER, KIELER, E. A. THAYSEN, THYGESEN and WULF, 1955). The deductions made by BENSHEIM (1960) seem very imprecise. He assigned certain neurotic states to specific periods of persecution. He distinguishes between an "outcast neurosis" brought about by the persecution in the years 1933 to 1939, and an "annihilation neurosis" caused by the stress in the period from 1939 to 1945.

But even scientists like BASTIAANS (1957) and v. BAEYER, HÄFNER and KISKER (1964), who tried to study the effects of persecution stress starting from more complex premises, were only able to detect weak statistical relationships. While in individual cases they were able to show conclusively the links between various traumatic experiences suffered during persecution and an inmate's later development, their statistical assumptions remain very global. BASTIAAN's attempt, by means of a seven-point scale, to quantify the degree of stress and to relate it to the degree of damage suffered by the victims of Nazi persecution yielded only moderate correlations because his scale covered very heterogeneous stress elements. The same objection applies to the work of v. BAEYER, HÄFNER and KISKER (1964), as the authors themselves admit.

In our study we chose a middle path between a casuistic-phenomenological and a global-statistical analysis of the persecutees' fates. It did not seem appropriate to us to carry out group statistical analysis of the worst experiences suffered by former inmates — incidentally, the phenomenon of "annihilation" stressed by v. BAEYER (1963) was not very often mentioned as being such an experience — because they are too subjective in character to permit this sort of analysis. It is, however, appropriate to isolate certain objective and subjective stress factors and to examine separately the various effects that they have on the development of the individual's life.

As objective, situation-dependent stress factors we have taken: work situations, duration of persecution and incarceration, loss of relatives, severity of the camp and illnesses suffered during imprisonment; and as subjective, individual-dependent variables through which the objective stress can be intensified or alleviated, we have taken: reason for persecution, age, sex, adaptation in the concentration camp and characteristics of individual personality development.

A description is given below of the stress variables that are used throughout the study to determine quantitatively the destructive influences of concentration camp incarceration. A great deal of attention is devoted to the type and frequency of the stress factors. Often it was impossible to do more than assign a quantitative index to a selection of these factors. The point of giving such a detailed description is to illustrate as many as possible of the stress situations which the persecutees faced. Furthermore, the detailed description of the various stress aspects is intended to provide insight into our indexing procedure.

1. Work Situation

A description of the work situation as an index of stress is still the most accurate way of characterizing the individual stress situation faced by an inmate. The severity of the work performed also gives a clearer indication of the stress individuals were expected to withstand than the severity of the camp conditions, because in harsh camps there was light work to do, while in camps where easy conditions prevailed some of the inmates could be worked to death. There is a very significant correlation between the remembered threat to life during incarceration and the severity of the work stress ($r = 0.30$), but poor correlation, on the other hand, with the severity of the stress imposed by camp conditions ($r = 0.05$).

The severity of the work situation is also a very practical individual stress variable because it could most readily be influenced by the initiative of the individual inmate himself. Through cunning manoeuvring and skillful adaptation to the mentality of the guards the persecutee could get himself assigned to perform easier types of work. In addition, a person's ability to push his fellow prisoners around was frequently a crucial factor in deciding whether he had to do hard or light work.

An inmate gave a very drastic example of this from his experience in Auschwitz: "Every morning, they made up work parties. A quarter of an hour before we moved off the strongest inmates came and took the weaker individuals by the scruff of the neck and threw them out of the privileged groups. Thus, the tough inmates got the easy jobs to do and the weak ones had to perform work which was so hard it could soon prove fatal."

The completely chaotic values in the concentration camp meant that the work performed in the camp was regarded as nothing more than an element in the "struggle for existence". An inmate who was able to get his way could often make sure that he was given "easy" work, while the weaker prisoner was assigned a harsh task to perform.

However, this was not always the case. It was not only the individual who faced situations from which there was no escape and in which he was completely subject to the whims of the SS; there were also camps in which there was in general little scope for personal manoeuvring. EITINGER (personal communication 1969), for example, reported the case of a young German Jew in Auschwitz who lived protected in a group of persons of the same faith. Because of an illness, he was transferred to the camp hospital and thus separated from his group. When he had recovered he was put in a barracks with some Ukrainian prisoners. He was completely isolated there because he did not understand the language of his fellow prisoners. Although he made a valiant effort, he was unable to gain a foothold in what was, for him, a totally alien environment and consequently, within a few days, he rapidly lost weight and died.

Only in exceptional cases, e.g. doctors, was it possible for a person to see any sense in the work carried out in the camps. The inmates quickly saw through the falsity of the motto propagated by the SS: "Arbeit macht frei", which implied that if an inmate worked hard he would be released sooner. In most cases the work

Table 4. Classification of the various work situations according to severity

1 Easy work	2 Moderately hard work	3 Hard work	4 Very hard work
1. Administrative work in an office	1. Light factory work	1. Work outside, not specified	1. Heavy digging (trenches, exca-vations, etc.)
2. Stock clerk	2. Craftman's work performed outside, unpaid	2. Work in forced labour camps	2. Forestry work
3. Library work	3. Light outside work such as cleaning up & snow removal	3. Heavy factory work	3. Work in quarries and gravel pits, cutting peat, mining (under-ground)
4. Work inside the camp	4. Laundry work	4. Construction work (build-ing houses, light road construction/ repairs)	4. Punishment squad
5. Kitchen work	5. Nursing work	5. Work outside the camp	5. Heavy carrying (when done by women)
6. Light crafts-man's work, done inside	6. Preliminary detention	6. Grave-digging	6. Punishment battalion
7. Special posts such as kapo, block leader, foreman	7. Quarantine	7. Agricultural work	
8. Quartered in priests' block, no work	8. Living in a ghetto, no work	8. Cleaning-up work (done by women)	
9. Time spend in reception camps		9. Removal (re-location) work	
10. Solitary con-finement, no work		10. Time spent in hiding places	

merely amounted to unproductive activity. To the inmates it was all chicanery. Occasionally, they were set to work doing something useful, e.g. working in arms factories. But in such cases, they realized that their work was helping to postpone the day when the regime would be defeated and they would be released.

In order to express the work situation in quantitative terms, all the types of work our interviewees had to perform were assessed for their probable degree of severity by several analysts and classified under 4 categories. The results of this classification procedure are shown in Table 4.

Table 4 shows that persecution situations not involving any actual work (e.g. solitary confinement without work) have also been included in the classification. The advantage of this procedure is that an individual measure of the stress suffered by each inmate can be obtained for the entire period of persecution, without any gaps. The index "severity of work situation", as well as the other measures of the stress situation, should always, of course, be considered in conjunction with certain modifying variables. One variable that can modify the stress is, for example, the inmate's previous work experience. It is probably true to say that in the case of an experienced forestry worker "forestry work" should not really be classified as "very hard work", whereas it certainly would fall in that category for an academic unused to physical labour.

Thus, in establishing the degree to which individuals were affected by work in the concentration camp, no general degree of severity was applied in each case. Instead, the degree of severity of the work for the person in question was put one notch lower when (a) the work was the same as that performed by the person in his normal working life, or (b) the person supervised the work. In general, the individual stress index was determined more precisely by taking into account the duration of the work of a particular degree of severity. The resulting classification according to persons exposed to "on the whole low" and "on the whole high" stress through work is given in Table 5.

The columns in Table 5 have the following significance:

Group A: inmates who on the whole were exposed to low work stress. Over a period of not more than two years the prisoners in this group had to perform less than 6 months of heavy and/or extremely heavy work. For periods exceeding two

Table 5. Severity and duration of the work stress (n=219)

Duration of imprisonment in months	A Number of persons performing predominantly light and/or moderately heavy work		B Number of persons performing predominantly heavy and/or extremely heavy work		Total number of persons	
3–24	25	(11.4%)	14	(6.4%)	39	(17.8%)
25–48	39	(17.8%)	36	(16.4%)	75	(34.2%)
49–72	37	(16.9%)	39	(17.8%)	76	(34.7%)
more than 72	17	(7.8%)	12	(5.5%)	29	(13.3%)
Totals	118	(53.9%)	101	(46.1%)	219	(100%)

years of imprisonment, people who had been exposed to less than 12 months of extremely heavy and less than 24 months of heavy and extremely heavy work were also included in this group.

Group B: Inmates who on the whole were exposed to severe work stress. Over a period of not more than two years the prisoners in this group had to perform more than 6 months of heavy and/or extremely heavy work. For periods exceeding two years of incarceration, people who had been exposed to heavy and/or extremely heavy work for more than 12 months were also included in this group.

The duration of the work stress was thus taken into account in our indexing procedure. However, considering the broad period of time spanned, this factor only permitted a relatively coarse classification between inmates exposed to "low" and those exposed to "high" work stress.

2. Severity of Camp Conditions

The reason for considering the severity of the camp conditions as an index of the stress situation is apparent from the following description given by one of our interviewees:

A Polish Jew who had spent 4 years in Theresienstadt and 5 months in Auschwitz was of the opinion that "compared with Auschwitz, Theresienstadt was a sanatorium. You can't really call Theresienstadt a concentration camp. It was a ghetto town in its own right with its own administration and laws. Admittedly, one bad thing about the place was that corruption was rife. The few months in Auschwitz were much worse than all the years in Theresienstadt".

The following description, given by a persecutee and already quoted above (p. 12), shows how such a statement about Auschwitz can in turn be relativized by the subjective experience of other persecutees:

"Life there (Auschwitz) was paradise compared to the ghetto (Lodz). We got real barley soup and margarine. Of course, the selection parades were terrifying. We always lived in dread of them. But, at all events, we did get something to eat."

Expressions such as "sanatorium" and "paradise" were frequently used by the ex-inmates to bring out the, relatively speaking, hellish character of other camps. In terms of subjective experience the inmates made a very clear distinction between the severity of the various camps. However, since the assessment criteria varied from person to person according to the individual need situation, the classifications of the camps according to their degree of severity were also subjectively very different. Therefore, in order to be able to use the severity of camp conditions as a stress index, objective characteristics were used. We are grateful to the "Institut für Zeitgeschichte (München)" (The Institute of Contemporary History, Munich), for having drawn up the list of characteristics which covers mainly the factors of "death quota", "methods of extermination", "medical experiments", "epidemics", "work stress", and "purpose of the camp as determined by the SS". The clearest classification of the camps was possible on the basis of the death quota.

Taking all the stress factors together, we obtained the following scale of severity for the camps:

a) Extermination camps (Belcec, Birkenau, Maidanek, Sobibor):

Medical experiments. Work and epidemics do not figure here as stress factors because these camps were used by the SS for the mass extermination of inmates. Almost 100% of the persons imprisoned in these camps died in the gas chambers.

b) Extremely harsh concentration camps (Auschwitz, Mauthausen, Stutthof, Bergen-Belsen):

Mass gassings, lethal injections, facilities for executing people by shooting them through the base of the skull, severe starvation, killing prisoners by immersing them in cold water, large-scale medical experiments, work in armament plants and factories. From 1943 onwards, more and more inmates died of dysentery, typhoid and spotted fever, particularly in Stutthof and Bergen-Belsen. More than 50% of the inmates were exterminated.

c) Harsh concentration camps (Sachsenhausen, Ravensbrück, Buchenwald, Flossen-bürg, Gross-Rosen):

Here the main emphasis was on shooting and gassing small groups of inmates. Medical experiments were much less frequent and on a much smaller scale. The work stress fluctuated between light factory work and extremely heavy work: tunnelling, building roads and in armament factories. Epidemics, particularly typhoid, were very frequent from 1944 onwards. About 30 to 50% of the inmates were exterminated.

d) Only Dachau can really be described as a concentration camp with moderately severe conditions:

Small groups of foreigners were shot or gassed. From 1942 onwards the SS occasionally carried out medical experiments. The work stress was relatively speaking moderately severe. Epidemics mainly occurred in 1945. Dachau was occasionally used by the SS as a collection camp for prominent prisoners.

The four classifications of the camps cover the total period during which they were in operation. However, following the notorious Wannsee Conference in 1942 the conditions in all the camps suddenly became even harsher; therefore, if an ex-inmate had experienced the incarceration conditions after that date we classified his degree of stress exposure one step higher up the scale. We were not quite certain how to classify the stress exposure of a persecutee who had spent some or all of his imprisonment in places of detention other than in one of the 13 most important concentration camps categorized by us. Altogether 38 concentration camps or satellite camps, 72 forced labour camps, 37 ghettos and 28 penitentiaries or prisons, named by persecutees as their places of detention, could not be classified according to their severity. However, this uncertainty is not of any great consequence because the interviewees usually only spent a short period of imprisonment in the non-classified camps. In general, on the basis of historical facts and information provided by the interviewees, these places of detention were classified as no more severe than the moderately harsh camp at Dachau.

The individual stress index was particularized by taking into account the duration of the degree of harshness to which the inmates were exposed in the camps. Here, the same classification principles were applied as for indexing the severity of the work-situation. As Table 6 shows, the result was a division of the inmates into those who "on the whole suffered low stress" and those who "on the whole suffered high stress" as a result of camp conditions.

The significance of the classification in Table 6 is as follows:

Group A: Inmates who on the whole suffered low stress as a result of camp conditions. Over a maximum period of two years of incarceration these persons spent less than 6 months in severe and/or extremely severe camps. For periods of incarceration in excess of two years persons who had spent less than 24 months in severe and/or extremely severe concentration camps were also included in this group.

Group B: Inmates who on the whole suffered a high degree of stress due to camp conditions. Over a maximum period of two years of imprisonment these persons spent more than 6 months in severe and/or extremely severe camps. For periods of incarceration in excess of two years, inmates who had spent more than 24 months in severe and/or extremely severe camps were also included in this group.

Table 6. Severity and duration of camp-induced stress (n=219)

Duration of incarceration in months	A Number of persons who spent most of the time in moderately severe camps		B Number of persons who spent most of the time in severe camps		Total number of persons	
3–24	27	(12.3%)	12	(5.5%)	39	(17.8%)
25–48	53	(24.2%)	22	(10.0%)	75	(34.2%)
49–72	60	(27.4%)	16	(7.3%)	76	(34.7%)
more than 72	15	(6.9%)	14	(6.4%)	29	(13.3%)
Totals	155	(70.8%)	64	(29.2%)	219	(100%)

Any inmate who had been imprisoned in an extermination camp was in each case regarded as having endured on the whole severe stress due to camp conditions.

The duration of the camp-stress situation was thus taken into account in the indexing. Considering the large period of time spanned, however, this factor only permitted a relatively coarse classification into those who had suffered "low" stress and those who had suffered "high" stress as a result of camp conditions.

3. Duration of Persecution and Incarceration

The duration of the period of incarceration is taken into account, by the German authorities at least, in determining the amount of "damages payable for loss of freedom". For each month of imprisonment the persecuted person is legally entitled to a certain rate of indemnification. A special pension is awarded for "damage to health" suffered as a result of incarceration.

It is true to say, in this connection, that the severity of the stress situation undoubtedly had a decisive influence in determining the directly apparent impairment of mental and physical health. As regards later rehabilitation into society, an important role was also played by the amount of time the persecutee had spent in isolation as a result of being persecuted. As is shown in the chapter on "Contact with Fellow Humans and Society" (see p. 138), nowhere can such strong correlations with the duration of incarceration be detected as in the sphere of interpersonal contact. The vast amount of experience, including stressful experience, which the persecutee was unable to share with the environment into which he was supposed to integrate once more, later proved to be a source of stress. The collapse of the Nazi regime very demonstratively vindicated the persecutees vis à vis the majority of Germans. In addition, the persecutees had stood up for their point of view and had suffered for doing so. But after 1945, very many of those who had been supporters of the old regime or who had gone along with it, were unable or did not wish to admit — not even privately — that they had made a serious mistake and that the persecutees had been right. They frequently refused to accept the moral obligation to show regret or admit guilt and once more treated the ex-persecutees as "outsiders", sometimes even as "criminals" from whom they kept aloof. The longer the persecutees had been isolated from society, the more they saw themselves stamped as "alien" or "marked" individuals.

Table 7. Duration and type of persecution situation (n=219)

Months	Incarceration in concentration camp		Incarceration in prison or penitentiary		Incarceration in forced labour camp or ghetto		Total period of persecution	
1– 6	25	(11.4%)	31	(14.2%)	14	(6%)	8	(3.7%)
7–24	94	(42.9%)	19	(8.7%)	29	(13.2%)	5	(2.3%)
25–48	45	(20.6%)	11	(5.0%)	23	(10.5%)	29	(13.2%)
49–72	20	(9.1%)	2	(0.9%)	2	(0.9%)	97	(44.3%)
73–96	10	(4.6%)	4	(1.8%)	0	(0.0%)	32	(14.6%)
97–144	6	(2.7%)	0	(0.0%)	0	(0.0%)	48	(21.9%)
not applicable	19	(8.7%)	152	(69.4%)	151	(69.0%)	0	(0.0%)

In addition, it should be mentioned that persons whom the Nazis liked to brand "pests of society" were the subject of humiliating defamatory campaigns before they were actually arrested. The aim of these campaigns was to single out certain groups of individuals, to identify them (e.g. by the star of David) and to alienate them from the population. The public insults, the boycott measures and the discrimination were followed by violence and terror (e.g. the Kristallnacht *), preliminary detention in prison — often accompanied by torture and solitary confinement — and finally incarceration in a concentration camp. Thus, the total period of persecution was often much longer than the period of imprisonment. This is demonstrated by Table 7, which shows the amount of time spent in concentration camps, forced labour camps and ghettos, as well as the time spent in prisons and penitentiaries, as a further characteristic of the stress situation. In addition, Table 7 lists the total period of persecution.

* Crystal Night, November 9, 1938, when the synagogues were burnt down — Translator.

Table 7 shows that persecutees spent more time in forced labour camps, ghettos or concentration camps than in prisons or penitentiaries. For most inmates the total persecution period was more than 4 years. The Table also shows that the most frequent term of imprisonment spent in concentration camps was from 6 months to 2 years. The next most frequent period of imprisonment was 2 to 4 years.

When calculating the correlations in the following chapters we took into account periods of incarceration and not total periods of persecution. It did not seem appropriate to us to correlate the total persecution period as a stress index with the disturbances suffered today by the ex-inmates, because the total persecution period varied greatly from individual to individual in a way which was difficult to analyse.

4. Extermination of Relatives

The number of relatives lost by a persecutee as a result of extermination measures often reflects the severity of the persecution in individual cases. For example, in the case of Polish Jews, it often happened that only one member of a family managed by chance to escape extermination. They were also the group worst off in the concentration camps. Deprived of all close friends and relatives in whom they might have been able to place some hope for the future, and barely able, because of the language barrier, to make themselves understood to the German SS, they occupied the position of outcasts, the dregs of society, among other inmates of the camps. Persecutees who were aware that their relatives had been exterminated were usually unable to forget — not even temporarily — the policy of total destruction pursued by the regime.

Table 8 provides as quantitative guide to the various fates suffered by parents, siblings, marital partners and children.

The data in Table 8 only permit us to imagine what the fates of their relatives may have meant to individual persecutees. Depending on the closeness of the ties with a particular member of his family, the individual persecutee was affected to a varying extent by that person's death. It was a particularly harsh blow for children and teenagers to learn that they would have to live in future without their parents. Others, whose spouses had been their last mainstay, plummetted to the very depths of

Table 8. The fate of the relatives of 219 persecutees (the figures in square brackets indicate how often the deaths of relatives were directly experienced or heard about during incarceration)

Relationship	Persecuted		Not persecuted
	Survived	Killed	
Parents (father, or mother, both parents)	6	119 [69]	94
Siblings	32	50 [17]	21
Marital partners	18	45 [16]	22
Children	9	28 [18]	22

despair when their partners were killed. Jews who had been sterilized by the Nazis and who then learnt that their only child had been murdered, were also completely broken in spirit.

Many persecutees experienced a strong feeling of "social depersonalization" ("Who am I?". "What am I doing in this world?") when, amidst the horrors of the concentration camp, they also had to bear the news of their relatives' deaths.

Like TRAUTMANN (1961) we found that many of the persons left behind were plagued by "feelings of guilt" and that they were painfully aware of the contradiction between the fact of their survival and the thought that "the others are dead". An inmate who may have had some sort of quarrel with his father or close friend shortly before the latter were killed was particularly tortured by self-reproach and the thought that he may have been responsible in some way for their deaths. Occasionally the horror of the inmate's own daily experience was so strong that it left no time or opportunity for sorrow on his part at the loss of his relatives. Sometimes the sorrow was eased by the solidarity of fellow-inmates. However, it came as even more of a blow to such inmates, following their release, to find that none of their relatives were left.

5. Physical and Mental Disorders

Illnesses suffered in the concentration camps were on the one hand a consequence of the stress situation in the camps, and on the other hand a specific source of stress in themselves. In view of the poor medical treatment and the murderous intent of the SS, including the hospital orderlies, which manifested itself in a variety of ways, any inmate who fell ill and had to be transferred to the camp hospital usually faced a direct threat to his life. However, the objective value of the information on illnesses suffered during incarceration is limited for the following reasons:

1. The information is based on what the inmates could remember about individual events, some of which took place as much as 10 to 20 years beforehand, and there were inevitably gaps in their memories.

2. The data given about the illnesses is for the most part not based on careful medical diagnoses but on impressions gained by laymen. Probably the only exception in this regard is the achievement of the French doctors at Mauthausen who managed to X-ray a large number of French deportees and to get the microfilms away from the SS doctors (VIC-DUPONT, FICHEZ, WEINSTEIN in MICHEL, 1955).

3. Many illnesses were not covered at all, e. g. internal disorders such as liver and kidney damage, tumours, etc.

4. Information on illnesses was for the most part given in connection with indemnification processes which, generally speaking, took account only of illnesses regarded by the interviewees and the doctors as directly due to the incarceration.

5. Usually only illnesses were reported which appeared likely to have a significant effect on the amount of indemnification to be paid. For example, menstrual disturbances occurred in almost all the female inmates (DÖRING, 1967), but since these usually receded again upon release, they were regarded as irrelevant to the medical diagnosis of the damage suffered.

Our data on the physical and mental disorders suffered during incarceration are given in Table 9. This information was gathered from a special random sample of 144 inmates who had undergone both medical and psychological examination.

Surveys of health damage suffered during the persecution period have been given by MICHEL (1955), PAUL and HERBERG (1963), v. BAEYER, HÄFNER and KISKER (1964).

Table 9. Physical and mental disorders suffered during incarceration (n=144)

Type of disorder	Men		Women		Total (n=144)
	young [a] (n=42)	old [b] (n=65)	young [a] (n=21)	old [b] (n=16)	
1. Head injuries caused by maltreatment	20 (48%)	36 (55%)	8 (38%)	3 (19%)	67 (46.5%)
2. Epidemics (typhoid, dysentry, spotted fever, etc.)	16 (38%)	14 (22%)	9 (43%)	6 (38%)	45 (31.2%)
3. Pulmonary-bronchial ailments (TB etc.)	11 (26%)	21 (32%)	4 (19%)	4 (25%)	40 (27.8%)
4. Cardiovascular ailments	12 (29%)	16 (25%)	5 (24%)	6 (38%)	39 (27.1%)
5. Rheumatic complaints	11 (26%)	15 (23%)	4 (19%)	7 (44%)	37 (25.7%)
6. Dyspeptic complaints	11 (26%)	14 (22%)	3 (14%)	4 (25%)	32 (22.2%)
7. Symptoms of hunger dystrophy	12 (29%)	10 (15%)	8 (38%)	4 (25%)	34 (23.6%)
8. Bacterial infections	8 (19%)	14 (22%)	6 (29%)	2 (13%)	30 (28%)
9. Injuries caused by maltreatment (excluding head injuries)	9 (21%)	9 (14%)	3 (14%)	— —	21 (14.6%)
10. Spinal column complaints	4 (10%)	8 (12%)	3 (14%)	5 (31%)	20 (13.9%)
11. Infections (malaria, jaundice, etc.)	3 (7%)	6 (9%)	2 (10%)	1 (6%)	12 (8.3%)
12. Brief, febrile infections	4 (10%)	— —	3 (14%)	2 (13%)	9 (6.3%)
13. Frostbitten feet	1 (2%)	1 (2%)	2 (10%)	1 (6%)	5 (3.5%)
14. Menstrual disturbances	— —	— —	11 (52%)	2 (13%)	13 (35.1%)
15. Permanent anxiety state	12 (28%)	23 (35%)	9 (44%)	8 (52%)	52 (36.4%)
16. Depressive moods	13 (31%)	17 (26%)	7 (31%)	7 (44%)	44 (30.5%)
17. Thoughts of suicide	7 (16%)	5 (8%)	1 (6%)	2 (12%)	15 (10.3%)

[a] "young" means less than 30 years old at start of incarceration.
[b] "old" means more than 30 years old at start of incarceration.

It is not possible to discuss here the differences in the frequency rates of illnesses as revealed in individual studies. The influences of the various study conditions will not be dealt with until the later chapters in which the present physical and mental condition is related to persecution-dependent factors (such as illnesses suffered in the camps) and to factors which are independent of the persecution (such as personality characteristics) and compared with the results obtained by other researchers. Of the disorders which inmates remembered from the time of their incarceration, head injuries resulting from maltreatment stand out above all others. Injuries to the facial skeleton and the epicranial aponeurosis, cranial bruising, concussions and slight contusions caused by the callous beatings by the SS were remembered by almost 50% of those interviewed, even though a long time had elapsed since the incidents. None of the other illnesses are mentioned by more than about one third of the ex-persecutees. Even the symptoms of hunger dystrophy such as cachexia, hunger edema and hunger polyuria, which seemed to many doctors to be the main form of disorder suffered by inmates when examined shortly after their release, are relatively rarely mentioned in the later surveys. This is probably because their consequences turned out to be less serious than at first supposed.

It is characteristic of the different stress patterns of the two sexes that men seem to have suffered more head injuries than women as a result of maltreatment while women on the other hand suffered more frequently from epidemics, hunger dystrophy and permanent anxiety states. Young women reported menstrual disturbances more frequently than older women and they suffered more head injuries as a result of maltreatment.

The correlation of the frequency of the disorders suffered in the camp with the duration of incarceration and the severity of camp conditions is not significant. On the other hand, where severe work stress was faced, there was a greater frequency of pulmonary and bronchial disorders and head injuries.

The more frequent head injuries suffered by inmates in severe work situations support and illustrate the correlation, described below, that was found between the severity of the work situation and the poor relationship of the inmate with his guards. Anyone who had to perform hard work was particularly prone to receiving head injuries, mainly because the guards administered particularly ruthless beatings to inmates in the underpriviledged position of having to perform such work.

Finally, the following description given by a former inmate will serve to demonstrate once more the often cited connection between the willpower to survive and the likelihood of falling ill in the camp.

B. was a house-painter by trade and he tried by every means at his command to get himself skilled work to do while he was imprisoned. Finally, he was detailed off to do painting work. He defined his situation as follows: "Although the work was hard and there were no proper tools or paints, I was able to keep myself from going under. I didn't smoke and I exchanged my cigarettes for food. My father, who was imprisoned with me, was in exactly the opposite situation. He became apathetic and was put to work moving heavy iron beams around. I tried all the time to cheer him up but he was no longer interested. I warned him in particular about the camp hospital, which was overcrowded, because most of the patients ended up in the gas chambers. But my father did not listen to me. He soon contracted cholera and died a few days later."

6. Reason for Persecution

In order to understand why the sociologically different groups of persecutees are sometimes alike and in other cases different in the way in which they have come to terms with their fate, it is necessary to examine the individual courses taken by the persecution. Table 10 shows different frequencies for the various groups of persecutees in most of the stress categories. The most important findings are framed. (To permit clear comparison and because the groups vary in size, we have also given the percentage figures; see Table 5.)

If, for the time being we disregard the stress values which can be expressed numerically, it is also possible, on the basis of the inmates' experience, to delineate different stresses in different groups of persecutees. The Jews were worst off in that the SS always made it clear to them that they were regarded as vermin and that their lives were correspondingly worthless. On the other hand, the political prisoners were given to understand that they had consciously chosen to be incarcerated in a concentration camp and that they had had the opportunity to change their ways. The conditions of imprisonment for the religious persecutees were greatley relaxed, at least for some of the time. In personal contact with them the SS guards often regarded them as comical or amusing and picked on them much less frequently than on other groups of persecutees as targets for their lethal aggressions.

Table 10. Reason for persecution and stress suffered (n=200; 19 persons could not be clearly assigned to any of the 6 categories)

Type of stress	Polish Jews		German Jews		Political and religious persecutees	
	male (n=64)	female (n=34)	male (n=33)	female (n=17)	male (n=42)	female (n=10)
Long period of severe work stress	38 59%	16 47%	15 (45%)	6 (35%)	14 (33%)	2 (20%)
Long period of severe camp stress	18 (28%)	6 (18%)	16 48%	7 41%	10 (24%)	2 (20%)
Total period of persecution more than 4 years	44 (69%)	27 (79%)	31 94%	15 88%	36 (86%)	9 (90%)
Time in concentration camp more than 3 years	6 (9%)	— —	8 (24%)	3 (18%)	25 60%	2 (20%)
Father or mother both died as result of persecution	44 69%	27 79%	22 (67%)	12 (71%)	1 (2%)	1 (10%)
Siblings died as result of persecution	22 (34%)	12 (35%)	9 (27%)	4 (24%)	—	— —
Marital partner died as result of persecution	27 (42%)	8 (24%)	5 (15%)	3 (18%)	—	— —
Children died as result of persecution	21 33%	5 15%	3 (9%)	— —	1 (2%)	— —

If the men and women are taken together, it is found that among the racial persecutees the Polish Jews were exposed to slightly more severe work stress than the German Jews, but these on the other hand suffered more severe camp stress and longer periods of persecution and detention than the Poles. Persecuted Jews from both countries were very frequently affected by the loss of members of their families. The loss figures are greater for the Polish Jews than for the German Jews.

The political or religous persecutees had easier work to perform and were exposed to less severe camp stress. Deaths of relatives as a result of persecution also occurred less frequently in their cases. However, they were persecuted and imprisoned for significantly longer periods than the Jews from Poland and Germany.

It is clearly impossible to weigh the stress values of the various fates of the various groups against each other without any more ado. For example, how can one weigh the loss of relatives against longer periods of imprisonment? When considering the various stresses to which the groups of persecutees were exposed, more attention should therefore be paid to the particular type of stress than to its presumed magnitude. Despite these restrictions, the figures given do permit us to assume that the political or religious persecutees — and particularly the women among them — suffered less stress than the racial persecutees from Germany and Poland.

As will be shown later on, there is little if any significant correlation between the duration of imprisonment and the disturbances suffered today by ex-inmates. This is understandable if one considers the opposed tendencies of duration of incarceration and stress experienced. The duration of incarceration is a statistically less important stress factor than the suffering actually experienced during imprisonment, because only a small percentage of the persecutees who were subjected to extreme stress managed to survive long periods of imprisonment. It must be assumed, therefore, that inmates exposed to extreme terror for long periods of time died.

Even from the point of view of the persecutees themselves, the Jews were in the worst position. They saw little if any chance of escaping death under the most ignominious circumstances. To protect themselves they were forced to suppress any expression of hatred towards the guards. Even the feeble hopes that they cherished of being able to survive the concentration camp were usually tempered by the feeling that a homeless and rootless existence awaited them after their release. The material basis of their lives had been destroyed, many of their relatives had been killed, and the rest of the world community seemed indifferent to the fate of the Jews, not to say openly anti-Semitic. The political and religious persecutees on the other hand were not face-to-face with death all the time. Many of them held middle or high ranks in the administrative set-up run by the inmates themselves and thus had more opportunity than the Jews to protect each other.

Summarizing, it can be stated therefore that both objectively and subjectively the Jewish persecutees suffered more than the political or religious persecutees.

7. Age

There can be no doubt that the age of the persecutees at the time when the Nazi terror engulfed them was a very specific and significant stress factor. Developmental psychology has revealed that there are certain age periods during which the susceptibility to crisis under stress is particularly pronounced. However, very few of the former inmates offered any information on whether their persecution was harder or easier to bear because of their age. The peculiarities of personality and the associated specific susceptibilities in various phases of a person's life tend to be lived rather than consciously experienced. The following remarks, made by a female Polish Jew, are an exception:

"As a young girl I was very impetuous. I was a member of a radical right-wing Zionist youth group. Our motto was 'blood and the sword'. But the ghetto robbed me of my youth. When I was 16 years old I was put in a ghetto with my parents. We had to work all the time and got very little to eat. It was in the ghetto that I got to know my future husband. If we had been older we would have suffered more. We came through the ghetto experience quite well because we were still young. If I had been married and given birth to my child in the ghetto, that would have been the worst thing that could have happened. It was ghastly the way children were killed in the ghetto."

However, the minutes of the interviews very rarely contain any complaint that the best years of a person's life were lost in the concentration camp. The age at the time of persecution is something that is taken for granted. But the age spread of the interviewees with whom we are concerned here was large. Since the incarceration was often preceded by a period of persecution and defamation, the age distributions differ for these two stress situations (see Table 11).

In the studies which take into account the fact that persecution can be especially significant at a particular age, special emphasis is placed on childhood and adolescence (KOLLE, 1958; BENSHEIM, 1960; v. BAEYER, HÄFNER and KISKER, 1964). BENSHEIM (1960), for example, discovered in racial persecutees a four-stage age-specific "scale of fear". According to his findings, children who were persecuted between 5 and 11 years of age developed during imprisonment "animal-motor primitive reactions"

Table 11. Age at start of persecution or imprisonment (n=219)

Age	At start of persecution		At start of imprisonment	
under 10	3	(1.4%)	1	(0.5%)
11–15	20	(9.1%)	10	(4.7%)
16–20	34	(15.5%)	30	(13.1%)
21–25	37	(16.9%)	37	(16.9%)
26–30	44	(20.1%)	44	(20.1%)
31–35	41	(18.7%)	49	(23.5%)
36–40	17	(7.8%)	18	(8.1%)
over 40	23	(10.5%)	30	(13.1%)

which they later retained. Adolescents ranging in age from 12 to 17 years are claimed by him to have suffered lasting damage from fear, particularly to the "vegetative-hormonal system". The persecutees in the 20 to 30 age group developed a "chronic anxiety state with depressive overtones" or became "asocial" as a result of "over-compensating for their anxiety". In the 30 to 40 age group BENSHEIM found a "chronic depression state with apprehensive paranoid overtones" brought on by the horrors of persecution. Unfortunately, these assumptions have not been systematically and statistically analysed. They are based on clinical impressions.

The age-specific disturbance areas in children and adolescents are seen differently by v. BAEYER, HÄFNER and KISKER (1964). According to their experience, the most decisive and serious event in this period of life was probably the destruction of natural family ties. This includes not just the separation from the mother but also any disruptions within the family unit.

Our comments on these results are given in the form of the findings presented in the various Chapters.

8. Sex

The group of persecuted persons interviewed by us was made up of 155 men and 64 women. It is not possible to compare the sexes as regards the extent of the subjectively experienced stress. External stress criteria cannot be applied to test whether men or women suffered varying degrees of damage under conditions of comparable external stress. The main reason why we have no valid criteria is that different standards had to be applied for men and for women. Thus, the only way to clarify the question regarding the significance of an inmate's sex as a stress factor is to carry out a phenomenological analysis of the stress situation on the basis of voluntary statements.

The persecution by the Nazis took the form of defamation, maltreatment, threats to life or incarceration and these measures had different effects on men and women because they saw themselves restricted in different areas of their lives. For a man it is nothing unusual to be at odds with the power of the state. Nevertheless, because of the extreme restrictions imposed on their possibilities for social expansion, the persecution was particularly hard for men to bear. The fascist authorities were extremely inflexible and rigorous in the way in which they went about depriving people of their rights, incarcerating them or exterminating them, and they gave their opponents absolutely no opportunity to argue with them. Particularly in concentration camps, where the persecutees were completely at the mercy of the despotic power of the SS, the isolation from society and the loss of status was, for male inmates in particular, a traumatic experience.

On the other hand, female persecutees were not so much depressed by the defamation campaign of the state nor by the fact that their opportunity for "aggressive" expansion was limited by the restrictions that were placed on their intimate lives. In the case of the racially persecuted woman, it was a particularly hard fate to bear if she was between the ages of 20 and 30 at the time of her ordeal, because it was at this time of her life that she would normally have laid the foundation for a family life of her own, but she was prevented from doing so by the race laws. Other women were particularly hard hit by the persecution measures when their families were destroyed, their husbands were transported and their children killed. They felt deprived of protection and life seemed devoid of meaning following the sudden loss of all their loved ones for whom they had lived and worked but who had also in turn given them moral and physical support.

Men and women differed greatly in the way in which they were affected by stress situations. This is illustrated most clearly by their different reactions to infringements of their intimate sphere.

An ex-persecutee found it particularly degrading to have to take a bath naked in full view of some SS men. A Jehovah's Witness felt utterly humiliated by the complete removal of all body hair. For an elderly German Jewish woman the most horrifying thing about life in a concentration camp was the vermin and the filth.

This type of humiliation was frequently cited by female persecutees, who regarded it as one of the main causes of their suffering, whereas the men, who were not particularly affected by such things, made little mention of it.

Furthermore, in the cold mechanistic atmosphere of the camp, the women's sexual experience came to an abrupt stop (TRAUTMANN, 1961). The fear of being raped by the SS and the constant wounds inflicted on their sense of modesty and intimacy made them negate anything connected with sexuality. The general incidence of amenorrhea is symptomatic of this. DÖRING's (1967) finding that "amenorrhea occurred in 100% of the women in the dreaded concentration camps" is confirmed by the reports at our disposal. DÖRING, too, believes that "the pitiless mental pressure in these camps must have been the reason for the sweeping occurrence of amenorrhea", particularly since menstruation usually started again soon after the women's release.

For the male inmates sexual frustration took a different form from that suffered by women because the men could usually find substitute activities. FRANKL (1959) and CAYROL (1959) report that absolutely no sexual activity took place: "We had no erotic dreams; our physical frailty, our agonies of hunger, our exhaustion and, added to this, sometimes the vivid memory of beatings received, all combined to make us incapable even for one moment of dreaming of a woman whom we could have loved or desired" (CAYROL, 1959). However, the records of our interviews with ex-inmates contain descriptions which complement the experiences related by FRANKL and CAYROL.

One particular persecutee had spent 4 years in prisons and penitentiaries and more than 3 years in Dachau. He gave the following report: "The main topic was not women but hunger. We dreamed about being hungry. I didn't miss not having any sex. I didn't even bother to visit the camp brothel. If you wanted to go, then you had to ask permission during rollcall. Everyone heard you. In the brothel, the individual rooms were fitted with spyholes. After about half an hour the guard started to scream 'That's it. Time's up. Get that man out of there!' The political persecutees declined on moral and religious grounds to visit the brothel. Many people went along just to have a talk with a woman, although the women were real prostitutes. Masturbation and homosexuality were widespread. On the whole, however, sexual thoughts and activity were suppressed by hunger, cold, work and exhaustion."

Another inmate claimed that "despite the starvation conditions" he "missed having sex". He went on: "I reject homosexuality. In any case, it did not get out of control in the camp. Its spread was in fact controlled by harsh disciplinary measures which the inmates themselves took. Many people had erotic dreams during the night or went in for masturbation. I secretly wanted to visit the camp brothel but the conditions accompanying such a visit put me off. The male or female SS guards used to watch the couples making love and kicked on the door with their boots if they thought the process was taking too long. To start with, it was mainly the older inmates or intellectuals who went to the brothel. Many took the prostitutes the packages which they had received from home and the women usually passed them on to starving persons."

Another persecutee reported: "The queers were bad, too. When they started to come into the camp in great numbers they seized all the power for themselves. Some of them had sexual relationships with the SS. They were given preferential treatment all round because they were not really enemies of the state like the Jews or the political prisoners. When homosexuality started to spread, a brothel was set up. However, the political prisoners did not use it because they knew it was staffed not by genuine prostitutes but by female inmates or girls who had been tricked and seduced.

In the concentration camp only people with full stomachs, i.e. the kapos, block leaders and similar types, had any sexual needs to satisfy. The political prisoners were always disciplined. Many inmates cracked up and indulged in sexual excesses and fantasies. It sometimes happened that a prisoner would have a fit and scream out all sorts of things, including obscenities."

III. Adaptation to Concentration-Camp Conditions

The ways in which persecutees adapted mentally to the terror situation encountered in the camps provide very clear clues to their later ability to come to terms with their fate. The variously reported behavioural and attitudinal characteristics of the concentration-camp inmate such as "mental primitivization" (KOGON, 1954), "cultural hibernation" (FRANKL, 1959), "regression to primitive-infantile instinctual urges" (BETTELHEIM, 1960) in fact mask a much broader range of reaction. Under the extreme pressures brought on by the constant threat of death hanging over them and by the total humiliation inflicted on them, the inmates may have appeared very much alike in their behaviour. They may all have seemed brutalized, hardened and "armour-plated", but deep down they were in turmoil. The frequently described levelling of individual differences was merely an external phenomenon; there was no levelling of individual experience. This fact is also apparent from previous scientific reports.

KRAL (1951), KOGON (1954) and v. BAEYER, HÄFNER and KISKER (1964), for example, describe different reactions depending on the duration of incarceration. The initial shock of imprisonment, which was accompanied by intense fear, was followed by an adaptation phase in which the inmate either sank into an apathetic-primitivized fatalistic state or developed active forms of adaptation. However, this description does not give a complete picture of the ways in which the inmates mastered their fate. KOGON (1954) saw that behind the uniformly rough outer shell of the concentration camp inmate fierce conflicts were raging, although these were barely perceptible to the mere onlooker. Even the future-oriented optimism of the political prisoners, who formed a tight-knit group, was frequently only a deceptive mask. Only when one of their fellows had committed suicide and his corpse lay at their feet — as KOGON puts it — did the prisoners begin to comprehend the inner torment he had suffered.

False, no longer viable attitudes dating from the time before incarceration soon crumbled: "The straitjacket of social mores was immediately discarded" (KOGON). Although the concentration-camp situation was one in which the inmates were pushed to the extreme limits of endurance, this did not bring about a levelling of individual differences. Men who had previously enjoyed high social rank now felt compelled to prove their strength of character. Many inmates reflected on their true strength, gained insight into the true nature of man and as a result became emotionally more mature. KOGON saw this in the "refinement of conscience" that took place and FRANKL (1959) discovered it in the "upsurge of a repressed turning to God".

It is quite impossible to list here everything that other people have written about the behaviour of concentration camp prisoners. It should be emphasized, however, that the modes of experience and the success in adapting were very different even under conditions of extreme stress and were not uniform as the conventional stress theory would have led one to expect. In addition, the modes of experience and the level of adaptation achieved to the camp situation are more closely related to the personality of the inmate than to external characteristics such as severity of the work stress, severity of the camp, hunger, sickness, etc. Even if the external forms of coping with the concentration-camp situation were reduced to a few survival tactics, the reasons for survival as seen by the inmates were highly varied.

1. Reasons for Survival as Recalled by Inmates

It seemed possible and appropriate, as a means of providing a quantitative guide, to list the reasons most frequently given by the interviewees to explain why they survived. The statements by the persecutees regarding the reasons for their survival were classified by three independent appraisers into 12 categories. Interviewees often gave no reasons for their survival, but equally often other interviewees cited more than one reason. Overall, therefore, the number of reasons exceeds the number of interviewees, as is evident from Table 12.

To us, the remarkable thing about this list of reasons for survival is the fact that "discipline and self control" figure in first place, and in particular come before "chance or luck". The importance of the inmate's inner attitude becomes even more apparent when one considers that, with the exception of "chance or luck" and "humaneness of individual guards", this factor plays a decisive role in all the other reasons for survival given. The knowledge that they had done something decisive to control what we have termed here "chance or luck" probably explains why hardly

Table 12. Reasons for survival as remembered by ex-inmates (n=219)

Reasons for survival	Frequency
1. "Discipline and self-control"	50 (22.8%)
2. "Chance or luck"	44 (20.1%)
3. "Cameraderie with fellow inmates"	43 (19.6%)
4. "Family memories"	31 (14.1%)
5. "Good work, good position/job"	31 (14.1%)
6. "Religious faith"	25 (11.4%)
7. "Active adaptation to camp conditions"	22 (10.0%)
8. "Good physical condition"	18 (8.2%)
9. "Humaneness of individual guards"	12 (5.5%)
10. "Retreat into one's own inner life"	9 (4.1%)
11. "Feelings of hatred and revenge towards Nazis"	8 (3.6%)
12. "Faith in political convictions"	3 (1.4%)

any of the interviewees mentioned external factors such as camp conditions, duration of incarceration, maltreatment, etc. The fact that there are certain links between the remembered reasons for survival and the personality characteristics of the inmates will be discussed in more detail in the chapter on "Basic Forms of Psychic Disturbance" (see p. 113).

This dry list of the most frequently quoted reasons for survival will now be illustrated by some of the persecutees' own reports on their experiences. The following answers were given in response to the question "Why did you survive?".

"I was quite an ordinary inmate. I never had any supervisory post. I was in good shape from playing sport and I had a strong will."

"I ate all the food that I was given and did not exchange any of it for cigarettes, as some people did. Also, there were times when life was relatively bearable. That was when I had some acquaintances or old-established privileged prisoners, whose word carried some weight, to protect me from the inhuman block leaders."

"I was always lucky enough to come across people who helped me. Usually they were kapos or hospital staff who had belonged to my former socialist group. When I went down with typhus and jaundice, they saved my life."

"One important reason could be that I met a woman who told me that she had met my father. The knowledge that my father was still alive gave me strength to survive. Otherwise it was a miracle that I escaped death."

"I used to say to myself 'what will be will be'. One doesn't live for ever anyway. But I also had a desire to experience the future and I never thought about the past. What good would it have done me when faced with the crematorium? I wanted to live and I was very careful in everything that I did. I thought: 'Keep working then nothing can happen'. I am a pious man, but my religious beliefs are somewhat on the modern side. If God wants me to live, then I live. My wife was unlucky, so was my daughter. I was fortunate. But, I always did whatever I could 'pour corriger la fortune'."

"I overcame everything thanks to my will to pull through. I deliberately overcame the terrible memories of people being tortured by forcing myself to become as hard as stone. I did not permit myself one single emotion otherwise I would probably not have made it alive."

"I never lost hope and I did not let anything get me down, although I was always scared that my turn would come. People's senses became dulled and they shut themselves off from the world around them."

"After I had been in Auschwitz for a few weeks I realized that I would have to do something to survive. I suffered particularly badly from hunger. Within a few days I was able to get myself put on potato-peeling duties. That's what saved me."

2. Personality of the Inmate and his Adaptation to the Concentration Camp Situation

Up to now, nowhere in the literature has a systematic analysis been made of the importance of the personality factor in regard to the inmate's behaviour during incarceration. The probable reason for this omission is that a merely superficial exploration makes it appear that the individual was very restricted in his freedom of behaviour in the concentration camp. Most investigators did not consider it necessary to carry out a more intensive study of this problem because, as appraisers, they were chiefly concerned with the outwardly apparent damaging forms of stress (such as beatings, illness, hunger, etc.). When, in fact, any report was given on a particular mode of adaptation, the investigators resorted to metaphor or relatively coarse classification categories such as "fatalistic attitude", "primitivization", "animal-like vegetation".

In our study of the persecutees' fates the pre-incarceration characteristics of the individual concentration-camp inmates and their survival tactics in the camps are considered in detail. These modes of behaviour are closely interrelated and they are also connected with the ways in which the inmates came to terms with their post-incarceration fate, as will be shown in detail in the following chapters.

Because of the extremely coercive character of the concentration-camp situation the modes of behaviour of the individual inmates were largely restricted to finding methods of adapting in order to survive. There were, of course, various ways in which to adapt to the situation, but success achieved in one way was closely related to the success achieved in another. This was also revealed by a factor analysis procedure in which sociological characteristics, stress and adaptation characteristics (see Appendix) of 210 interviewees (the information was incomplete in 9 cases) were related to each other. With one exception, the resulting factors have been ignored because they agree with the remarks made on p. 25 (reasons for persecution).

The one factor we have retained — we have called it the "adaptation to concentration camp conditions" factor — is of central importance because it reveals the structural relationships of the various adaptation characteristics to each other (see Tables 13 and 14):

Table 13. The factor of adaptation to concentration camp conditions

Characteristics	"Inmate successfully adapted to camp situation" (Pole A)	"Inmate did not manage to adapt to camp situation" (Pole B)	Loading
Interpersonal contact with fellow prisoners	Actively sought contact	Difficulty in making contact	0.77
Attitude towards fellow prisoners	Comradely attitude	Indifference	0.74
Activity displayed during incarceration	Active throughout	Passive throughout	0.67
Relationships with guards	Adapted to guards	Did not adapt to guards	0.39

Table 14. Intercorrelations and loadings for the characteristics of the adaptation factor

	1. Actively sought contact	2. Comradely attitude	3. Activity	4. Adaptation	Factor loading
1. Actively sought contact	—	0.46	0.44	0.26	0.77
2. Comradely attitude		—	0.31	0.16	0.74
3. Activity			—	0.31	0.67
4. Adaptation to SS					0.39

As is clear from Table 13, the differences in the degree of adaptation achieved by the inmates can be related back, above all, to the varying degree of initiative taken in making contact with others and to differences in the amount of comradeship displayed. From a statistical point of view, active "survival tactics" and the ability to adapt to the SS are less important characteristics when it comes to distinguishing between the inmates and their ability to cope with camp conditions. This is also what one would expect, because the inmates had to display a certain amount of "obedience" and "discipline", even submissivness (if only feigned) in order to survive. The "activity displayed during incarceration" and the "relationships with the guards" were therefore probably factors which in reality the survivors were able to vary less than might appear to us nowadays.

In the following we have listed the characteristics of successful adaptation (Pole A) together with the modes of behaviour on which assessment of these characteristics was based:

Actively sought social contact (132 interviewees): "Took an active part in a politically organized group", "Had frequent contact with persons of similar religious beliefs", "Was able to strike up associations with various groups", "Had many contacts as a result of holding a supervisory position", "Visited other barracks".

Comradeliness (149 interviewees): "Comforted fellow prisoners", "Showed new inmates how to protect themselves", "In his position as block leader, looked after the well-being of those in his charge", "Occasionally shared his food with others when they were in dire need".

Activity (134 interviewees): "Through his activity as a barber always tried to establish connections and to exploit these connections for himself and others", "Was popular with the guards because he was a good organizer", "Worked out escape plans and got away once", "Made sure he got the work he wanted and had himself transferred to camps where the extermination risk was low", "Carried on trading activities in the camp", "Made every possible effort to get work in the camp kitchen and was finally successful".

Adapted to guards (108 interviewees): "Forced the guards to respect him because of his brisk, clever manner", "Opportunistic submission", "Was granted special privileges in his position as supervisor", "Was frequently protected by the guards from being punished".

The failure to adapt (Pole B) is characterized by the following modes of behaviour:

Difficulty in making contact (87 interviewees): "Odd character", "Mistrusted everyone", "Was only interested in forming special advantageous relationships with the guards", "Was locked up with criminals, with whom he wanted nothing to do".

Indifference (70 interviewees): "Uncomradely attitude towards fellow prisoners", "Always an outsider", "Only looked after his own interests", "Was rejected and retired into a shell".

Passivity (85 interviewees): "Clung onto other prisoners", "A mere hanger-on in politically organized groups", "Completely apathetic, wanted to die", "Attributed his survival to chance or fortune", "Fatalist", "Tried to seek safety in illness".

Did not adapt to guards (111 interviewees): "Was frequently punished", "Was always given the worst work", "Was hostile and stubborn towards the guards", "Always got the worst of things", "Was frequently tortured because of disobedience".

Further differentiation of the adaptive behaviour in concentration camps was obtained through analysis of the intercorrelations of the characteristics of adaptation (see Table 14).

Proceeding first of all from the factor loadings, we find that the survival tactic that involved adapting to the SS guards stands out most from the other modes of adaptation. Its factor loading (0.39) is significantly lower. It is very poorly correlated with comradeliness (r=0.16), but it is very significantly correlated with general activity (r=0.31).

The relatively high degree of correlation between general activity and adaptation to the SS can be interpreted in two ways. First, it was one method of getting along with the guards if one toed the line, worked hard and took an active part in the self-administration of the inmates' affairs. But on the other hand, such behaviour was only possible with the benevolent tolerance of the SS. The relatively low correlation between comradeliness and the ability to adapt to the mentality and demands of the guards is due to the fact that activity aimed at assisting other inmates often involved conflict with the guards.

The tactic of trying to maintain the best possible relationships with the guards exhibits the following correlations with characteristics other than the adaptation factor:

Persecutees who adapted to the guards were more frequently German (1% significance) and had easier work conditions (1% significance).

Among the reasons for these correlations is probably the fact that the SS guards were less prejudiced towards German Jews than towards Polish Jews and no language barrier existed between them and the Germans. From the point of view of the inmates, a long period of persecution, such as was typically the case for the German inmates, and relatively light work stress were both factors which enabled the prisoners to get to know and adapt to the guards. With long exposure to the SS guards, the inmates gradually lost their fear of them, particularly once they got to know their weaknesses and knew how to exploit them (see also BETTELHEIM, 1960).

The mode of survival characterized chiefly by activity is significantly correlated only with light work stress (5% significance).

Again, there are two possible interpretations here. On the one hand, the main result of the inmate's activity was that he managed to reduce the stress of his work situation; on the other hand, the reduced work stress gave him more opportunity for activity.

"Comradeliness" and "active initiative in making social contact" are the most crucial elements determining the adaptation factor. Their factor loadings are highest. They also have a very high intercorrelation ($r = 0.46$). In contrast to the characteristics "adaptation to the SS" and "activity" neither comradeliness nor the active seeking of social contact are significantly correlated with the severity of the work stress (in both cases $r = 0.0$). This means that even though the inmates may have been given easier work to perform, they did not allow this to corrupt them into displaying a less comradely attitude towards their fellow prisoners. There are significantly negative correlations between the degree of camp stress, comradeliness and the active seeking of social contact.

Persecutees who exhibited comradeliness (1% significance) and actively sought social contact (5% significance) were exposed to less camp stress.

We can deduce from this that in extremely harsh camps the inmates were so strongly compelled to adopt egoistical survival tactics that solidarity with fellow prisoners was a trait which could only develop in, relatively speaking, easier camps. Activity and adaptation to the SS were also restricted by severe camp conditions, but not to the same extent as the seeking of social contact and comradeliness.

In order to obtain a general view of the conditions on which the overall adaptation achievement in the camps depended, a single adaptation value was calculated for each persecutee. For this purpose all four characteristics were regarded as equal. Inmates who had zero, one or two characteristics of successful adaptation (100 interviewees) were regarded as having achieved poor adaptation. Inmates with three or four characteristics of successful adaptation were regarded as having adapted well (110 interviewees). When these global indices of good adaptation to camp conditions were correlated with 60 characteristics of the inmate's pre-concentration camp personality, sociological background and stress situation, it was found that in almost all cases only the personality characteristics showed significant correlations with the adaptation achievement. The success in achieving adaptation to the camp situation does not depend to any significant extent on sex, age, reasons for persecution, origin or marital status, nor on the persecution and fate of relatives, or on the duration of persecution and imprisonment.

The fact that severe work and camp stress greatly restricted the inmate's opportunities for adaptation has already been indicated by the significant negative correlations with the individual characteristics of adaptation (see p. 34 et seqq.). This fact is confirmed by the finding that the severity of the work and camp situation also exhibits significantly negative correlations with the overall adaptation achievement. However, it is clear from the reports that the factor "submission to fate" should also be considered, since the weaker and more dispirited inmates allowed themselves to be given the worst work and to be incarcerated in the harshest camps.

Because of the multiple correlations of the inmate's adaptation performance with aspects of his basic personality, it is therefore also possible to state that the development of successful survival tactics in the camps is not a consequence of external fate but, instead, is the expression of a dynamic personality.

Inmates who adapted well to the camp situation, who were active, comradely and outgoing had the following characteristic experience and behaviour patterns prior to incarceration [2]:

> The mother was open-minded and receptive (10% significance)
> The mother was cooperative and tolerant (0.1% significance)
> Relationships with siblings were harmonious (10% significance)
> Psychosocial development was harmonious (5% significance)
> The break with the parental home was successful (5% significance)
> Good relationships existed with people of the same sex and age (5% significance)
> They were successful in their careers (5% significance)
> They took an active part in the general life of society (1% significance)
> They reacted with active countermeasures to the onset of persecution (0.1% significance)

In the case of the inmates who adapted badly to camp conditions, who were passive, uncomradely and low in social contact, we find that they had precisely the opposite experience in the time preceding their incarceration. Their relationships inside and outside the family were less happy and successful than in the case of the inmates who were able to cope with the camp situation.

These empirical findings lend further credence to the psychodynamic theories of development which assume that a person's later behaviour in life is based very largely on the modes of experience and the modes of coping with life which are developed in earlier stages of his existence. Of 14 characteristics relating to the interviewees' experiences within their parental family, including their relationship with their father, the most significant characteristic from the point of view of later behaviour proved to be an affectionate and understanding method of upbringing exercised by the mother. The development of an unshakeable trust in the mother is a prerequisite and a starting point for the later formation of a trusting and realistic attitude towards the rest of humanity. The early experience of stable interpersonal relationships forms the basis for satisfactory contacts later in life.

---

[2] The characteristics are arranged in psychogenetic sequence and not according to their statistical significance.

In the statements made by the persecutees who were well adapted both before and during incarceration we find, for example, the following descriptions of how their mothers were remembered:

"There was an affectionate relationship between us. Also, she always took a great deal of interest in my success."
"My mother was energetic and spirited. Thanks to my good relationship with her I also acquired these characteristics."
"I got on very well with my mother. My harmonious relationship with her gave me the basis of confidence I needed throughout my long life, even though the Nazis killed her very early on."
"When things got really bad in Auschwitz I used to think of my mother. This gave me the confidence and the power to survive the concentration camp unscathed."

It was found that the inmates who were able to look back on a "good" relationship with their mothers were the ones who did not buckle under the stress of imprisonment. Thanks to their "positive" memories they were able to give their lives an historic dimension which formed the basis for hope in the future. One persecutee put it like this:

"In the concentration camp I felt that, since I had had such a promising start in life, it was worth making the effort to survive so that I could afterwards demonstrate what I was capable of."

The open-minded, receptive character of the mother, the mainly harmonious relationships with siblings, and the general impression that the psychosocial development had proceeded normally are the main elements in these memories of a cooperative harmonious relationship between mother and child. There are intercorrelations between these variables but it is not possible to sort them out on the basis of the memories recounted by the inmates. However, it can be said in summary that the inmates who were able to hold their own under camp conditions were those who could look back on a childhood in which their most important needs had been satisfied.

A satisfactory childhood also made it possible for the individuals in question to develop successful means of mastering life outside the family. They were able to break away from the parental home, and unlike others they achieved this break without much difficulty. Reflecting their relationships with their siblings, they were easily able to make contact with male or female friends. They were popular with those around them and there were no barriers to success in their occupation and to the development of socially integrative activity.

It is remarkable that, as regards sthenic-active behavioural attitudes, the greatest differences in personality development between the inmates able to cope and those unable to cope with the concentration camp situation occurred from late puberty onwards. The ability to bear up under the stress of incarceration was not determined by such variables as empathy with the opposite sex or a harmonious married life, but by occupational success, activity in the affairs of society, and initiative upon onset of persecution. Everything which the successful inmates needed to survive the concentration camp with the minimum of damage, namely an outgoing attitude, comradeliness, activity and adaptibility, had all been acquired and moulded in the time prior to imprisonment in the normal course of coming to grips with jobs and society. The self-confidence they had gained and the security which this gave them became apparent at the onset of persecution. They did not passively accept the fate which the Nazis wished to impose on them, instead they took active countermeasures in the form of attempts to escape or offered resistance on arrest and during interrogations.

The present differences in attitude and behaviour between the inmates who adapted well to the camp situation and those who did not are thus to be seen not only as a continuation of the character development which started out differently **very** early on, but also as the effect of the varying degrees of damage inflicted by the concentration camp experience. Even today the inmates who came through the rigours of incarceration well are, with a high degree of significance, much more expansive, reliable, cheerful and full of confidence than those who were worse affected by the persecution and who despondently put up with all the Nazi bullying.

These points will be dealt with in detail in the following chapters.

CHAPTER 3

Late-Appearing Damage to Health

Outline of Problem

The medical scientific literature published to date on the late injuries which manifest themselves after concentration camp incarceration is primarily characterized by the fact that the interviewers' contact with the former persecutees came either in the course of a medical consultation or in connection with an appraisal for pension purposes. Thus, there is a decisive preselection of the cases reported. In fact, only the sick or those who feel sick are covered.

We could overlook this selection factor with its false conclusions if it should turn out that the number of healthy individuals is relatively small. Then a more serious fact might be that the results of the most comprehensive investigations were obtained in the course of medical appraisal procedures. In the situation as it existed at the time, many investigators, who were expected to produce hundreds of appraisal reports in the space of a few years, not only lacked the time needed to carry out a careful examination and to determine the precise medical history, they also failed to check the phenomena which MATUSSEK (1961) termed the "compulsive urge to adapt to the symptom". By this is meant the fact that the applicant for a pension generally described his complaint from one particular aspect, namely the one which to his layman's mind seemed to offer the quickest and most effective way of reaching his goal, which was to achieve the best possible pension. We are not referring here to a conscious and tendentious falsification of the symptoms — although this happened — but instead to the usual attitude encountered in every medical examination, i.e. a patient who goes to the doctor with "stomach ache" will only mention those facts which, in his opinion, are related to the symptom bothering him.

All the examining doctors, however, whether they had a lot of time or too little, whether they described their findings in detail or not, were under pressure to reach a clearcut decision on the extent to which the injury in question was related to the persecution situation. The doctor therefore had to develop his own theory as to whether and to what extent a causal relationship existed between sickness and incarceration. In other words, the examining doctor often had to come to a decision before the problem had been properly and scientifically analysed. This phenomenon is reflected in the large discrepancies between the findings and the theories on late injury following concentration-camp incarceration. V. BAEYER, HÄFNER and KISKER have given a detailed list of the contradictions contained in the literature and correctly pointed out that the differences are not solely due to the time when the examination was conducted or to the different methods of investigation. But they were unable to offer any further reasons for these discrepancies. We lean towards the assumption that the appraisal situation, in which most of the theories and findings reported so far in the medical literature were obtained, is to blame for the widely differing views.

This raises a second problem to be looked at in this chapter, namely the contrast between the findings reached in an appraisal situation and those obtained in an interview situation.

There is a third problem connected with the diagnoses made for former concentration camp inmates. The main question here is whether for this group of people a specific pattern of late injury symptoms requires a special diagnosis. Some authors assume that it does and therefore also speak of a "concentration-camp syndrome" (HERMANN and THYGESEN, 1954; THAYSEN and THAYSEN, 1955; STRÖM, EITINGER, GRÖNVIK, LÖNNUM, ENGESET, OSVIK and ROGAN, 1961; PAUL, 1963) or an "asthenia syndrome" (SEGELLE and ELLENBOGEN, 1954; TARGOWLA, 1955; FICHEZ, 1957; RICKET and MANS, 1958) or of a "concentration camp neurosis" (BENSHEIM, 1960). We shall therefore be asking the question: What symptoms are apparent approximately 15 years after the inmates' release and what should they be termed?

The fourth problem to be dealt with in this chapter is the question of the stress factors which are correlated with the present pattern of symptoms. This question is usually answered in a relatively general way. The present injury is related back solely to the concentration camp experience and little attempt, if any, is made to differentiate between stress factors. Also, in those cases where a differentiation was attempted — at least partially — no significance values were calculated so that it remained unclear whether certain correlations exist and, if so, how significant they are.

This omission makes it particularly difficult to assess the correlations of the relationships between the present injury and the pre-concentration-camp personality. General expressions such as "Never ill prior to incarceration", "No special problems during development", "Neurotic childhood development", and similar, can provide little information on the importance of personality factors for the stress experienced in the camps.

We then attempt to determine statistically the correlation of the present patterns of symptoms with the various sociological and psychological characteristics, including those of personal development.

Finally, we deal in this chapter with the problem of what factors determined the amount of pension to be awarded for late injury in the case of former concentration-camp inmates.

The results presented in this chapter were obtained from the following groups of persons (Table 15, page 42).

Of the total of 245 former persecutees interviewed 188 were selected. This smaller group is composed of 170 persons who had submitted an application for indemnification of illness or injury resulting from concentration camp incarceration (applicants) and 18 persons who had not made any such application (non-applicants). The medical documents relating to the indemnification procedure were not available for the other 57 persons in the overall group. Therefore these people could not be considered in connection with the problems discussed in this chapter.

The indemnification documentation for the 170 applicants was evaluated for the medical information it contained. The results were contrasted with those obtained in the interviews, although it should be pointed out here that in 26 cases no interview could be conducted because of the death, prolonged absence, unknown whereabouts or direct refusal of the person in question, or because the information was so sketchy that it could not be evaluated. However, the medical reports of these 26 persons have not been used in the later analysis of pension procedures.

The group of 144 applicants interviewed by us is highly representative of the total group of 245 (see Appendix p. 261).

In order to determine the late injury suffered we chose a factor analysis method of the kind described in detail in Chapter 1 "Study Methods". We did this because we wished to supplement and expand the large number of tables giving statistics of the symptoms (MINKOWSKI, 1946; HERMANN and THYGESEN, 1954; HELWEG-LARSEN, HOFFMEYER, KIELER, THAYSEN and THAYSEN, THYGESEN and WULFF, 1955; RICHET,

Table 15. Persons covered in this chapter (n=188)

Group	Number
Persons who had been medically examined in connection with indemnification procedures	170
Psychological interviews were conducted for 144 persons in this group	
Persons not medically examined in connection with indemnification procedures (psychological interviews conducted in each case)	18
Total	188

GILBERT-DREYFUS, FICHEZ and UZAN, 1955; BASTIAANS, 1957; RICHET and MANS, 1958; EITINGER, 1961; ENGESET, 1961; KLIMKOVA-DEUTSCHOVA, 1961; DÖRING, 1963; v. BAEYER, HÄFNER and KISKER, 1964) by carrying out a study which did not simply enquire into the percentage frequency of individual symptoms but also into the dimensions on which several symptoms are based. This procedure was all the more appropriate since most of the studies carried out to date have concentrated merely on establishing with sufficient accuracy the symptoms falling within their particular scope and have used these to arrive at a diagnosis.

This is particularly true with regard to the difference between psychic and physical symptoms. Usually the authors who had to prepare reports on chiefly physical symptoms gave an inadequate assessment of the psychic symptomatology and vice versa. Where, however, both aspects were considered, as in the studies prepared by EITINGER (1961), the individual physical and mental symptoms were recorded and their percentage frequency determined, but the question was never posed as to whether and what symptoms are closely connected. Thus, there was too great a risk of designating an arbitrarily selected group of symptoms as a "concentration camp syndrome".

We therefore asked ourselves the question: Which injury dimensions stand out in a joint assessment of physical and psychic symptoms exhibited by ex-inmates? These injury dimensions could then probably be given the highest weighting — at least from a statistical point of view — among the late injuries.

I. Late Injury Following Incarceration

1. Healthy Persons

For the reasons stated in the chapter on "Study Methods", we cannot give an accurate figure for the percentage of healthy ex-inmates. Of the 66 persons who refused to be interviewed (see "Study Methods" p. 2) we can be certain that 7 individuals who declined to cooperate with us did so because they felt well and therefore were not interested in our study. We can only assume that these 7 persons were not the only ones out of the 66 who refused to be interviewed for the reasons just given. It is not possible therefore to come to any accurate conclusion about persons who refused to be interviewed because they felt healthy. We can only say with certainty that a much larger number of persons refused to be interviewed for other reasons. Also, with regard to the total number of ex-inmates, we are inclined to believe, for reasons which will be described in more detail later, that the number of ex-inmates who remained healthy is very small.

Only 18 persons out of the total group of 245 failed to submit an application for indemnification. The persons in question were 16 Jews and 2 priests. 12 Jews emigrated, 3 to the USA and 9 to Israel. The remaining 4 are now living in Germany. This group mentioned the following complaints in the course of psychological interviews (Table 16):

Table 16. Number of physical and psychological complaints mentioned by 18 non-applicants

Physical complaints	absol. number	Psychological complaints	absol. number
Dyspeptic complaints	5	Anxiety dreams	6
Spinal column complaints	3	Nervousness, irritability	5
Headache	2	Depressive moods	4
Hearing and vision defects	2	Anxiety states	3
Pulmonary-bronchial complaints	1	Partial or temporary amnesia	1
Stomach disorders	1	Tiredness	1
Rheumatic complaints	1		
Gynaecological complaints	1		
Sterility	1		
Total	17	Total	20

It is apparent from the Table that the persons who made no application for a pension for possible damage suffered to health were in no way free from complaints. When a comparison is made with the overall group of applicants it is found, however, that the average frequency of somatic complaints is much higher in the case of applicants (3.1 complaints per person, as established in the interview) than in that of non-applicants (0.9 complaints per person). It can be stated therefore that judging by the number of complaints, the non-applicants are physically healthier than the applicants. The same is true of the mental health status of the two groups. Applicants had far more complaints (3.8 per person, as established by interview) than non-applicants (1.1 complaints per person). The values for the applicants are, however, average values for the entire group of applicants. It is possible that the differences between the two groups would be reduced if only applicants with low disability ratings were used in the comparison. Out of 170 applicants, 16 (9.4%) were deemed to have suffered a less than 25% reduction in working capacity as a result of persecution-related damage to health. Such a loss of capacity is legally regarded as equivalent to a state of health which does not prevent the average person from functioning, i.e. it does not possess any "pathological value". There can therefore be no entitlement in this case to indemnification.

In order to be able to determine the "pathological value" of the complaints of non-applicants more accurately, we will compare this group with those applicants who had the lowest reduction in working capacity (less than 25%). The subjective complaints mentioned in the interviews are taken as the basis for the comparison.

Table 17 demonstrates the frequency of the complaints mentioned by applicants with a persecution-related reduction in working capacity of less than 25% (Table 17):

Table 17. Physical and psychological complaints of 16 persons suffering less than 25% reduction in working capacity as a result of persecution

Physical complaints	Absolute quantity	Psychological complaints	Absolute quantity
Cardiovascular complaints	7	Anxiety dreams	9
Vegetative complaints	5	Mistrust, difficulty in making	
Head complaints	5	social contact	9
Stomach complaints	5	Internal agitation, irritability	8
Pulmonary-bronchial complaints	4	Sleep disturbances	8
Dental complaints	3	Depressive moods	7
Spinal column complaints	3	Anxiety states	6
Rheumatic complaints	2	Tiredness, apathy	5
Hearing and sight defects	2	Feeling of isolation	5
Intestinal disorders	2	Temporary or partial amnesia,	
Injury to limbs following		poor concentration	4
maltreatment	2	Paranoid ideation	3
Urological complaints	1	Feelings of hatred	2
Gynaecological complaints	1	Disturbed vitality	1
Total	42	Total	67

The Table shows that the 16 applicants likewise complained of far more somatic and psychic problems than the non-applicants. The number of psychological complaints is particularly high in the case of the applicants. As will be discussed in Section III (p. 78) very low pensions are awarded precisely in the case of psychic disturbances, so we can expect to find persons with exclusively psychic complaints in the lowest pension brackets.

Non-applicants thus differ clearly from applicants as regards their subjective complaints. Even those applicants who were assessed as having suffered the least reduction in working capacity, which did not entitle them to any idemnification, have far more complaints than non-applicants. However, since we did not carry out a detailed medical examination either of the applicants or of the non-applicants we cannot make any absolutely reliable statements on the different "pathological values" of the respective states of health of the two groups.

However, from the figures given it is possible to assume that non-applicants, in view of the lower frequency of their complaints, are in general healthier than applicants and would not have stood very much chance of obtaining a pension. Whether this is why the non-applicants declined to submit an application for indemnification for damage to health or whether other motives were involved is a matter which will be clarified by closer examination of these persons.

The group of 18 non-applicants can be divided into two subgroups:

a) Healthy persons

Among the 18 persons there were 4 former persecutees who did not complain of any health problems or any bad effects at all resulting from incarceration. The four people were a priest and three Jews. The priest had been incarcerated for 4 years under severe conditions and he suffered from a hearing defect which was unrelated to his concentration camp days. Since he did not have any other complaints he did not see any need to make an application for indemnification.

The three other persecutees were a detective officer, a lawyer and a waiter. The detective and the lawyer were altogether imprisoned for only a short time with relatively light working stress. The waiter, a qualified mechanic, had been incarcerated for two years — including a short period in Auschwitz — but had always had a bearable job to carry out which, in his opinion, helped him to survive almost entirely unscathed.

b) Sick persons

The remaining 14 persons did not feel healthy and related all their problems back to the concentration camp. Nevertheless, they did not apply for indemnification.

In 7 cases it was not possible to explain exactly why no application had been made because the persons in question gave either no information or only inadequate information on this point, for example: "I am not interested in compensation", or "my lawyer is to blame for my not having applied for compensation".

The remaining 7 interviewees who felt unwell and who regarded their complaints as related to the persecution they had endured, explicitly refused to apply for a pension. In their cases we find a motivation that can be interpreted as representing two extreme variants of their adjustment to their concentration camp past.

1. Emphasis on concentration camp past. Three of the former persecutees characterize this particular variant. They refer very emphatically to their past as concentration camp inmates and try to extract as much personal recognition and prestige as possible from the fact of their incarceration. However, they feel they can only achieve this by refusing to accept any form of financial compensation for their sufferings. They strictly avoid becoming in any way dependent on their former persecutors, say by applying for a pension and exposing themselves to all the time-consuming bureaucracy that this would involve.

"For me, as a priest, money cannot make good the damage suffered. I think it would be unbecoming for a priest to make such an application and I also do not think it right to take payment for one's sufferings." It is his opinion that the symptoms manifest in his case such as stomach complaints (ulcer), depressive moods, anxiety dreams and nervousness are directly connected with the stresses of persecution.

Another person, a Jew, wants nothing to do with any money "that the Germans would pay for my blood, at least not until everyone has been compensated". Following a sterilization operation carried out on him during incarceration he now suffers from dyspeptic symptoms, depressive states, anxiety dreams and nervousness.

An academic, also persecuted on racial grounds, stated, "I am not in the least interested in having my damaged health officially certified. I want to avoid getting into permanent conflict with doctors. I am frequently tortured by anxiety states which are triggered by the least little thing, for example when someone knocks on the door, when the telephone rings or when people shout. A panicky feeling of disaster suddenly overcomes me. When this happens, I hear the terrible bellowing of the German guards. At one time I wanted to start a course of psychiatric treatment, but I was afraid that it would be far too upsetting for me.

In my opinion money can do nothing at all to help one cope with the after-effects of the concentration camp experience. In fact, I think it a rather questionable practice to accept money for this. One might go so far as to suspect an unacceptable motive behind Germany's offer to make good concentration camp sufferings with money. The just demands of the people who were persecuted cannot be fully satisfied by cash payments. It is not enough to provide material compensation while internally, morally, the entire issue is being skirted. Germany is not yet in a position to make up for the past."

2. Disavowal of concentration camp past. This attitude is easiest to identify from the fact that the persons who fall into this category spend as little time as possible thinking or worrying about their concentration camp past; above all, they do not want to discuss it with other people.

A female Jew, now living in Israel, gave the following report: "The only thing I suffer from at present is migraine, otherwise I am completely healthy. This is why I chose not to make any application for compensation — I am not interested in it. Of course, one never forgets what happened — it is impossible to forget. But I am trying to put it out of my mind. I don't want to think about it nor do I want to discuss it any more."

Another racial persecutee said:

"I didn't apply for a pension because it was too much trouble. Probably no one would believe I was ever in a concentration camp. You have to be able to prove and certify everything. I can't do that. It would just stir everything up again. You may not be able to believe it, but I actually told the authorities in writing that I didn't want a pension."

A Jew, now living in Israel, made the following comments:

"I don't think I would be eligible for a pension. Anyway, I'm not going to do anything about it. Also, I think the public is making too much fuss about the events that took place in the camps. Look at all the commotion which is associated right now with the Eichmann trial." Although he lost part of a finger as a result of forced labour and although he suffers from dyspepsia and occasional depressive moods, he refuses to admit that he has suffered permanently in any way from his concentration camp experiences. He rarely thinks about that period in his life. He also avoids newspaper articles on the subject.

A female Jew stated right at the start of the interview that she did not like talking about her persecution. She said:

"What I have to relate is of no interest to scientific research. You know, the memories are too painful for me to be able to talk about them easily." When questioned about the state of her health she felt that she did not suffer from any particular symptoms. But, in the course of her interview she spontaneously remarked, "I don't feel well these days. I am in a constant state of inner agitation. For years I have had nightmares about the SS and the camp police. Sometimes I cry for hours without knowing why."

From these descriptions we can assume that these persons are attempting to overcome their terrible experiences by repressing them and also by avoiding any investigations which would inevitably bring back memories of the past. They would rather forego a pension than upset the delicate equilibrium they have struggled to establish.

Summarizing, it can be said that in view of the above-mentioned methodological difficulties (refusal on the part of the interviewees to cooperate) it is not possible to give an exact percentage for the number of "healthy" former inmates. It is our opinion, however, that the percentage is very low. However, as will be shown in the individual chapters, there are two points to be considered here: Firstly, the designation "healthy" is a highly relative term. Even the supposedly healthy persons were not entirely free from symptoms, some of which at least were in all likelihood connected with their concentration camp imprisonment. Secondly, the inmates who came through the experience of imprisonment unscathed were generally those who were exposed to above average "bearable" conditions or who managed to engineer such conditions for themselves in the camps.

2. The Results of Medical Examinations and Psychological Interviews

As far back as 1961 we expressed the view that a medical examination conducted for the purposes of pension assessment is by no means the best method of obtaining accurate data for a comprehensive diagnosis. V. BAEYER, HÄFNER and KISKER took full account of these doubts and gave technical directions on how the difficulties to be expected with this group of people should be handled in the situation of a medical examination.

We feel, however, that even the best medical examiner is unable, except in very rare cases, to eliminate the "compulsion to fit the symptoms to the examination situation", as MATUSSEK described this effect. We were able to confirm this suspicion by contrasting the somatic and psychological complaints spontaneously expressed both during medical examinations and during psychological interviews (see Tables 18 and 19).

We deliberately took the complaints and not the diagnoses as the basis for the comparison, because the various examining doctors arrived at different diagnoses for one and the same complaint.

From these Tables it is apparent that:

In the situation of a medical examination far more somatic complaints were mentioned than in an interview situation. This almost certainly is due to the fact that the interviewer did not expressly enquire after somatic problems while the examining doctor was chiefly interested in precisely such complaints in order to assess the person's eligibility for a pension.

In the interview situation far more psychological complaints were mentioned than somatic problems. Characteristically, the difference between the medical examination and the interview situation is least obvious in the case of complaints the ex-inmate felt could be related to physical injury. This applies in particular to disturbances of memory and concentration as well as to tiredness and apathy.

On the other hand, there is a striking difference in favour of the interview situation when it comes to such complaints as "mistrust", "shyness" and "difficulty in

Table 18. Somatic complaints (n=144)

Complaints	Mentioned in medical examinations	Mentioned in psychological interviews	Level of significance [a]
Vegetative complaints	86 (59.7%)	48 (33.7%)	h.s.
Dental complaints	53 (36.8%)	19 (13.3%)	h.s.
Rheumatic complaints	48 (33.7%)	24 (16.8%)	s.s.
Cardiovascular complaints	95 (66.0%)	68 (47.2%)	s.s.
Head complaints	64 (44.4%)	42 (29.3%)	s.s.
Hepatic/bilious complaints	35 (24.3%)	16 (11.2%)	s.s.
Urological complaints	24 (16.8%)	8 (5.6%)	s.s.
Spinal column complaints	48 (33.7%)	30 (20.8%)	s.
Defective sight/hearing	35 (24.3%)	21 (14.1%)	s.
Pulmonary-bronchial complaints	57 (39.6%)	41 (28.7%)	s.
Intestinal complaints	27 (18.7%)	13 (9.1%)	s.
Stomach complaints	61 (42.6%)	50 (34.8%)	—
Complaints resulting from mistreatment	22 (15.3%)	19 (13.3%)	—
Neurological complaints	11 (7.6%)	8 (5.6%)	—
Chronic anginose throat conditions	9 (6.3%)	0 (0%)	—
Circulation problems (following frostbite)	5 (3.5%)	4 (2.8%)	—
Skin eruptions	1 (0.7%)	0 (0%)	—
Gynaecological complaints (38 women)	14 (37.8%)	10 (27.0%)	—

[a] The difference between the figures for the medical examinations and the psychological interviews was tested for significance using the four-field chi-square test (h.s. = 0.1%; s.s. = 1%; s = 5% level of significance).

Table 19. Psychological complaints (n=144)

Complaints	Mentioned in medical examinations	Mentioned in psychological interviews	Level of significance [a]
Mistrust, shyness, difficulty in making social contact	6 (4.2%)	62 (43.4%)	h.s.
Feeling of isolation	2 (1.4%)	54 (37.8%)	h.s.
Anxiety dreams	28 (19.4%)	75 (52.5%)	h.s.
Feelings of hatred	0 (0%)	31 (21.6%)	h.s.
Paranoid ideation	1 (0.7%)	21 (14.7%)	h.s.
Inner agitation, irritability	41 (28.5%)	72 (50.2%)	h.s.
Depressive mood	43 (29.9%)	61 (42.6%)	s.
Sleep disturbances	45 (31.3%)	46 (32.2%)	—
Anxiety states	29 (20.1%)	33 (22.9%)	—
Temporary or partial amnesia	32 (22.2%)	39 (27.3%)	—
Tiredness, apathy	30 (20.8%)	36 (25.2%)	—
Impaired vitality	11 (7.6%)	9 (6.3%)	—
Thoughts of suicide	6 (4.2%)	5 (3.5%)	—

[a] The difference between the figures for the medical examinations and the psychological interviews was tested for significance using the four-field chi-square test (h.s. = 0.1%; s.s. = 1%; s = 5% level of significance).

making social contact". These were recorded in only 4.2% of the cases in medical examinations but in 43.4% of the cases in psychological interviews. It is also remarkable that in the situation of a medical examination there was absolutely no mention whatsoever of feelings of hatred while, on the other hand, 21.6% of the interviewees spoke of such feelings. One could, perhaps, take the view that feelings of hatred are of no consequence as regards the development of clinically relevant symptoms, but such an opinion ignores the possible correlation with other psychic symptoms such as mistrust or shyness and, furthermore, it overlooks the particularly interesting fact that the patients did not mention this point at all to the examining doctor. Thus, it is quite possible that a very significant factor in a complete pattern of symptoms is being ignored.

This becomes even more apparent when one compares the interview situation with the situation of the psychiatric examination because, of all the medical examinations, this latter comes closest to the interview. In a comparison of persons who were both interviewed and psychiatrically examined, it was found that the following complaints were more frequently mentioned in the interview situation:

Feelings of isolation   (1% significance)
Feelings of hatred   (1% significance)
Mistrust, shyness and difficulties   (10% significance)
in making social contact
Paranoid ideation   (10% significance)

It can be seen from these findings that in the situation of a medical examination the patient felt less free to relate to the doctor all the changes that the had noted in his personality since his period of incarceration. Indeed, what applicant is prepared to regard the doctor, particularly a German doctor, as so objective and understanding that he can confide in him all his hatred, some of which must also be directed against the person of the doctor? This is most unlikely to happen in a situation where the applicant wants something from the doctor, namely the most favourable possible assessment of the pension payable for the health damage suffered.

This varying behaviour with regard to the complaints mentioned suggests that the difference between the examination situations is largely the reason for the discrepancies in the findings and thus for the associated divergence in the diagnoses advanced so far in the literature.

It was tacitly assumed that the examinee would complain in the same way about the same problems in every examination situation. Such an a priori concept is methodologically most doubtful in the case of the catalogue of complaints compiled in connection with the "concentration camp syndrome", because here the complaints are almost without exception characterized by two particular features. Firstly, the complaints chiefly concern exhaustion symptoms which correspond to the late sequelae of extreme stress as expected by the examiner and the examinee. Secondly, they are symptoms which can only be described and which are difficult to check objectively, at least as regards severity. Perhaps this is the reason why HERMANN and THYGESEN (1954) and EITINGER (1961) used physiological findings, which were not confirmed by other investigators, to support their theories (loss of weight or neurological symptoms). These physiological facts were intended to compensate for the subjectivity of the damage suffered.

3. Illness Dimensions in the Case of Injury Suffered by Ex-Persecutees

The differences between the complaints mentioned in two different examination situations, as described in the last section, suggest that it would be logical to subject both series of complaints to a factor analysis. With the aid of this statistical operation we wish to attempt an analysis of the structural relationships between the somatic and psychic complaints recorded in the two examination situations.

In so doing we have ignored the fact that the dates when the initial medical examinations were conducted diverged quite considerably in some cases. The medical examinations were conducted between 1946 and 1960 and the interviews between 1958 and 1962. However, we were able to ignore this factor because it was clear from the medical documentation available to us that a continuous check had been carried out on the medical complaints and that no statistically significant change in the overall pattern of complaints had been discovered. In other words, the complaints mentioned to the examining doctor in 1946 still existed unchanged in 1960. This means that the assumption frequently made in the literature that certain physical and psychological disorders would only manifest themselves after a more or less lengthy interval of time or would only last for a few years after the inmate's release and then disappear forever, could not be confirmed by the complaints and illnesses established in our test subjects.

There were two reasons why we based our calculations on the complaints rather than on the diagnoses. Firstly, different doctors arrived at different diagnoses for one and the same pattern of complaints — particularly in the case of late psychic injury. Secondly, we did not carry out tests of our own to verify the diagnoses. The interviewees merely described their complaints to us. If we had taken the diagnoses together with the complaints in our calculations, this would have falsified the results.

For technical reasons (see Appendix), however, we had to ignore symptoms which were reported by less than 15% of the persons interviewed. This left us with 14 somatic and 12 psychic characteristics for 144 former inmates (106 males, 38 females) which were included in the factor analysis. In addition, we also took account of age and sex. This gave us the chance to establish whether certain complaints are age- or sex-dependent. In the light of previous factor analysis of clinical data, there seemed little point in including any more variables in the analysis because this would have distorted the pattern of symptoms in favour of extra-clinical data. All other variables, i.e. the subjective and objective, psychological and sociological characteristics considered by us, were correlated with the established factors either statistically or by means of the chi-square test. This calculation procedure yielded the four factors listed in Table 20.

Table 20. Four-factor structure of psychic and somatic complaints

Factors	
Factor I:	Psychophysical syndrome (State of exhaustion)
Factor II:	Gynaecological disorders
Factor III:	Internal disorders
Factor IV:	Psychic syndrome (Mistrust)

Factor I: "Psychophysical Syndrome"

We call this factor the "psychophysical syndrome" because it involves complaints experienced in both the physical and mental spheres. This sets the factor apart from the other three, which cover either purely physical (gynaecological and internal) disorders or purely psychic disturbances.

Instead of defining this factor in terms of the various physical and psychological symptoms which it contains, it can perhaps best be described as denoting a state of exhaustion with depressive overtones. This factor bears the closest resemblance to the group of symptoms described as the "concentration camp syndrome", the "asthenia syndrome" and the "concentration camp neurosis". The symptoms do not coincide exactly, as can be seen from Table 39. In this Table we have compared the symptoms described by various authors under the concept "concentration camp syndrome" or related names. We could only consider those authors who gave statistics for the complaints mentioned.

Table 21. Characteristics of the "psychophysical syndrome" (Factor I)

Characteristic	Loading
Head complaints	0.61
Memory and concentration disturbances	0.58
Tiredness, apathy	0.56
Depressive mood states	0.53
Anxiety dreams	0.49
Sleep disturbances	0.49
Inner agitation, irritability	0.39
Vegetative complaints	0.38
Disturbed vitality	0.38

It does not serve any purpose to argue about the designation of this syndrome, because it is most unlikely that a uniform nomenclature will ever be adopted. Depending on their specialization and personal training, different doctors will include either the stress to which the persons in question were exposed (concentration camp syndrome, concentration camp neurosis, etc.) or the complaints (asthenia, psychasthenia, state of exhaustion, depressive exhaustion) or perhaps even both ("asthénie postconcentrationnaire et troubles psychiques").

However, it should be borne in mind that designations which give the impression that this is a characteristic syndrome found in all former concentration camp inmates are deceptive. In fact, this pattern of symptoms, which can best be described as a "depressive exhaustion syndrome", does not occur as a late injury in all former inmates nor is it observed only in concentration camp inmates. PAUL (1963) observed a similar syndrome in former persecutees who were never imprisoned in a concentration camp. V. BAEYER, HÄFNER and KISKER discovered a state of exhaustion in a control group of young recruits. Furthermore, the stress which precedes such states of exhaustion does not necessarily have to be of external origin such as concentration camp incarceration, persecution or the stress of recruit training. The cause can also be sought in inner stress forces of which the person in question may quite often be

Table 22. Overview of the frequency of complaints recorded in various examinations conducted on former persecutees

	KLIMKOVA-DEUTSCHOVA, E.:	HERMANN, K., and THYGESEN, P.:	EITINGER, L.:	HERMANN, K., and THYGESEN, P.:	PAUL, H.:
Examination period:	1945–1961	1951–1953	1957–1961	1964	1958–1962
Persons:	200 former concentration camp inmates and members of combat units	120 former members of the resistance (concentration camp inmates)	100 persons incarcerated in German concentration camps, Norwegian and Japanese camps	225 former members of the resistance (concentration camp inmates)	50 former persecutees (not concentration camp inmates) of various national origins
Origin of cases:	Examination to assess eligibility for compensation	Follow-up examination at request of an accident insurance institute (re-assessment of compensation)	Follow-up examination at request of the Association for Disabled Servicemen (Kriegsinvalidenverband) (re-assessment of compensation)	Follow-up examination for scientific purposes	Examination to assess eligibility for compensation
Complaints	%	%	%	%	%
Lassitude	40		85		
Nervousness, lassitude			78		
Poor memory	14.5	87	78	57	88
Dysphoric mood			72		
Emotional instability		36	70		92 (mood affected)
Sleep disturbances	41		61	65	84
Anxiety	36	62	55		68 (during day)
Feelings of inadequacy			54		
Loss of initiative			54		
Headaches	53.5		53		98
Vegetative complaints	42		48		
Giddiness	24		43		92

	1	2	3	4	5
Anxiety dreams	10		36	67	82
Depressions	34.5	67	36	67	
Trembling	23		21		
Alcohol abuse			19		
Reduced alcohol tolerance			14		50
Diffuse pain and paresthesia			14		
Tinnitus			11		
Affective instability (irritability)	25	73		80	100
Oversensitivity to noise		43			68
Inability to concentrate		78		62	
Vertigo (height-induced)					80
Difficulties in making social contact					66
Weepiness				more than 90	66
Easily tired					64
Excessive sweating				71	56
Hypersomnia during the day	12				
Hypertension	57				
Disturbance of elementary postural reflexes	18				

unaware. V. BAEYER (1961) aptly characterized the inner reasons for a state of exhaustion in the case of average psychiatric illness as "self-contradiction of the will to achieve". The fact that he also discovered this component in former concentration camp inmates and related it back to an instinctive defence reaction against all types of work after years of exposure to horrifying work stress is completely in keeping with our findings.

The exhaustion reaction is not just a transitory phase through which the inmates pass directly after their release as v. BAEYER, HÄFNER and KISKER (1964) supposed. Instead, it can be a symptom which is still manifest 15 years after release. We there-fore do not feel it is justified to interpret an exhaustion syndrome merely as a super-ficial, transitory phenomenon which masks the actual personality change induced by the concentration camp stress. The persistence of such symptoms is determined not only by the pre-incarceration personality and by the concentration camp stress but also by the present internal and external life situation.

This assumption is supported by the fact that although the catalogue of symptoms for Factor I lists anxiety dreams, there is no specific mention of significant anxiety experienced in everyday life. Theoretically the opposite could be the case because anxiety states are also explicitly mentioned as belonging to the table of complaints both in medical examinations and in interviews (with approximately the same fre-quency in both cases, i.e. about 21%). The fact that in this illness dimension anxiety dreams prevail over daytime anxiety permits us to conclude that certain problems are abreacted more subconsciously than consciously.

If this is borne in mind, it is no wonder that the subject of "concentration camp dreams" is usually, but by no means always, the terror experienced in a Nazi concen-tration camp. Even Communists who regard Russia as a paradise of freedom and who personally experienced the horror of a Nazi concentration camp as the very epitome of inhumanity are nevertheless capable of dreaming that they are prisoners in a Communist concentration camp, as we discovered in several explorations. Initial-ly, the interviewees spoke only of concentration camp dreams, thus intimating that in the dreams they were reliving the terrible experiences of their incarceration. But when, in the middle of a discussion with a former inmate, we suddenly asked whether the dreams always concerned only Nazi camps the interviewee replied in astonish-ment, "How did you know that I also dream about Communist camps?" However, we were unable to follow up this phenomenon.

It is sufficient to state here that the feeling of being suppressed and tortured, as it features in the relatively frequent symptom of the concentration camp dreams, is not a simple reliving of the concentration camp experience. Instead, it also always involves a personality-specific mode of coming to terms with past and present con-flicts.

A diagram (Fig. 1) of the frequency distribution of the characteristic complaints of Factor I ("Psychophysical syndrome") shows how many former inmates exhibit how many characteristic symptoms.

The distribution shows that this factor, which of all four factors is the one that most closely resembles the "typical" incarceration-induced late injury referred to in the literature, occurs by no means as frequently as is sometimes assumed. The distribution of the 9 characteristic complaints of Factor I shows (Fig. 1) that only one former inmate exhibits the "psychophysical syndrome" in its pure form. That is to say, this person mentions all 9 symptoms of the syndrome. On the other hand, there are no less than 6 people who do not mention any of the characteristic complaints of this factor. Further examination of the distribution of the complaints reveals that the greatest accumulation of complaints (namely 7, 8 and 9) is only represented by 27 former persecutees (18.7%) while on the other hand the lowest accumulation (0, 1 and 2) is represented by 37 persons (25.7%).

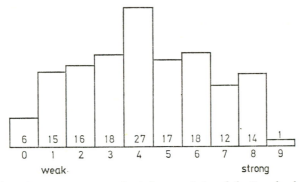

Fig. 1. Distribution of 144 persons over the 9 characteristics of the "psychophysical syndrome" factor

Certainly, the number of complaints, which in this factor is identical with the number of subjectively expressed but, in objective medical terms, not absolutely verifiable complaints, is not an unqualified measure of the severity of the affliction. But the approximately "normal distribution" of the frequency of the complaints shows that the factor of the "concentration camp syndrome", which is much described in the literature on the camps, is not as frequently encountered in its pure form in this particular group, which was not selected according to medical criteria, as is often stated (EITINGER, 1961). Above all, it must be assumed in connection with this factor that the pattern of symptoms is not solely related to the persecution suffered. We will return to this assumption in a later section and try to establish whether it is correct or not (p. 61 et seq).

Factor II: "Gynaecological Disorders"

Table 23. Characteristics of "Gynaecological Disorders" (Factor II)

Characteristics	Loading
Feminine sex	0.79
Gynaecological complaints	0.76
No dental complaints	0.44

The characteristics of this factor show that a sex-specific disorder, characterized above all by gynaecological complaints of various types, is to be observed in former concentration camp inmates.

The factor is composed of 3 intercorrelated characteristics. It was clear that "feminine sex" and "gynaecological complaints" (disturbed menstrual cycles, adnexitis, parametritis, etc.) must occur in one factor because, of course, only women can have gynaecological complaints. However, not all the women mention such complaints.

The inclusion of the characteristic "no dental complaints" is unusual. However, it can be taken as a negative confirmation of the sexual specificity of the factor. "Dental complaints" correlate with the characteristic "male sex". The reason for this finding is that, in the camps, men suffered more head and face injuries than women and therefore complained more frequently of dental problems after their release.

As far as the "gynaecological complaints" are concerned, this form of disorder deserves special attention. The following findings might after all have been possible:

We could, for instance, have found a sex-specific factor in men, e.g. cardiac complaints, or women could also have reacted with other "sex-specific" disorders (e.g. headaches) instead of with genital disorders. But the finding that women reacted with gynaecological complaints points to the long-known fact that under the emotional and physical pressure of the camp situation women react primarily by developing gynaecological disturbances (e.g. amennorhea). However, these findings go beyond the disturbances observed during the actual period of incarceration in that the complaints noted among our sample group are late injuries which in most cases are irreversible.

Using specially selected patients, DÖRING (1963) determined gynaecological complaints in 74 (93.7%) out of 79 former female inmates who were examined by him between 1958 and 1961. In our largely unselected sample of 38 women almost half (44.7%) mentioned gynaecological complaints. This emphasizes the fact that women tend more than men to react with genital disorders.

Factor III: "Internal Disorders"

This illness dimension is composed of the following characteristics (Table 24):

Table 24. Characteristics of "Internal Disorders" (Factor III)

Characteristics	Loading
Cardiovascular complaints	0.62
Hepatic/bilious complaints	0.56
Pulmonary-bronchial complaints	0.50
Age (1960 — over 45)	0.47

This factor, too, which represents a type of late injury suffered by ex-inmates, contains exclusively physical complaints. On the one hand the factor comprises purely internal disorders and on the other it includes an age-specific characteristic.

As regards the individual disorders, there is a connection on the one hand between cardiovascular complaints, pulmonary-bronchial complaints and age and on the other hand between hepatic-bilious complaints and cardiovascular complaints.

This finding should not be all that surprising since cardiovascular complaints are connected in a variety of ways with pulmonary-bronchial complaints and age (e.g. emphysema) and can also go together with hepatic-bilious complaints (e.g. congested

liver). There is no significant correlation between hepatic-bilious complaints, pulmonary-bronchial complaints and age. It is also worth noting that no other internal
or other physical disorder prevailed as the "type disorder" when all the psychic and
somatic complaints were jointly calculated. This is worth bearing in mind since 42%
of the interviewed and medically examined persons complained of stomach troubles,
36% mentioned dental problems, and 23% had trouble with their spinal columns.

As regards the age characteristic, we can say that the internal disorders are age-
specific insofar as the stated constellations of symptoms appear preferentially in the
higher age groups of former concentration camp inmates. One might see here a paral-
lel to Factor II in which a sex-specific factor was determined.

The distribution of the three somatic complaints over the entire group is as follows (Fig. 2):

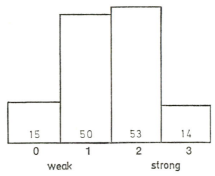

Fig. 2. Distribution of 132 persons over the 3 characteristics of the factor "Internal Disorders".
The characteristic "Age", which is a constituent element of the factor, has not been included
in the diagram because it is not a complaint characteristic. This eliminates 12 person under 45
who, furthermore, exhibited none of the three complaints

The diagram shows that the extreme positions are represented with almost equal
frequency. Of our total sample, 15 persons made no mention at all of the complaints
that constitute Factor III while 14 complained of all 3 disorders.

Factor IV: "Psychic Syndrome" (Mistrust)

This factor is identified by the following characteristics:

Table 25. Characteristics of the "Psychic Syndrome" (Factor IV)

Characteristics	Loading
Mistrust	0.65
Feeling of isolation	0.48
Paranoid ideation	0.48

In contrast to the preceding factors, this one contains exclusively psychic symptoms. One might also term it a "social disorder" because its characteristics reflect the
relationship of the individual to his fellow humans. Mistrust correlates with the
feeling of isolation and paranoid ideation. The relationship between the feeling of
isolation and the paranoid ideation is not significant. Both characteristics, which are

independent of each other, are grouped around the symptom "mistrust". Clinically this accentuation may easily be overlooked, but it could be very significant as regards the present situation of former inmates of concentration camps.

On the one hand, there is the person who is mistrustful, particularly of Germans, and who because of this mistrust cuts himself off from the world despite a strong desire to make social contact (see Chapter "Contact with Fellow Humans and Society", p. 124). Here the mistrust is coupled with paranoid ideas. On the other hand, there is the person who is also mistrustful and who as a result holds himself aloof from others; however, because he chooses to remain aloof and does not seek contact with others, he does not suffer a paranoid reaction.

While the mistrust that is associated with paranoid ideation can be regarded as neurotic — and pre-incarceration personality traits play a role here — the second type of mistrust can be interpreted rather as a "learning effect" resulting from the concentration camp situation.

The most important feature of this factor is that it stands out as an illness type in its own right from an overall grouping of somatic and psychological complaints. The disturbance in the ability to make social contact, which results from the experiences of incarceration and is strongly stressed by VENZLAFF (1958), v. BAEYER, HÄFNER and KISKER (1964) inter al., is significantly confirmed by the way in which this illness dimension manifests itself.

It is furthermore remarkable that of the large number of psychic symptoms contained in the list of complaints, only mistrust stands out as a single factor by itself. This is all the more remarkable since the list includes depressive moods and anxiety symptoms and these play such a large role in the statistics of symptoms.

The distribution of the characteristics of Factor IV is shown in Fig. 3:

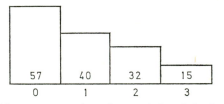

Fig. 3. Distribution of 144 persons over the 3 characteristics of the factor "Psychic Syndrome"

In 57 cases (39.6%) none of the characteristics was present, at least one was present in 40 cases (27.7%) and two or more characteristics were represented by a total of 47 persons (32.6%).

Summary

1. The proportion of former inmates entirely free of complaints in the group, which was not selected according to medical criteria, is relatively small.

In addition to those without complaints, there are also many former inmates with a relatively small number of complaints. Although these complaints are obviously related to the period of concentration camp incarceration, these people made no application for indemnification of health damage suffered. The motivation of this behaviour is reflected in two extreme attitudes, which are interpreted either as the desire to emphasize or the desire to expunge the concentration camp past.

2. A comparison of the complaints described in medical examinations and in psychological interviews reveals that the symptoms mentioned depend on the examination situation. Therefore the complaints recorded in both situations were taken as the basis of the factor analysis.

3. A factor analysis was conducted in order to clarify the question of the inner connection between the psychological and physical complaints. The intention was to determine the illness dimensions behind the individual symptoms.

The calculation yielded 4 factors which can primarily be distinguished as follows: one is a psychophysical syndrome, two involve purely somatic illnesses and the last one comprises purely psychic symptoms. Age and sex were shown to be factors predisposing to illness.

The presence of various illness dimensions indicates that there is no single uniform illness reaction to the period of incarceration in a concentration camp. Above all, diagnostic expressions such as "concentration-camp syndrome", "concentration-camp neurosis", etc. are misleading.

II. Genesis of the Illness Syndromes

In this section the illness dimensions discovered by factor analysis will be related to the facts which may be of importance in determining the choice of symptoms. It is, after all, necessary to ask why this particular inmate developed psychic symptoms while another inmate was stricken with a cardiovascular disorder or some other form of late injury. In the following, we have deliberately considered only illness dimensions and not individual complaints (except in the case of "sex"). It has been found that individual complaints exhibit very few, if any, statistically significant connections with concentration camp stress and with characteristics dating from the prepersecution period. This is not to say, however, that there is absolutely no correlation between individual complaints and stress. It is just that the illness dimensions, which constitute more comprehensive categories and contain several structurally related individual complaints, are better suited to bring out the relationship between late injury and concentration camp stress or personality development.

The correlations of the characteristics with the illness dimensions obtained by factor analysis were established as follows:

By calculating the factor values (see chapter on "Study Methods", p. 10) we determined for each of the persons included in the factor analysis just how strongly they represent or do not represent a particular factor. On the basis of the degree of representation it was possible to form two groups of persons for each factor. One group consisted of persons who were strongly representative of the factor and the other of individuals who represented the factor weakly or not at all. Using the four-field chi-square test it was then possible to relate the illness dimensions to the various types of stress, sociological characteristics and life histories of the persons investigated.

The statistically significant results will be listed and discussed below. Although the significant correlations discovered can in no way be interpreted as causal relationships, we cannot say that causal connections are totally improbable. However, in our discussion of the findings, we have only indicated possible causal connections in those cases where they seem plausible from a clinical standpoint.

1. Sociological Characteristics

The distribution of our sample group among the various sociological categories is shown in Table 26.

Table 26. Sociological characteristics (n=144)

Characteristics	Number	%
Sex:		
male	106	73.6
female	38	26.4
Age in 1960:		
up to 40	21	14.6
41–45	19	13.2
46–50	24	16.4
51–55	35	24.3
56–60	20	13.9
over 61	25	17.4
Reasons for persecution:		
racial	104	72.2
political	30	20.8
religious	10	7.0
Country of origin:		
Germany	73	50.7
Eastern Europe	71	49.3
Country of residence:		
Germany	118	81.9
Israel	18	12.5
USA	8	5.6

a) Sex

In the factor analysis of the complaints it was found that "Gynaecological disorders" (Factor II) are a sex-specific illness dimension in their own right. Furthermore, the correlation matrix revealed other relationships between female sex and certain somatic and psychological complaints following release. For example, female ex-inmates nowadays complain more frequently than male inmates of:

Vegetative disturbances (1% significance)
Anxiety states (1% significance)
Cardiovascular problems (5% significance)
Hepatic-bilious trouble (5% significance)
Men complained more frequently of:
Dental trouble (5% significance)
"Psychic syndrome" (Factor IV) (10% significance)

These findings reveal a very complex but nonetheless clear picture of the state of health of the sexes.

The health complaints suffered by the women consist primarily of disturbances of the sexual functions. In addition, women suffer more frequently than men from anxiety states and vegetative disturbances; what is more, they exhibit a higher incidence of cardiovascular and hepatic-bilious disorders. As a result, the women are found to have suffered more comprehensive and severe injury than the men. This has not so much to do with differing stress situations as with a sex-specific reaction. Astonishingly enough, this fact has been virtually ignored in the literature published to date.

b) Age

In the factor analysis of the complaints, age proved to be an important characteristic of the illness syndrome "internal disorders" (Factor III).

Most of the former persecutees who now suffer from this group of disorders were over 45 years in 1960. It was therefore concluded that these disorders should be regarded as an age-specific syndrome. It is not possible to determine more precisely the extent to which age has a causative or merely a predisposing role to play.

Apart from the case of Factor III ("internal disorders"), factor analysis failed to reveal any further connections between age and illness syndromes. Admittedly, it should be remembered at this point that the age element was used only in a dichotomous framework (persecutees under 45, those over 45), i.e. only a coarse differentiation was made. Age may play an important part in the other syndromes as well when a breakdown into differentiated age classes is made. Such a procedure yielded the following results:

Persecutees who were under 40 years of age in 1960 represent the "psychophysical syndrome" (Factor I) more frequently than those who were over 60 in 1960 (1% significance).

This syndrome (Factor I) is found more frequently in the age range up to 45 than in the age range over 56 (5% significance).

Altogether, all those under 50 (in 1960) complained more frequently of the "psychophysical syndrome" (Factor I) than all older age groups (1% significance).

"Gynaecological disorders" (Factor II) are distributed uniformly throughout all age groups.

The "psychic syndrome" (Factor IV) is distributed uniformly throughout all age ranges, with the exception of the extreme age groups. The syndrome occurs more frequently in persons under 40 years of age (in 1960) than in those over 60 (5% significance).

These findings indicate that, with the exception of the "gynaecological disorders" (Factor II), age is also of importance in all the other syndromes. It is typical of the "psychophysical syndrome" (Factor I) that it is mostly found in persons under 50 years old (in 1960). The "psychic syndrome" (Factor IV) differentiates only between the two extreme age ranges, namely persons under 40 (in 1960) and those over 60.

Before these findings are interpreted, i.e. before the influence of age on the illness syndromes can be properly assessed, it seems necessary to examine the distribution of the various groups of persecutees among the different age groups. It is possible that age and the reasons for persecution are closely linked, so that connections between certain age groups and certain illness syndromes may also depend on connections between the reasons for persecution and the illness syndrome.

A check shows that age and reasons for persecution are in fact linked in a certain way. Up to the age of about 45 years the persons examined had almost all been persecuted on racial grounds. Racial persecutees also continued to predominate in the 46 to 55-year age group. In this range the second largest group is made up of political persecutees. In the age range over 56 years the breakdown was 50% racial persecutees and 50% political and religious persecutees. Most of the political perse- cutees are found in the 46+ age group. Religious persecutees belong almost without exception to the 56+ age group (in 1960).

We can say, therefore, that both age and the reasons for persecution play an important role in the psychophysical syndrome, but it is not possible to decide which of these is the more significant characteristic. Similarly, we must leave unanswered the question of what causal links exist between these characteristics and the illness syndrome. The connections are too complex.

Persecutees suffering from internal disorders are not characterized by any specific grounds for persecution. Age and reasons for persecution are thus not linked in their case. From this it can be deduced that age is more important than the reasons for persecution in the development of internal disorders.

Persons exhibiting the psychic syndrome — racial and political persecutees — are differentiated by age only in the extreme age groups. Persecutees under 40 (in 1960) represent the syndrome more frequently than persecutees over 60.

c) Reasons for Persecution

The persons studied by us can be divided into the following groups according to the reasons for their persecution and incarceration in concentration camps:

1. Racial persecutees 72.2%
2. Political persecutees 20.8%
3. Religious persecutees 7.0%

Their links with the illness syndromes determined by factor analysis are as fol- lows:

Racially persecuted individuals suffer more frequently from the "psychophysical syn- drome" (Factor I) than do political and religious persecutees (1% significance).

Racially persecuted persons suffer more frequently from the "psychic syndrome" (Factor IV) than do religious persecutees (5% significance).

There is no difference between the groups of persecutees as regards "gynaecological dis- orders" (Factor II) and "internal disorders" (Factor III).

Overall, the group of religious persecutees suffered the least injury to health. This is illustrated by the following finding:

Religious persecutees represent the "psychic syndrome" (Factor IV) less frequently than political persecutees (5% significance).

These findings may be interpreted as follows. While all three groups are equally affected by purely physical complaints, the Jews stand out from the religious and political persecutees primarily because they exhibit a greater incidence of Factor I ("psychophysical syndrome"). Secondly, the Jews are also more severely afflicted by Factor IV ("mistrust") than religious persecutees who, in turn, are less mistrustful than political persecutees.

d) Country of Origin

The group of persons under examination breaks down, according to country of origin, into persecutees from Eastern Europe (49.3%) and persecutees from Germany (50.7%). These are distributed over the four illness syndromes as follows:

Persecutees of Eastern European origin complain more frequently of the "psychophysical syndrome" (Factor I) (5% significance).
Persecutees from Germany complain more frequently of "internal disorders" (Factor III) (5% significance).
Persecutees from Eastern Europe and Germany are afflicted equally frequently by "gynaecological disorders" (Factor II) and the "psychic syndrome" (Factor IV).

The two groups thus differ from each other with respect to two illness syndromes. Persecutees from Eastern Europe complain more frequently of the exhaustion syndrome and persecutees from Germany more frequently of internal disorders. v. BAEYER, HÄFNER and KISKER (1964) support our findings insofar as they also recorded a series of complaints, which are contained in Factor I, more frequently in persecutees of Eastern European origin. The complaints in question are headaches, giddiness, anxiety dreams, sleep disturbances and irritability. However, since these results have not been statistically checked and since they were also determined without including somatic findings, caution is necessary in making any comparisons.

e) Present Country of Residence

Since there were so few of them, the persons now resident in the USA and Israel were taken together. The following results were found:

Former inmates who are now living in Germany complain in greater numbers of "internal disorders" than persecutees residing in the USA and Israel (1% significance).
None of the other syndromes make any discrimination on the basis of the present country of residence.

The highly significant finding that the inmates living in Germany are more severely affected by internal disorders is probably due to the fact that these persons were prevented by their illness from emigrating.

v. BAEYER, HÄFNER and KISKER (1964), who also investigated persecutees from various countries (Israel, France, USA), discovered a lower incidence of psychosomatic symptoms (headache, gastro-intestinal complaints, irritability, emotional instability) in the persecutees living in Germany. Our results do not contradict those of v. BAEYER et al. insofar as we found a high incidence of internal disorders in the persons living in Germany.

v. BAEYER, HÄFNER and KISKER (1964) indicate that the symptoms may have sociocultural overtones, although they point out that, since there is a risk of preselection, the findings may not be too reliable. While we are also unable to exclude this possibility, we nevertheless feel that another interpretation is more appropriate, namely that only younger and physically healthier persons could face the risk of emigration. Those who remained behind in Germany are older and physically weaker (see also the chapter on the motives for emigration of Jewish persecutees and their ability to cope with life, p. 229).

2. Persecution Stress

a) Severity of Work Situation

The severity of the work in the concentration camp was shown by the following correlation to be an important stress factor:

Persecutees who were exposed to severe work stress in the camps nowadays complain more frequently of the "psychophysical syndrome" (Factor I) and of the "psychic syndrome" (Factor IV) (5% significance).

These findings are significant on two counts:

1. The severity of the work situation is a better indicator of the stress faced in the camp than the type of camp itself.
2. The severity of the work situation is only correlated with psychophysical and psychic disturbances. Although one would tend to associate severe work more with purely physical injury, this is not the case.

We can conclude from this that the two psychic reaction forms among our 4 factors are related to severe work stress in the camps. Both the "exhaustion syndrome" and the "syndrome of mistrust" are clearly correlated with work severity. It still remains to be examined whether there are any reasons why precisely these persons had to perform particularly harsh work.

b) Severity of Camp

As can be seen from the chapter on "Persecution and Stress" the severity of the camp situation, as a stress index, is made up of several individual stress elements. When this index is related to the illness syndromes established by factor analysis, we find, just as for the duration of incarceration, that there are no significant differences.

This finding does not show that the severity of the camp had no influence on the course of illness, but only that for low camp stress the frequency of illness amoung survivors was just as high as for severe camp stress.

c) Influence of the Duration of Incarceration

Of the sample group investigated, 50% were incarcerated for between 3 and 48 months and the other 50% for more than 48 months.

None of the four illness dimensions exhibited a statistically significant correlation with the duration of incarceration. Even comparisons of extreme groups failed to reveal any differences.

This result indicates that the injuries to health in the form of the syndromes established by factor analysis did not occur more frequently with increasing duration of incarceration. The probability that an inmate would suffer injury to health during a short period of imprisonment was just as great as after a long period of incarceration.

These findings are surprising because the examining doctors concluded, understandably, that the duration of incarceration was an illness-determining factor. RICHET and MANS (1963) also regard the duration of imprisonment as decisively important. They assume that the incarceration accelerated the aging process and that one year of concentration camp imprisonment was equivalent to 4 years of normal aging. This very arbitrary formula is not confirmed by our findings, because if the duration of imprisonment was so important there ought to be some differences with regard to the duration of incarceration in the dimensions established by us.

d) Loss of Relatives

The extent to which an inmate was personally affected by persecution and incarceration was also influenced by the loss of close members of the family. Knowledge of the death of a close relative could destroy an inmate's hope of survival and in most cases made the future appear devoid of meaning. This attitude made itself apparent in apathy and passivity, which without doubt contributed greatly to the external stress. The following findings were made:

During their incarceration, persecutees who represent the "psychophysical syndrome" (Factor I), the "psychic syndrome" (Factor IV) and the "gynaecological disorders" (Factor II) endured the loss of relatives (parents, siblings, marital partners and children) more frequently than those inmates who do not represent these syndromes (1%, 5% and 10% significance).

Persecutees with "internal disorders" (Factor III) lost fewer relatives during their period of incarceration (10% significance).

From these findings it can be concluded that the persons with "internal disorders" tended to be the least affected by losses of relatives. The removal of this psychic stress must be seen against the background of the findings mentioned in section (e), which demonstrates the lack of any psychic complaints but points out the importance of hunger dystrophy.

The persons who represent Factor I were clearly worst affected by loss of relatives, followed by those representing Factor IV and those representing Factor II. Here again, we find the fact which was mentioned during the discussion of the work severity — although the reliability of the finding clearly decreases from Factor I through to Factor IV — that the persons with psychic disturbances are more severely affected by one important element of the overall stress situation.

e) Illnesses Suffered during Incarceration

The stress to which concentration camp inmates were exposed is also expressed in the form of the illnesses suffered. When calculating the correlation with the illness dimensions obtained by factor analysis, the following findings were made:

Persecutees who represent the "psychophysical syndrome" (Factor I) suffered during incarceration more frequently from:

Cardiovascular disorders (5% significance)
Depressive moods (5% significance)
Permanent anxiety (5% significance)
Head and face injuries (10% significance)
Thoughts of suicide (10% significance)

Persecutees suffering from "gynaecological disorders" (Factor II) were more frequently affected during incarceration by:

Amenorrhea (10% significance)

Persecutees with "internal disorders" (Factor III) suffered more frequently during incarceration from:

Hunger dystrophy (1⁰/o significance)
Pulmonary-bronchial affections (1⁰/o significance)
Infectious diseases *(sensu stricto)* (1⁰/o significance)
Bacterial infections (5⁰/o significance)
Dyspeptic complaints (5⁰/o significance)
High-fever infections (10⁰/o significance)

Persecutees who represent the "psychic syndrome" (Factor IV) complained during incarceration of:

High-fever infections (5⁰/o significance)
Depressive moods (5⁰/o significance)
Infectious diseases *(sensu stricto)* (10⁰/o significance)
Head and face injuries (10⁰/o significance)
Limb injuries caused by maltreatment (10⁰/o significance)

The clearest correlations between illness suffered during incarceration and late injury are revealed in the case of "internal disorders" (Factor III).

Persons with internal disorders suffered far more than others from hunger dystrophy, pulmonary-bronchial affections and infectious diseases. It is also striking that nowhere else, except for this illness dimension, do the ex-inmates recall or mention hunger dystrophy when discussing their case histories. Also, there is no mention, either here or in the case of women with "gynaecological disorders" (Factor II), of any psychic symptoms. Since it is unlikely that only these two groups suffered from hunger dystrophy disorders, it is obvious that the inmates' statements regarding the illnesses suffered during incarceration reflect a retroactive subjective evaluation of the individual complaints. There can be no doubt that all the illnesses mentioned did actually exist, but which ones were remembered and mentioned may also depend on the personality of the individual. The following interpretation is possible:

Former inmates who exhibit an exhaustion syndrome as their particular form of late injury had more psychic than somatic complaints even during their period of incarceration. Apart from cardiovascular disorders — interestingly enough these are not correlated with the internal disorders suffered following release, which are obviously an age-dependent reaction — and head injuries, these persons suffered mainly from anxiety, depression and thoughts of suicide. While the inmates nowadays exhibiting the mistrust syndrome also suffered from depression, we find that anxiety and thoughts of suicide are associated with persons exhibiting Factor I ("psychophysical syndrome"). Both symptoms could be related in that the persons exhibiting them were exposed to more stress than other inmates not only because of the harshness of the work situation, as shown in the preceding section, but also because of the more severe maltreatment (head and face injuries). This is the source of their anxiety and thoughts of suicide. But we should also ask whether these persons, in view of their personality structure, were unable to obtain easier work for themselves and thus indirectly "brought on" the "most severe camp stress situation", namely the work. Furthermore, the fact that of all the illnesses suffered during incarceration — which have not been covered in their entirety — these persons nowadays remember the stated psychic complaints probably has something to do with their present condition, anxiety and depression being important parts of the syndrome.

Differences in personality also play a role here, as is illustrated by the fact that while persons with the "mistrust" syndrome were exposed to severe work stress — possibly because of the same inability exhibited by those listed under Factor I — and also were badly maltreated during incarceration (injuries to limbs), they never suffered any anxiety or experienced suicidal thoughts during this period. Here, again, this finding must be seen in connection with the present pattern of symptoms. Neither symptom nowadays plays any detectable role in these persons.

In conclusion, it should be mentioned that in a check made of the medical histories with regard to psychic and somatic illnesses, 88.9% of the persons in question stated that they had never been seriously ill prior to incarceration. There are various ways of interpreting this finding. The most probable interpretation is that against the background of the illnesses suffered in the post-concentration-camp period the illnesses suffered before incarceration seemed unimportant and thus were not mentioned or were not remembered. Certainly, in some cases one of the reasons for this was probably the fear that if any mention was made of earlier illnesses, the present complaints would not be regarded as persecution-related and would thus not have qualified the sufferer for a pension. In the case of those persons who mentioned pre-concentration-camp illnesses (7.6%), all the disorders grew worse in the period following incarceration. In our opinion, not too much value should be attached to individual observations according to which certain disorders (e.g. ulcers) disappeared as a result of incarceration.

3. Developmental Influences of Childhood and Adolescence

Some of the above-mentioned findings gave rise to the question of what effect certain pre-incarceration developmental influences had on later illness symptoms. It has already been pointed out that certain personality traits may perhaps be responsible for the type of stress suffered in the concentration camp. Apart from BASTIAANS (1957), this highly important question has not been empirically studied anywhere in the entire literature on concentration camps. There is no doubt that this is largely because of the above-mentioned difficulties associated with the examination situation. Even with our methodological procedure there are limits to the amount of detail we can give in answering this question. Within these limits, however, we found some very informative clues:

Persecutees with the "psychophysical syndrome" (Factor I), in contrast to those who do not represent the syndrome, yield the following data:

Both parents felt part of a minority group (5% significance).
The standard of living of the parental family was characterized by material prosperity (5% significance).
The father was an understanding and cooperative parent (10% significance).
The father was open and receptive to the world around him (10% significance).
A poor emotional relationship existed with the mother (10% significance).

The findings yield a picture of a generally undisturbed and normal development with good general conditions of existence, but this obviously applies only to the external framework of development. There is in fact a sharp contrast with the emotionally fluctuating mother-child relationship which is sometimes even marked by rejection. However, this finding is no more than a trend. It is difficult to judge to what extent this relatively disturbed relationship with the mother had an effect on the development of personality, since we were unable to gather any further information. Nevertheless, we can assume that the poor mother-child relationship would tend to produce a somewhat less stable psychic state. Under conditions of extreme stress this tendency could manifest itself in the form of greater susceptibility to psychic complaints. This assumption is supported by further findings on the significance of mother-child relationships which are described in the chapter on "Basic Forms of Psychic Disturbance".

Prior to their incarceration, persecutees with "gynaecological disorders" (Factor II), compared with women without such disorders, were unmarried (despite being of marriageable age) or were married without children (5% significance in each case).

While no far-reaching interpretations can be made on the basis of this finding, the following possibility comes to mind: women who suffered from gynaecological disorders as a late consequence of incarceration were in fact already impaired in their sex-specific role before persecution started.

Persecutees with "internal disorders" (Factor IV) are characterized by the following features:

More frequently than others they had completed their occupational training prior to persecution (1% significance).
The father felt part of the majority group (1% significance).
Their style of life was not influenced by any explicit Weltanschauung prior to persecution (5% significance).
Their own standard of living prior to persecution was one of material prosperity (10% significance).

All that these results tell us about the family conditions is that these persons grew up under a *majority-related paternal* influence. This is understandable if it is remembered that these interviewees were chiefly of German origin. We can draw more conclusions from the two other findings, particularly the highly significant finding that occupational training was completed before persecution started.

This result suggests that, to a certain extent, the situation of external security contributed to a greater degree of inner stability. This would be significant in that it might help the individual to ward off or at least reduce his susceptibility to psychic complaints brought on by the stress of persecution. Persons exhibiting this factor do, in fact, suffer only from somatic and not from psychological complaints.

Therefore, as regards the period of persecution and also the chances of finding work following release, we should not underestimate the importance of the phase during which the conditions for a secure existence were created. On the one hand, with the advantage of completed occupational training and also occupational experience an inmate was able to do much to improve his personal lot in the concentration camp; on the other hand, returning to his old job following release from the camp made it easier for the inmate to reintegrate into society.

Persons representing the "psychic syndrome" (Factor IV) are characterized by the following features, in contrast to those who do not exhibit this syndrome:

The father had a narrow outlook and was reticent (5% significance).

In the period prior to persecution the first marital partner was chosen from within the occupational group (5% significance).

Relationships with siblings were on the whole harmonious (10% significance).

The person's own psycho-social development was harmonious (10% significance).

These findings indicate that the individual's development was undisturbed and that siblings enjoyed an harmonious relationship with each other. There is no information on the parent-child relationship but there are indications that disturbances existed. We can see this from the finding relating to the father. Obviously, as a result of certain prominent personality characteristics, he provoked criticism and opposition. From this one can draw certain conclusions about maladjusted attitudes towards authority which would have been a negative factor for the persons in question during the time of their persecution and imprisonment.

The interpretation suggests itself that persons whose development was moulded in this way would deep down have resisted the extremely authoritarian behaviour of their persecutors. The result of this was that externally (toward the persecutors) they were socially rigid and unable to adjust. This interpretation is further supported by the finding that these persons cling more frequently than others to early behavioural attitudes (from the period prior to persecution) (5% significance). Possibly, as a result of this, they provoked their persecutors into maltreating them (see p. 66).

The statements made by these persecutees about a harmonious development during childhood and adolescence are probably, in view of the persecution stress, a positively embellished memory of the past.

The finding regarding the choice of marital partner is worth noting. It shows that a racially persecuted person tended to choose his partner from the group that shared his convictions, and a Jehovah's Witness tended to select his marital partner from among persons of the same faith.

This behaviour points possibly to far-reaching disturbances in the ability to relate to other people, since to the criterion of personal affection were added idealistic or even ideological selection principles. As members of a racial, political or religious minority these persons felt remote from society. They document this attitude and still live very much according to this belief even today. To their mistrust of society around them as the authoritarian majority has been added a feeling of isolation and a paranoiac view of the world.

Summary

The successful attempt at interpreting presently extant psychic and somatic complaints as injury types or illness dimensions permits us to conclude that there is a specific injury dynamic that varies from dimension to dimension.

For the individual types, the following statistically significant correlations were established both with the various forms of stress and with sociological and psychological features:

a) Psychophysical syndrome (Factor I). Ex-persecutees who now exhibit this syndrome were under 50 years old in 1960 and thus belong overall to the younger group of persecutees. They include, for the most part, racially persecuted individuals, particularly of Polish origin, and they come from minority-related families with a good standard of living. The dominating parent was the father, with whom they had a relationship characterized by honour and respect. The relationship with the mother was not so positive. From this we may perhaps conclude that the individuals in this group were more susceptible to psychic disturbance under extreme stress. The stress to which they were exposed during incarceration is characterized by the loss of relatives, severe work situations and predominantly psychic disturbances (anxiety, depressions, thoughts of suicide).

b) Gynaecological disorders (Factor II). Women with gynaecological disorders are characterized by the fact that prior to incarceration, although they were of a marriageable age, they were either unmarried or married without children. However, this finding is really too unrelated to permit the conclusion that gynaecological complaints can only be traced back to specific dispositions. Instead, there is more reason to believe that women reacted with greater intensity than men to the emotional and physical stresses of persecution and incarceration. This is indicated not only by the sex-specific symptoms but also by the fact that women complain more frequently of both somatic and psychological problems. In view of the frequency with which anxiety states were suffered, it can be assumed that some of the somatic complaints (e.g. cardiovascular complaints) are of a functional nature.

c) Internal disorders (Factor III). Ex-persecutees who represent this syndrome tend to be of German origin, are presently resident in Germany and are over 50 years of age (1960). They grew up in families in which the father was majority-related. Their Weltanschauung was not strongly developed or rigidly oriented. More frequently than other persecutees, they had completed their occupational training before the onset of persecution. As a result, it was concluded that the occupational experience they had gathered stood them in good stead and permitted better adaptation both during their incarceration and following their release. The stress to which they were exposed during imprisonment primarily took the form of purely somatic illnesses, particularly hunger dystrophy. They were not exposed to the severest type of work stress during incarceration and were also less affected by the loss of relatives. Nowadays, just as during the time when they were imprisoned, only somatic disorders but no psychic complaints are diagnosable.

d) Psychic syndrome (Factor IV). The inmates who represent the sphere of psychic complaints comprise racially persecuted persons of German origin and also political persecutees. As regards age distribution, the only differentiation is that persons under 40 (1960) exhibit the syndrome more frequently than persons over 60 (1960). As concerns family conditions, the father in particular stands out as being taciturn and having a narrow outlook on life. This probably led to authority conflicts in the children and thus in the members of this group of ex-persecutees. In addition, the father's restricted world view seems to have sown the seed of the inmates' later mistrustful attitude. The relationship with siblings was on the whole good. In retrospect, these people felt that their development had been undisturbed and harmonious.

It is worth noting that, prior to persecution, marital partners had tended to be selected from minority groups. One possible interpretation of this finding is the assumption that persons exhibiting this syndrome were less adaptable and flexible in their interpersonal relationships and thus their free choice of marital partner was hampered before the onset of persecution. The lack of adaptability in particular is brought out clearly by the way in which these persons clung to earlier behavioural patterns during their incarceration and also following their release. The lack of social mobility and the authority problems derived from their relationships with their fathers were the probable reasons why these individuals had the more severe types of work inflicted on them in the camps. This interpretation is also borne out by the fact that these inmates tended to be mistreated more frequently than others. Conflicts with authority and adaptation difficulties, however, provide only a partial explanation of this syndrome. The interpersonal experience in the concentration camp and the problems of reintegration into society after release must all be considered as additional determining factors.

From these characteristics of the four illness dimensions we can now draw the following general conclusions on the nature of extreme stress and its effects on health:

The human organism obviously reacts in different ways to such extreme stress. There is no specific late-injury syndrome. The reactions can take the form of psychic, psychophysical or purely somatic illness syndromes. The choice of the mode of reaction depends both on the severity of the stress and on the development of the individual's personality prior to persecution. The more physically oriented syndromes occur preferentially in persons who had to withstand severe camp stress (harsh work, loss of relatives). In the case of the purely somatic complaints (gynaecological complaints and internal disorders) these stresses were not so severe.

This should be sufficient proof that the psychoreactive disturbances were the result of more severe stress than the somatic illnesses. The importance of this fact is in no way lessened by the finding that personality traits also played a role in determining the severity of the stress; because of family influences, namely their relationship with their parents, certain persons were unable to adapt to the extreme terror conditions of concentration camp incarceration in the same way that other people were obviously able to do. The lack of adaptability during imprisonment which is found in psychoreactively disturbed persons — in contrast to people with somatic illnesses — is also borne out by the finding that these persons suffered just as much, if not more, from psychic complaints (anxiety, depression, thoughts of suicide) as from physical illnesses during incarceration. People now suffering from physical complaints do not mention any psychological symptoms during incarceration.

III. Compensation for Injury to Health

In this section we attempt to explain the factors that determine the amount of compensation (pension) paid to former inmates of concentration camps for damage suffered to health. From documentation and the personal statements of 170 former persecutees we have data on the medical examination and indemnification procedures followed over a period of 16 years (1945–1960). The majority of the applications concerning pensions for damage suffered to health were made in the first half of this period up to 1952 (see Fig. 4).

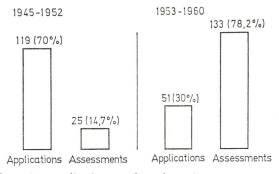

Fig. 4. Number of pension applications made and pension assesments prepared in various periods of time (n=170 persons)

From the Figure it can be seen that while most applications were submitted during 1945 to 1952, most assessments were made in the period from 1953 to 1960. This is an indication of the time taken to process the applications. On average, the processing extended over a period of 4 to 6 years. If an appeal was lodged against an assessment, this added a further processing delay of 1½ to 2½ years until the appeal procedure was completed. It is not difficult to see that, because of the extremely long drawn-out procedure, a pension application in itself could be a special form of stress for the ex-persecutee. However, this particular factor was to a large extent ignored, if it was recognized at all, by the indemnification authorities who obviously felt that it was a stress the ex-inmate could reasonably be expected to bear.

In order to gain a clearer idea of the factors that determined the amount of pension awarded, this chapter is further subdivided into two sections. First we shall try to establish all the influences exerted on the compensation procedure by factors external to the illness itself. It is necessary to identify these influencing factors and to establish how important they are before we can examine the next problem, namely the extent to which the amount of pension depended on the type and degree of severity of the health damage suffered.

1. Influences not Dependent on Illness

a) Date of Pension Application

It can be assumed that the longer the time that has elapsed since the inmate's release, the less importance will be attached to the persecution-relatedness of his complaints. As a result, we considered it justifiable to regard the date when the application for a pension was made as one of the factors determining the amount of pension awarded. No information on specific late injuries which might have reduced

Fig. 5. Frequency with which the persecution-relatedness of somatic illnesses was rejected in the period 1945 to 1960 (based on medical reports prepared by public health offices)

the validity of this assumption was available, since the most important publications did not appear until after 1954. Up until that time it had simply seemed logical to question the relationship between persecution and injury to health, the further apart these two phenomena occurred. However, as regards the amount of pension awarded, it was of decisive importance whether damage to health was recognized as being brought on by persecution or not. We tested our hypothesis by examining the frequency with which the persecution-relatedness of illnesses was rejected in the years 1945 to 1960. The results apply only to somatic disorders, since psychiatric illnesses were for the most part not diagnosed in our sample until 1955 to 1960.

It is clear from Figure 5 that, in the period from 1945 to 1950, on average about one third of all somatic illnesses were rejected in the reports prepared by public health offices as being unrelated to the persecution situation. Between 1950 and 1954 the percentage of rejections dropped sharply and then rose again in 1955. Between 1955 and 1960, i.e. about 10 years after the inmates' release, almost 50% of all the somatic illnesses were rejected as not being persecution-related. For the persecutee this means that the period immediately following his release, as well as the period after 1954, were relatively unfavourable times in which to apply for a pension for damaged health. This fact may perhaps be explained as follows:

In the period immediately following the inmates' release the examining doctors were very wary about recognizing health injury as being brought on by the persecution situation. In the years immediately following 1945 only a few foreign-language publications were available on the consequences of concentration camp incarceration. It was not until the number of pension applications swelled and the specific pensionable illnesses became known that more comprehensive, better founded knowledge was gained about the relationship between extreme stress and health damage. Also, the examining doctors' willingness to recognize health damage as a consequence of persecution increased only gradually over the years.

Once the peak of the pension application wave had passed and the number of applications started to decline, a change also occurred in the attitude of the examining doctors. They became more and more critical in their assessment of the persecution-relatedness of somatic illnesses because of the length of time that had elapsed between incarceration and date of application. To an increasing extent, illnesses which had previously been regarded as persecution-induced were diagnosed as diathetic illnesses which had become manifest during the post-persecution period.

b) Differing Assessments by the Examining Doctors

Another factor governing the amount of pension awarded was the different way in which the various groups of doctors assessed the damage to health. The examinations of 170 former concentration camp inmates now living in Germany, Israel and the USA (New York) were carried out in the main by 4 sorts of doctors: general practitioners, specialists in internal diseases, psychiatrists and Public Health Department doctors.

There was no difference between the proposed pensions on the basis of the country in which the examination was made. Doctors in Germany proposed essentially the same pensions as those in the USA (New York) and Israel.

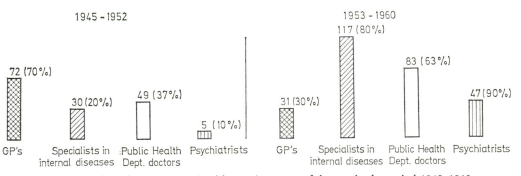

Fig. 6. Number of persons examined by various sorts of doctors in the period 1945–1960

Figure 6 shows the proportions of the various sorts of doctors involved.

It can be seen from Figure 6 that in the early years most of the former inmates were examined by general practitioners and Public Health Department doctors.

From 1953 onward the examinations were carried out mainly by specialists in internal diseases and Public Health Department doctors. General practioners did very little examining. Most psychiatric examinations were not carried out until after 1952.

If the 4 groups of doctors under discussion are characterized according to their diagnostic procedures, we find certain differences (Fig. 7).

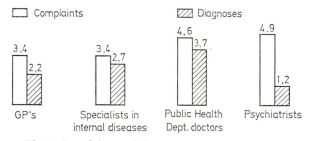

Fig. 7. Complaints and diagnoses per person (n=170)

It can be seen that psychiatrists and general practitioners make fewest diagnoses. Public Health Department doctors have the greatest frequency of diagnoses per person. This is not really surprising since these doctors dealt with the broadest spectrum of health damage.

The greatest differences between the complaints and diagnoses per person are found in the case of psychiatrists. Although the psychiatrists examined people with a wide range of psychic complaints, they made the fewest diagnoses of all 4 groups of doctors. This may possibly indicate a considerable lack of certainty on their part in making a diagnosis. It is for this reason that in particular late psychic injuries without any organic basis are increasingly becoming the focal point of discussions on the

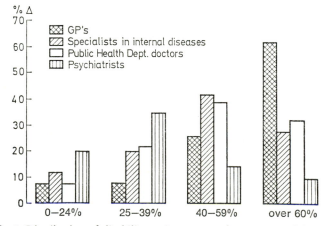

Fig. 8. Distribution of disability ratings among the 4 groups of doctors

consequences of concentration camp incarceration. The problem is not just that late psychic injuries are on the increase, but also to find a suitable diagnostic method that will include and classify such injury. As will be shown in the chapter on "Psychiatric Diagnoses", almost every psychiatrist who deals with the problem of late injury in former inmates has his own diagnostic approach.

A comparison of the average pension rates established by the four groups of doctors for the persons examined by them reveals a number of differences (Fig. 8).

It will be seen from Figure 8 that general practitioners allow the highest pension rates. More than half of the persons examined by them were classified as having suffered a more than 60% loss of earning power. Doctors from the Public Health Department found a loss of earning capacity in excess of 60% in 32% of the cases examined by them, while specialists in internal medicine reached such an assessment in 27% and psychiatrists in only 9.6% of their cases.

The difference between the last three groups of doctors and the general practitioners is very striking and statistically significant (1% significance). The closest agreement on the amount of pension exists between the Public Health Department doctors and the specialists in internal diseases. They most frequently assessed the loss of earning capacity at between 40 and 50%. Psychiatrists most often determined a 25% to 39% loss of earning capacity in the persons examined by them.

Summarizing, it can be said that general practitioners make relatively few diagnoses per person yet propose the highest pension rates. Public Health Department doctors and specialists in internal medicine make the most diagnoses but set the pension rates lower than those proposed by general practitioners. In fact, they tend to fall somewhere between the two extremes of the general practitioners and the psychiatrists — the latter make the least diagnoses and also award the lowest pensions.

When interpreting these results it must be remembered that general practitioners were on the whole consulted soon after the persecutees' release (see Fig. 7) while psychiatric examination was not invoked to any great extent until after 1952.

One of the reasons for the high pensions proposed by the general practitioners may be that, as family doctors, they were in general more kindly disposed towards their patients than specialist doctors and Public Health Department doctors. They often had a special relationship of trust with their patients and were well acquainted with their background of persecution. It was therefore natural for them to allow their own subjective opinion of the degree of persecution stress to dictate the pension rate that they suggested. In addition, it is possible that the general practitioner may not have been able to make such fine diagnostic distinctions as the specialist doctor and therefore, in cases of doubt, he tended to opt for a higher pension assessment.

As already mentioned, the psychiatrist faced the problem not only of properly diagnosing and classifying the complaint but also of establishing the extent to which the late-appearing or persisting psychic complaints were related to the persecution situation. In most cases the psychiatrists put their patients in the lower pension bracket, namely only slightly above the 25% impairment at which pension eligibility commenced. This phenomenon is impossible to understand when one remembers the severity of the stress to which the psychically disturbed individual was exposed. Not only was the psychically disturbed person "hit" by the harshest type of work during incarceration, but even after his release he was still "punished" by the examining doctors who awarded him the lowest pension.

It seems certain that the scientific concept according to which the examining doctors proceeded is also involved here.

c) The "Concept" Followed by the Examining Doctors

By "concept" is meant the opinions and attitudes of the doctors on which their assessment and compensation of the health damage suffered by ex-inmates were based. This "concept" is not a well-founded, absolutely binding and authoritative medical opinion nor is it a social prejudice, but it nevertheless has a certain influence on the way in which the doctors reached their decisions.

The doctors who examined the group of persons under study in this book did not base their opinions on the quasi-theoretical conclusions that "hunger dystrophy" (HELWEG-LARSEN, HOFFMEYER, KIELER, THAYSEN and THAYSEN, THYGESEN and WULF, 1952; HERMANN and THYGESEN, 1954), "premature senility" (FICHEZ and KLOTZ, 1961) or "cerebral damage" (GRÖNVIK and LÖNNUM, EITINGER, 1961) were the causes of the late injury. Nevertheless, they do prefer to use categories according to which the health damage is regarded and explained as a disturbance of a purely somatic nature. We have already discussed this in connection with the "compulsion to fit the symptoms to the examination situation" (see discussion on the effect of the examination situation, p. 47).

The persons examined adapted to this "concept" during their medical examination by mentioning more somatic than psychic complaints. The former persecutees were unable to give full expression to the entire range of their present complaints except in a situation other than that of a medical examination.

Admittedly, the reason for this was not simply that the persecutees tended to adapt to the examination situation, but also because they hesitated to admit to any psychic problems (e.g. mistrust or feelings of hatred).

However, these are factors which depend on the persecutees themselves and which could possibly have had some influence on the pension assessment procedure.

d) Behaviour and Attitude of the Persecutees

Most persecutees adapted to the somatic "concept" in the situation of the medical examination in order to comply with the doctors' prejudice and to avoid being awarded a poor pension. This behaviour can definitely be described as adaptive. It differs from the two following attitudinal variants which can be described as extremes.

1. The first group includes persons who refrained from applying for a pension even though their health was impaired. We have already mentioned these individuals further above (see p. 45).

2. The second group includes persons who appealed against the pension assessment because they felt that the pension awarded to them was unjustifiably low. Altogether 28.2% (48 out of 170 applicants) appealed against the first pension assessment. In two cases 1.2%) the appeal was dismissed and in one case the revision procedure is still not complete. In the remaining 45 cases the appeal procedure resulted in a number of changes for the second pension assessment (Table 27).

Altogether, 48 (28.2%) out of 170 applicants lodged an appeal against their pensions. About half of the appellants (52%) failed to get their pensions revised; but,

Table 27. Results of appeal procedure (the percentages are based on n=48 appellants)

Assessment	absolute number
No change in pension rate	25 (52%)
Pension rate increased	16 (30.6%)
Pension rate lowered	4 (8.3%)

in a good third (30.6%) of the cases the pensions were increased; in 8.3% of the cases the pension rate was lowered.

In order to form a better opinion of whether the appeals were justified or not we compared the appellants with the non-appellants as regards sociological characteristics and state of health:

The characteristics of age, sex, country of residence and grounds for persecution did not reveal any statistically significant differences.
Similarly, no statistically significant differences were discovered as regards somatic and psychic complaints.

This means, in the first instance, that the dissatisfaction with the pension which gave rise to the appeal was not related to the type of illness or complaint pattern. On the basis of our material it is difficult to say with any certainty which other factors could be responsible. The following trends were observed:

Appellants suffered less from headaches (10% significance)
Appellants had more paranoid ideas (10% significance)
Appellants exhibited more feelings of hatred (10% significance)

Although these findings cannot be regarded as statistically significant, their content is important enough to permit the following possible interpretations:

The finding that appellants suffered from fewer headaches may be connected with their specific method of getting rid of aggression. Instead of allowing the obviously present aggression to take the form of headaches (directed against oneself), aggressive feelings are expressed by the appellants in the form of dissatisfaction and formal opposition (appeal against pension assessment) towards the pension authorities.

In connection with the other findings it is clear that the aggressive feelings towards former persecutors manifest themselves in a variety of ways:

In the case of non-appellants the aggression is expressed as (or converted into) psychosomatic complaints. In the case of appellants the aggression is expressed by a specific social behaviour, i.e. these persons live it out more directly.

There are two possible interpretations for the frequent occurrence of feelings of hatred and paranoid ideas:

On the one hand these can be seen as the expression of asthenic-aggressive personality traits. On the other hand they constitute the reaction to the unsatisfactory outcome of the appeal procedure. After all, 60.3% of the appellants failed to obtain any increase in their pension rates.

As regards the attitude of the persecutees to the examination and pension assessment procedures, the following statements can be made:

The behaviour both of the non-applicants and of the applicants who adapted to the medical examination situation has to a certain extent made it difficult to research into late injury in former inmates of concentration camps. Both groups in fact impede the process of obtaining adequate and complete data on late psychic injury.

It is for this reason that the "psychic syndrome" (Factor IV) as a social disease was more or less ignored for a long time in the examinations conducted by the indemnification authorities. It was not until psychiatrists (STRAUSS, 1957; KOLLE, 1958; MATUSSEK, 1966; v. BAEYER, HÄFNER and KISKER, 1964, inter al.) devoted themselves more intensively to this problem that it was duly recognized as a late injury.

Checking of the sociological characteristics sex, age (in 1960), country of residence and their correlation with the size of pension awarded, yielded no significant findings.

All that could be established was that every racial persecutee was awarded a higher pension than the political and religious persecutees (5% significance).

This is not a surprising result, since racial persecutees were exposed to the most severe stress during persecution and incarceration and nowadays suffer from the worst symptoms of health damage.

2. Dependence of the Amount of Pension on the Type of Disorder

The examining doctors did not base their assessment of the patients' loss of earning power on the subjective complaints voiced but, instead, on the diagnoses which they themselves made. Therefore we cannot proceed from the complaint-based illness dimensions established by factor analysis but must take individual diagnoses as our starting point. In so doing, however, we run into the problem that most doctors did not propose a separate pension rate for each illness (diagnosis), but one single rate for all the illnesses taken together. It is thus no longer possible, after the event, to establish clearly to what extent the individual illnesses contribute to the overall magnitude of the pension rate.

Altogether, in our material, the Public Health Department doctors made individual pension assessments for 33.4% and specialists in internal medicine for 45.5% of the illnesses regarded by them to be persecution-induced. General practitioners made only global pension assessments. In addition, not all the illnesses mentioned were recognized as being brought on by persecution, therefore the amount of data available and thus also its representativeness are limited. Nevertheless, in the following we shall attempt to check the relationship between the pension rate and the illness on the basis of individual proposed pensions.

The individual pension rates proposed by the Public Health Department doctors were used for this purpose. They coincide with those put forward by the specialists in internal medicine.

a) Magnitude of individual pension rates for somatic illnesses. Of 26 different somatic illnesses, 15 had to be ignored because too few individual pension rates had been proposed in these cases. Individual pension rates were suggested for the remaining 11 forms of illness (Table 28).

It can be seen from Table 28 that the highest pension rates were proposed in the case of specific internal diseases. Tuberculosis and cardiovascular lesions were the illnesses for which the highest pensions were awarded. Psychosomatic complaints such as gastritis, ulcers and vegetative dystonia are rated exactly at the 25% disability limit.

Table 28. Average disability rating proposed for persecution-induced somatic illnesses (170 persons)

Diagnoses	Average persecution-related disability rating %
Tuberculosis (pulmonary)	59.8
Cardiovascular complaints	39.3
Static anomalies	38.5
Arthrosis	28.0
Gastritis, ulcers	25.8
Vegetative dystonia	23.8
Pulmonary-bronchial complaints	23.6
Affections of connective and sustentacular tissue	21.7
Chronic hepatocholecystopathy	20.3
Spondylosis	19.3

All the disabilities rated below the 25% mark are legally regarded as non-pensionable. In our material it was mainly the cases of spondylosis and chronic hepatocholecystopathy that were termed "not unduly morbid conditions which can still be overcome by the average individual".

b) Magnitude of individual pension rates proposed for psychiatric illnesses.

Out of 5 different psychiatric diagnoses, 4 can be evaluated as regards the individual pension rates proposed. Individual pension rates were suggested by psychiatrists for 85.1% of the persecution-related illnesses. This is the highest figure for any of the examining doctors.

In addition, psychiatrists stand out because in only 26.7% of the cases — a low figure — did they reject the claim that a particular psychiatric complaint was persecution-related. This is all the more remarkable since most psychiatric examinations were not carried out until after 1955, at a time when the rejection rate in all other medical examinations was distinctly higher. We can conclude from this that psychiatric disorders became more and more significant as manifestations of late injury as time went by after the inmates' release.

Table 29. Average disability ratings proposed for persecution-related psychic disorders

Diagnoses	Average persecution-related disability rating %
Organic brain damage	41.1
Neurotic reaction	31.7
Chronic-reactive depression	29.6
Neurasthenia	28.9

The individual disability ratings suggested for the various psychiatric disorders are given in Table 29.

Table 29 shows that very much higher pensions were proposed for organically determined psychiatric illness than for reactive disturbances and asthenic states.

Although psychiatric illnesses became increasingly important after 1955, higher pensions were awarded for organic brain damage than for reactive changes. This finding lends further support to the assumption that the examining doctors tended to seek somatic reasons for the disturbances.

The disability ratings proposed for the persecution-related reactive disturbances coincide with the results obtained by v. BAEYER, HÄFNER and KISKER, who also recorded a 25—30% disability. The authors are of the opinion that the low pension rates for reactive disorders reflect German practice in assessing such complaints. In Norway, Denmark and Holland much higher disability ratings were established (THYGESEN, 1955; BASTIAANS, 1957; STRÖM, EITINGER, GRÖNVIK, LÖNNUM, ENGENS, OSVIK and ROGAN, 1961).

In our sample group, 94 out of 170 persons expressed an opinion on their satisfaction or dissatisfaction with the pension awarded them. 74 (78.7%) were dissatisfied with the amount and only 20 (21.3%) felt their pension was adequate. It would be a simple matter to write off the large number of dissatisfied individuals as neurotic quibblers. However, it would be more scientifically accurate to assume that the traditional appraisal concept, especially as employed in Germany, is false, so leading to underassessment and hence inadequate compensation of psychoreactive disturbances.

Summary

1. On the basis of material on file and interview data gathered from our sample group we were able to establish that illness-dependent factors as well as factors that were not related to illness were of decisive importance in determining the amount of pension.

2. The willingness of the examining doctors to recognize the persecution-relatedness of a particular complaint varied from period to period and, as a result, the time when a pension application was made was a very important factor in determining the amount of pension. In addition, there were variations in the pension rating as a result of differences in the approach preferred by the various sorts of doctors.

3. The personal attitude of the persecutees to the examination situation is in many, sometimes extreme, ways a decisive determinant in the pension assessment procedure.

4. The type of illness also has an effect on the size of the pension awarded. It is noticeable that the lower pension rates awarded in the case of psychic disturbances do not do justice to the proven severity of the stress situation, which was one of the main causes of this type of illness.

CHAPTER 4

Psychiatric Diagnoses

Outline of Problem

The late injury dimensions discussed in the preceding chapter included two factors characterized by chiefly psychic complaints, a fact which indicates the importance of psychological damage as a consequence of incarceration in a concentration camp. In this chapter, therefore, we intend to study how the doctors, and particularly the psychiatrists, who examined the group interviewed by us approached this phenomenon. How were the symptoms of late psychic injury determined and evaluated?

Psychiatric diagnoses were made for 66 (38.9%) of the 170 medically examined persons in our sample, thereby indicating that slightly more than a third of the inmates stood out as having some form of psychic complaint. This finding approximates to that of STRAUSS (1961), who detected psychiatrically relevant damage in about a third of the persons (n = 1000) he examined. Apart from this result, there are no reliable data on the proportion of psychic illnesses diagnosed in the total number of medically examined former inmates. In examining the question of late psychic injury, with which we are concerned in this chapter, we must first of all study whether our figure of almost 40% provides an acceptably reliable indication of the frequency of late psychic injury. This will be determined by analysing the criteria according to which an applicant was psychiatrically examined.

I. Examination and Compensation

1. Selection Criteria for Psychiatric Examination

Table 30 (page 82) lists the reasons which led to an individual undergoing psychiatric examination.

It can be seen from Table 30 that most psychiatric examinations were carried out as a result of referrals of patients by non-psychiatrists. We were unable to establish in greater detail what criteria the various doctors applied in referring people to psychiatrists. Certainly, the pattern of symptoms alone was not the decisive reason, because for the same pattern of complaints one doctor called in a psychiatrist while another doctor did not. We can conclude from this that a certain number of former persecutees — it is not possible to say how many exactly — were not psychiatrically examined, although strictly speaking they should have been.

One fifth of the psychiatrically examined persons, on their own initiative, submitted an application for indemnification for the psychic injury they had suffered. This group can be broken down into two different subgroups. The majority (13.6%) applied for compensation for their psychic complaints. The minority (4.6%) started

Table 30. Reasons why ex-inmates were psychiatrically examined (n=66)

Reasons	abs. number	%
On initiative of examining doctor		
a) Referred to a psychiatrist by a non-psychiatrist	38	57.6
b) Psychiatrically examined by a non-psychiatrist	14	21.2
On persecutee's own initiative		
a) Explicit reference made to psychic complaints in the application for compensation	9	13.6
b) Appeal against pension assessment pointing out that psychic complaints had been overlooked	3	4.6
Not clear/not applicable	2	3.0

by claiming compensation for somatic injury but then discovered in the course of the medical examinations that their psychic symptoms were not properly taken into account by any of the doctors. They therefore appealed against their pension assessment and practically forced the authorities to have them psychiatrically examined. The following detailed example serves to illustrate what course all this took in the individual case.

In 1955 a racial persecutee applied from Israel for compensation for a persecution-related injury to the right eye and also for general physical weakness. Prior to persecution — so he claimed — he had been healthy. During the time that he was persecuted he contracted typhus and suffered various infections on his hands and legs. Shortly before the end of the war his right eye was injured by a stone thrown by guards while he was trying to escape. Since that time he has been almost totally blind in that eye. In an official medical report prepared in 1956 in Jerusalem by a specialist in internal medicine, the following diagnoses were made:

a) Loss of sight in right eye (direct result of persecution);
b) Neurocirculatory asthenia with a tendency toward fluctuating blood pressure (predisposition, not a result of persecution).

The first pension assessment was handed down in 1957. He appealed it in 1958 because he felt the assessment of a 30% disability rating for the injury to his eye was too low. In addition he claimed that he was suffering from TB and had also contracted a stomach disorder as a consequence of his persecution. In order to pursue his case for indemnification more efficiently he returned to Germany from Israel.

In 1958 a specialist in lung diseases and a specialist in internal medicine diagnosed an inactive case of pulmonary tuberculosis; a general practitioner diagnosed colitis mucosa, Römheld complex, adhesion of the diaphragm, hyperthyroid complaints, vegetative instability and a tendency to become depressed; another general practitioner diagnosed gastritis. In addition, also in 1958, an X-ray specialist detected a fibrosis on the left ear lobe. On the basis of these attestations, a medical clinic was asked to prepare a medical report for submission to the Oberlandesgericht (Provincial Supreme Court). The report contained the following diagnoses:

a) Slight pleuritic residues,
b) Pulmonary lesions,

c) Hypertension,
d) Hypoacid gastroduodenitis,
e) Suspected liver cell damage.

The pulmonary lesions were considered to have been brought about by the persecution situation, but the other illnesses were not held to be persecution-related. In 1959, in a letter to the Regional Indemnification Office, the applicant requested that he be further examined at a psychiatric hospital because the psychological damage which he had sustained had not been taken into account. He attached a certificate from a general practitioner, issued in the same year, confirming that he was suffering from a chronic persecution-related depressive state associated with a reduced ability to work, apathy, inhibitions, feelings of inadequacy, dejection and hypochondriac complaints.

The Indemnification Office replied to this medical claim, informing the applicant that: "It must be assumed that the asthenia diagnosed by Dr. P. (general practitioner) is the same condition described by Dr. S. (specialist in internal medicine) as chronic depression associated with reduced ability to work. Since this complaint was not regarded as persecution-related, either in the pension assessment or in the two judgements, although the court was aware of Dr. P.s findings of a psychic disorder — and in fact extracts of these findings were quoted to the court — there is no cause to find that Mr. H. is suffering from any neurological-psychiatric complaint since judgement has already been passed on the psychic problems."

The person in question filed an appeal against this assessment. The appeal was accompanied by a report from a neurologist in which the psychic problems were attributed to damage to the frontal part of the brain.

As a result of this appeal, an examination was carried out in 1960 in a psychiatric hospital. The examination failed to reveal brain damage nor did it discover any reasons for supposing a chronic depression. According to the examining doctors, the patient should instead be described as suffering from a neurosis resulting from psychasthenia. The neurosis was taking a sensitive-paranoiac course marked by anxiety with slightly querulous traits and it expressed itself in the form of a tendency to tire easily, concentration disturbances, uncertainty, lack of drive and occasionally in somatic complaints.

It was further argued in the report that the complaints had previously been much less severe, which would hardly be the case for a persecution-related neurosis. Finally the report stated: "It is not possible to confirm that any loss of working capacity has been brought on by the neurosis nor is it likely that the neurosis can be ascribed to the persecution situation." The neurotic disturbances were for the most part seen as resulting from the stress of trying to obtain a secure existence, i.e. they were explained away as a pension neurosis.

Through his lawyer, the applicant requested the Indemnification Office to examine his petition once more. When the Indemnification Office advised him to take legal action to settle his claim the applicant, together with his lawyer, had a personal interview with the Vice-President of the Indemnification Office. In the subsequent report issued by the medical service of the indemnification authorities it was stated that: "Apparently the judges and thus also, of course, the examining doctors at the psychiatric hospital, were unaware of the judgement handed down by the Federal Supreme Court on 18. 5. 1960 according to which psychic damage can still be recognised as persecution-related after a certain period of time has elapsed if the persistence of such damage is due to a corresponding predisposition ... According to recent medical publications it is therefore possible that a future examination, carried out in connection with the appeal, may find the claim to be justified. In this case a once-only payment either to compensate for the hardship suffered or by way of settlement is advocated."

A settlement was reached with the Indemnification Office and no legal proceedings were instituted.

This case yields many exemplary points. To start with, it is clear how difficult it was for the person in question to have the authorities recognize his justified entitlement to a proper medical examination. Such cases are probably so few and far between because other persecutees did not possess such determination. After all, in this particular instance the medical examinations dragged on over 5 years and in this period the applicant changed his lawyer 8 times.

Secondly, the course of the examination procedure shows up the almost autistic diagnostic approach of the various doctors. One specialist in internal medicine diagnosed "neurocirculatory asthenia with a tendency to fluctuating blood pressure"; one general practitioner found a "chronic depressive state" while another detected "vegetative instability" and "tendency to become depressed"; a neurologist certified the presence of "damage to the frontal part of the brain with psychic sequelae"; finally, in the psychiatric hospital a "psychasthenic" neurosis was diagnosed. Clearly, the examining doctors were relatively helpless when it came to diagnosing late-appearing psychic injury. This can be taken as further proof of the arbitrary and random selection of the psychiatrically examined persecutees.

The uncertainty of the doctors in the face of the psychic sequelae of concentration camp incarceration is also evidenced by the long time which elapsed until a psychiatric examination was carried out in each case. The delay was very long, especially in the years immediately following the inmate's release, the average time being 4 years.

After 1952, but particularly after 1955, the problem of late psychic injury came increasingly to the fore as a result of the growing number of publications and the accumulation of experience on the subject. The time between application and psychiatric examination gradually grew shorter. More and more applications for compensation of psychic disturbances were made. According to an estimate made by the local Indemnification Office, the percentage of persons who had been awarded a pension on the grounds of psychic complaints had risen by 1960 to about 60% of the total number of applicants.

Summarizing, we can say that, in our opinion, the percentage (38.9%) of persecutees suffering from psychiatric illnesses does not reflect the actual occurrence of psychic disturbances. The true percentage is quite clearly higher than this figure. Apart from the unknown number of non-applicants with psychiatric complaints, this statement is supported by the above-mentioned finding that it was the attitude of the doctors that determined whether or not a specialised psychiatric examination was considered necessary in the case of certain psychic complaint patterns.

This assumption is borne out by the fact that the psychiatrist was only brought into the examination procedure at a very late juncture, after much time (on average 2.5 years) had gone by.

2. Problems of Diagnostic Classification

In Chapter 3 (pp. 50-51) we drew attention to the lack of uniformity in diagnosing late psychic injury. Many authors therefore resort to a newly created nomenclature, as shown in Table 31 (page 86).

While the diagnostic concepts listed in the Table were specially created to characterize late injury arising from incarceration, the doctors who examined our 66 cases used conventional terms common in everyday psychiatric practice.

The diagnostic designations which deviate very little, if at all, from the pattern of complaints and which, according to the "labelling", would seem to be closely related, have been grouped by us under generic headings. Accordingly, the psychiatrically examined cases from our sample break down as follows:

1. Organic brain damage	24 diagnoses	
Damage to brain substance (following contusio cerebri)		7
Vascular brain damage		7
Post-encephalitic symptoms (following typhus)		5
Traumatic epilepsy		2
Epileptic fits		1
Vasomotor-induced cerebral seizures		1
Post-concussion disturbances		1

2. Neurasthenia	24 diagnoses	
Neurovegetative dystonia		6
Nervous overexcitability		5
State of nervous exhaustion		4
State of neurasthenic inadequacy		4
Psychasthenia		2
Neurocirculatory asthenia		1
Asthenia		1
Vasovegetative phenomena		1

3. Chronic-reactive depressions	19 diagnoses	
Reactive-depressive mood states		7
Chronic-reactive depression		7
Depressive states		4
Psychological depression		1

4. Neurotic reaction	14 diagnoses	
Chronic anxiety states		5
Traumatic anxiety neurosis		2
Psychoneurotic reaction		2
Long-lasting neurotic reaction		2
General neurosis		1
Chronic anxiety depression		1
Psychoreactive disturbances		1

5. Psychoses	2 diagnoses	
Schizophrenia		1
Endogenous depression		1

Since more than one diagnosis was made in 14 instances, the total number of diagnoses is higher than the number of cases. The combination of organic brain damage and chronic-reactive depressions occurred particularly frequently (6 cases).

Over a third of the persons for whom a psychiatric diagnosis was made can be grouped under the generic heading "organic brain damage". The examining doctors are of the opinion that in these patients the late psychic injury can be related back to cerebral lesions. A check of the findings reached by the examining doctors and on which they based their diagnosis reveals the following:

Number of persons	24
Neurological findings (more or less pronounced): Reflex anomalies, encephalography	14
Subjective complaints: Headaches	20
Poor memory	14
Giddiness	10

Epileptic fits	2
Fainting fits	2
Most frequent medical history:	
Head injury resulting from mistreatment	18
Typhus	5

From this it is clear that the most frequent finding on which the diagnosis of "organic brain damage" was based was the mention of headaches, closely followed by a particular type of concentration camp stress, namely head injury. On the other hand, the neurological findings recorded in the files were only established in slightly more than 50% of the cases. This would seem to indicate that certain examining doctors assumed the existence of some sort of cerebral lesion even when there was no other neurological evidence apart from headaches. Head injuries suffered during incarceration were then causally related to headaches still experienced today.

In agreement with v. Baeyer, Häfner and Kisker (1964), it is possible to conclude from these findings that neurological symptoms as an expression of late cerebral injury are not as frequent as, for example, Eitinger (1961, 1964) discovered in his material. The diagnosis of some sort of cerebral lesion, which is given somewhat too frequently in relation to the neurological findings, was obviously made in many cases because the causal significance of concentration camp stress, particularly head injury, seemed more plausible both to the examining doctors and the indemnification authorities if an "organic connection" could be postulated.

Table 31. Designation of post-incarceration late injury

Author	Year	Number of persons	"Syndrome"
Hermann and Thygesen	1954	120	Concentration camp syndrome
Segele and Ellenbogen	1954	2300	Asthénie post-concentrationnaire et troubles psychiques
Targowla	1955	not stated	Syndrome of deportation asthenia
Bastiaans	1957	300	State of psychosomato-traumatic weakness
Fichez	1957	not stated	Chronic progressive asthenia
Venzlaff	1958	not stated	Suffering-induced personality change
Bensheim	1960	not stated	Concentration camp neurosis
Eitinger et al.	1961	100	Concentration camp syndrome
Trautmann	1961	not stated	Extermination camp syndrome
Klimkova-Deutschova	1961	200	Concentration camp syndrome
Chodoff	1963	23	Late injury associated with concentration camp syndrome
Krystal and Niederland	1965	2000	Survivor syndrome

In the following discussion of late psychic injury we shall also take into account the psychic complaint patterns associated with cerebral lesion in order to determine whether the psychic symptoms of persons with brain damage differ from the main group of other late psychic injuries. Because they are so infrequently mentioned, we must exclude the endogenous psychoses from the overall group. They are, in any case, characterized by an unambiguous group of symptoms. At this point, in view of the frequency of schizophrenia and endogenous depressions recorded in our unselected group, we would merely make the following remarks:

The figures for the frequency of schizophrenia in the normal population fluctuate between 0.7% and 1% and for endogenous depressions the figures range between 0.4% and 1.6%. Consequently, our findings are important for the following reasons: In a medically random group of surviving inmates of concentration camps the proportion of psychoses is not higher than in the average population. This probably indicates that the early discovery (BONHOEFER, 1947) that the number of psychoses is not increased by external stress is correct. However, this statement only applies to the survivors of concentration camps. It is quite possible, indeed probable, that the persons who developed psychoses under the stress of incarceration did not survive the Nazi terror.

It would seem logical to compare the frequency of the psychiatric diagnoses made in our sample group with those of other authors. Unfortunately this is not possible. Even in our 66 cases a definite trend is evident towards a "personal" diagnostic approach so that any comparison with the results of other authors would be a semantic rather than a factual comparison, because the different terms do not always refer to different psychiatric realities, as was seen above in the case of the "concentration camp syndrome".

3. Persecution-Relatedness of Psychiatric Illnesses

Table 32 indicates whether the examining doctors regarded the late psychic injuries as persecution-related or not. In compiling this table we took the opinion of the last doctors to examine the ex-inmates, because their judgement was the one which had most influence on the preparation of a pension assessment. Often, the judgements did not coincide with those made previously. To illustrate this, let us just mention the one case of endogenous depression that was diagnosed in our material. This endogenous depression was declared to be persecution-related by the doctors who last examined the individual in question, but another clinic had previously come to the opposite conclusion.

It is clear from Table 32 that the majority of the psychic illnesses were regarded as persecution-related by the doctors. Disregarding psychoses, because they occur too infrequently in our material, the tendency to disallow the claim that a complaint was persecution-related was strongest in the case of the diagnoses grouped under the concepts of "neurasthenia" or "neurotic reaction" (in each case the ratio was about 2 : 1 between recognition and non-recognition of the claim). Nearly all the examining doctors agree on the persecution-relatedness of "chronic-reactive depressions".

This finding is remarkable insofar as the non-German literature on the subject tends to regard the neurasthenic symptom patterns (often grouped under the concept

Table 32. Medical opinions on the persecution-relatedness of psychiatric illnesses

Psychiatric diagnoses	persecution-related	not persecution-related
Organic brain damage	20	3
Chronic-reactive depression	18	1
Neurotic reaction	10	4
Neurasthenia	16	8
Psychoses:		
Schizophrenia	1	—
Endogenous depression	1	—

"concentration camp syndrome") as typically persecution-related problems. German doctors seem to be more inclined to regard the symptom patterns grouped under the concept "chronic-reactive depressions" as typically persecution-related.

However, the evaluation of the pension rating proposed by the examining doctor and also the decision whether this proposal can be accepted are matters which fall within the jurisdiction of the indemnification authority or the relevant legal instance (in court proceedings and settlements). In the following, we shall examine how closely the opinions of the examining doctors and the legal decisions handed down by the authorities coincide with regard to the persecution-relatedness of psychiatric illnesses (see Table 33).

Table 32 shows that the opinions of the doctors in the case of "organic brain damage", "neurasthenia" and "endogenous psychoses" were accepted. The greatest

Table 33. Assessment of the persecution-relatedness of psychiatric illnesses by doctors and indemnification authorities. (The totals for the indemnification authorities are not always the same as those given for the doctors because some indemnification procedures were still in progress at the time when we analysed the file documentation)

Psychiatric diagnoses	Doctors		Indemnification authorities	
	related to persecution	not related	related to persecution	not related
Organic brain damage	20	3	16	3
Chronic-reactive depressions	18	1	14	5
Neurotic reactions	10	4	4	5
Neurasthenia	16	8	13	9
Psychoses:				
Schizophrenia	1	—	1	—
Endogenous depression	1	—	1	—

disagreement occurs in the figures for "chronic-reactive depressions". Here, almost one quarter of the 19 diagnoses were held by the indemnification authorities to be not persecution-related. In contrast, the examining doctors accepted all but one case of chronic-reactive depression as persecution-related.

In the case of "neurotic reaction" there is also an increased tendency on the part of the indemnification authorities to reject the possibility of a link between the symptoms and the persecution stress, although here the data are the least reliable in view of the still unconcluded proceedings.

Summarizing, it can be said that even if examining doctors show a tendency to regard mainly organically induced psychic disturbances as persecution-related — and therefore also to evaluate patterns of psychic symptoms, in the absence of neurological findings, as an expression of organic brain damage — they are also open-minded enough to recognize neurotic reactions, but particularly chronic depressions, as persecution-related disorders. The indemnification authorities do not go along with this. Instead, they show a clear tendency to regard chiefly organic brain damage as persecution-related even if the proof is often inconclusive.

II. Experience-Reactive Syndromes

1. Experience-Reactive Syndromes and Complaint Patterns

Below we deal in detail with the patterns of psychic illness which we group together under the heading "experience-reactive syndromes". As will be made clear later on, this choice of terminology is not intended to signify that the pattern of clinical symptoms depends solely on the incarceration endured. In our comparison of the various experience-reactive patterns, which is intended to show that it is justifiable to arrive at various diagnoses, we have also included cerebral lesions, although these are not experience-reactive disturbances. It will be seen further below why this is a reasonable step to take. On the other hand, we have ignored the endogenous psychoses, whose pattern of symptoms differs distinctly from that of other illnesses. In addition, they are too few in number to be used in statistical analyses.

Before we turn to examining the distribution of the complaints among the individual diagnoses, it is necessary to study whether persecutees with only one psychiatric diagnosis differ from those for whom several diagnoses were made on the basis of the symptoms discovered. Table 34 (page 90) shows the percentage frequency of complaints for both these groups as well for the overall group.

The distribution of the complaints among persons for whom single and multiple diagnoses were made does not reveal any significant differences. Anxiety symptoms alone occur noticeably more frequently in persons for whom several psychiatric diagnoses were made. This finding does not, however, justify the assumption that a systematic difference exists between the two groups. Nor does a comparison of the mean complaint frequencies reveal any differences worth mentioning.

The mean frequency values are as follows:
for persons with a single diagnosis, 5.5 complaints,
for persons with several diagnoses, 6.0 complaints.

Table 34. Distribution of complaints for single and multiple diagnoses

Complaints	Single diagnosis (n=50)	Multiple diagnosis (n=14)	Total (n=64)
Anxiety dreams	35 (69%)	12 (86%)	47 (72%)
Anxiety states	19 (37%)	10 (71%)	29 (45%)
Paranoid ideation	8 (16%)	1 (7%)	9 (14%)
Feelings of hatred	9 (18%)	4 (29%)	13 (20%)
Inner agitation, irritability, nervousness	34 (67%)	9 (64%)	43 (66%)
Disturbances of memory and concentration	24 (47%)	9 (64%)	33 (51%)
Mistrust, shyness, poor social contact	19 (37%)	6 (43%)	25 (38%)
Feeling of isolation	17 (33%)	4 (29%)	21 (32%)
Depression and compulsive brooding	37 (73%)	9 (64%)	46 (71%)
Sleep disturbances	32 (63%)	10 (71%)	42 (65%)
Disturbed vitality	10 (20%)	4 (29%)	14 (22%)
Thoughts of suicide	4 (8%)	1 (7%)	5 (3%)
Tiredness and apathy	30 (59%)	6 (43%)	36 (55%)

Further proof of the similar distribution of complaints in the two groups is provided by the consistently high and very high correlations between persons with a single diagnosis (e.g. "chronic-reactive depression") and persons with combined diagnoses in which this single diagnosis is included (e.g. "chronic-reactive depression" and "neurotic reaction"). Table 35 lists the correlation coefficients obtained by the rank correlation procedure [3]. The complaints which were "detected only by a psychiatrist" and the grouping "all complaints" were calculated separately.

With one exception ("neurotic reaction" compared with "neurotic reaction and other diagnoses") all rank comparisons of the complaints are highly significant. On the basis of complaint frequency, persons with several diagnoses thus differ little, if at all, from persons with only one diagnosis. Even when the complaints which were detected only by psychiatrists are analysed, this agreement remains the same.

Since the persons with several different diagnoses obviously do not represent an independent pattern of illness, we disregard them from now on. We limit our studies to persons with one diagnosis. Table 36 lists the percentage frequencies of 13 complaints against 4 psychiatric diagnoses.

Despite the relatively low number of persons in each diagnostic group, it is possible to make the following deductions from Table 36. There are no clear accumulations of complaints that would be exclusively typical for only one diagnostic concept in each case. Some complaints occur relatively frequently in all 4 syndromes (depres-

---

[3] For each group of diagnoses a rank of complaints was formed according to the frequency of the complaints. The correlations were established with the aid of these ranks.

Table 35. Correlational comparison of persons with single and multiple diagnoses with regard to the frequency of their symptoms

Diagnoses	all complaints	complaints detected only by a psychiatrist
"Chronic-reactive depression" compared with "chronic-reactive depression and other diagnoses"	0.97 (0.1% sign.)	0.91 (0.1% sign.)
"Neurotic reaction" compared with "neurotic reaction and other diagnoses"	0.66 (1% sign.)	0.77 (0.1% sign.)
"Neurasthenia" compared with "neurasthenia and other diagnoses"	0.79 (0.1% sign.)	0.80 (0.1% sign.)
"Organic brain damage" compared with "organic brain damage and other diagnoses"	0.82 (0.1% sign.)	0.80 (0.1% sign.)

Table 36. Distribution of 13 complaints among 4 psychiatric diagnoses

Complaints	Chronic-reactive depression (n=9)	Neurotic reaction (n=9)	Neur-asthenia (n=17)	Organic brain damage (n=15)	Total (n=50)
Anxiety dreams	9 (100%)	7 (78%)	11 (65%)	8 (54%)	35 (69%)
Anxiety states	6 (67%)	5 (56%)	5 (29%)	3 (20%)	19 (37%)
Paranoid ideation	0 (—)	4 (44%)	3 (18%)	1 (7%)	8 (16%)
Feelings of hatred	1 (11%)	3 (33%)	2 (12%)	3 (20%)	9 (18%)
Inner agitation, irritability, nervousness	9 (100%)	8 (89%)	11 (65%)	6 (40%)	34 (67%)
Disturbances of memory and concentration	6 (67%)	2 (22%)	9 (53%)	7 (47%)	24 (47%)
Mistrust, shyness, poor social contact	2 (22%)	6 (67%)	8 (47%)	3 (20%)	19 (37%)
Feeling of isolation	4 (44%)	2 (22%)	7 (41%)	4 (27%)	17 (33%)
Depression and compulsive brooding	9 (100%)	7 (78%)	13 (76%)	8 (54%)	37 (37%)
Sleep disturbances	8 (89%)	8 (89%)	11 (65%)	5 (33%)	32 (63%)
Disturbed vitality	0 (—)	5 (56%)	5 (29%)	0 (—)	10 (20%)
Thoughts of suicide	1 (11%)	1 (11%)	1 (6%)	1 (7%)	30 (59%)
Tiredness and apathy	6 (67%)	7 (78%)	9 (53%)	8 (54%)	4 (8%)

sive mood, anxiety dreams, inner agitation — irritability — nervousness, sleep disturbances, tiredness — apathy), others occur relatively infrequently in all 4 syndromes (thoughts of suicide, paranoid ideas, feelings of hatred).

Only persons diagnosed as "depressive" exhibit no paranoid ideas and no disturbed vitality, in contrast to persons classified under "neurotic reaction". In these points the persons with chronic-reactive depressions and those with organic brain damage resemble each other most closely.

Table 37 lists the values of the rank correlations. Using a rank of symptom frequencies per diagnosis, these values were calculated separately for all complaints (right upper part of Table) and for those which were only recorded by a psychiatrist (left lower part of Table).

Table 37. Rank correlations between four psychiatric diagnoses

Diagnoses	Chronic-reactive depression	Neurotic reaction	Neur-asthenia	Organic brain damage	Average
Chronic-reactive depression	—	0.68	0.89	0.88	0.81
Neurotic reaction	0.87	—	0.83	0.66	0.66
Neurasthenia	0.80	0.88	—	0.74	0.85
Organic brain damage	0.87	0.47	0.84	—	0.73
Average	0.85	0.80	0.81	0.76	—

All the correlations are statistically significant (from $r = 0.68$ onwards with 1% significance). The symptom patterns of chronic-reactive depression and of organic brain damage resemble each other most closely. Those of neurotic reaction and organic brain damage are the least similar. Further differentiation of the content of Table 37 does not seem appropriate in view of the consistently high correlation coefficients.

This impression that the illness patterns are to a large extent similar becomes even stronger when all four syndromes are considered simultaneously. When all the complaints are taken into account, the agreement for all 4 psychiatric diagnoses (calculated after KENDALL) is $W = 0.81$; when only the complaints determined by psychiatrists are considered, the agreement is $W = 0.83$. Both values are statistically very significant (0.1% significance).

The result of this statistical analysis can be summarized as follows:

1. On the basis of the psychic complaint patterns, there are no differences worth mentioning for former concentration camp inmates with one or more psychiatric diagnoses.

2. Furthermore, there are no clear associations of specific complaints with the psychiatric diagnoses (experience-reactive syndromes). Even if the syndrome of organic brain damage is included in the comparison, statistically highly significant similarities are found between all four diagnostic concepts. This indicates that the

diagnosis "organic brain damage" was not always made on the basis of different psychic complaints, but because of a certain theoretical conception regarding the cause of the symptoms. Either these doctors were convinced that only organic brain damage could produce psychic disturbances, or they made this diagnosis in order to increase the ex-inmate's prospects of obtaining a pension. As shown above, in the case of the diagnosis "organic brain damage" the likelihood that the problem was persecution-induced was greatest and the chances of obtaining a pension were thus best.

3. These statements apply both to the complaint patterns which were established only by psychiatrists and to the symptoms mentioned in the course of the interviews.

These findings pose the question whether the different psychiatric diagnoses do, in fact, relate to different forms of experience-reactive late injury. In addition, however, it also seems justified to ask whether there are in fact any qualitatively different and psychiatrically clearly diagnosable reactions to the experience of incarceration. The above observations at least make it seem doubtful that the diagnosing doctors share uniform and comparable views on the various illness patterns.

2. Symptom Patterns and Genesis of Experience-Reactive Syndromes

a) Differences in the Symptom Patterns

Since no clear differences were found to exist between the psychological complaints of the four psychiatric diagnosis groups under discussion here, we will now examine whether any differences can be discovered when other variables are considered.

A comparison of the four diagnosis groups on the basis of several sociological characteristics yields the following results:

The diagnosis "chronic reactive depression" is made more frequently for female persecutees than for male (5% significance).

The diagnosis "neurotic reaction" is made more frequently for male Jewish persecutees who were less than 35 years old at the time of their release and who nowadays reside preferentially in Israel and New York (5% significance).

The diagnosis "neurasthenia" is made more frequently for male persecutees who were born in Germany, are still living in Germany and were persecuted on political or religious grounds (10% significance).

No statistically significant connections are revealed for the diagnosis "organic brain damage".

These findings can be interpreted as follows against the background of detailed individual case analyses.

The fact that "chronic-reactive depression" is diagnosed more frequently in female persecutees does not mean that the women in our sample group actually suffered more frequently or more severely from depressive illness than the men. The depressive reactions of the women merely manifest themselves in different connections and in different forms from those of the men. For example, the men's depressions tend to come to the fore more frequently in the sphere of their work or career. On the other hand, the women experience their depressions more intensely in the sphere of marital and family life or social contact. Within these spheres, the women are more aware of their depressed state and they tend to be more willing and able to express this situation to the doctor. The more obvious character of female depression seems to be the reason why this experience-reactive disturbance is more frequently diagnosed in women. This interpretation is supported by the observation that the individual symptom "depressive mood" in fact occurs with equal frequency in men and women.

The "depressive mood" plays an important role in the representatives of all four diagnosis groups. It is not possible to detect qualitative differences between the depressive mood of persecutees with the diagnosis "chronic-reactive depression" and that of persons with the diagnoses "neurotic reaction," "neurasthenia" or "organic brain damage."

We are unable to offer any plausible explanation of the findings made for the persons grouped under the headings "neurotic reaction" and "neurasthenia". Let us merely stress at this point that this syndrome does not deviate from the syndrome "chronic-reactive depression" as regards type and frequency of the complaints.

Persons with the diagnosis "organic brain damage" occur in approximately equal numbers in all age groups and countries of residence and they include racial, political and religious persecutees of both sexes. Persons with this diagnosis mention relatively few psychic complaints either to the examining doctor or in the interview situation, but on the other hand they do not individually exhibit more somatic, in particular neurological, symptoms than the persons in the other diagnosed group. Their only conspicuous characteristic is a greater irritability, a lack of self-control and aggressiveness, but all this only comes clearly to the fore in the interview. In certain cases one gains the impression that they live out their urge to be aggressive and destructive within the protection, so to speak, of their diagnosis. The following remarks, for example, are typical:

"My nerves have completely had it. Every so often it just comes over me — then I have to scream."

"I know what I went through has left me slightly wrong in the head. My neighbours know it, too. They keep out of my way. They know that I easily lose control of myself when I am irritated."

However, the impulsive aggressiveness of these interviewees can equally well be turned against themselves in an uncontrolled manner:

"I got my share, too. No matter which way I look at it, I am one of the underprivileged classes."

"We Jews were also to blame. Perhaps more than the others. We failed."

It seems that the behaviour of these persons is not simply determined by the actual brain damage itself, but rather by the awareness or the suspicion that they are no longer quite "right in the head". This fact relativizes the finding made above that the psychic complaint pattern of all four groups is nearly the same. The persons with the diagnosis "organic brain damage" resemble each other more than they resemble persons in the other diagnostic groups because of the stated aggressive behaviour patterns, quite apart from the neurological findings described above.

b) Differences in Stress Exposure

We next examine whether the different psychiatric diagnoses can perhaps be explained by analysing the period of persecution. We will restrict ourselves here to those cases where the diagnosing doctors recognized that the disorders were persecution-related.

We first of all consider whether the persons diagnosed as suffering from psychiatric complaints were exposed to more severe stress during incarceration than those persons in whom the doctors found no psychic damage. A statistical comparison of the characteristics reveals the following:

No differences can be detected as regards work stress, camp severity, duration of incarceration or loss of relatives.

On the basis of objectivized stress characteristics it is thus not possible to discover any indications that the persons for whom psychiatric complaints were diagnosed were more severely affected by concentration camp incarceration than other persecutees.

The results are similar when the four syndrome groups are contrasted with one another using the same stress characteristics. The work stress and the severity of the camp as well as the loss of relatives do not reveal any differences between the four groups. The following difference is established for the time variable:

Persons with the diagnoses "chronic-reactive depression" and "organic brain damage" more frequently spent *less* than 4 years in concentration camps.

Persons with the diagnoses "neurotic reaction" and "neurasthenia" on the other hand more frequently spent *more* than 4 years in concentration camps (5⁰/o significance).

We can discover no plausible explanation for this finding. However, it is worth noting that the persons diagnosed as having depressive complaints, and particularly those with organic brain damage, had been imprisoned for less than 4 years in the camps. This last finding, in particular, contradicts a generally current view that the duration of incarceration is proportionally related to the organic brain damage.

Detailed analysis of the subjective patterns of experience and reaction during incarceration as reported in the interviews does not reveal any important differences between the persons diagnosed as suffering from psychiatric disorders. With the exception of the interviewees for whom "organic brain damage" was diagnosed, who all refer more frequently to mistreatment, beatings and head injuries, there are no indications that any regular relationships exist between stress experienced in concentration camps and psychiatric diagnoses.

These negative findings deserve to be given special emphasis here, all the more so because, as we continue our investigation, we will find in many cases that the opposite is true. For a large number of the sequelae of concentration camp incarceration, which will be described below, it is possible to trace their genesis right back to the stress situation.

Even analysis of the developmental influences preceding the onset of persecution failed to reveal any changes in this picture. Ex-persecutees who were classified by the doctors as "chronic-reactive depressive", "neurotic" or "neurasthenic" come from the same family backgrounds and were exposed to the same developmental influences as the total group of all persecutees. Even when the three diagnosis groups are compared with one another, no differences are apparent.

Summarizing, we can say therefore that the former inmates of concentration camps for whom psychic disturbances were diagnosed do not differ from the overall group studied as regards comparable data for developmental period, persecution period and period following release. With the exception of the psychiatric diagnosis

made in their cases, nothing seems to differentiate these persons from the other persecutees. In other words, the psychiatric diagnosis of these illnesses seems to a large
extent to depend on the personal conventions of the examining doctor.

3. Dimensions of the Psychic Complaints

In the light of the above findings, it is necessary to repeat the question whether
there are in fact any distinguishable forms of experience-reactive disturbances in
former concentration camp inmates. This question is important to the extent that a
merely theoretical differentiation of psychiatric syndromes, unsupported by any corresponding illness patterns, would be of no practical use.

We now attempt, with the aid of a factor analysis, to reveal the interconnections
between the psychic complaints. In so doing, we ignore the psychiatric labelling of
the complaint patterns.

All 13 of the complaints listed on p. 91 from all 64 psychiatrically examined persecutees are used in the analysis. Again, the two psychoses have been omitted. Details
on the methodology of the factor analysis procedure are given on p. 10. Statistically
and psychologically the optimum result of this analysis seems to us to be the 4-factor
structure given in Table 38.

Table 38. 4-factor structure of psychic complaints

Factors	Characteristics	Loading
Factor I: Poor social contact	Mistrust, shyness, poor social	0.67
	contact. Paranoid ideation	0.52
Factor II: Disturbed vitality	Disturbed vitality	0.61
	Sleep disturbances	0.50
	Inner unrest, irritability, nervousness	0.44
Factor III: Anxiety	Anxiety dreams	0.68
	Anxiety states	0.67
	Sleep disturbances	0.57
Factor IV: Depression	Depression and compulsive brooding	0.78
	Tiredness and apathy	0.56
	Poor memory and concentration disturbances	0.39

Factor I ("Poor social contact") covers the turning away by the individual from
his social environment. Fellow humans are seen as hostile and threatening forces and
are anxiously avoided. The individual cannot consciously experience, let alone give
active expression to his own feelings of hatred and his strong aggressiveness, which
are the real causes for his poor social contact. There is no equivalent to this factor
in the psychiatric diagnoses of the cases under consideration here.

Factor II ("Disturbed vitality") covers psychosomatic reactions. The state of
psychic conflict gives rise to a series of physical symptoms accompanied by — ap-

parently — unfounded restlessness and irritability. The individual is psychologically in a constant state of alert. Behind this is a repressed fear which is not consciously perceived.

Factor III ("Fear") covers the state of deep anxiety. Anxiety states and anxiety dreams determine the daytime and nighttime pattern of this form of reaction. The anxiety experienced — in a more external sense — tends to promote social contact rather than to destroy it. The subject of this factor corresponds to the psychiatric syndrome of "neurotic reaction".

Factor IV ("Depression") covers the state of a very depressed, listless basic mood. The individual's thoughts circle compulsively around always the same problems or experiences. His consciousness is not free to absorb and process the real world around him. This factor corresponds to the psychiatric syndrome of "chronic-reactive depression".

The results of this factor analysis are significant for several reasons. On the one hand, they reproduce thematically two important diagnostic criteria in psychiatry ("anxiety" and "depression") and thus they would appear to contradict the criticism levelled above at the medical diagnoses. However, this contradiction does not exist in reality, because in the preceding sections we have not shown that different psychic reaction forms *do not exist;* all we have said is that they cannot be adequately and uniformly covered by the psychiatric diagnoses applied.

This holds true in particular for the dimension we have called "poor social contact". To a large extent this corresponds to the "psychic syndrome" (mistrust) described in Chapter 3 (pp. 57—58) as a social disorder. The first and most important feature to point out here is the occurrence of the contact factor. Previous psychiatric diagnoses of persecutees make no mention of an illness pattern centred around a "reactive" falling out with the social environment. Admittedly v. BAEYER, HÄFNER and KISKER (1964) refer to the importance of disturbed social contact as a consequence of concentration camp incarceration, but they see no reason to regard this as the core of an independent illness pattern. In this respect, the efforts made by these authors to follow chiefly the traditional diagnostic approach in classifying the experience-reactive syndromes of the persecutees seem to us to obscure the extraordinary importance and peculiarity of the persecution-related contact problems observed in former inmates.

Factor II ("disturbed vitality") corresponds to some extent to the "psychophysical syndrome" described on pp. 51—55 as a state of exhaustion. However, when psychic complaints alone are considered, the anxiety characteristics and depression characteristics stand out from the more comprehensive "psychophysical syndrome" as a dimension in their own right. A further statistical-correlational analysis of these factors does not seem warranted in view of the poor representativeness of the psychiatrically examined persons.

The most important results of this analysis of the psychic complaints of former inmates of concentration camps can be summarized in two points:

1. So far neither scientific theory nor medical practice has been able to provide any adequate and generally applicable knowledge on the dimensions, i.e. the inner relationships, of the psychic complaints of former inmates.

The medical diagnoses of late psychic injury, which are based exclusively on conventional but by no means uniform criteria, do not do justice to the specific manifestations of these late injuries. It is particularly disadvantageous that the everyday areas of life such as social contact, family life and occupation have not as yet received proper attention in the medical examinations of ex-persecutees.

2. Persecutees who were psychiatrically examined seem to have been selected on a quite arbitrary basis. Persons who were diagnosed as suffering from a psychiatric complaint do not differ from the overall sample of persecutees either as regards the stress to which they were exposed in the camps or with respect to their psychic symptoms. Persons with personality changes brought on by organic brain damage constitute a certain exception here.

These two points show (1) that it is necessary to broaden the psychological criteria applied in analysing late psychic injury, i.e. the investigation should be extended to an accurate study of areas largely obscured by current psychiatric nomenclature; (2) the question of what late psychiatric injury, if any, has been suffered should not just be studied in the group of persons who were designated as psychiatrically ill by a psychiatrist. Instead, we must include in our investigation all the persons in our sample, even those who are supposedly psychologically healthy. Both these requirements will be met in the following chapters.

Summary

1. In the group of 170 medically examined persecutees under investigation here, psychiatric reports are available for 66 persons (38.9%). The criteria by which persons are selected for psychiatric examination seem to be by and large "arbitrary". The actual percentage of psychiatrically sick persons among former inmates is probably much higher.

2. The categories of late psychiatric injury diagnosed in former persecutees are confusing because they are so numerous and so unclear. Therefore, we reduced the number to five generic concepts: organic brain damage, chronic-reactive depression, neurotic reaction, neurasthenia and psychosis.

3. In most cases the diagnosing doctors recognize that the late psychic injury is persecution-related. As regards the diagnoses "organic brain damage" and "neurasthenia", the suggestions made by the examining doctors were generally accepted by the indemnification authorities. There is a higher quota of rejection by the indemnification authorities in the case of "chronic-reactive depression" and "neurotic reactions".

4. Former concentration camp inmates do not display any clear links between certain complaints and the psychiatric diagnoses. This is also the case for persecutees for whom several different diagnoses were made and it makes no difference whether the complaint patterns were established by a psychiatrist or by means of an interview.

5. Even taking into account other psychological and sociological variables, it is not possible to find a logical basis for the psychiatric diagnoses. The psychiatric classifications used for the symptoms of the persecutees are obviously of little practical value because the diagnoses are not based on objectively verifiable differences within the group of persecutees.

6. Factor analysis of all complaints, including psychic problems, showed that at least four substantially different dimensions of psychic illnesses can be assumed to exist. They centre around the following illness symptoms: difficulty in making social contact, disturbed vitality, anxiety, depression.

CHAPTER 5

Basic Forms of Psychic Disturbance

Outline of the Problem

The last chapter described the psychiatric diagnoses made for former concentration camp inmates. The categories used were neither uniform nor sufficiently differentiated to permit all late psychic injury to be adequately covered. It is therefore not surprising that only one third of the cases in our study were diagnosed as suffering from some degree of psychic disturbance.

The results of the foregoing chapter cause us to ask whether the use of better differentiated categories would have revealed late injuries in ex-inmates who would be regarded as "psychologically unremarkable" according to the coarser and by no means unequivocal diagnostic approach of psychiatry. Such disturbances are to be expected, if only because there is scarcely any area of psychological experience which has not been described by one or the other author as adversely affected — see Table 39 (page 100).

The spectrum of the disturbance areas listed in Table 39 makes in clear that it is left to the examining doctor to decide whether he wishes to regard the individual symptom patterns as clinically relevant or as a general, fairly frequent reaction form of the individual's personality. Since the boundaries are of their nature fluid, we will try to use those categories of psychological health which are relevant for the maximum possible number of ex-concentration-camp inmates.

In addition to merely establishing whether a particular characteristic is present or not, we are also interested in whether and how the designated categories are inwardly connected. In answering this question, we will attempt to establish how far the complaints of former inmates are also located outside the narrow clinical sphere.

To find the answers to this question we conducted a factor analysis of 30 characteristics, based on interviews with 210 interviewees, which characterize the psychic state of these persons. In addition, 7 Rorschach ratings and 18 questionnaire items for 82 persons were put through a separate factor analysis (see Appendix, p. 255).

For the interview characteristics, three factors were found which remained relatively constant throughout all the extractions (see Table 40, page 100).

Other factors which were revealed by the analysis are neglected here because they either consisted of a single variable with a non-relevant amount of variance or they proved to be psychologically uninterpretable or inconstant.

Analysis of the Rorschach data and questionnaire data also yielded three main factors, only one of which (emotional sensitivity) will be discussed in this connection. The two remaining factors are described in the chapter on "Contact with Fellow Humans and Society". (All technical data are given in the chapter on "Study Methods").

Table 39. Focal points in the psychiatric diagnoses of former persecutees

Focal points of the described symptom patterns	Authors
Depressive pattern	
Chronic-reactive depression, grief, resignation, cheerlessness, renunciative attitude, thoughts of suicide, feelings of guilt	HERMANN and THYGESEN, TARGOWLA, STRAUSS, KOLLE, VENZLAFF, BENSHEIM, EITINGER, TRAUTMANN, KLIMKOVA-DEUTSCHOVA, CHODOFF, v. BAEYER, HÄFNER and KISKER, LESNIAK, KRYSTAL and NIEDERLAND
Asthenic pattern	
Apathy, adynamia, lack of initiative, tiredness, exhaustibility, low vitality, limp state	MINKOWSKI, TARGOWLA, BASTIAANS, FICHEZ, STRAUSS, VENZLAFF, BENSHEIM, EITINGER, KLIMKOVA-DEUTSCHOVA, v. BAEYER, HÄFNER and KISKER
Disturbances in the emotional affective sphere	
Hypersensitivity, irritability, explosiveness, excitability, emotional instability, insensitivity, deadening of the emotions, affective paralysis	HERMANN and THYGESEN, FICHEZ, BENSHEIM, EITINGER, MINKOWSKI, BENSHEIM (?), TRAUTMANN, KLIMKOVA-DEUTSCHOVA, LESNIAK, et al.
Anxiety symptoms	
Anxiety states, phobic reactions, fearfulness, anxiety dreams (sleep disturbances)	HERMANN and THYGESEN, VENZLAFF, BENSHEIM, TRAUTMANN, v. BAEYER, HÄFNER and KISKER, KLIMKOVA-DEUTSCHOVA, KRYSTAL and NIEDERLAND
Disturbances in the intellectual sphere	
Poor memory, disturbed concentration, reduced attentiveness, amnesia and hypermnesia	HERMANN and THYGESEN, TARGOWLA, EITINGER, KLIMKOVA-DEUTSCHOVA, KRYSTAL and NIEDERLAND
Disturbed social contact	
Isolation, dissociability, communication disturbances	FICHEZ, VENZLAFF, v. BAEYER, HÄFNER and KISKER, KRYSTAL and NIEDERLAND
Disturbed self esteem	
Feelings of inferiority and inadequacy, lack of self confidence, reduced self esteem, shift of identity	FICHEZ, VENZLAFF, EITINGER, KRYSTAL and NIEDERLAND
Paranoid symptoms	
Mistrust, hostility	STRAUSS, VENZLAFF, v. BAEYER, HÄFNER and KISKER

Table 40. Factors for the interview characteristics

Factors	
Factor I	Resignation and despair
Factor II	Apathy and inhibition
Factor III	Aggressive irritable moodiness

I. Manifestation and Genesis

Factor I: Resignation and despair

This factor is typified by the characteristics listed in Table 41.

Table 41. Factor of "resignation and despair"

Characteristic	Loading
Visible despair brought on by concentration camp fate	0.68
Period of incarceration now seen as senseless and destructive of life	0.65
Present mood tends to be one of depression	0.64
No signs that the concentration camp experience had a "maturing" influence	0.61
Emotional susceptibility almost totally lacking	0.49

The factor is characterized by resignation which can go as far as becoming despair. The lives of the persons represented here are marked by the brutal senselessness of the concentration camp experience. These people are haunted by memories of that terrible period in their existence and try, mostly in vain, to put them out of their minds. Emotional involvement is avoided so that in extreme cases these people give the impression of being untouched by the problems and conflicts of modern life. The future does not seem to exist for them. As a result, the time since their release has remained by and large without form or content. It is striking that this state of resignation and despair is not overlain by any hypochondria nor does it go together with self-pity or suicidal tendencies.

The subject matter of this form of experience is very like, although not completely identical with, the depression patterns often described in the literature (HERMANN and THYGESEN, 1954; TARGOWLA, 1954; KOLLE, 1958; EITINGER, 1961; LEVINGER, 1962; KRYSTAL and NIEDERLAND, 1965).

Similarities with the above factor that are psychodynamically more relevant can be found in e.g. VENZLAFF (1958). He writes of a "breakdown of the ordered structure of personality", a phenomenon seen as deriving directly from the destructive influences of the period of persecution.

The psychic state described by the factor "resignation and despair" strikingly mirrors the effect exerted on personality by the fact that life now appears senseless and aimless. The associated emotional vacuum and reduced emotional susceptibility can either be interpreted as persisting "affective paralysis" (TRAUTMANN, 1961) or as a protective mechanism and an attempt to achieve "a restrictive defence against a possible revival of traumatic experiences by reality and memories" (v. BAEYER, HÄFNER and KISKER, 1964).

The psychic significance of the factor "resignation and despair" is revealed, amongst other things, by the lack of any clear correlations with purely somatic damage. This is matched by the observation that persons in whom "resignation and despair" are very pronounced are usually awarded disability pensions which are only slightly, if at all, higher than those granted persons with few or no symptoms of this psychic disturbance. This finding supports the fact mentioned in the chapter on "Psychiatric Diagnoses" (p. 97), that people with psychic disturbances are awarded inadequate pensions, particularly if these disturbances are not clinically prominent.

A graduation of the factor "resignation and despair" showing how many of the 5 characteristics which make up this factor apply to each of the 210 interviewees is given in Fig. 9.

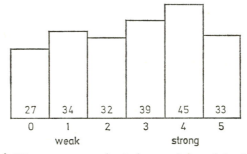

Fig. 9. Distribution of 210 persons over the 5 characteristics of the factor "resignation and despair"

All 5 characteristics are present in 33 of the interviewees (15%). No characteristic of this factor, i.e. a total lack of any resigned attitude, was detected in 27 of those interviewed (12%). All the other former inmates tended more or less towards one or the other of the two extremes: 93 persons (44.3%) had 0–2 characteristics, 117 (55.7%) had 3–5 characteristics.

Fig. 9 shows that not all former persecutees exhibit resignation or despair. Some of them show no signs of any such psychic state. But this does not mean that the persons in whom this factor is weak or even absent are psychically healthy. They may be suffering from other disturbances.

In order to carry out a statistical examination of the connections between the attitude of resignation and other areas of life, the 210 interviewees were dichotomized using Factor I. For this purpose the 93 persons (44.3%) with 0–2 characteristics (weak representation of this factor) were taken together and contrasted with the 117 persons (55.7%) with 3–5 characteristics (strong representation of this factor).

On this basis, the following statistically significant differences can be established between the groups of persecutees (chi-square test):

Persecutees who represent the factor "resignation and despair" are more frequently Polish Jews than Germans persecuted for political or religious reasons (1%), more frequently Polish Jews than German Jews (5% significance), and also more frequently female than male (5% significance). However, there is *no* difference between these persecutees as regards age (not even when extreme groups are compared).

The more pronounced manifestation of "resignation and despair" in Polish Jews may, among other things, be connected with the fact that they were exposed to particularly major upheavals in their lives. Rather like women as opposed to men, Polish Jews in contrast to German persecutees were in general more deeply rooted in and integrated with their family environment. The persecution experience, with all its accompanying destructive phenomena, thus meant for them a correspondingly far-reaching process of uprooting and disintegration. In addition, the Polish Jews in the group we examined were unable to return to their familiar environment. The psychic correlation of these facts is resignation and despair.

Such an interpretation is supported in the literature by observations that "uprooting depressions" (H. STRAUSS, 1957) and "alienation reaction" (KOLLE, 1958) are specific reactions in Polish Jews.

The second significant finding, namely the stronger degree to which women are affected, is also confirmed in the analyses of physical health (Chapter on "Late-Appearing Damage to Health") and of social contact behaviour (Chapter on "Contact with Fellow Humans and Society").

This finding can be interpreted as an indication that women in general tend much more than men to react in an all-out manner to stress. Partial malfunctions and disturbances seem more typical for men, particularly in regard to the way with which they cope with their persecution experience, and these can be compensated for by still functional behavioural patterns. On the other hand, above a certain level of subjective stress, women tend more often to react by giving way to total despair and to the belief that life is totally devoid of meaning.

Examination of the connections with characteristics from other areas of life (see also Chapter on "Contact with Fellow Humans and Society", "Marriage and Family", "Occupational Reintegration") yields further concrete facts on the attitude of resignation and despair. The following findings are statistically significant:

Persecutees who represent the factor "resignation and despair" are more frequently lacking in social contact today (0.1% significance), more frequently exhibit a rejective attitude towards their fellow humans (0.1% significance), are more frequently uninterested in public affairs (1% significance), more frequently live in needy circumstances (5% significance).

The close correlation with the listed areas of life emphasizes once again the importance of the factor under discussion here. The significance of these connections is unequivocal. Former inmates exhibiting clear symptoms of resignation, hopelessness and despair are also impaired in all areas of social communication. In a way, this situation is not surprising, since people who are still suffering as described from the persecution inflicted on them cannot be expected to muster sufficient hope and effort to relate once more to the lives of others. Thus, while the psychic disturbance of resignation and despair expresses primarily the relationship of the persons in question to themselves, it also reflects their relationship with other persons. This disturbance is a psychic condition of the post-incarceration period; it incorporates all the experiences to which the individual has been exposed since his release from imprisonment, in particular the reciprocal relationship with human society.

As regards the correlation of this psychic disturbance with the stress of concentration camp incarceration, the following statistically significant results are obtained when persons with a weakly resigned attitude are contrasted with those in whom the attitude is strongly expressed:

Persecutees who represent the factor "resignation and despair" were more frequently exposed to severe work stress in the camps (0.1% significance);
were more frequently incarcerated in harsh camps (1% significance), and had lost father and mother significantly more frequently as a result of persecution (5% significance);
do *not* differ as regards duration of incarceration.

These findings are clear and can be interpreted as showing at least that the present psychic condition has been brought about by a combination of the deprivation, threats and losses suffered during persecution. Persons who nowadays stand out because of their strongly pronounced attitude of resignation and despair also, from an objective standpoint, suffered more during the period of persecution (harsh work stress, severe camp conditions, loss of father and mother) than persons who nowadays do not have such a resigned or despairing attitude.

The clearest index of the severity of persecution is provided by the degree of work stress endured in the camps. More than all other conditions, the type of work to be performed determined whether an inmate held up or collapsed during incarceration. Harsh physical labour (for example in a quarry) usually represented as severe a threat to life as, say, a serious infection.

The correlation between the severity of camp conditions and the attitude of despair indicates that not just the work but also the other circumstances in the harsh camps, some of which after all were extermination camps, contributed towards the later development of a resigned attitude.

In addition, the correlation with the loss of their parents also helps to explain why the persecutees in question were unable to come to terms with the experience of their incarceration, even in the different conditions of existence following their release. The annihilation of their parents finally destroyed any chance they may have had of re-establishing relations with particularly important persons from the past.

In this connection, it is very important to note that the absolute duration of incarceration contributes nothing to our understanding of why these persons now exhibit this attitude of resignation and despair. The development of this attitude is obviously only marginally affected, if at all, by a long or short period of incarceration. This confirms the low significance of the duration of incarceration, as already found in the study of medically relevant late injuries.

An analysis of the statements and data on the period of incarceration itself reveals that the disturbances described above did not arise only after the inmate was released but probably were present in incipient form during the time the person was imprisoned. The correlation of the factor "resignation and despair" with the factor of "adaptation in the concentration camp" described in the chapter on persecution stress (see p. 34) reveals that persons who now exhibit despair and resignation suffered from socio-communicative and behavioural disturbances even while they were incarcerated:

Persecutees who represent the factor "resignation and despair" were less frequently able to adapt successfully in the camps (0.1% significance).

This factor is represented mainly by Polish Jews and women and, in addition, this group suffered the greatest stress in the concentration camps. There is thus much evidence to support the assumption that such disturbances are a direct result of concentration camp stress. (Additional data in confirmation of this finding are given in the chapter on "Contact with Fellow Humans and Society" see p. 132).

Despite this clear correlation, it must be stated that not *all* former inmates are characterized by this attitude of resignation and despair. In studying the genesis of this psychic problem, it seems reasonable to take into account also the development period prior to the onset of persecution.

We can, in fact, find several statistically significant differences between the ex-persecutees as regards developmental influences:

Persecutees who represent the factor "resignation and despair" report more frequently that their parents' marriage was harmonious (5% significance);
more frequently describe the general conditions of existence during their childhood and youth as "good" (5% significance);
seem more frequently to have been able to make contact with partners of the same or opposite sex during their youth (5% significance in each case);
more frequently describe their father as cooperative in his approach to upbringing (5% significance) and more frequently as open-minded and receptive to the world around him (10% significance);
report more frequently that they enjoyed a good emotional relationship with their father as well as with their mother (10% significance).

These findings would appear to indicate that resignation and despair stand out against a background of positive childhood development as the consequence of severe and terrible concentration camp experiences. The severity of the disturbance manifest today is clearly contrasted with the positive influences of the development period. A causal interpretation, according to which a person could only react with resignation and despair to severe internal and external stress if he or she had had a happy and harmonious childhood, cannot be upheld on the basis of the facts available, but neither can it be totally rejected.

One should also consider the possibility that psychically highly disturbed ex-inmates may perhaps tend to idealize their early past. If such idealization tendencies had any effect in bringing about the correlations described above, they are typical only for the attitude of resignation and despair and not for other psychic disturbances, for which no corresponding findings were made.

Factor II: Apathy and inhibition

A second form of psychic disturbance exhibits the constellation of characteristics listed in Table 42.

This factor denotes general passivity. Ex-persecutees representing this factor are to a great extent dispirited and exhausted. They no longer take any pleasure in their previous occupations and above all no longer have any faith in themselves. Instead, they observe and worry about themselves with hypochondriacal intensity. Achievement is replaced by a dejected plaintiveness and an anxious recording of physical and mental failure.

Table 42. Factor of "apathy and inhibition"

Characteristic	Loading
Lack of drive	0.74
Plaintiveness	0.59
Easily tired	0.56
Hypochondriacal complaints	0.53
Dejection	0.41

Similar characteristics of this form of reaction have frequently been diagnosed in the earlier literature on concentration camps under the heading "asthenia". They are at the core, for example, of the "asthenic syndrome of deportees" (TARGOWLA, 1954), of "chronic progressive asthenia" (FICHEZ, 1954) or of a "psychosomato-traumatic state of weakness" (BASTIAANS, 1957).

Although the asthenic symptoms were also seen as having a psychic element, they were usually taken primarily as an expression of somatic injury. This emphatically postulated somatic etiology (HERMANN and THYGESEN, 1954; TARGOWLA, 1955; RICHET and MANS, 1956; FICHEZ, 1957; SEGELLE and ELLENBOGEN, 1958) may have contributed to the greater number of diagnoses of asthenic conditions.

The occurrence of the psychic disturbance described above makes it clear that the theory of the physical dependence of psychasthenic states needs to be severely modified, because this psychic disorder is detected in ex-persecutees as long as 15 years after their release. At that time, the acute deficiency and weakness symptoms of a physical nature that had been observed immediately after the release from imprisonment had to a large extent receded. Thus, even clear representatives of the factor "apathy and inhibition" do not exhibit neurological or other physical disturbances any more frequently than persons who represent this factor slightly or not at all.

No correlations exist with the factor "psychophysical syndrome" (see p. 51) nor with the factor "internal disorders" (see p. 56). Even the average disability rating tends to be only slightly higher in apathetic-inhibited persons than in persons who do not exhibit this psychic disturbance.

Graduation of the factor "apathy and inhibition" on the basis of the five constituent characteristics gives the following distribution for 210 interviewees:

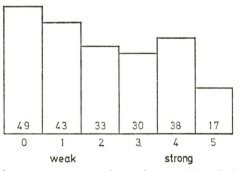

Fig. 10. Distribution of 210 persons over the 5 characteristics of the factor "apathy and inhibition"

This factor is strongly pronounced in 17 interviewees (8.1%), while 49 persons (23.3%) do not exhibit any of the characteristics of this form of reaction. When the scale is dichotomized, 125 interviewees (59.5%) represent the factor weakly and 85 persons (40.5%) strongly.

There are no specific accumulations of this factor within the individual persecution groups:

     Sex
     Age (including extreme groups)   Country of residence
     Country of origin   Reasons for persecution

do *not* correlate with the psychic disturbance of "apathy and inhibition". This psychic disturbance is thus more or less uniformly distributed throughout all sociological sub-groups. Thus, it is typical for the total population of ex-persecutees.

On the other hand, there are clearer correlations with other areas of the inmates' lives today. It is found, for example, that the representatives of the factor "apathy and inhibition" are much more severely impaired in all socio-communicative areas than former persecutees in whom this psychic disturbance is only weakly, if at all, manifest. In this respect there are no fundamental differences between this factor and that of "resignation and despair".

A significant difference results, however, when an attempt is made to determine more accurately the relevant value of the characteristic "mistrust" which is found in representatives of both fundamental disturbances. This value can be determined in the unequivocal representatives of both factors. It is found that in connection with resignation and despair the mistrustful turning away from other human beings is a central phenomenon and a direct expression of the loss of trust in oneself and in one's fellow men. Overstating slightly, we might even go so far as to say that in resigned and despairing persecutees it is the breakdown of trust in the world around them that causes all further socio-communicative disturbances.

"As far as I am concerned, other people are dead. It is my experience that I can expect nothing from them."

On the other hand, the apathetic-inhibited inmates primarily remain socially aloof and the mistrust is more the result of an increasing degree of alienation from other persons over the years. The actual causes for this alienation are the inmates' dejection, inferiority complexes and lack of drive. Thus the mistrust shown by these "low-drive" persons does not express a fundamental lack of faith in mankind as it does in the persons with the "resignation" syndrome, but instead represents a reaction to the desired but absent human contact and intimacy.

"I don't know why, but people don't seem to want anything to do with me. I am very reserved; it's not really worth making an effort; they only think of themselves."

The low drive, which manifests itself in inhibited activity and a lack of aggression, is also responsible for the on average lower standard of living of persons with pronounced "apathy and inhibition" traits. For, after all, lack of activity coupled with a dejected and plaintive attitude, are not the best of qualifications for advancement in a career.

The psychic disturbance of "apathy and inhibition" seems to be less clearly determined by the objective stress of persecution than the "resignation and despair" syndrome. The only correlation is with the severity of the work stress during incarceration.

Persons who represent the factor "apathy and inhibition" were exposed more frequently to severe work stress in the camps (5% significance).

Other persecution-related stress characteristics such as

> severity of the camp,
> duration of incarceration,
> number of relatives lost,

do *not* yield any differences.

From this it is apparent that the connection between persecution stress and "apathy and inhibition" is not as clear as that between stress and "resignation and despair"; these findings indicate that personality-specific characteristics also play a role in shaping the present pattern of symptoms. It is therefore probably not a matter of chance that persons who nowadays are characterized by pronounced "apathy and inhibition" also exhibited socio-communicative and adaptation difficulties in the camps more frequently than persons who exhibit none or only a few of the characteristics of this psychic disturbance:

Persons who represent the factor "apathy and inhibition" were more frequently unable to adapt in the concentration camp (5% significance).

An attitude tending towards passivity and evasion, which is also an essential co-determinant of the "apathy and inhibition" pattern, can be traced back to the development period preceding incarceration.

Persons representing the factor "apathy and inhibition" had an authoritarian mother who had a poor emotional relationship with her children (10% significance in both cases), and were mainly passive, even during their adolescence, before the onset of persecution (10% significance).

Despite all the caution that is dictated by the low level of significance, this finding nevertheless permits us to assume that the influence of a strict and not very loving mother contributed to the passivity which now predominates in the interviewees in question.

The unequivocal representatives of this factor exhibit early on, among other things, a clear lack of accomplishment, frequently coupled with a renunciatory attitude and a tendency to encapsulate themselves from society, e.g. from their classmates. This withdrawal into themselves was also the most frequent reaction to the stress of incarceration, but in most cases it proved to be an inadequate defence for the individual. The collapse of this defensive attitude under the conditions of incarceration resulted in even greater despondency, which remained a determining factor in the inmates' lives even after their release.

Factor III: Aggressive-irritable moodiness

The third basic form of psychic disturbance observed in ex-inmates of concentration camps is a factor with the constellation of characteristics listed in Table 43.

The psychic state which is evident in this factor is more dynamic and obvious than in the two preceding factors. It is marked by pent-up aggressiveness which is either directed against the outside world in the form of somewhat diffuse irritability and dissatisfaction, or it can also be turned against the individual himself in the form of

Table 43. Factor of "aggressive-irritable moodiness"

Characteristic	Loading
Irritability	0.78
Dissatisfaction	0.73
Self-pity	0.55
Emotional instability	0.47
Hypochondriacal complaints	0.44

hypochondria. All the individual's attention and love is directed towards his own person, his fate and his present state, and the world around is expected to share this attitude.

The regressive tendency which is apparent here also manifests itself in the individual's exaggerated expectations of the amends to be made by his fellow humans, who are called to account for the persecution suffered and all its stresses.

"I was the one that was imprisoned, not the others. That's my basic position. I suffered for the rest and now I want atonement. But money is not enough."

The stronger the need for recognition of the wrongs suffered, the weaker the ability, in general, to express it adequately. The inadequate expression of aggression provokes opposition from other people and in turn strengthens the tendency to hypochondria and self-pity.

"Aggressive-irritable moodiness" thus reflects, to some extent, the rejection of the persecutee by the world in which he lives; this is in contrast to the attitude of "resignation" where the persecutee turns away from the world around him. In addition, "aggressive-irritable moodiness" still permits social communication, and even constantly provokes such communication, whereas the attitude of resignation and despair expresses a more far-reaching breakdown in interpersonal contact. Accordingly, the mood of resigned individuals is usually a monotonous one of depression and dejection while that of the aggressive-irritable individuals tends to be more fluctuating and unstable.

This unstable mood as an accompanying phenomenon of uninhibited expression of aggression is also reflected in a factor which was obtained from a factor analysis of 7 Rorschach and 19 questionnaire items involving 82 persons (see Chapter 1, p. 7 and Appendix, p. 255). We call this the "affectivity factor", and it comprises the characteristics listed in Table 44.

Table 44. Factor of "affectivity" (from Rorschach and questionnaire data)

Characteristic	"Affective stability" (Pole A)	"Affective instability" (Pole B)	Loading
Inhibition or repression of aggression (Rorschach)	pronounced	not pronounced	0.67
Affective adaptation (Rorschach)	achieved	not achieved	0.65
Ability to make contact (Rorschach)	little affected	clearly affected	0.56
Outward-oriented aggressiveness (Rorschach)	not evident	evident	0.53
Affective instability (Rorschach)	barely evident	clearly evident	0.46
Assessment of social environment (Rorschach)	tends to be negative	none made	0.45
Inward-oriented aggressiveness (Questionnaire)	clearly evident	barely evident	0.45

The factor divides into two poles: "affective instability" (Pole B) and "affective stability" (Pole A). The condition of affective instability is characterized above all by an extensive lack of emotional and intellectual control mechanisms. Affective impulses come to the surface in an uncontrolled manner. There is practically no tendency to direct aggression against oneself as well. Interviewees who represent this pole are to a large extent helpless in the grip of their aggressiveness. They are constantly at loggerheads with the world around them. The conflict situations that arise from the reactions of the environment generally contribute to further instability of the affective state.

Persons who represent Pole A ("affective stability") are not so openly aggressive. Here the aggressive tendencies take the form of verbal criticism or emotional depreciation of the world in which they live, but there are no uncontrolled, violent outbursts. Thus, these persons appear on the surface to be relatively well adapted emotionally and to have achieved affective stability. But this stability is generally attained by inhibiting and repressing aggressive tendencies and consequently quite often results in disturbances in other psychic areas.

So far, with the exception of work by MATUSSEK (1961), TRAUTMANN (1961), HOPPE (1962), v. BAEYER, HÄFNER and KISKER (1964), relatively little mention has been made in the literature on concentration camps of reaction forms with an aggressive content. This may be because most authors gained their medical experience of ex-inmates in the situation of a medical examination conducted for the purpose of assessing pension entitlement. In such a situation, however, the examinee will suppress his aggressions in order not to jeopardize the outcome of the examination. (See also the list of complaints recorded in the medical examination and interview situations, p. 48). This assumption is also supported by the fact that the case which HOPPE used to describe the dynamics of chronic aggression in ex-inmates had been observed during a long course of analytical treatment.

Another reason why the phenomenon of an aggressive reaction to persecution seems to have been largely ignored is that it does not really fit in any known clinical scheme. Even authors who recognize the specific relationship between incarceration and aggressive behaviour patterns only regard these as individual symptoms and do not attempt to correlate them with other corresponding behaviour patterns.

The 5 characteristics which constitute the factor "aggressive-irritable moodiness" are distributed as follows among 210 former inmates:

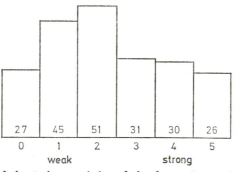

27	45	51	31	30	26
0	1	2	3	4	5
weak				strong	

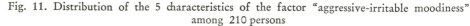

Fig. 11. Distribution of the 5 characteristics of the factor "aggressive-irritable moodiness" among 210 persons

26 interviewees (12.4%) represent the factor "aggressive-irritable moodiness" in full with all five characteristics. No signs of this factor are discernible, on the other hand, in 27 interviewees (12.9%). When the scale is dichotomized, 123 interviewees (58.6%) exhibit the factor weakly (0–2 characteristics), while in 87 interviewees (41.4%) it is very pronounced (3–5 characteristics). "Aggressive-irritable moodiness" occurs *equally*

in men and women,

in persecutees born in Germany and those born in Poland,

in Jews and in political or religious persecutees.

A difference is only apparent as regards the extreme limits of the inmates' present ages, and even then it is no more than a slight tendency.

At the time of the interview (1960) persecutees who represent the factor "aggressive-irritable moodiness"

were more frequently older than 61 and less frequently younger than 40 (10% significance).

Thus, we see first that "aggressive-irritable moodiness" does not have any special affinity with any particular group of persecutees. The tendency for this factor to be exhibited more frequently by older interviewees can probably be interpreted as a general developmental-psychological phenomenon. Accordingly, a loss of adaptability, frequently accompanied by irritability, dissatisfaction and hypochondriac tendencies, could also be expected in a normal population of uniform age.

The correlations of the "aggressive-irritable" factor with other social-communicative areas are less pronounced than in both preceding forms of disturbance. The strongly aggressive and irritable persecutees also exhibit disturbances in their marital and social lives, but the element of mistrust, which is typical for the other two factors, is missing. In addition, no differences can be discovered between the present standard of living of representatives of the "aggressive-irritable" factor and of persons who do not represent this factor.

In contrast to representatives of the "resignation and despair" factor, who avoid all contact because of their mistrustful attitude, it is noted that the aggressive-irritable persecutees actively seek contact but then destroy it through their aggressive mood. Nevertheless, considered overall, the disturbance of interpersonal contact is not as far-reaching in this group of persons as it is in those typified by resignation and despair.

Qualitative analysis also reveals a clear distinction between the contact and social-communicative disturbances of apathetic-inhibited and aggressive-irritable interviewees. For ex-inmates representing the factor of "aggressive-irritable moodiness", the cause of the social disturbance is to be seen in the *unadapted* contact activity, while for representatives of the "apathy and inhibition" factor the cause is a *lack of* contact initiative.

As was the case with the "apathy and inhibition" factor, no consistent correlation with the various forms of incarceration stress can be found for aggressive-irritable moodiness. Thus *no* statistically significant differences exist between interviewees exhibiting pronounced and weak aggressive-irritable moodiness for the following stress dimensions:

Duration of incarceration,

Degree of severity of the camp,

Number of relatives lost.

On the other hand, the correlation of the psychic disturbance discussed here with work stress as well as with the adaptation to conditions in the camp proved to be very significant:

Persecutees who represent the "aggressive-irritable moodiness" factor were more frequently exposed to harsh work stress in the camps (1% significance), and failed more frequently to adapt to camp conditions (1% significance).

As with the other two basic psychic disturbances, the interpretation that first suggests itself for this finding is that the more severe stress and the threat to life imposed by the work situation in the camps resulted in a correspondingly stronger aggressive-irritable reaction today.

Such an explanation, which approximately follows the "frustration-aggression-hypothesis" (J. DOLLARD, 1939), ignores the possible interpretation which we have described above, namely the importance of personality in determining the type of work situation.

According to this, the clear present-day disturbance in the ability to handle aggressiveness could have been present during the period of incarceration and would have impeded the inmate's ability to achieve optimum adaptation to camp conditions, i.e. also to achieve the best work conditions.

With regard to how this attitude came about, we can only report one single significant finding, a developmental characteristic, from all the material discussed here:

Persecutees who represent the factor "aggressive-irritable moodiness" more frequently had a poor emotional relationship with their mother during childhood (5% significance).

The validity of this finding is increased by the fact that there is no equivalent disturbance in the relationship with the father. It is thus at least probable that the genetic roots of this psychic disturbance are also to be sought in an emotionally disturbed relationship with the mother. The genesis of this attitude would then be seen as the individual's form of reaction to an early feeling that he had been given a raw deal and that he had been unfairly treated, particularly by his mother. It is possible that the persons in question reacted to this experience even in their mother's presence with dissatisfaction and hypochondriacally tinged displays of this dissatisfaction. The experiences of persecution may then have re-activated this behaviour as a reaction form and it now determines the ex-inmate's attitude towards society.

A comparison of the findings on the developmental period of the aggressive-irritable individuals and the apathetic-inhibited persons reveals that the former merely had a poor emotional relationship with their mothers while the latter mention that their mothers were authoritarian. This might indicate that the apathetic-inhibited persons were manoeuvred into a more passive attitude by their authoritarian mothers — a fact which is confirmed by a study of their adolescence — while the aggressive-irritable types suffered chiefly from the unstable emotional relationship with their mothers and therefore did not react passively but in an irritable-aggressive manner.

These two differing effects of the mother-child relationship are in turn fundamentally different from the relationships of the "resigned" individuals to their mothers. In their case, it is almost impossible to detect any type of disturbance in their relationships with either parent. On the contrary, their childhood is described as harmonious and ideal. But, for all that, the stress characteristics in this group of persons are more severe than in the two other groups. We can probably conclude from this that resignation and despair are the most unequivocal persecution-related reactions, while aggressive-irritable moodiness can also be determined by developmental influences in childhood.

Of course, in advancing this interpretation we do not intend to claim that the present psychic disturbance of aggressive-irritable moodiness is exclusively determined by early childhood experiences. This detail is merely mentioned as an aid to understanding why some persons react to the stress of incarceration and persecution with hypochondriacally tinged aggressive-irritable moodiness, while this specific form of reaction to a relatively comparable situation is not detected in other persons.

II. Psychic Disturbances and Reasons for Survival

In the following, we will examine whether the three basic psychic disturbances described here are correlated with specific reasons for survival, as they were subjectively remembered by the ex-persecutees. Through further questioning, an attempt was made to obtain additional data on the three factors.

The subjectively experienced and stated reasons for the inmates' survival were given in the chapter on "Stress Imposed by Concentration-Camp Incarceration" (see p. 32). To answer the questions with which we are concerned here, we will pick out only those reasons for survival which are significantly correlated with the three fundamental psychic disturbances (Table 45).

Persons who today have a mainly resigned and despairing outlook on life stated that they survived the experience of incarceration largely through luck or chance. It is hardly likely that these persons were more favoured by luck or chance in the camps than the other persecutees. Instead, their feeling that they do not owe their survival to their own efforts and strength to resist annihilation tends to express the

Table 45. Reasons for survival and fundamental psychic disturbances

Reasons for survival	"Resignation and Despair"		"Apathy and Inhibition"		"Aggressive-Irritable Moodiness"	
	strong	weak	strong	weak	strong	weak
	Number of Persons					
"Chance or luck"	31 [b]	13	19	25	23	21
"Family memories"	21 [a]	9	16	14	14	16
"Active adaptation to camp conditions"	9	13	3	19 [c]	8	14
"Religious faith"	9	16	6	19 [b]	8	17
"Discipline and self-control"	27	19	17	29	15	31 [a]

[a] 5% significance;   [b] 1% significance;   [c] 0.1% significance

depth of their resignation and the doubt they have in themselves and their own abilities. It seems that these persons were most strongly aware of the irrationality and absurdity of state-planned and state-organised murder. The traces of this experience are evident today in their inability to give any sense or purpose to their lives.

The second reason for survival which is frequently given by these persons, namely the memories of their families, can be seen in this context as an attempt to remember something rational and comforting in the terrible world of death and destruction. The persons in question, mainly Polish Jews and women, see p. 102, were obviously more strongly family-oriented than other persecutees. The fact that they also suffered more frequently from the loss of relatives may have contributed additionally to the shaping of their attitude of resignation and despair (see also p. 103).

The group of persecutees who are nowadays apathetic and inhibited is characterized by the fact that these persons hardly mention "active adaptation to camp conditions" and "religious faith" as reasons for their survival. This finding indicates that a reaction form materialized in the concentration camps which we must call somatic-intellectual-psychological passivity. This powerful fatalism is found most frequently in persecutees who nowadays most strongly exhibit the psychic disturbance of apathy and inhibition.

It is striking how infrequently persons whose psychic condition is now characterized by aggressive-irritable moodiness mentioned "discipline and self-control" as the reasons for their survival. Conversely, people who believe they owe their survival to discipline and self-control suffer little, if at all, from aggressive-irritable moodiness. The correlation seems plausible because persons who do not lose their self-control under conditions of extreme stress can probably also cope with the resistance and frustrations encountered in life after their release without having to resort to the somewhat regressive adaptation mechanisms of aggressive-irritable moodiness.

As regards the connection between remembered reasons for survival and the inmates' present psychic states, we can say in conclusion that the significant correlations point to the existence of psychodynamic continuity between former and present forms of coping with stress.

III. Symptom-Free Survivors of Incarceration

So far, we have described three fundamental forms of psychic disturbance. These disturbances are not equally present in all the interviewees. Some persecutees have symptoms of all three fundamental disturbances while others exhibit very few or even no such disturbances.

In the total sample of 210 interviewees there are 25 persons (11.9%) in whom four or all five characteristics, i.e. a total of 12 to 15 characteristics, of each of the three forms of disturbance can be detected. Similarly, the total sample contains 25 persons (11.9%) in whom at most one symptom of each form of disturbance, i.e. a total of at most three symptoms, can be detected.

Thus there are two contrasting extreme groups of persons with psychic disturbances; one group can be described as "rich in symptoms" and the other as relatively "symptom-free". By contrasting these two groups we will attempt to investigate what essential qualities and what accompanying phenomena are exhibited by persons who survived incarceration without suffering any of the more pronounced symptoms of psychic distress today.

This investigation is intended to complement the findings made so far. Let us first consider the pre-concentration-camp period in order to gain a clearer view of the genetic aspects.

Persecutees who are nowadays relatively symptom-free usually had a mother who felt part of the social majority group; mothers of those with many symptoms, on the other hand, felt more frequently that they belonged to a social minority (5% significance), and were characterized during their adolescence by their chiefly active attitude, while persons now displaying many symptoms were mainly passive during adolescence (5% significance).

These two findings can be interpreted and correlated with one another as follows:

The social integration of the mother into the society around her seems to make it possible for the child to grow up without disturbance and also to develop more actively and with confidence. In contrast, a mother who feels alienated within a large social group, because she relates to the values and behavioural standards of a special group, seems unable to provide her child with as much self-assurance and confidence.

It is interesting to note that the father does not play a correspondingly important role in this regard. Even the purely emotional relationships between the child and its parents seem to be of subordinate importance for the connection discussed here between the expression of activity in adolescence and the later formation of psychic symptoms.

The varying degree to which activity was developed, and also the varying capacity for self assertion, are even more clearly evident in the two extreme groups at the very start of the persecution:

Persecutees who are today relatively free of symptoms were active at the start of persecution whereas persecutees who nowadays exhibit many symptoms were passive (1% significance).

The persons who are nowadays free of psychic symptoms took a series of counter-measures at the start of persecution ranging from active resistance to flight, going underground or attempting to emigrate. These active reactions to the onset of persecution are to a large extent lacking in persons who are now psychically disturbed. Quite helpless to do otherwise, they usually weakly and passively allowed themselves to be arrested and incarcerated. This passive behaviour expresses an attitude which can be verbalised approximately as follows: "You can't fight against fate. The others are stronger than I am. What can I do as a weak individual human being?"

It seems relevant to link this attitude with the minority-orientation of the mothers of these interviewees. The mothers, too, lived in a world which they experienced to some extent as alien and overpowering and with which they sought to come to terms mainly by adopting a passive, withdrawn and non-aggressive posture.

However, it can be seen that, as the persecution progressed, less success in adapting was achieved by being passive than by facing up to the world with an active, self-assertive attitude. This is particularly true for the conditions of life encountered in the concentration camps. Various statistically significant differences can be established for the inmates' behaviour in the camps (the four following variables constitute the factor "adaptation to concentration camp conditions"; they are listed individually here to bring out the differences):

Persecutees who are nowadays relatively free of symptoms
more frequently state that they owe their survival to their active efforts to survive (0.1% significance),

more frequently took the initiative in making social contact with other inmates (1% significance),

managed more frequently to adapt to the guards (1% significance),

did *not*, on the other hand, differ from the other extreme group in their attitude to their fellow inmates (comradeliness or indifference).

The correlation between the active attempt to adapt to concentration camp conditions and the relatively symptom-free reaction to the stress situation is very clear. On the other hand, refusing to make any active effort to face up to the world, and trying instead to survive a dangerous situation by adopting a passive attitude of submission and evasion, carried the penalty that a large number of psychic disturbances developed.

This comparison of the extreme groups shows again very clearly that, by adopting an active posture and attempting to assert himself, the inmate had a better direct chance of reducing the stress than by trying to survive passively and unnoticed. This relationship is apparent in the following finding:

Persecutees who are nowadays relatively free of symptoms
more frequently had easier work to perform during incarceration (0.1% significance),

but do *not* differ from the persecutees with strongly pronounced symptoms as regards duration of incarceration, severity of the camp and loss of relatives.

Here too, as in a large number of other findings, it is evident that the stress imposed by the actual work situation is the most important index of individual suffering during incarceration. The duration of incarceration and the type of camp are less important stress indices. In our opinion, they do not in any way help to explain the later reaction forms and patterns of symptoms. On the other hand, two important facts become apparent when we study the work stress to which former inmates were exposed. Firstly, we find that persons who were active and self-assertive before and during captivity were more frequently assigned easier work. Secondly, persons who were exposed to low work stress in the camps are nowadays much more likely to be free of psychological symptoms.

The pattern which is revealed by these findings can be formulated approximately as follows. The ability to take an active part in moulding the world around one and also to be self-assertive is a permanent personality characteristic, which manifests itself relatively early on in a person's development and is observed even under conditions of extreme stress. Such ability goes together with great psychological stability. This personality pattern is also seen in the period following an inmate's release; in fact, in a certain sense, it only manifests itself to its full extent in the post-incarceration period. This is borne out by the following findings.

Persecutees who are nowadays relatively free of symptoms are characterized in the period between 1945 (release from concentration camp) and 1949/50 (start of legal indemnification and pension procedures) by an active attempt to adapt to the new environment (0.1% significance),

managed to become firmly established again much sooner than other persecutees (1% significance).

It thus seems that the energetic attempts to come to terms with a new environment and the relatively rapid final choice of a particular place to live are factors that have a favourable influence on the ex-inmate's ability to cope with his experience and regain his psychological health. In the post-incarceration period, the form of adaptation is again characterized by self-assertiveness. In their contact with the authorities, in their jobs and also in their social contact with friends and neighbours, the persecutees who are nowadays relatively free of symptoms frequently tend to express their point of view firmly, sometimes even quite aggressively. In all social areas they are nowadays much more open-minded, successful and better integrated. Through their behaviour some of them have succeeded in obtaining jobs where they are able, as MATUSSEK pointed out in 1961, to find a socially oriented outlet for their aggression.

In contrast, persons who nowadays suffer from severe psychic disturbances typically exhibit — as they did while imprisoned — an evasive, submissive behaviour pattern. Thus, they are nowadays usually unsuccessful, dejected and lonely in their marriages, in social contact and in their jobs.

Summary

1. In the foregoing study, the question was asked as to what complaint dimensions can be detected in former inmates outside the narrow psychiatric-clinical sector. In order to clarify this problem, 30 characteristics which describe the psychic state of these persons were examined by factor analysis. In this procedure, 3 basic forms of psychic disturbance were obtained and discussed.

2. The first fundamental psychic disturbance was termed "resignation and despair". This disturbance takes in the psychic condition in which the sufferer sees life as devoid of sense and purpose. In this condition all emotional involvement with the environment is avoided. There no longer seems to be any vital link with the future.

3. The second fundamental psychic disturbance was called "apathy and inhibition". This disturbance is based on a general state of passiveness which manifests itself in lack of drive and lack of self assurance. In contrast to the "resignation and despair" disturbance, the sufferer in this case feels primarily that he is a failure and a worthless individual.

4. The third basic psychic disturbance was that of "aggressive-irritable moodiness". This psychic disturbance is based essentially on pent-up aggressiveness which is discharged in uncontrolled outbursts against the person's environment or is hypochondriacally directed against his own body. A separate factor analysis of the data of a projection test (Rorschach) and a questionnaire revealed that former inmates of concentration camps who are nowadays conspicuously aggressive and irritable, are emotionally unstable and do not possess adequate control or inhibition mechanisms.

5. The lack of any correlation with late somatic injury indicates the mainly psychologically determined character of all three types of disturbance. On the other hand, there are clear correlations between the three basic forms of psychic disturbance and impairment in other areas of life. This holds true, in particular, for all forms of social co-existence and for the intimate sphere of marriage, right through to participating in political life and the general life of society.

However, these relationships are less relevant for the dimension of "aggressive-irritable moodiness" than for the two other forms of psychic disturbance. "Aggressive-irritable moodiness" still contains a certain measure of social activity which permits a favourable prognosis to be made for ex-inmates who suffer from this disturbance.

6. On the question of how far the basic psychic disturbances are determined by the stress experienced in the camps, it is possible to say that the severity of the work stress played an important role in all three cases. In addition, the severity of the camp and the loss of parents contributed to a particularly harsh fate in the case of the persecutees characterized by "resignation and despair".

7. Former persecutees who nowadays show clear signs of resignation and despair claim more frequently than others that they owe their survival to chance or luck. Persons who are nowadays largely free of any symptoms of "apathy and inhibition" claim more frequently than others that they owe their survival to their ability actively to adapt to the camp conditions. Persons who nowadays by and large exhibit no characteristics of "aggressive-irritable moodiness" believe more frequently than others that they survived because of their discipline and self-control.

8. In the case of all three forms of disturbance behavioural attitudes were evident even during the period of incarceration which pointed towards the psychic impairment as it is manifest today. This fact brings out the effectiveness of certain personality-specific characteristics that were developed before the onset of persecution.

In representatives of the factor "resignation and despair", the later psychic disturbances seem to develop against a background of a generally harmonious and protected childhood. In contrast, representatives of the other two forms of psychic disturbance were more frequently exposed to negative developmental influences. For example, their relationship with their mothers was more frequently disturbed, although the disturbance was not the same in all cases. The father did not figure in this connection.

9. In a final comparison, persecutees who were relatively free of symptoms were contrasted with those who had many symptoms. It was found that the capacity for active adaptation and self-assertion was developed early on and was generally sustained even under extremely harsh conditions of existence. The ability actively to come to terms with the outside world goes together with a relatively symptom-free reaction to the experience of incarceration. On the other hand, a passive wait-and-see attitude, as practised from early childhood onward, led to severe psychic disturbances with many symptoms in the post-incarceration period.

CHAPTER 6

Contact with Fellow Humans and Society

Outline of Problem

The factors of the fundamental psychic disturbances which were described in the last chapter also imply disturbances in the sphere of interpersonal contact. Neither the resigned and despairing nor the apathetic-inhibited or aggressive-irritable individual is able to experience a mutually satisfactory relationship with other persons and society. It is therefore no wonder that the majority of the persons who represent the above disturbances must be described to a greater or lesser extent as "lonely", "mistrustful", and "not interested in life around them".

In this chapter, therefore, we will analyse the problem of interpersonal contact in more detail. We are not interested here in the intrapsychic events, but solely in the relationships between the former persecutee and his environment and society. We will start by omitting the aspect of marriage, because this area of contact is a special phenomenon of interpersonal relationships and is therefore discussed in a special chapter.

The significance of disturbances in interpersonal contact is already apparent from the fact that in the concentration camp situation the inmates were forced into contact with each other in a wide variety of ways, yet this contact was perverted under the pressure of such factors as hunger, torture and terror.

The literature published to date has also referred to the disturbances in interpersonal contact resulting from incarceration in a concentration camp. MINKOWSKI (1946) states that during the period of imprisonment "emotions were anaesthetized and contact with one's neighbour was lost". V. BAEYER, HÄFNER and KISKER (1964) regard "the insecurity of interpersonal and social relationships ... as the most important element in the experience-reactive syndromes of persecutees". VENZLAFF (1958) talks of a syndrome which is characterized, among other things, by "a reduced ability to take an active part in shaping one's life as a result of serious disturbances in the interpersonal and social spheres".

In order to determine the connection between incarceration and disturbances in social relationships we carried out two factor analyses:

The first was based on 25 characteristics of 210 interviewees (see chapter on methods, p. 4). For our calculations we selected those interview categories which provide data on interpersonal and social contact (see Appendix V). The analysis revealed that the most important factors were those described below as "ability to cope with society" and "attitude to fellow humans".

In a second factor analysis we based our calculations on 26 relevant data concerning the subjective way in which fellow humans were experienced. The data were taken from the questionnaire and the Rorschach test (see Appendix). Both methods were used for 82 of the interviewees (see chapter on methods, p. 7). The factors brought to light by this analysis procedure are referred to below as "feeling of belonging to society" and "view of own position in society".

I. Dimensions of Interpersonal Contact and Experience

1. Ability to Cope with Society

The most significant contact dimension proved to be the factor of the "ability to cope with society". It comprises the characteristics listed in Table 46.

Table 46. Factor of "ability to cope with society"

Characteristic	"Social integration" (Pole A)	"Social isolation" (Pole B)	Loading
Self-assertiveness outside the family	active, expansive behaviour	passive, evasive behaviour	0.73
Form of aggression	open aggressiveness	inhibited aggression	0.60
Interest in one's environment	open-mindedness, openness	taciturnity, narrow outlook	0.60
Isolation and rejection of society	not apparent	apparent	0.57
Participation in general life of society	participation	lack of interest	0.56
Personal contacts	contacts also outside the family	few if any contacts	0.48
Standard of living	materially well-off	materially needy	0.47

This factor delineates the basic problem of former inmates in their relationship to the society in which they live. In the extreme variations two forms are contrasted with each other, that of "social integration" (Pole A) and that of "social isolation" (Pole B). We now explain what exactly these two forms of social behaviour represent.

The pole of "social integration" constitutes receptiveness and active turning toward other people. The most important components of social reintegration seem to be an active effort to come to terms with society, and the ability to release aggression. In keeping with the special situation of ex-inmates of concentration camps, even relatively uncontrolled aggressiveness is better for the process of social reintegration than a complete lack of aggression. The following example will serve to illustrate this statement:

"If anyone treats me badly, I yell. This is a serious problem. I try to restrain myself, otherwise people won't let me into their homes. But, when Nazi matters are involved, I find it almost impossible to control myself."

However, the aggressive feelings do not have to surface in such an uncontrolled and explosive manner as in this case. They can also find adequate expression, as the following report shows:

"I prefer to remain in the background. If someone annoys me, I usually hold my tongue and keep my thoughts to myself. But, if it gets too much for me, I tap the person on the shoulder and say 'Look here, I don't really agree with that'."

Further characteristics of "socially integrated" persons are an interest in the world around them and a receptive attitude to social life. This interest and participation in social life also reflects the extent to which the individual identifies with the existing society, and this must be taken as a very important indication of social integration:

One person was watching the news on television when the interviewer arrived. He commented on Mikoyan and Kennedy as they appeared on the screen and added some detailed remarks about politics.

In the final analysis, the successful resocialization of former persecutees is characterized by concrete personal contacts and a sound financial existence:

A Jewish interviewee who had married a non-Jewish wife after his liberation reported that he nowadays moves in an "appropriate social circle". "Through my father-in-law I even have contact with people from the diplomatic corps. When choosing my friends I make no distinction between Jews and non-Jews. De facto, most of my friends are German. I never have any difficulties with people whom I meet for the first time."

However, this form of unlimited social contact is somewhat rare. It is usually the case that interpersonal contact is restricted to certain groups of persons, usually fellow-sufferers and persons of the same beliefs, with whom the individual was incarcerated.

"As a former political persecutee I feel the need to meet up with my old comrades. We often spend an evening together. The feeling of camaraderie that we experienced in the concentration camp was something unique. When we meet we all agree not to talk about the concentration camp days. The first person to do so has to pay a Mark. The money soon piles up."

Even "socially integrated" persons, in the sense described here, are not able to face all their fellowmen with equal lack of inhibition. On the contrary, they frequently avoid anybody to whom they are not bound by any feeling of relatedness or similarity. It is, however, important that they have at least found a way of making some sort of contact with other people.

The determining factors which make it possible for ex-inmates to find their way back into society are aggressive self-assertiveness and receptiveness towards the world around them.

On the other hand the pole of "social isolation" is characterized in its most extreme form by an almost complete lack of aggressiveness and drive. As the following examples show, the most significant characteristics of ex-persecutees nowadays leading lonely existences are a passive attitude and the inability to release aggression:

An ex-persecutee mentioned injustices that had taken place in the post-war period and that had also affected some of his personal friends. He said that he had boiled with rage but did not dare to open his mouth. Nor does he dare to write to the newspaper because he is afraid. One has no choice but to live in fear. The police are capable of anything.

Another interviewee reported that he had recently caught a thief in his shop but let him go again because he wanted at all costs to avoid having any contact with the authorities. For the same reason, he refuses to take any action on his — justified — claims for indemnification.

This attitude goes hand in hand with a withdrawal from social life and a lack of interest in social affairs, which in this form seem quite specific for the "social isolation" of former persecutees.

For example, a former political persecutee now lives totally with-drawn from the world. He just wants to be left in peace. Therefore he never associates with his colleagues outside working hours and he refuses to give any thought to politics. "Don't bring that up. It leaves me cold."

Another ex-persecutee is so preoccupied with his concentration camp experience, almost to the exclusion of all else, that he is prevented from participating in present-day life. He stated: "I feel that all my earlier interests have 'burnt out'. I no longer have any desire to go to theatres and concerts, although previously I derived a great deal of pleasure from these. The only thing I enjoy doing is reading about the Third Reich."

This turning away from all aspects of social life is matched, in the sphere of inter-personal relationships, by the inability to make contact with other people. While attempts at making contact are frequently undertaken, but then fail to meet with success, there are also cases where the individual withdraws and shuts himself off entirely from the world around. One final example will demonstrate this inability to establish and maintain any links with other persons.

"I was persecuted because of my Jewish origins. Now I frequently have to change my place of residence for reasons of health. My social experience with other people is the same in all the towns or cities where I live. Scarcely do we get to know someone before the acquaintanceship comes to an end. My wife and I always take possession of the people we get to know. We don't get to meet many people, and then we always expect too much. When we start to talk about the Nazi period, it always puts an end to the social relationship. That's the way it always is for us."

While in this case the marriage remained as the sole mode of interpersonal contact, many "socially isolated" persons lack even this. The persons in question have a disharmonious marriage or are even separated from their marital partners. From the point of view of careers, the persons representing this pole tend to be unsuccessful (see chapter on "Occupational Reintegration", p. 160, and the Chapter on "Marriage and Family", p. 185).

Figure 12 shows how the 210 interviewees are distributed over the listed characteristics. The extreme form of "social integration" exists when all the characteristics

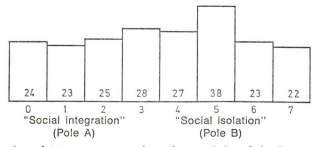

Fig. 12. Distribution of 210 persons over the 7 characteristics of the factor "ability to cope with society"

of pole A occur together. Similarly, the extreme form of "social isolation" is determined by the joint occurrence of all the characteristics of pole B.

According to the characteristics of pole A, 24 interviewees (11.5%) are socially integrated. Complete social isolation is exhibited by 22 interviewees (10.5%). The remaining persons tend towards either of these two poles. If the number of persons with characteristics 0–3 (socially integrated) and those with characteristics 4–7 (socially isolated) are added, we find a ratio of 100 : 101, i.e. a slight preponderance of the "socially isolated" individuals.

The socio-communicative dimension illustrated covers only the aspect of interpersonal behaviour. The factor "attitude to fellow human beings" crystallized out independently of this.

2. Attitude to Fellow Human Beings

This factor comprises the characteristics listed in Table 47.

Table 47. Factor of "attitude towards fellow human beings"

Characteristics	"Sociability" (Pole A)	"Rejection" (Pole B)	Loading
Attempts to understand and forgive	apparent	not apparent	0.68
Attitude to fellowmen	mainly trusting	mainly distrustful	0.65
Reproaches and accusations	not apparent	apparent	0.61
Prejudices towards fellowmen	not pronounced	pronounced	0.58
Hostility	not pronounced	pronounced	0.55
Interest in environment	open-minded, receptive	narrow-minded, restricted outlook	0.47

The extreme groupings of the characteristics are designated as "sociability" (Pole A) and "rejection" (Pole B). While the real relationship with one's fellowmen manifests itself in the factor "ability to cope with society", the factor "attitude towards one's fellow human beings" reflects the inmate's inner view of the other person.

Pole A must be defined as an active attempt to achieve an inner acceptance of other people. In keeping with the positive character of the main variables of the factor the ex-inmate does not blame those around him today for what he went through during his persecution or for the destructive experiences associated with that period of his life.

The reason for the persecution is not seen in the moral inferiority of all Germans but in the historical situation of Germany around the year 1933 or in the criminal inclinations of a few power-mad deluders of the people.

"It was the cruelty and inferiority complex of the upper echelons of the party leadership that led to our being persecuted. People were organised and trained to become subhuman and they were rewarded for cruelty. These individuals were the flotsam and jetsam of society. You find such a stratum in any nation."

These excuses enable the ex-persecutee, at least potentially, to establish contact with other people.

"My relationship with other people was intensified by the experience of incarceration. I now have more understanding for them."

This attitude need not necessarily, however, result in total integration into society. Despite a friendly disposition towards other persons, there is often a clear desire to remain aloof from concrete partners. The apparent attempt to achieve social rapprochement may mask rejection tendencies. An externally friendly and accepting disposition towards other people, the credibility of which however remains indeterminate, is quite frequently found in persecutees with a particular Weltanschauung because, for such persons, love of one's neighbours and of one's enemies are important elements of their faith (see chapter on "Weltanschauung und Incarceration", p. 218).

"If someone offends me, I forgive him. I never get angry. I just think it is stupid to let myself be provoked."

The persons who achieve a trusting "turning toward" others also show signs of having a deeper and more mature understanding of their fellowmen. These interviewees have succeeded in coming to terms with their personal persecution fate without any serious traces of being depressed or resigned and thus they have found a new starting point for a fruitful encounter with their fellow human beings.

A German lawyer who had been persecuted on political grounds nowadays stresses that he does not regret the enforced experience of incarceration: "A person can only arrive at his true and divinely ordained self through suffering. Even in moments of crisis the essential truth prevailed in me — my faith was unshakeable and I was firmly confident that there was a meaning to everything. I have a realistic attitude. Other people criticize too much, but that is unnecessary."

The pole of "rejection" can be more clearly accentuated and its content brought into sharper relief. For persons who represent this pole an initial determining fact is that their social thought, feeling and values are even today still to a great extent determined by their personal experiences during persecution. For them, as ex-inmates, other people frequently continue to be what they were during the period of persecution, namely potential or actual enemies and annihilators who have to be treated with the utmost caution. This mistrust, which was acquired under conditions of extreme stress, seems to have had such a strong effect in shaping the personality of a certain group of individuals that it can no longer be dropped even though the conditions of existence are no longer the same:

"Since the days when I was persecuted I have found it more difficult to establish relationships with other people. I don't trust any German until I am absolutely certain that he was not a Nazi. At large gatherings I often feel that the people are hiding behind masks and I ask myself whether perhaps this person or that was one of the murderers."

A former political persecutee expressed the opinion that all the bad things about the Nazis were being forgotten too quickly and only the good aspects were being remembered. "The Nazis are everywhere in the bureaucratic system. We are being persecuted again today and again we have to become resistance fighters."

In contrast to former inmates of concentration camps whose mistrustful attitude takes the form of anxious repulsion and hostile depreciation of other people, there are other interviewees whose negative attitude is characterized by accusation and reproach:

"I no longer have any ideals or goals. Everything has been smashed. I cannot absolve them of their guilt, nor can I forgive them, because they murdered my family. I'm like a broken twig. Anything is possible in Germany once the Americans leave. I have completely lost my faith in the Germans."

This form of accusation is evidence of a socially negative attitude which is based on a distorted view of the other person. The distortion is caused by the fact that the world around is viewed and experienced solely from a hostile standpoint.

Figure 13 shows the distribution of the 6 characteristics over the 210 interviewees dealt with here:

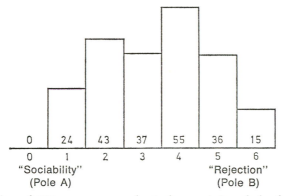

0	24	43	37	55	36	15
0	1	2	3	4	5	6

"Sociability"   "Rejection"
(Pole A)   (Pole B)

Fig. 13. Distribution of 210 persons over the 6 characteristics of the factor "Attitude to fellowmen"

Figure 13 shows clearly that all six rejection characteristics are present in 15 interviewees (7%) and that in no case are they completely lacking. When the number of persons with 0–2 characteristics (sociability) is related to the number of those with 4–6 characteristics (rejection of others) — leaving aside the middle group with 3 characteristics — a ratio of 67 : 106 is obtained. This means that persons whose relationships with their fellowmen are characterized by mistrust, reproach, accusation and reticence are almost twice as numerous as those who, despite their concentration camp sufferings, have a reconciliatory, understanding and receptive attitude towards other people.

The fact that the two dimensions of "ability to cope with one's environment" and "attitude towards one's fellowmen" are not connected indicates that it is probably possible to achieve a degree of external re-integration and adaptation, but without at the same time being able deep down to adopt an open, trusting manner towards others.

Both the forms of contact described here are observable socio-communicative phenomena. The subject plane of interpersonal relations is illuminated by a methodoligical approach which attempts to analyse contact relationships indirectly.

3. Feeling of Belonging to Society

A factor analysis of 26 questionnaires and Rorschach data obtained from 82 former persecutees (see statement of problem, p. 119 and chapter on "Study Methods", p. 7) yielded the factor "feeling of belonging to society" as the first contact dimension. It comprises the characteristics listed in Table 48 (page 126).

Table 48. Factor of "feeling of belonging to society"

"Feeling of belonging" (Pole A)	"Feeling of alienation" (Pole B)	Loading
I do not think that I have changed as a result of incarceration	I think that being incarcerated has made me different from other people	0.66
Being incarcerated has not alienated me from other people	Being incarcerated has alienated me even more from other people	0.66
My sufferings have not made it difficult for me to achieve contact with other people	My sufferings have made it difficult for me to achieve contact with other people	0.65
I more frequently become aggressive	I rarely or never become aggressive	0.57
Being incarcerated has not made me more withdrawn in my contact with other people	Being incarcerated has made me more withdrawn in my contact with other people	0.53
Sometimes I also strike up acquaintance by taking some of the initiative myself	I never really manage to strike up acquaintance by taking the initiative myself	0.45
I do not feel at a disadvantage today compared with other people	I feel at a disadvantage today compared with other people	0.43
I have personal contacts outside my family and my close circle of acquaintances	I only have personal contacts within the family and with people whom I know well	0.43

The extreme poles are characterized as a "feeling of belonging" and a "feeling of alienation". Under the "feeling of belonging" the ex-inmates emphatically deny that their concentration camp experiences have in any way affected their present-day relationships with other people. The persons who represent this pole either reject the notion that their period of incarceration can have any influence whatsoever on their social relationships so long after the event, or they are surprised by such a line of questioning. When asked whether, as a result of the concentration camp stress, they now experience life differently from other people, whether they have become alienated from their fellowmen or whether their suffering makes it difficult for them to gain access to society, they answered as follows:

"No, no. I don't think so."

"No. But unless a person has actually lived through it all, he will not be able to understand or believe it."

"I don't know how other people feel, but I don't think it is likely that I feel any differently now from before as a result of my imprisonment."

They stress their re-integration into society and do not feel in any way at a disadvantage. At the same time they describe themselves as very active and even aggressive in their contact with other people:

"I always manage to make acquaintances because I make an effort too."

"I have certainly become less reserved — I'm certainly more restless."

"If you insulted me, I would throw you out."

This activity is also reflected in the initiative in making contact which these persons seem to develop in their interpersonal relationships. They state that they have many contacts outside the sphere of their families:

"I make contact very quickly and very easily. I take the initiative. I can acclimatize myself very quickly. I'm always surrounded by people. I'm never lonely."

"I take part in amateur dramatics. In fact, I play leading roles."

"Yes, of course I have good friends."

Many of the statements almost go as far as rejecting even the slightest suggestion that the inmates may have been affected by their incarceration. One might almost say that in many cases persons representing the "feeling of belonging" absolutely refuse to think about their concentration camp past.

On the other hand, the "feeling of alienation" is characterized by the awareness that one is different and strange and unable to form close relationships with one's fellow-men. The interviewees who represent this pole feel that they have been scarred for life. They feel isolated and believe that the experiences through which they have lived make it difficult for them to establish contact with other people today. This is demonstrated by the following replies:

"I find it difficult to get close enough to people to strike up friendship."

"I have, of course, become more critical in my judgement of people and in many cases I think to myself 'I wonder what you've got on your conscience?'"

"I've become a little bit shy of people. You should have seen me before, laughing and dancing! Now I never go anywhere."

These interviewees lack the initiative to bridge the gap between themselves and their fellowmen. They restrict their contact to their own family or to groups with which they feel an affinity:

"I'm no longer someone who must have company at all costs. I want peace and quiet because I need it ... I stay with my family."

"I always hold back ... In my opinion a person can only reveal his innermost feelings if, in fact, he has nothing worth revealing or if he has never been hurt as a result of his openness."

The lack of initiative and energy is also expressed by the fact that these inter-viewees rarely exhibit any aggression, although they feel at a disadvantage compared with others:

"I realize that since I have aged prematurely, there is no longer very much that I can achieve in life."

"It is nowadays impossible for an ex-inmate to find acceptance anywhere."

"If anyone annoys me, I usually leave the room."

"I usually keep quiet and think to myself, 'that's not right, what he is doing'."

Summarizing, it can be said that the "feeling of alienation" is characterized by the almost resigned and apathetic way in which the inmates relate all their present socio-communicative problems to the period of incarceration. Also, none of these interviewees seem to take any initiative of their own.

The distribution of 82 interviewees over the 8 characteristics of the factor de-scribed is shown by Figure 14 (page 128).

It is apparent from Fig. 14 that only 13 (16%) persons unequivocally represent the factor "feeling of belonging". On the other hand, the "feeling of alienation" is characteristic for 36 (44%) of the interviewees.

The "feeling of belonging to society", which is represented by certain ex-inmates of concentration camps, is correlated as follows with the already described dimensions of interpersonal contact:

Persecutees who represent the pole "feeling of belonging" are also more frequently "socially integrated" or "sociable";

Persecutees who represent the pole "feeling of alienation" are also more frequently "socially isolated" or "reject" other people (1% significance in each case).

Further differentiation of these very significant correlations indicates new ways of interpreting the phenomena of interpersonal contact that have been described:

The present open and trusting attitude towards one's fellowmen can most likely be regarded as a sign of inner stability based on a true overcoming of the concentration camp past. The persecutees who are now able once more to turn in a trusting

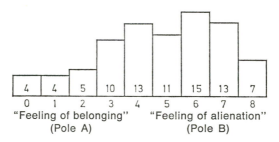

Fig. 14. Distribution of 82 persons over the 8 characteristics of the factor "feeling of belonging to society"

manner towards their fellow human beings have acquired sufficient distance from their concentration camp past to eliminate the need either to disclaim or play up their role as former concentration camp inmates. They exhibit no psychic disturbances and are for the most part "partially successful" in their careers. It was precisely this group of persons who were "partially successful" in their careers which also proved to be psychically the healthiest of all the inmates in another context (see chapter on "Occupational Re-integration", p. 160).

On the other hand, two separate groups can be distinguished in those interviewees who are nowadays "socially integrated". In one group active self-assertion is frequently accompanied by the demonstration of their role as former concentration camp inmates. These interviewees are "successful" or at least "partially successful" in their careers. Following their release, it seems that their main aim was to make an intense effort to adapt externally to the world around them. To do this they also played on their concentration camp past whenever they deemed it necessary.

A second group seems to have achieved their present "social integration" only by forgetting their concentration camp past and leaving it behind them. These interviewees emphatically deny any suggestion that their concentration camp past in any way affects their present lives. Frequently they disavow their role as ex-inmates. At the same time, they show no clear ability to adapt to a job but are most frequently represented in the "partially successful" group. Since these interviewees also seem to be largely free of any psychic complaints, it can be said that repressing one's concentration camp past does not necessarily have a negative effect on the ex-inmate's ability to cope with life today.

On the other hand, the present failure to achieve successful interpersonal relationships and the turning away from the possibilities offered by life today — as is evidenced by the poles "social isolation" and "rejection" — may be the result of a fixation on the period of incarceration or on events that took place in the past. The interviewees who ascribe their present failures in the socio-communicative sphere solely to their period of internment are at the same time more frequently "resigned and despairing" or "apathetic and inhibited".

Both methods of coming to terms with life, i.e. the refusal to think of the concentration camp past or being fixated on it, could be unsuccessful attempts to cope with the experience of incarceration. In the next chapter ("Occupational Re-integration", see p. 169) we go into this in more detail.

4. View of Own Position in Society

The factor "view of own position in society" crystallized as a further dimension. It is made up of the characteristics listed in Table 49.

Table 49. Factor of "view of own position in society"

"Satisfaction" (Pole A)	"Dissatisfaction" (Pole B)	Loading
I do not want any more recognition than I now get for what I went through in the concentration camp	I really think ex-concentration camp inmates deserve more recognition for what they went through than they get	0.66
Even if I am provoked, I do not usually get aggressive	If I am provoked I can become aggressive	0.56
In many respects I am better off than other people	I am worse off than other people in all respects	0.54
I feel other people show sufficient respect for me as an ex-concentration camp inmate — or: I don't want to be respected as an ex-concentration-camp inmate	Other people do not show sufficient respect to ex-concentration-camp inmates	0.51
No uncontrolled expressions of aggression, or almost none (0–1), are apparent in the Rorschach test	Several (2–4) uncontrolled expressions of aggression revealed by Rorschach test	0.41

If the factor "feeling of belonging to society" deals more with the social processing of the period of incarceration, this new factor covers the way in which the ex-inmate experiences the reaction of other people to his own particular concentration camp fate.

The pole labelled "satisfaction" is characterized by a forbearing-peaceable attitude. The interviewees who represent this pole nowadays no longer expect any recognition for the incarceration that they suffered:

"No, I no longer want any recognition for my concentration camp experience. After all, we did not enter the camps voluntarily."

"We don't want anyone to know about it."

"Whenever I describe incarceration in a concentration camp I always talk about other people's experiences. The reaction is then much more instructive for me. I don't need other people's sympathy."

In addition, these interviewees claim to be completely lacking in hostility, even if they are provoked by their fellowmen:

"If I am provoked, I keep quiet, go my own sweet way and keep everything to myself."

"If someone made me angry, I would certainly say something. But there is rarely any reason for anger. It has always been my view that a person should be able to control himself."

"No one can insult me because I never defend my honour."

The almost exaggerated unassumingness and lack of aggressiveness becomes more readily understandable if it is remembered that 40% (8) of these interviewees are Jehovah's Witnesses. These claim that they are better off than most of their fellowmen:

"I have everything that I need and spiritually I am far better off than most other people — I have my faith."

"I no longer need recognition of my concentration camp experience because I did it all for God. Nor am I interested in what other people think about it."

The "satisfaction" pole, which on the one hand expresses the simple wish and intention not to attract attention and not to stand out from the crowd, must, however, be very specifically interpreted in the case of the Jehovah's Witnesses. The apparently stoic attitude of this group of persons is in keeping with their view that only Jehovah controls the fates of people here on earth.

This conviction is the basis for their imagined superiority over the rest of mankind. They believe that it is not possible to change the world and that it will remain a vale of tears until God sees fit to intervene; therefore the worse things seem, the happier they become, because the more signs there are of the end of the world, the closer salvation must be. Under these circumstances, there can be no evil in the world that will shake the Jehovah's Witnesses out of their "satisfied" state. They are thus clearly contrasted with the political persecutees who mainly represent the pole of "dissatisfaction".

The pole of "dissatisfaction" is characterized by an exigent and aggressive attitude towards other people. The interviewees who represent this pole are dissatisfied with their environment in all respects because it does not accord them enough respect as ex-concentration-camp inmates.

"Respected? Far from it! Other people refuse even to consider the problem of guilt — they just don't want to know about it."

"Not respected, but pitied!"

"My neighbour recognizes what I went through. But some people say 'If he hadn't got involved, they wouldn't have locked him up'. Others just look the other way and don't want to have anything to do with me although they know that I was interned in a concentration camp."

"Other people think those times are over. But, for people like myself who were involved in what went on, those times are not forgotten."

The interviewees feel that, because of the suffering that they had to endure during their incarceration, they deserve more recognition now. They also stress that they are worse off materially and from the point of view of jobs and health than the majority of other people. Their demanding attitude is coupled with an explosive aggressiveness:

"I react violently and my heart pounds. Sometimes I shout and then I feel ashamed that I was too violent."

"I get terribly worked up. At the beginning I used to shout my head off, but not any more."

"Yes, I want recognition so that those times won't be forgotten."

"I don't want personal recognition but I do think the action of resisting the regime should be recognized. The need for resistance did not come to an end with the closing of the concentration camps."

The psychic reality which is evident behind this "dissatisfaction" thus differs from case to case. Some people want amends for what they suffered, others want relief and still others want a reward for their resistance. It should be noted that this pole is mainly represented by political persecutees and German-born Jews now living in Germany.

The political persecutees regard their aggressive-demanding attitude as fully justified. They are convinced that the world should be changed in accordance with their political views — which vary quite considerably from individual to individual — and are therefore dissatisfied with existing circumstances. For many of these persons the period of incarceration is taken as a means of justifying the "martyr's role" which enables them forcibly to drive home their demands.

German Jews also have the opportunity to adopt an accusing attitude towards their environment here in Germany; this posture may be necessary for them to maintain their psychic equilibrium (see MATUSSEK, 1961).

The distribution of the 82 interviewees in relation to the 5 characteristics is shown in Fig. 15.

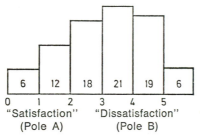

Fig. 15. Distribution of 82 persons over the 5 characteristics of the factor "view of own position in society"

This overview shows that 18 (22%) of the interviewees represent the pole "satisfaction" while 25 (30%) of the interviewees are clearly "dissatisfied" with society's attitude towards them.

While this dimension is in no way connected with the factor "ability to cope with society" it is significantly correlated with the factor "attitude to fellow humans":

Persecutees who represent the pole "satisfaction" are more frequently "sociable"; persons who are nowadays "dissatisfied" more frequently have a "rejecting" attitude (5% significance).

This correlation shows clearly that in some persecutees the external "dissatisfaction" with other people, society and existing conditions in general hides a deep-rooted mistrust and feelings of hostility. In this case the "dissatisfaction" appears to be an external projection of the individual's basic attitude of mistrust.

Even more striking is the connection between the factor "view of own position in society" and the basic types of psychic disturbance. While no statistically significant links could be established with the factors "apathy and inhibition" and "aggressive-irritable moodiness" the following correlation exists with the factor "resignation and despair":

Persecutees who represent the pole "dissatisfaction" are more frequently also "resigned and despairing" (1% significance).

This finding shows that the ex-inmate's dissatisfaction with society's attitude towards him cannot be covered by the above-mentioned intrapsychic categories, because if this were the case one would tend to expect a correlation with aggressive-irritable persons. The "dissatisfaction" which comes to the fore in such cases is, instead, the expression of hopelessness and despair. For these persons the subjectively experienced failure of their fellowmen to recognize the sufferings which the ex-inmates endured in the concentration camps is taken as a confirmation of the absolute senselessness of the concentration camp period and thus also of their present existence. The only response they can muster is that of "resignation".

The demonstrated correlation, however, hides the fact that no less than 10 (12.5%) of the interviewees represent the pole of "dissatisfaction" without exhibiting any of the basic forms of psychic disturbance. They are neither "resigned and despairing" nor "apathetic and inhibited" or "aggressive and irritated". Nevertheless, they are to a high degree "dissatisfied" with their fellowmen or with existing society. These persons are probably affected by the situation described by MATUSSEK (1961), namely that society cannot be fair even to ex-inmates because it failed to come to grips with the problem of the concentration camps at the time when these were actually in operation. To this extent, therefore, the "dissatisfaction" of ex-persecutees may also constitute an appropriate reaction to the inability of society to grant these people the recognition and thanks to which they are entitled.

II. Types of Contact in the Various Groups of Persecutees

1. Sex-Specific Differences

In our surveys, we found no statistically significant differences between men and women as regards the described dimension of "ability to cope with society" and "attitude to fellow humans". Men and women represent, in equal proportion, the poles of "social integration" and "social isolation" as well as the poles of "sociability" and "rejection". A very significant difference exists only in the attitude to public affairs:

Women are more frequently uninterested and men more frequently involved in public affairs (1% significance).

This is by and large what one would generally expect to find, and it is not a characteristic restricted to the sample of ex-concentration-camp inmates examined by us. Despite historical developments in recent decades, the role of the man in our civilization is still much more strongly determined by his interest in public affairs than is the role of the woman.

Specific differences can be established by analysing the questionnaire data. As regards the factor "feeling of belonging in society" the two sexes differ significantly from each other in the following way:

Women more frequently experience a "feeling of alienation" and men a "feeling of belonging" (5% significance).

Essentially this difference reveals that women imagine more frequently than men that they have become alienated from other people as a result of their concentration camp experience; they believe that their incarceration sets them apart from other people and they are now more reserved in their dealings with others.

There are no differences between men and women as regards the factor "view of own position in society".

Probably the main result of the findings listed here is the stronger belief held by women that their interpersonal relationships have been impaired, although in external behaviour they do not necessarily differ from men. For women, more distinctly than for men, the period of incarceration has created a gap between them and their fellowmen. They see insurmountable barriers between themselves and others who have not been through the same experiences.

If one also takes account of sex-specific trends revealed by the Rorschach test, an even clearer picture can be obtained. In this case, women, as opposed to men, exhibit:

A stronger need for interpersonal contact, but they are hampered in their ability to make contact by their weaker rational control and their greater degree of emotional instability (see Appendix).

Interpreting this finding together with the above-mentioned differences yielded by analysis of the questionnaires, it can be said that women apparently have less opportunity than men to process the overwhelming experience of incarceration in a rational manner. Instead, all aspects of their lives are permeated and affected by this experience and, as we have already stressed in the chapters on "Late-Appearing Damage to Health" and "Psychic Disturbances", they reacted more drastically and enduringly to the concentration camp suffering. Thus, a basic existing need for contact with other people cannot develop so freely because it is again and again impeded and hampered by the feeling that the concentration camp experience has made them different from others.

2. Age-Specific Differences

In our random sample all we could find was a slight difference (trend) between young and old with regard to the 4 dimensions of socio-communicative behaviour and experience:

Young (under 50 in 1960) ex-inmates are more frequently "socially integrated",
Old (over 50 in 1960) ex-inmates are more frequently "socially isolated" (10% significance).

This finding, which is no more than a trend, cannot really be interpreted as
specifically related to the concentration camp experience because isolation is probably more a fundamental problem of ageing and can also be observed in a normal
population.

On the other hand, significant differences can be detected in the statements made
by the interviewees about themselves. Persecutees who were older than 50 in 1960
differ significantly in the following matters from persecutees who were younger
than 50 in 1960:

Older inmates believe more frequently than younger ones that as a result of their experience they have become alienated from their fellowmen (5% significance).
Older inmates believe less frequently than younger ones that it is possible to rely on the
friendliness of one's fellowmen (5% significance).
Older inmates claim less frequently than younger ones that they occasionally make an
effort to gain new acquaintances (5% significance).

These findings can be supported by differences which are revealed in the Rorschach test.

According to this test the younger inmates, compared with the older ones, exhibit:

Stronger inwardly directed but also outwardly directed aggressiveness; less rational
adaptation and a poorer capacity for introversion and for coping with the experience of
incarceration (see Appendix).

The listed findings may indicate that older inmates are basically more reserved
and mistrusting than younger inmates and nowadays remain more aloof from persons who were not interned in concentration camps. Compared with the younger
inmates they appear more rigid and less flexible; this finding (trend) was already
made in the preceding chapter in connection with the discussion of the factor
"aggressive-irritable moodiness". In contrast, the younger inmates tend to live out
their conflicts and direct their aggressions to some extent against themselves and
they are emotionally more involved. Although their reaction to the period of incarceration thus displays certain neurotic traits, these tend to be reflected in their
present socio-communicative behaviour in the form of greater initiative in seeking
contact and a more sociable attitude towards their fellowmen.

3. Reasons for Persecution

There is only a slight difference (trend) as regards the described dimensions of
interpersonal behaviour and experience between political and religious persecutees
on the one hand and racial persecutees on the other:

Religious and political persecutees are nowadays more likely to be "socially integrated";
racial persecutees tend more to be "socially isolated" (10% significance).

This is substantiated by a single finding, namely:

Political and religious detainees are more frequently interested in public affairs while
racial persecutees are more frequently uninterested (1% significance).

This highly significant connection is not surprising in so far as political detainees exhibited strong interest in public affairs right from the start. Their political engagement nowadays constitutes an important bridge to society. Even if these persons work off certain difficulties more strongly on their environment, they still retain the possibility of attaining greater stability through their active interest in public affairs.

If, in addition, we consider a series of individual findings from the questionnaire and Rorschach test, a very clear picture emerges:

Political persecutees believe more frequently than racial persecutees that it is possible to rely on other people being friendly (5% significance).

Political persecutees mention less frequently than racial persecutees that they only have contact with members of their own family (5% significance).

Political persecutees exhibit strong mistrust of their fellowmen less frequently than racial persecutees (5% significance).

The evaluation of the Rorschach tests (see Appendix, p. 255) shows that political persecutees, compared with racial persecutees, exhibit less anxiety in their social contact behaviour but also have less desire to seek contact.

Although political persecutees seem to be hardly less impaired in their observable contact behaviour than racial persecutees, the subjective experience of both groups appears to be relatively different. Political persecutees do not have such strong feelings of mistrust towards other people. They are able to integrate the incarceration into their lives and are also able, in their own way, to feel that they belong to society. The situation is quite different for Jews now living in Germany. Their main difficulty is in the socio-communicative sphere where they have to overcome the problem of living together with their persecutors. Almost inevitably, this co-existence must be characterized by uncertainty and mistrust.

4. Country of Origin

Differentiating former inmates of concentration camps according to their country of origin is a relatively complex matter. Besides ethnological peculiarities, the period of incarceration was also different for Germans and Eastern Europeans, and it was experienced in different ways by these groups, so that it is difficult to draw any conclusions about the causation of their present contact behaviour.

Although the existing literature on concentration camps does touch on the question of the country of origin of ex-persecutees, the data given are not statistically significant.

As regards the dimension of socio-communicative behaviour and experience described by us, we can find only one significant difference between persecutees of German and Eastern European origin, namely in the factor "attitude to fellowmen".

Persecutees of German origin more frequently represent the pole "sociability" and persecutees of Polish origin more frequently the pole of "rejection" (5% significance).

The main reason for this finding is probably the fact that Polish Jews, unlike all other groups, have always lived in an alien socio-cultural environment since their liberation from the camps. Their stronger rejection could therefore be interpreted as a reaction to the greater social strangeness of their present environment. It should also be remembered, however, that the ghetto experiences of earlier centuries are fresher in the memories of Polish Jews than in those of other Jews, who were practically all assimilated prior to the start of persecution. This hypothesis becomes even more plausible if we consider the following additional findings:

Persecutees born in Germany more frequently take an interest in public affairs than those born in Poland (1% significance),

they are more likely to be engaged in activities outside the family sphere (5% significance),

they tend to have a broader spectrum of contact in both private and personal spheres (10% significance).

Distinguishing between German and Polish Jews on the basis of the questionnaire results revealed the following differences:

Polish Jews believe more frequently than German Jews that because they were incarcerated in a concentration camp they now have difficulty in making contact with other people (5% significance).

Polish Jews state more frequently than German Jews that they sometimes take an active part in striking up acquaintance with others (5% significance).

Polish Jews, more frequently than German Jews, mention the members of their own family as the persons with whom they have any contact (5% significance).

The Rorschach test (see Appendix, p. 255) revealed that:

Polish Jews have a marked desire to make contact with others yet at the same time suffer anxiety in their social relationships so that, in their case, a pronounced attempt to make contact is contrasted with poor ability to sustain such contact.

Summarizing, in contrast to persecutees of Polish origin, those of German origin are generally more interested and responsive, as well as more successful and less disturbed in their socio-communicative behaviour. On the other hand, Polish Jews make a greater attempt to seek contact, although their actual contacts are to a great extent limited to their own families.

These findings can essentially be interpreted as follows:

On the one hand, the different socio-cultural background of the groups to which we have already referred is important. While Poles above all lived a very strongly tradition-bound and family-oriented existence in ghetto-like seclusion, the German Jews were to a large extent assimilated. This may be the reason for the more pronounced family-oriented contact behaviour of Polish Jews, which still prevails today.

Their lesser interest in public affairs and thus their unreadiness to identify with the majority may be due to the fact that nowadays in Germany, but also in the USA and Israel, they are living in a more alien world than persecutees who were born in Germany. Polish Jews have been uprooted in two ways. They suffered more than Germany Jews from being torn, on the one hand, from the warm security of their families and, on the other, from the familiar linguistic and socio-cultural security of their homeland.

It is therefore no small wonder that, despite their apparent isolation, they should experience a strong desire to make contact. This phenomenon has already been referred to in another context (see chapter on "Late-Appearing Damage to Health"). In the case of the Polish Jews the hypothesis seems likely that the need for contact, which may have built up during the period of incarceration, no longer finds any adequate form of expression. The deep uncertainty felt by these people and their mistrustful attitude prevent them from behaving in a free and natural manner towards their fellowmen.

5. Country of Residence

It is just as impossible to correlate the present country of residence unequivocally with the present contact behaviour. Firstly, the choice of future place of residence following release from imprisonment may have depended on specific personality characteristics of the inmates. Secondly, the national peculiarities of a country determine the contact behaviour of its inhabitants.

While it was not possible to determine any statistically significant differences in the described contact dimensions, a series of individual findings were made for the countries of residence, USA, Israel and Germany, which were studied by us:

Concentration camp inmates now living in the USA or Israel have a broader range of contact than those now living in Germany (5% significance).

Thus, former persecutees lead a relatively more isolated existence in Germany than those in the USA or Israel. As the questionnaire results show, they also seem to be more strongly affected by this isolation:

Jews living in Germany feel more frequently than Jews living in the USA that they have become alienated from their fellowmen as a result of the incarceration experience (1% significance).

The following differences exist between Jews now living in Israel and those now living in Germany:

Jews nowadays living in Germany
feel more frequently than the others that they have changed as a result of incarceration (1% significance),
believe less frequently that one can rely on the friendship of one's fellowmen (1% significance),
are more frequently mistrustful of their fellowmen (1% significance),
more frequently have a negative opinion of their environment (1% significance),
more frequently feel at a disadvantage compared with other people (5% significance).

In agreement with the result of the interviews, which showed that inmates now living in Germany more frequently suffer from disturbed contact behaviour, they are also more distrustful, more reserved and more socially alienated.

This finding seems to indicate that the Jews in general in the USA and in Israel, but probably also in other western countries, have been more successful in coping with their concentration camp past than the Jews in Germany which, for them, is still the country of their persecutors.

III. Influence of Earlier Periods in Inmates' Lives

Following the description of interpersonal relationships and their differentiation according to sociological groupings we will now turn to the question of the possible genesis of present-day social disturbances in former persecutees. The main factor to consider here is the stress of incarceration. The overwhelming horror of this intrusion into a person's life seems a plausible cause of severe difficulties in the socio-communicative sphere. However, as in the preceding chapters, it is necessary to include data on personal development in the analysis.

1. Stress of Persecution

The general hypothesis that the stress of incarceration can be regarded as a genetic force in the development of present-day social disturbances can be narrowed down to the following question:

Could certain forms of stress also have brought about certain disturbances in the sphere of interpersonal contact?

The following connections are found between concentration camp stress (work severity, camp severity, duration of incarceration) and the dimensions of interpersonal contact:

Persecutees who are nowadays "socially isolated"
more frequently had to perform harsh work in the camps (0.1% significance),
were more frequently incarcerated in severe camps (5% significance),
were more frequently incarcerated for longer periods of time (10% significance).

Persecutees who nowadays have an attitude of "rejection"
more frequently had to perform harsh work in the camps (5% significance),
were more frequently incarcerated in severe camps (5% significance),
were more frequently incarcerated for longer periods of time (5% significance).

No correlations exist between the factors "feeling of belonging to society" and "view of own position in society" and the stress characteristics.

These findings show that only the present interpersonal contact behaviour and the attitude towards one's fellowmen are statistically correlated with certain stresses of incarceration. It is striking that here again the severity of the work situation exhibits the clearest correlation with today's disturbances. The present-day state of "social isolation" is particularly dependent on the severity of the work to which a person was exposed. The following interpretation may be advanced here:

Today's "social integration" is characterized by the ability for self-assertion, activity and interest. "Social isolation" is characterized by passiveness and lack of interest. It can be assumed that the severity of the work ruined the mental and physical health of the inmate to such an extent that after his release he was simply too weak to assert himself or develop any activity.

This assumption is also supported by the findings described in the chapter on "Basic Forms of Psychic Disturbance" (see p. 101). In all 3 factors, particularly the factor "resignation and despair", the severity of the work was the decisive stress element.

On the other hand, it must also be considered that personality factors might be involved. As described in the preceding chapter, the inmates were able up to a point to influence the type of work which they were expected to perform. It is very likely that particularly flexible, active and self-assertive inmates were able to get themselves easier work.

The effect of the various forms of stress on the present-day attitude of ex-inmates to their fellowmen is less specific. The attitude of rejection and hostility seems to depend less on certain stress results and is more a personality-specific reaction to persecution and incarceration.

Even more than the attitude to one's fellowmen, the present subjective experience of ex-persecutees — insofar as it is covered by the factors "feeling of belonging to society" and "view of own position in society" — is independent of certain measurable or observable effects of the period of incarceration. It should probably be borne in mind here that no adequate stress characteristics could be determined at the level of present-day subjective experience.

As revealed by factor analysis, interpersonal behaviour during incarceration took the form of a uniform dimension "adaptation in the concentration camp" with the pole "successful adaptation" contrasted with "unsuccessful adaptation" (see chapter on "Stresses Imposed by Concentration Camp Incarceration", p. 34).

The following highly significant correlations exist with the described factors of present-day interpersonal behaviour:

Persecutees who exhibited "successful adaptation" during incarceration are nowadays more likely to be "socially integrated" or "sociable".

Persecutees who failed to achieve adaptation during incarceration are nowadays more likely to be "socially isolated" or to have a "rejecting" attitude (0.1% significance).

No correlations exist between the factor "adaptation in the concentration camp" and the factors "feeling of belonging to society" and "view of own position in society".

These findings show that ex-persecutees who nowadays can be described either as active and adapted, as expressed by the pole "social integration", or as mentally well-balanced and relatively free of prejudice, as expressed by the pole "sociability", were also successful in establishing social contact during the period of incarceration. Similarly, former persecutees who nowadays either have barely any contact at all or are filled with mistrust and resentment, were also passive, and their ability to achieve interpersonal contact was disturbed even during incarceration. The conspicuous character, i.e. the high statistical significance, of the correlations is surprising. The most likely interpretation here is that the present-day social behaviour must have been moulded by more than just the stress of the concentration camps. It is also necessary to consider the possibility of formative influences that pre-date the period of persecution.

2. Developmental Influences of Childhood and Adolescence

Of the many characteristics that were collected in our study to determine the peculiarities of personality during childhood and adolescence, the following were found to be relevant as regards present forms of contact:

Persecutees who are nowadays "socially integrated"
more frequently had mothers and fathers who felt that they were part of the majority group in their country of residence;
correspondingly, those who are nowadays "socially isolated" more frequently had mothers and fathers who felt that they belonged to the minority group (0.1% and 5% significance).

If we compare only the extreme manifestations of the contact factors with early developmental data we find the following additional correlations:

Persecutees who are now "socially integrated"
more frequently had open-minded, responsive mothers who were cooperative in their methods
of bringing up their children;
correspondingly, those who are nowadays "socially isolated" more frequently had mothers
who were unresponsive, narrow-minded and authoritarian (0.1% and 5% significance).
Persecutees who are now "sociable" in attitude more frequently
had mothers who felt part of the majority group in their country of residence;
correspondingly, persecutees who nowadays have a "rejecting" attitude more frequently had
mothers who were minority-related (5% significance).

In the findings listed, one is struck in particular by the prominent role played by
the mother. Even with regard to an external aspect of family existence, namely the
feeling of belonging to the existing majority or minority group, the mother comes
more strongly to the fore, although one might have expected the father to play a
determining role here. Nevertheless, this is the only characteristic where there is any
correlation at all between the influence of the father and present-day contact
behaviour.

Thus it can be said that former persecutees whose parents grew up in a social
community without any perceptible pressure from an opposed group are nowadays
better integrated socially. Leaving aside the group affinity of the father, persecutees
whose mothers felt part of the majority group are also nowadays less mistrustful
than persecutees whose mothers were clearly oriented towards the standards of the
minority. If, as a result of the parents' association with a minority group, the children felt "different from the others", which must have been the case, then their
"social isolation" and "rejection" of others — all of which was intensified by the
concentration camp experience — must probably be regarded as an inevitable
sequela.

The mothers of former persecutees who can now again be regarded as "socially
integrated" are further characterized by general open-mindedness and a cooperative
attitude in bringing up their children. On the other hand, present-day "social isolation" is correlated with a reserved mother and an authoritarian upbringing. It is
interesting to note here that it is not so much the actual mother-child relationship
that seems to dominate the picture but rather the personality of the mother as this
is experienced by the child. One might say that the social behaviour manifest today
is most strongly influenced by identification with the mother.

The following findings relating to salient features of the adolescence of former
persecutees, should also be considered in conjunction with the relationships already
described:

Persecutees who are nowadays "socially integrated"
more frequently were able to achieve a successful break with their parental home,
had a harmonious development,
had good relationships with figures of authority outside the family;
correspondingly, persons who are nowadays "socially isolated" were
more frequently unable to break away successfully from the parental home,
had a disturbed development,
had poor relationships with figures of authority outside the family (1%, 5% and 5% significance).

We find here also a significant correlation with the factor "view of own position in society".

Persecutees who represent the pole "satisfaction"
more frequently had good relationships with authority figures outside the family;
Persecutees who represent the pole "dissatisfaction"
more frequently had poor relationships with authority figures outside the family (5% significance).

It is striking that neither the earlier relationships with persons of the same age and sex nor with persons of the same age of the opposite sex appear to be in any way correlated with the present social behaviour. On the other hand, the relationship with authority figures outside the family is of relatively great importance.

These findings should perhaps be interpreted as a direct continuation of the parents-child or mother-child relationships. In the final analysis it is the parental home that not only moulds the relationship with authority figures outside the family but also guarantees a harmonious childhood development or a successful break with the parental home.

Summary

1. Two factor analyses, the data for which were obtained either from the interviews or from a questionnaire and the Rorschach test, yielded four relevant factors for the present-day interpersonal relationships of former concentration camp inmates.

2. The interview data revealed two separate and important dimensions. The first ("ability to cope with society") is characterized by active self-assertiveness and initiative in making social contact (pole of "social integration") as compared with passive lack of drive (pole of "social isolation"). The second dimension ("attitude to one's fellowmen") comprises the poles "sociability" and mistrustful "rejection" of other people.

3. The factors obtained from the questionnaire and the Rorschach test also provide two independent dimensions. The factor "feeling of belonging to society" is characterized by the poles "feeling of belonging" and "feeling of alienation". Persons representing the "feeling of belonging" emphatically reject the possibility that the period of incarceration had any effect on their present contact behaviour, while those representing the "feeling of alienation" equally emphatically see a causal relationship between this state and incarceration. The significant correlations of this factor with the factors "ability to cope with society" and "attitude to one's fellowmen" show that some of the interviewees can nowadays only achieve "social integration" by repressing or disavowing their concentration camp past, while on the other hand "social isolation" and "rejection" of one's fellowmen may be caused by a fixation on the past.

The factor "view of own position in society" expresses how the inmates experience the reaction of their fellowmen to their concentration camp past. In this factor we find the two extreme poles of the dissatisfied, aggressive, demanding persons (pole of "dissatisfaction") contrasted with the satisfied, non-aggressive, non-demanding persons (pole of "satisfaction").

4. Of the various sociological characteristics examined, those of sex, age, country of origin and present country of residence proved to be significant for the present contact behaviour. Women feel more strongly than men that their interpersonal relationships were adversely affected by the concentration camp experience. Older inmates, compared to younger ones, above all remain more aloof from persons who did not suffer the experience of incarceration. Persecutees born in Eastern Europe nowadays clearly exhibit more pronounced disturbances of interpersonal contact than those born in Germany; in this case a role may be played by the difficulties encountered in adapting to a new socio-cultural environment. Persecutees now living in the USA and Israel are less mistrustful and less socially isolated than those living in Germany. It must be assumed that the latter's ability to make contact it inhibited by the fact that they have to live together with their former persecutors.

5. Important connections are also found to exist between the present-day contact behaviour and the stress of the concentration camp. In general, it can be said that the difficulties in the sphere of social behaviour are directly related to the severity of the stress. Severe work stress is nowadays specifically related to passiveness, isolation and lack of aggressiveness.

6. The most striking of the characteristics of personality development is the importance of the mother in the development of later disturbances in interpersonal contact. In this connection the personality of the mother, the way she sees herself, and the role which she plays in society seem to be of greater importance than the concrete child-mother relationship. The identification with the mother can thus be seen as having a strong moulding effect on the individual's present contact behaviour.

CHAPTER 7

Occupational Reintegration Following Incarceration

Outline of Problem

The relationship with one's fellowmen and society, as described in the preceding chapter, is an important indicator of successful or unsuccessful reintegration. In this chapter we wish to examine the question of a person's occupation as a particular form of social reintegration. Of course, an occupation is primarily an activity that is carried out for the purpose of earning one's daily bread and also to satisfy one's capabilities and interests. But, in addition, it is a link with other people and society as a whole. This contact with others and with society takes various forms depending on the type of occupation and the success that is achieved in pursuing it. When this fact is borne in mind, the failure of the literature on the sequelae of incarceration to mention this subject appears doubly unfortunate. In fact, the literature barely touches on the problems of occupational reintegration, probably because investigators were primarily interested in somatic and psychological disorders and did not pay any attention to the problems of social reintegration experienced by former inmates.

Therefore this chapter starts out by describing the general phenomena connected with the occupations of ex-inmates, then it turns to the question of how successful these persons are nowadays in their occupations and what it takes to be successful. In order to achieve greater comparability within the study group in this chapter, the sample was standardized in two directions. Firstly, statistical comparisons were made only for male interviewees. This restriction is necessary because women have different occupational problems from men. Occupational achievement and success can be deduced relatively clearly in the case of men from the type of work, salary level and similar data. However, the type of work performed by women ceases to be objectifiable at the latest at the moment when they marry and start to run a household. We have therefore restricted our statements to the occupational development of male persecutees.

The second step towards standardizing the sample was taken by ignoring, to a large extent, male inmates who were persecuted on religious grounds. In the case of Catholic priests and also, to some degree, of Jehovah's Witnesses, their occupation cannot be clearly separated, if at all, from the other dimensions of their lives. In these cases, the individual merges by and large with his profession. Therefore we have not included these persons in this part of the investigation. We have also left out 16 former persecutees for whom either incomplete or insufficiently reliable data were available on the questions of interest here. This left us with 133 male interviewees in whom to analyse the occupational problems faced by former concentration camp inmates.

I. Problems of Reintegration

1. Choice of Occupation

The range of variation in the occupations selected by the inmates following their liberation corresponds approximately to the conditions that existed in the same group of interviewees prior to persecution. Thus, at first sight, there do not appear to be any persecution-dependent categories of occupation. However, if the frequency of the various occupations before and after incarceration is compared, some differences do stand out (see Table 50):

Table 50. Occupations pursued before and after persecution (n=133)

Occupations	Before persecution %	After persecution %
Salaried employees	9	26
Artisans	12	22
Shopkeepers	11	16
Businessmen	15	10
Members of the professions	10	5
Workers	26	4
Civil servants	2	4
Pensioners	—	13
Undergoing training	15	—

The largest quantitative changes occur in the categories "workers" (26% : 4%), "salaried employees" (9% : 26%) and "artisans" (12% : 22%). The number of workers declines considerably after persecution and that of salaried employees and artisans increases noticeably. Only 10% of the workers from the persecution period remained workers after their release.

However, this shift in the occupational structure must not be taken as solely due to the persecution, because to some extent it corresponds to a general trend.

As is evident from Table 51, for the period between 1950 and 1961, the entire male population of the Federal Republic of Germany exhibits a trend away from wage-earning to salaried employment.

These statistics show that the number of salaried employees rose by 3.8% between 1950 and 1961 while the number of workers declined by 4.8% during the same period. However, in the group studied by us, the general trend away from wage-earning jobs to salaried employment is particularly pronounced. The number of salaried employees rose from 9% to 26% while the number of workers dropped

Table 51. Gainfully employed males in the Federal Republic of Germany during the period from 1950 to 1961 (Yearbook of Statistics for the FRG)

Occupational categories	1950 Number	1961 Number
Salaried employees	2,011,474 (14.2%)	2,001,300 (18.0%)
Workers	8,034,632 (56.8%)	8,605,100 (52%)
All occupations	14,125,413 (100%)	16,533,200 (100%)

Table 52. Types of occupation pursued by persons now living in Germany (n=85)

Types of occupation	political persecutees (n=29) Number	German Jews (n=27) Number	Polish Jews (n=29) Number
Professions, civil servants, salaried employees	14 (48%)	11 (41%)	2 (7%)
Businessmen, shopkeepers	2 (7%)	7 (26%)	22 (76%)
Artisans, workers	7 (24%)	4 (15%)	1 (3%)
Pensioners	6 (21%)	5 (19%)	4 (14%)

from 26% to 4%. Admittedly, the two periods in question (the persecutee statistics are for the period from about 1940 to 1960 and the Federal statistics for 1950 to 1961) are not entirely comparable.

One interpretation of this intensification of an already familiar trend is that after their release the ex-inmates tended quite generally to make particularly great efforts to secure an economically and materially sound existence. In this sense, the choice of the occupations of salaried employee and artisan, which were preferred by the ex-inmates, can be seen as an attempt to attain greater occupational security.

In the period under study, the numbers in the professions declined by 50% (from 10% to 5%). The professions recorded for the pre-persecution period were those of doctor, lawyer, artist and journalist. In the post-persecution period only doctors and lawyers are found, while the artistically creative professions are missing altogether. This general survey of the occupational categories of ex-inmates can be further differentiated by considering various groups of persecutees. For this purpose, (see Table 52) we have compared three groups of persecutees now living in Germany (48 interviewees now resident in Israel and New York have not been considered here).

The groups of persons born in Germany — German Jews and political persecutees — are very similar as regards the distribution of occupational categories. The salaried occupations are the most numerous. On the other hand, Polish Jews who now live in the Federal Republic of Germany are most commonly in business.

These differences represent the different occupational situations of the various groups. The differences are only to a limited extent based on the type of occupation pursued in the pre-persecution period because, of the Polish Jews now living in Germany, only one interviewee remained in the occupation he had pursued prior to persecution. Leaving aside those who are now pensioners and those who were still undergoing training before persecution started, this means that 4% of the Polish Jews did not change occupations. On the other hand, applying the same restrictions, 53% of the political persecutees and as many as 67% of the German Jews remained in the same occupations.

These findings indicate fundamental differences in the occupational adaptation of the three groups of persecutees now living in West Germany. Taking the preferred types of occupation as the basis, these differences can be briefly outlined as follows:

Polish Jews living in Germany nowadays mainly pursue the occupations of businessman or shopkeeper. This indicates the relatively poor degree of assimilation of this group of persecutees, because although these occupations presuppose a certain amount of intimacy with the socio-cultural environment they do not require any integration in the stricter sense into the given society. Thus, among the ex-persecutees born in Poland there is not one who feels really at home living in Germany.

In contrast to this group, the German Jews who remained in Germany usually return to the occupation which they had prior to persecution. They pick up their occupation again at the point where the onset of persecution forced them to leave off. This is evidence of a stronger trend towards social reintegration than is found in Polish Jews.

Other forces are involved where the political persecutees are concerned. Prior to persecution these persons were almost exclusively employed as artisans and workers but nowadays they are chiefly salaried employees and civil servants. One might say that they have advanced socially to some extent and the interviewees themselves feel that this is so. In addition, the fact that former political persecutees now work preferentially in civil service and administrative positions is evidence of greater integration — compared with the pre-persecution period — into present-day society. A large number of this group of persons, who in their youth consciously revolted against the then existing forms and representatives of governmental power, are now employed in the civil service of the present State.

The differences observed between the three groups of former persecutees are characteristic for the persons living in West Germany. These group-specific forms of adaptation could not be determined in persons living in the other countries of emigration examined by us, namely Israel and the USA.

2. Occupational Progress Patterns

In our analysis of the various types of occupation we have so far not considered the success achieved by individuals in their occupations. The level of achievement is revealed by the various progress patterns recorded for the period 1945 to 1960.

These progress patterns are oriented around the relevant occupational level attained. The occupational level is defined by the degree of material success, social prestige and permanent security attained. Four typical progress patterns can be distinguished:

Pattern A: found in 36 cases (27%). Occupational level rises continuously. Occupational position constantly improved. Income and occupational stability increase.

Pattern B: found in 32 cases (24%). Maximum occupational level rapidly reached after 1945 and maintained without fluctuations.

Pattern C: found in 16 cases (12%). Pattern characterized by an initial rise followed by a decline. The occupational level attained soon after release cannot be maintained.

Pattern D: found in 49 cases (37%). Monotonous pattern, no upward trend. No improvement achieved in the occupational position after release.

All four patterns occur in approximately the same ratio in persecutees from different countries of origin and residence. The only statistically significant difference that can be detected is on the basis of age:

Persons exhibiting progress patterns A and B were frequently younger than 45 at the time of release (1% significance).

Age thus seems to be an important determinant for positive occupational progress following release. We will deal with this in more detail below.

If, instead of just considering the occupational progress attained after release, we compare the occupational level reached before and after persecution, the following picture emerges (see Table 53). (In the case of persons who had not completed any occupational training at the start of persecution, the potential as evidenced by the occupational training, e.g. education, was taken as the basis of the comparison):

Table 53. Comparison of occupational level before and after persecution (n=133)

Occupational level	German Jews (n=44) %	Polish Jews (n=60) %	Political persecutees (n=29) %	Total (n=133) %
Occupational level distinctly higher now than before	11	5	14	11
Occupational level same now as before	39	48	49	41
Occupational level stagnating, full potential not reached	32	9	10	22
Occupational level distinctly lower now than before	18	38	34	26

Table 53 shows that about half (52%) of the former inmates have nowadays attained an occupational level corresponding to or even higher than that achieved prior to persecution. The other half of the interviewees (48%) have now attained an occupational level inferior to that preceding persecution. More ex-inmates exhibit a clear occupational regression (26%) than a clear occupational improvement (11%). The breakdown according to three groups of persecutees does not reveal any significant deviations from the total group.

3. Standard of Living

The occupational level does not always correspond to the standard of living. In addition to one's own occupational achievements, the standard of living is also dependent on such things as pensions, spouse's income, inheritances, private gifts, etc. We have therefore attempted to classify the standard of living of the ex-persecutees in the following Table (see Table 54):

Table 54. Present standard of living (n=133)

Standard of living	German Jews (n=44) %	Polish Jews (n=60) %	Political persecutees (n=29) %	Total (n=133) %
wealthy, well-off	5	—	3	3
good standard of living	60	60	55	59
limited means but not needy	30	37	41	35
needy	5	3	—	3

The distribution is concentrated mainly in the category "good standard of living". This means that the majority of ex-persecutees enjoy a good solid middle-class standard of living.

In altogether 38% of all the interviewees covered here the standard of living was lower and corresponded approximately to the economic conditions prevailing in the lower middle class.

We must limit ourselves here mainly to the bare essentials of existence. The extreme variants of this scale are only represented by, in each case, 3% of the interviewees.

No statistically significant differences can be found in the individual groups of persecutees or in the three countries of residence: Germany, Israel, USA. Nor do the age distributions deviate significantly from each other.

4. Premature Disability

Persons who dropped out of the work force completely before reaching the statutory age limit of 65 are described as prematurely disabled. Fig. 16 shows the age distribution of 133 interviewees.

In the case of 133 male interviewees the average age at the time of the investigation (1960) was 50, with a range from 29 to 69 years.

Of these 133 men, 19 (14%) suffered some form of disability before reaching age 65. This percentage is relatively low. Given the severity of the concentration camp stress one might have expected a higher percentage of prematurely disabled persons. However, when discussing this finding, we should not forget that this sample group is not totally representative. It is still theoretically possible that a dispro-portionately high percentage of prematurely disabled persons might be found among the ex-persecutees whom we were unable to interview.

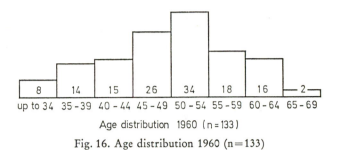

| 8 | 14 | 15 | 26 | 34 | 18 | 16 | 2 |

up to 34 35-39 40-44 45-49 50-54 55-59 60-64 65-69

Age distribution 1960 (n=133)

Fig. 16. Age distribution 1960 (n=133)

Given the material available, all we can say therefore is that it is not neces-sarily typical for ex-inmates to age prematurely and thus to become unfit for work. Many of them still feel able to work even when close to retirement. Indeed, many of them expressed the desire to go on working. On the other hand, there are per-sons who consider themselves unable to work long before they turn 65 and who therefore consider themselves unjustly treated when their applications for an early pension are refused.

It would be wrong to play these observations off against each other in order to construct a theory. The efforts of those people who wish to see all the ex-inmates treated in the same way and given an early pension are closely related to the fact that insufficient medical attention has been given to the question of the individual's fitness for work.

As long as the fitness for work is judged solely by the relatively coarse criteria of somatic disturbances, while psychic disturbances are ignored, the problems of impaired capacity for work and premature disability will be one-sidedly and there-fore wrongly assessed (see p. 160).

Of the 19 persons in our sample of interviewees who had been granted early pensions, 18 are now living in Germany and one in New York. The percentage of persons with early pensions is about equal in the three groups of persecutees. The average disability age on the other hand fluctuates slightly (see Table 55).

Table 55. Disability age of persons with early pensions living
in Germany (n=18)

Persecutee group	Number	Average disability age
Political persecutees	6 (21%)	48 years
German Jews	5 (19%)	53 years
Polish Jews	7 (19%)	45 years

The German Jews are closest to the normal pension age at the time when they become prematurely disabled. The Polish Jews are the first to take an early pension.

Slight differences can also be detected in the distribution of these early pensioners among the various types of occupation (see Table 56).

Here again, the scant data available prevent us from making any too far-reaching interpretations. All we can do is stress the remarkable fact that in relative terms the highest percentage of persons with early pensions are found in the professions (doctors, lawyers, artists, etc.) and among the workers.

Of the businessmen and civil servants only about 15% in each case take an early pension. In the case of salaried employees and artisans the proportion drops to as low as 3%. We can therefore assume that these occupations either permit or even require the ex-persecutees to come to terms in some way or another with the experience of incarceration and this is beneficial for the physical and psychic ability to work.

Table 56. Prematurely disabled persons as distributed among the various types of occupation (n=19)

Type of occupation	Number of interviewees	Proportion on early pension
Professions	13	6 (46%)
Workers	9	4 (44%)
Civil servants	6	1 (16%)
Businessmen	40	6 (16%)
Artisans	30	1 (3%)
Salaried employees	35	1 (3%)

II. Occupational Success and Failure

1. Measuring Occupational Success

It does not seem either sensible or possible to analyse here in detail all the individual differences in the occupational problems faced by ex-persecutees; therefore we shall merely study certain prominent forms of occupational success in order to correlate them with other areas of the inmates' lives.

In determining the occupational success achieved, special attention is focused above all on the psychologically relevant peculiarities of the ex-inmates' lives. These peculiarities are determined by the inmates' need to reorient or re-adapt their careers in general against the background of a more or less total uprooting in all areas of life.

Therefore, we are not so concerned here with the type of occupation pursued or its social evaluation. Instead, we are more interested in a general view that takes in both the subjective effort to achieve a degree of occupational success appropriate to one's individual abilities, given the limitations of the situation, and also the objective results of this effort.

In order to determine the forms of occupational adaptation we are justified in considering, initially, only the data from the post-incarceration period: this is shown by the results of a factor analysis which we will now briefly outline.

This factor analysis comprises all comparable occupational data of 133 male interviewees. Facts relating to the occupational development prior to persecution and data on the period of persecution itself, particularly the period of incarceration, have been included in the analysis (see Appendix, p. 256). The tabular presentation of the four-factor structure gives the following picture:

A significant result of this factor analysis is that the various biographical-historical periods (pre-persecution period, persecution period and incarceration, as well as the period following release) are to a large extent self-contained dimensions of life as far as the work and occupational situation is concerned. We will qualify this statement and provide more details at the appropriate points below.

The independent and self-contained character of the factor "occupational success following release" makes it a suitable starting point for an operational definition of an inmate's present day occupational success. For this purpose we have compiled the constituent characteristics of this factor in Table 58.

Table 57. Four-factor structure of the analysis of inmates' work and occupations

Factors	Pole A	Pole B
I Occupational success following release	Successful adaptation to work	Occupational failure
II Work stress during persecution period	Light work stress in concentration camp	Severe work stress in concentration camp
III Occupational training prior to persecution	Successful occupational development	Disturbed occupational development
IV Social stratum to which parents belonged	Upper middle class	Lower middle class

Table 58. Factor "occupational success following release"

Characteristic	"Occupational success" (Pole A)	"Occupational failure" (Pole B)	Loading
Reintegration	successful reintegration	difficulties in reintegrating	0.83
Occupational level	same or higher level compared with pre-persecution period	lower level than in pre-persecution period	0.82
Occupational progress	upward trend since release	sometimes up sometimes down, or even no upward trend at all following release	0.80
Standard of living	materially well-off	materially needy	0.79

All ex-inmates whose occupational data were considered in the analysis tend toward one of the two poles. Further graduation is possible if for each individual person we determine how many of the four characteristics constituting this factor are positive. The following distribution is obtained (Fig. 17):

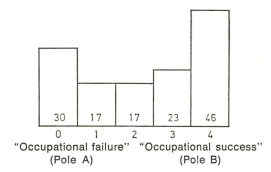

30	17	17	23	46
0	1	2	3	4

"Occupational failure"   "Occupational success"
(Pole A)   (Pole B)

Fig. 17. Distribution of 133 persons among the 4 characteristics of the factor "occupational success following release"

The occupational situation of 46 former persecutees coincides nowadays with that represented by Pole A above, while 30 former inmates exhibit a degree of occupational success corresponding exactly to Pole B. The remaining 57 persons fall between these two poles. In order to simplify the later steps in this analysis we will combine the 5 above listed grades into three groups:

A. Interviewees with 4 characteristics of Pole A: good occupational success   46 persons
B. Interviewees with 2 or 3 characteristics of Pole A: partial occupational success 40 persons
C. Interviewees with 0 or 1 characteristic of Pole A: no occupational success   47 persons

These three groups can be outlined as follows on the basis of the occupational variables which characterize them:

A. Persons with good occupational success. They all succeeded in reintegrating into an occupation after release. They either returned to the type of work which they had prior to incarceration or they built up a new occupational existence. In all cases they have attained an occupational level which is at least as good as that which they enjoyed before persecution. After release their careers followed a stable and constantly upward-tending course. All enjoy a good standard of living.

B. Persons with partial occupational success. The clearest feature in all these cases is the *great effort* to reintegrate into an occupation. Although 86% of these interviewees built up a new occupational existence or returned to their old occupation, the progress made by more than half of these people (54%) was unstable up to 1960 and did not continuously improve. Compared with the status prior to the onset of persecution 40% of these persons had declined to a lower occupational level or were stagnating at a level inappropriate to their potential. Nevertheless, 70% of them were financially comfortably off. Although overall these persons exhibit a clear trend towards occupational stability and success, each member of this group has at least one occupational problem that he cannot completely master.

C. Persons without any occupational success. Only one of the 4 occupational characteristics was positive for just one person in three (34%). None of the characteristics were positive for any of the rest (66%). Occupational progress following release was uncertain in all cases, unstable and did not consistently follow an upward trend. The present standard of living is poor and the economic conditions are restricted. The occupational level attained prior to persecution was not achieved by any member of this group following release.

Summarizing, it can be said that: 34.6% of the ex-inmates have achieved good occupational success since their release, 30% have achieved partial success and 35.4% have achieved no success at all. This distribution is the same, without any significant differences, in Germany, Israel and New York. Thus the country of residence has no detectable effect on the degree and form of the occupational success. Nor can any statistically significant correlations be established between occupational success and country of birth (Germany and Poland). Similarly, the question of a connection between occupational adaptation and the reasons for persecution (Jewish persecutees and political persecutees) cannot be statistically verified. Thus, from the ex-inmates in our sample group, we are unable to confirm the observations of ROSEN (1959), and VERNOFF et al. (1962) according to whom Jewish males exhibit, comparatively speaking, the maximum achievement motivation and a correspondingly high degree of success in their occupations. We are unable to decide here whether this is due to the selection of our material or to the fact that Jewish males lost an apparently specific occupational quality as a result of incarceration.

2. State of Health

It is logical to assume that there is a connection between the above-mentioned differences in occupational adaptability and the individual's physical state of health. In order to test this hypothesis we will first consider those interviewees who applied for a pension for damaged health and for whom, consequently, a medical report was made. Finally, we shall examine several non-applicants with regard to the complaints expressed by them in the interviews and attempt to establish why they chose not to apply for compensation.

a) Applicants

Of the 133 male interviewees considered here, detailed health documentation and disability ratings are available for 101 (75%). Of the remaining 32 interviewees, 11 were non-applicants. In the case of 21 interviewees we were unable to inspect their files. These persons have, therefore, been left out. The applicants are distributed as follows among the three occupational success groups:

Table 59. Applications for pensions to compensate for damaged health (n=133)

Occupational group	Number	Proportion of applicants Number
A successful	46	34 (74%)
B partially successful	40	27 (68%)
C unsuccessful	47	40 (85%)

The percentage of applicants is highest (85%) in the unsuccessful group and lowest in the partially successful group (68%).

The application for a pension for damaged health tells us nothing, however, about the actual extent of the health damage. This is usually expressed by the disability rating as determined by the examining doctor.

Although the quantification of health damage in terms of percentages is not an entirely problem-free procedure, it can nevertheless serve as a rough guide. Table 60 therefore compares the total disability rating with the degree of occupational success.

Table 60. Distribution of disability ratings

Occupational group	0–24%	25–39%	40–59%	60% and more	Mean percentage
A successful	9	10	6	9	39
B partially successful	6	4	11	6	43
C unsuccessful	7	9	14	10	44

The lowest average disability rating (39%) is found in the case of the successful ex-persecutees, while the unsuccessful persons had the highest average rating (44%). However, this difference is not statistically significant. But this means that success in one's occupation and the extent of health damage as diagnosed by the doctor — expressed by the disability rating — are not statistically correlated.

This important finding can be interpreted in various ways. To start with, it is possible that occupational success and the state of a person's health really are two independent variables. But then one would have to consider whether the medical diagnosis may be deficient in some way and thus cannot accurately take account of the relationship between these two variables. So far it would seem that the medical diagnoses and pension assessments have considered only somatic and not psychic disorders. Most doctors do not have the proper training or even the correct theoretical approach (see "Compensation of Late Injury", p. 75) to be able to make a correct assessment of psychic disturbances.

The ex-inmates who are unsuccessful in their occupations seem to run the greatest risk of being awarded an inadequate pension for damage suffered to their health. This is indicated among other things by the following finding:

Persons who failed to make a success of their occupations after release from the camps appeal against the amount of pension awarded them more frequently than do persons who are successful or at least partially successful in their occupations (5% significance).

Thus, persons who are unsuccessful in their occupations are the ones who most frequently receive a pension assessment with which they are not satisfied and against which they therefore lodge an appeal. One could conveniently dismiss this finding by assuming that the persons in question are suffering from a pension neurosis, but the majority of our studies so far do not support such a stance.

With the exception of the statistical review by KOLLE (1968), who reported that out of 218 cases of neuropsychiatrically examined ex-inmates 6.1% exhibited "tendentious, pension-oriented neurotic behaviour", no investigator has found any significant incidence of persons suffering from a pension neurosis (see Chapter on "Late-Appearing Damage to Health").

The doctors who tend to diagnose a neurotic desire for a larger pension are mainly those who believe that every person who is physically healthy, i.e. who does not have any obvious symptoms, must be able to work. For the reasons stated above, the many and varied psychically based work disturbances are not recognized here.

b) Non-Applicants

Finally, we consider the occupational integration of ex-inmates who did not make any application for compensation of damaged health. Of the total of 18 non-applicants whose state of health has already been discussed on pages 43–47, 11 male interviewees are included in the present random sample.

In the chapter on "Late-Appearing Damage to Health" we have already examined the actual state of health of the non-applicants and their motives in refusing to try for a pension. We would only point out here that all non-applicants, independent of their personal reasons for renouncing their entitlement to a pension, are characterized by a strong effort to get on in their occupations.

Nor do the persons in question give up this effort even when faced with permanent resistance. Therefore, the feature which most clearly characterizes the occupational progress pattern of this group is the above-average frequency with which they change their occupation or place of work. The following description of the occupation pattern of one of the non-applicants will make this behaviour clear:

The interviewee, the son of Jewish parents in Germany, was born in 1925. He attended elementary school (Volksschule) where he achieved average marks. He would have liked to become an electrician but he had to train to be a mechanic because, as a Jew, he was unable to find the desired apprenticeship position.

In 1943, at the age of 18, he was put in the Theresienstadt concentration camp and then, 18 months later, was transferred to Auschwitz. At the time of his release he was in a fairly good state of health. The reason for this, according to him, was that he had soon managed to find work in the camp as a mechanic and had thus been able to make himself useful to the SS. As a result, he enjoyed a few small privileges and was given additional rations in the camp. When he learned that both his parents had died in concentration camps, he went to Berlin and tried, as he said, to find "easy work which would bring in a lot of cash".

To start with he did odd jobs around a circus and then he took a job as a waiter in a café-restaurant.

In 1946 he got himself a very advantageous position in the Jewish Agency. He worked here until emigrating to Israel in 1948.

In Israel he started out with a temporary job in the post office and then worked as a cook in the army. After he left the army he worked as a waiter in various places. In 1956, together with a partner, he tried to open a restaurant for tourists in Jerusalem. When this experiment failed he went back to being a waiter, for a while on a ship and then finally in a large hotel in Jerusalem. The interviewee is nowadays fairly comfortably off.

As regards his health, he complained of occasional stomach trouble, but nothing which could not be treated by simple means.

A similar tendency to change jobs repeatedly is also found — with one exception — in the other male non-applicants. However, this job mobility is not an expression of their adaptability but of their constant search for the best possible position — especially in financial terms. For these persons the long drawn-out and laborious pension procedure is a tiresome and even humiliating business. They prefer to renounce any claim to a pension in favour of re-building their lives and occupations themselves, without any assistance from their ex-persecutors.

3. Age

a) Influence of Age on Occupational Success

It must be assumed that age is also a determining factor in the degree of occupational success achieved by ex-inmates. Table 61 compares the age distribution of the three occupational groups:

Table 61. Age in 1945 (n=133)

Occupational group	up to 20	21–25	26–30	31–35	36–40	41–45	46 and over
A successful	—	7	8	8	10	7	6
B partially successful	8	5	12	4	8	2	1
C unsuccessful	—	5	3	10	13	7	9

Statistical examination of this distribution reveals the following differences:

Persons who are partially successful in their jobs are younger than those who are successful, and significantly younger than unsuccessful persons (1% and 5% significance).

There is *no* difference between the successful and unsuccessful groups as regards their age.

A possible explanation for this finding is that the various age groups were affected in qualitatively different ways by the onset of persecution.

For the younger interviewees the start of persecution constituted in almost all cases a serious incursion in their lives at a time when they were either deciding on or training for an occupation. Therefore, in the post-incarceration period we find that young persecutees display increased job insecurity. This is not so much a symptom of fundamental failure on their parts but rather the expression of their conflict in trying to solve the problems of adapting to an occupation following release.

Older interviewees, on the other hand, were overtaken by persecution almost always at a time when they had established themselves, to a greater or lesser extent, in their chosen occupations. The interruption of their lives and jobs at this point in their development therefore leads either to a complete breakdown of their ability to work any more (the people who are unsuccessful in their occupations today) or to a reintegration into the working world with all the vigour that they displayed prior to persecution (the people who are successful in their occupations today).

This interpretation is supported by the following finding:

Persons who are nowadays successful in their work returned to their old pre-persecution occupations more frequently than those who are nowadays unsuccessful in their jobs (5⁰/₀ significance).

There are two possible ways in which to interpret this finding. On the one hand it is conceivable that ex-persecutees who were able to return to their pre-incarceration occupation had on average a better chance of making a success of their lives upon release from imprisonment. On the other hand, it is also possible to conclude that it is an attribute of occupationally successful individuals that they cling to what they once learned; in other words they have achieved such close identification with a particular occupation that, even under different environmental conditions, they return once more to the old job.

It goes without saying that the factor of age alone cannot adequately clarify such a complex phenomenon as the occupational reintegration of ex-inmates of concentration camps. We will therefore now analyse the individual lives of particularly young and particularly old ex-inmates in order to bring out further factors which are also responsible for the differing degrees of occupational success achieved following the inmates' release.

b) Occupational Progress Patterns of Young Persecutees

In order to establish the various component causes of the different degrees of progress made by inmates following their release, we will consider here male persecutees who were less than 25 years old in 1945. Our group of interviewees contains 25 persons in this age category. Seven of them were successful in their jobs, 13 partially successful and 5 unsuccessful.

Because of the relatively low number of interviewees, we will not try to establish quantitative differences but will concentrate instead on the qualitative aspects. The age-independent factors behind the varying degrees of occupational success will be discussed in detail further below, therefore we merely mention the salient points here.

One point to be made is that the differences in the ability to get on in a job, which manifested themselves in young persecutees between 1945 and 1960, do not seem to be causally related to the objective degree of persecution stress. Nor can we find any indication that education, present state of health or intelligence (as far as this could be assessed without performing any tests) are important factors in the occupational success of young ex-persecutees. However, the following differences in personality stand out.

The young ex-inmates who are successful in their occupations are characterized chiefly by extreme restlessness and compulsive drive. They get themselves some sort of job soon after their release. They are interested neither in the type of occupation nor in material success. What matters to them above all else is to be active. Behind this almost compulsive development of activity one senses an attempt on their part to reconnoitre their environment and to detect and counter all possible dangers in good time. The way in which these persons come to terms with their potentially hostile environment is not by offering active resistance but by adapting cleverly and — towards themselves as well — ruthlessly to the environmental conditions.

The occupational success which follows "automatically" in the wake of this process of adapting, without really being consciously sought, does not provide any apparent satisfaction. The attitude towards job and fellowmen still continues to be determined by agitation and restlessness. A good job and material security are not enough to permit the individual to enjoy his achievements. The quest goes on. Continuation courses are taken and jobs changed in an attempt to find better protection against new dangers. In the process the individual finds no enjoyment in what he has attained nor does he manage to identify with a particular occupation. Rest and enjoyment, stability and identification with the job are avoided rather than sought.

This state is clearly expressed in the words of a German-born Jew now living in Israel:

"I am always on the defensive, even if no one wants to harm me and even if no one is persecuting us. And I am always intent on looking after my own interests, even if it means acting illegally."

The occupational patterns of young persons who are only moderately successful in their jobs are similar to those outlined above. However, in their cases the hectic and compulsive element is usually missing.

In contrast to the clearly manifest achievement motivation observed in successful individuals, the persons who are only partially successful in their work have great, often excessive ambitions. These people frequently state that the onset of persecution interrupted them in the implementation of their actual career plans. They are not satisfied with what they have attained, in fact they would like to be something entirely different. As a result, these interviewees are usually unable to identify with their chosen occupation. But, unlike the first group, they suffer from this situation and look around for something else to identify with. In general, it is true to say that the young persecutees who are only partially successful in their occupations are most intensely aware of the conflict inherent in their situation.

It is precisely in this respect that they differ clearly from the occupationally unsuccessful individuals. The people who are failures in their work are only able to form a very fragmentary view of their occupational situation. Even though they are generally aware of the state of economic misery in which they live and although they voice general dissatisfaction with this state of affairs, they are unable to make any realistic attempts to change the situation. It is a characteristic feature of these interviewees that they are married to energetic, usually working wives. However, their wives' dynamic approach to work does not have a calming effect on these interviewees, instead it tends to act as an impertinent and insulting provocation. The tendency always to feel at a disadvantage or to imagine that one has been unjustly treated is particularly pronounced in these persons. One of these interviewees expresses this feeling as follows:

"I'm a Jonah. I never seem to escape having bad luck. All my life I've had nothing but problems and I can't see that things will ever change for me."

c) Occupational Patterns of Older Persecutees

This group comprises 16 interviewees who were older than 46 in 1945. Of these, 6 were very successful in their occupations following release, 9 where unsuccessful and one was only partially successful. We will ignore this latter individual because he is not sufficiently representative and thus we will compare only older male per-secutees with good and bad occupational achievements (15 interviewees).

Older ex-persecutees who were able to make a success of their occupations fol-lowing release had also been conspicuously industrious prior to persecution, a fact which is reflected in their adaptable, flexible and success-motivated attitude. The marriages of these interviewees take second place to their jobs. They either marry a woman with money or a hard-working sober woman who accepts it as quite natural that the man should be utterly devoted to his work and career. By the time when persecution commenced, these interviewees had already built up a solid occupational base which, in some instances, protected them for quite some time from severe acts of persecution. They were incarcerated at a relatively late date in pro-ceedings. During incarceration these men usually discovered that it paid to have a work and success-oriented attitude even under concentration camp conditions.

This attitude was carried over without interruption into the post-incarceration period. Immediately after their release they investigated various ways and means of earning money. Since in most cases these persons did not have any moral in-hibitions to prevent them using even illegal means to earn money (black market, pimping) they soon managed to secure a sound material existence and a successful career. This attitude varies little throughout the rest of their lives. Family and marriage, even a second marriage, play a subordinate role. The period of persecu-tion itself left hardly any mark, if at all. The theme that determines their lives is the urge to achieve material and social success. While they do manage to gain mate-rial success, social success eludes them or it merely takes the form of an external prestige which cannot blind the persons in question to the fact that deep down they are lonely.

In this respect the pattern of the occupationally successful older interviewees is similar to that of the unsuccessful individuals. These, too, are socially isolated and lonely at the end of their lives. On the other hand, there is one very important point in which the two groups differ conspicuously from each other, namely the difference in the subjective importance of the pursued occupation. In the case of the older men who are nowadays successful, their occupation prior to persecution and in particular the material aspect of that occupation was primarily a means of coming to terms with their environment. On the other hand, the persons who are nowadays unsuccessful identify themselves much more closely with the sense of their occupation, regardless of its material value. For them their occupation was an im-portant part of their lives which they could not give up without a second thought. Their social role and thus their contact with their environment were in no small part made possible trough their identification with their occupation. It is therefore little wonder that the persons who are nowadays successful comprise mainly busi-nessmant, while chiefly intellectuals, artists and artisans are to be found in the second group.

As a rule, the persecution affected the latter much more severely than the men in the first group. None of these interviewees was physically capable of finding his way back into employment immediately after being released from the camp. Those who do try it after a more or less long recovery phase soon give up again in bitter resignation. Resignation and bitterness are combined with a reproachful attitude towards society. The individuals in question feel betrayed and abandoned by their environment. The resulting feeling of loneliness is blamed on the lack of under-standing and callousness displayed by their fellowmen. Instead of a realistic attempt to cope with their environment they indulge in unreal pipe dreams and illusory hopes. Like the unsuccessful young interviewees the older ones are also as a rule married to more active and dynamic women. Often their wives are their only means of moral support.

These differences point up emphatically the importance of predominantly psy-chological personality traits for the attainment of occupational success following release. We will analyse these relationships in more detail in the following.

4. Psychic Disturbances

The correlation between disturbed working ability and psychic disturbance is considered separately below. In order to determine the individual extent of the psychic disturbance we have taken 30 characteristics, which were also included in the factor analysis in Chapter 5 "Basic Forms of Psychic Disturbance" (see Appendix, p. 253), and checked how many disturbances can be detected for each person.

The following differences are statistically significant:

Persons who were unsuccessful in their occupations following release are clearly more psychically disturbed than persons who were partially successful in their occupations (1% significance) and than persons who were successful in their occupations (5% significance).

No statistically significant difference can be detected between successful and partially successful individuals.

This finding confirms the close correlation between occupational failure and psychic disturbance in former inmates. It is striking that the converse is not true, i.e. that occupationally successful persons should be psychically the healthiest. On average the weakest form of psychic disturbance is exhibited instead by persons who were only partially successful in their jobs and who have so far never achieved any completely satisfying success in their work. This indicates that complete devo-tion to the process of adapting to one's occupation, as is typically observed in per-sons who are successful in their work, may have to be paid for in psychic distur-bances. We will return to this relationship later (see p. 167).

The above-described difference between the three occupational groups is also apparent in the correlation with the factors discussed in the chapter on "Fundamen-tal forms of psychic disturbance".

Persons who were unsuccessful in their occupations are the strongest representatives of the factor "resignation and despair". In this respect they differ clearly from persons with only partial occupational success (1% significance) and also from successful persons (5% signifi-cance).

The same statistical differences are found for the factor "apathy and inhibition"; persons with no occupational success are more apathetic and inhibited than partially successful (1% significance) and successful persons (5% significance).

Also, in the case of the factor "aggressive-irritable moodiness" it is found that the un-successful individuals are the ones who suffer most. They display this psychic disturbance much more frequently than partially successful persons (1% significance) and also tend to be more aggressive and irritable than successful persons (10% significance).

These findings may be summarized as follows:

In ex-inmates lack of job success often occurs together with a lack of hope, depressive inhibition and chronically dissatisfied, irritable moodiness. These psychic disturbances occur least frequently in ex-inmates who are nowadays only partially successful in their jobs. In the successful individuals, who are more psychically disturbed than the only partially successful persons, aggressive-irritable moodiness seems to be more typical than resignation and despair.

There seems little sense to us in regarding the occupational failure as the cause of the psychic disturbances or vice versa in asserting that occupational failure is only the result of the disturbed psychic state. It is, instead, more reasonable to regard both forms of disturbance — psychic disturbance and work disturbance — as having a common root and to see in them only two externally different aspects of a common basic disturbance typically found in ex-inmates. These findings once more emphatically underscore the reservations already expressed about trying to assess the work capability of ex-persecutees solely on the basis of their physical condition. A shift in emphasis towards a more careful consideration of the psychic situation when establishing the degree of disability thus seems absolutely necessary.

5. Handling of Aggression

The way in which the ex-inmates work off their aggression is of particular importance for the analysis of their adaptation to their occupations, because in order to be successful in one's work it is essential to have a certain degree of controlled aggressiveness. It can be seen from this statement that the term "aggressiveness" is used here in a wider sense than merely that of hostility. By aggression is also meant, in this context, the general quality of tackling life and facing up to problems. This does not necessarily have to be a hostile-destructive process.

a) Development of Activity Following Release

Let us first consider aggression in the general form of the activity developed by the ex-inmates and let us examine its connection with job success. It is found that the correlation between these two phenomena is not constant, but changes in a characteristic way in the course of time. Table 62 illustrates the distribution for the first adaptation phase:

Table 62. Coming to terms with the environment in the first phase of adaptation 1945–1946
(n=133)

Occupational group	Attempted orientation Activity Number	Collapse Passiveness Number
A successful	35 (76%)	11 (24%)
B partially successful	26 (65%)	14 (35%)
C unsuccessful	32 (70%)	14 (30%)

A statistical examination of this distribution does not yield any significant differences between the groups. The development of activity in an attempt to cope with the environment, as observed in the first two years after release, is thus not obviously correlated with the occupational success achieved up to 1960.

However, very significant differences are discovered about five years later at the turn of the decade 1949/1950. Table 63 illustrates the corresponding distribution.

Table 63. Coming to terms with the environment in 1949/50 (n=133)

Occupational group	Effort to adapt to environment Activity, own initiative Number	Activity, supported Number	Disturbances in adaptation to environment Uncertainty Helplessness Number	Evasion Withdrawal Number
A successful	19 (41%)	19 (41%)	8 (18%)	— —
B partially successful	11 (28%)	20 (50%)	9 (23%)	— —
C unsuccessful	4 (9%)	6 (13%)	32 (68%)	5 (11%)

A statistical examination of this distribution gives the following results:

Five years after their release occupationally unsuccessful persons make fewer attempts to adapt to their environment than partially successful or successful persons (1% significance in each case).

At that time there are no differences between partially successful and successful persons.

A comparison of the above-listed categories indicates the process-like character of environmental adaptation in ex-persecutees. Differences such as those discovered in the ex-inmates in 1946 at the end of the first adaptation phase still provide no clue as to whether the persons in question will be successful or not in their later lives. But, by the turn of the decade, in 1949/1950, there is a clear relationship between active coping with the environment and later success in one's occupation. At this time, unsuccessful men display with significantly greater frequency an uncertain evasive attitude in their attempt to come to terms with their environment.

As the adaptation process continues, these differences in the amount of activity developed become even more pronounced. Over the next 10 years (up to 1960) successful men do not slacken — or at least not perceptibly — their active efforts to adapt. On the other hand, between 1950 and 1960, it is found that the men who are only partially successful in their occupations do not continue to make such intense efforts to adapt to their environment. We will show, further below, that this slackening off in the attempt to achieve external control of their environment often goes together with inner control of the problems of adaptation and can therefore also be positively evaluated.

In the case of the persons who achieve no success at all in their occupations, the ability to adapt actively to their environment diminishes more and more, but it is not accompanied by intellectualization of the problems of adaptation. On the contrary, the final state reached by these interviewees is usually marked by elements of depressive hopelessness and a feeling of uselessness.

In the next section we examine a specific form of handling aggression, namely visibly and audibly expressed hostile aggressivity.

b) Externalized Aggression

All verbal or physical forms of conflict in the socio-communicative sphere are expressions of aggression. The 133 male interviewees in the three occupational success groups are distributed as follows among four categories of individually predominant forms of aggression:

Table 64. Predominant forms of aggression (n=133)

Occupational group	Externalized aggression		Inhibited aggression	
	uncontrolled explosive	controlled stable	reserved inhibited	no visible expression of aggression
	Number	Number	Number	Number
A successful	7 (15%)	7 (15%)	32 (70%)	— —
B partially successful	9 (23%)	9 (23%)	20 (50%)	2 (5%)
C unsuccessful	16 (34%)	3 (6%)	23 (49%)	5 (11%)
Total	32 (24%)	19 (14%)	75 (56%)	7 (5%)

Table 64 shows that a reserved-inhibited form of aggression is most common in the ex-persecutees examined by us (56.4%); in a quarter of the persons examined the aggression is uncontrolled and explosive; in 14.3% the aggressive behaviour is controlled and stable. No visible forms of aggression can be detected in 5.3% of the ex-inmates.

Judging by the numerical distribution alone, it would seem that the inhibited-reserved method of getting rid of aggression is typical for ex-inmates of concentration camps. This attitude occurs particularly frequently in men who have successfully adapted to their occupations. It is, in fact, found in 70% of this group. The difference between this and the other two comparison groups is statistically significant at just below the 5% significance level (trend). The category "uncontrolled, explosive expression of aggression", on the other hand, seems to be particularly untypical for occupationally successful persons because it is more frequently observed as a trend in the other two occupational groups.

The men who were only partially successful in their jobs stand out because of the relative, even though not quite statistically significant, frequency with which they represent the category "controlled and stable expression of aggression".

On the other hand, the unsuccessful individuals display the greatest deviation from the overall distribution in the category "uncontrolled and explosive expression of aggression". In this respect they tend to differ most clearly from the successful persons. The complete lack of any expression of aggression is also a distinguishing factor between these two groups, even if it is not statistically significant.

Thus, inhibition and control mechanisms in the socio-communicative sphere would seem to be important accompanying phenomena, perhaps even essential conditions for successful job adaptation in ex-inmates. However, these mechanisms only promote adaptation when they do not entirely suppress the individual's aggressive impulses but instead help him to sublimate or transpose his aggression.

An example of the situational transposition of aggression is provided by the following description given by a successful textile businessman:

"When important customers come, then I sometimes do the selling myself. A lot of Germans also come to me and want to buy. Sometimes one of them starts to curse, perhaps because he knows I am a Jew. I keep quiet and listen to it all, but when he's gone I slap an extra 10% on the price."

This ability to shift the aggression elsewhere is as good as completely lacking in ex-inmates who are unsuccesful in their occupations. It is characteristic for them that they either entirely repress their aggressive-destructive urges or that they are helplessly at the mercy of these forces. Some individual cases are examined in the following section to bring out these relationships clearly.

c) Three Typical Forms of Handling Aggression

The individual cases described by way of illustration below are not extreme variants but "average cases" of the sort frequently found among ex-inmates of concentration camps. The biographical data of the development and persecution period are touched on only briefly so that the main emphasis is placed on the relationships between the handling of aggression and occupational success following release.

Representative of persons who are successful in their occupations.

Mr. F., a Jew born in Poland, now living in Munich, was 46 years old at the time of the interview. He talks quickly and quietly, barely opening his mouth. He treated both interviews that we conducted with him as an unpleasant duty which he had to get over with. Nevertheless, his statements are precise and detailed.

His first marriage, to a German woman, took place soon after his release from imprisonment. The marriage was dissolved 10 years later at the wife's instigation. He is now remarried to a woman 10 years his junior. They have no children. Together with his second wife he has built up a hairdressing salon for men and women, which is in a favourable location and is doing well. The interviewee has 5 employees working for him and has a comfortable income.

He describes himself as almost completely unable to concentrate, agitated and restless. Almost every evening he dreams about concentration camps and often wakes up. Although he frequently does not get enough sleep he works without a break from morning through to evening. He goes to his salon at 7 o'clock in the morning and cleans and tidies up. Any handyman jobs that are needed around the salon or at his house he carries out himself after working hours. On Sunday, when he cannot go to work, he suffers agonies. He wants to buy himself a garden which he can look after in his spare time.

He needs ceaseless, automatic activity, so he says, in order to ward off the flood of concentration camp memories that threatens to break in on him. Reading, which was once his favourite occupation, is now impossible because each moment of contemplation and rest triggers anxiety and despair in him. Only when driving his car does he manage to relax a little.

He believes that the people around him are unaware of his agitation. He gets on well with everyone. In particular, he never has any problems with his clients because he always gives in to them. He even has an ex-SS man among his clientele. According to him they both respect each other. He can never get angry with anyone. He wants harmony. If one of his employees comes two hours late to work one day, he cannot bring himself to tell the person off. But if an angry word should slip out once in a while, he regrets it immediately and patches things up again. Whenever anyone wants money from him he gives it without any questions. Yet he has not got any real friends. Even his wife does not understand him. They do not quarrel very often. "I give in, just to keep the peace and make sure that everything stays fine."

The following means of handling aggression are typical for this and similar cases.

1. There are no observable social aggressions. The interpersonal contact behaviour exhibited by the interviewees appears to be "adapted".

2. The non-aggressive adaptation succeeds at the expense of attaining mastery over the past. The experiences of the persecution period are repressed.

3. While this act of repression permits considerable activity to be developed in the occupational sphere, it makes it impossible to have any real live contact with one's fellowmen and a series of psychic symptoms is the price that has to be paid.

Representative of the unsuccessful group:

Mr. T. was born the eldest son of Jewish parents in Poland. At the time of the interview he was 45 years old and was living in Munich. He first married at the age of 20. His wife lost her life during the persecution.

The interviewee stated that he was a trained car mechanic and that before the start of the persecution he had operated his own taxi. Immediately after his release he returned to his job of driving and worked for a secret emigration organisation taking emigrants for Israel to a transit camp in Salzburg.

In 1947 the pulmonary TB which he had picked up during imprisonment flared up again and he required treatment in a sanatorium up to 1951. Upon leaving the sanatorium he worked as a street trader or hawked goods in markets. When this work got too much for him he tried to set himself up in a steady business. However, he had to give this attempt up after a short while and so all his efforts to stabilize his economic position were unsuccessful.

In 1951, following his discharge from the sanatorium, he married a 17-year-old German girl, but the marriage was dissolved two years later at the wife's instigation.

After this, the interviewee travelled illegally to Yugoslavia. Legal entry was refused to him because of a customs offence. In Yugoslavia he got to know is third wife, a Croatian from a Jewish family, and after living in Yugoslavia for about 4 1/2 years he returned with his wife to Munich. In Munich he tried once more to set himself up as a street trader but, in his own words, he returned home every evening so exhausted from his dealings that he gave up work entirely and since 1959 has been living simply on the pensions which he and his wife receive.

He wants to emigrate to Israel, but in order not to arrive there empty-handed he wants first to earn enough money in Germany so that he can buy and operate his own taxi in Israel. So far, he has no idea how he can put this plan into effect.

He emphatically rejects all Germans and nowadays avoids all contact with his environment. The only "crime" he ever committed, so he thinks, was to marry a German wife (the 17-year-old girl). But neither he nor his wife have any Jewish acquaintances either.

He has a lot of trouble with his health. His main problem are his "nerves". He recounted a series of incidents in which he had lost control of "his nerves". Once he was talking with another trader at a market who mistook him for an ex-member of the Nazi party and made some particularly flagrant anti-semitic comments. He immediately beat this man so severely that he drew blood. On another occasion, he thought he recognized a particularly brutal SS man out in the street. He wanted to approach this person but he had a fit and fell unconscious.

Another time, he chanced to meet a sick old man whom he wanted to help. So he went to the municipal council and forced the chairman "under threat of grievous bodily harm", as he himself described it, to allocate coal to the old man and also provide other aid.

After each of these clashes he felt completely washed out and had to stay in bed for days and weeks at a time.

The relationship here between the handling of aggression and occupational success is characterized by the following points:

1. The aggressive impulses cannot be controlled and directed. They drive the interviewee time and again to destructive outbursts or impotent collapse.

2. The ability to work is severely restricted. The interviewee is unable to work continuously over a long period of time. At the age of 44 he has withdrawn entirely from the working world.

3. Like the ability to work, the interviewee's capacity for social contact is also affected by the particular form of aggressive reaction described above. While the eruptive outbursts of aggression certainly bring him into contact with other people, they make it impossible for him to achieve a stable relationship with his environment. The interviewee thus, finally, himself withdraws from any contact and seeks isolation.

4. This occupational and social isolation goes together with a general lack of realism. For example, he believed that he would soon be able to lead a new and happier life in Israel, unspoiled by job problems, although practically all the conditions necessary to transform this dream into reality were lacking.

Representative of the persons with some success in their jobs.

Mr. W. was 37 years old at the time of the interview. He was born in Berlin, the second son of Jewish parents, and is now living in New York. He is married to a Moroccan Jew and has two children. His attitude towards the German interviewer was friendly but aloof.

The interviewee stated that he had been a talented student, but because of the increasing persecution he had been compelled to break off his studies at high school and at a music academy to report for forced labour in an arms factory. In 1943 at the age of 17 he was deported to Auschwitz. Just before the end of the war, while being transported to Dachau, he was able to escape.

He made his way illegally to France. After a short period of rest he worked for a short while at several different jobs and was very disturbed to discover that everything associated with work reminded him of his concentration camp days and therefore elicited resistance and rejection in him. With the aid of acquaintances he found a job on a Jewish newspaper as editor and compositor. Finally he gave instruction to Jewish children before they emigrated to Israel.

Then, he himself went to Israel "to do something for Israel" as he put it. But already after one year, which he spent as a soldier in the Jewish army, he returned to France and worked in various towns and for various employers. Simultaneously he worked hard to arrange his emigration to the USA because he felt that neither in Europe nor in Israel could he, in his own words, "find the difficult way back into society".

In 1952 he received an immigration permit for Baltimore (USA). He lived there for several months with a cousin, worked in a factory and then moved to New York with his first $ 100 which he had saved by living and eating frugally. In New York he tried, with the aid of Jewish acquaintances from Germany, to get established in an occupation. He worked in various import and export firms but always felt, after a short while, that the work was getting too much for him. In order to get rid of this feeling of uncertainty, he took part on his own initiative in language courses and studied business administration. In addition, he tried to fill the gaps in his knowledge by reading textbooks. Despite all his efforts, he still felt uncertain in his job and this upset him greatly.

In his contact with other people, just as in his work, his sole aim, as he himself puts it, is "to find my way back to normal circumstances". Upon his release from incarceration he felt a strong urge to mix in society. However, he had difficulties in understanding the attitudes of other people. Even today, he is still trying to find out what life is all about and what makes people behave the way they do.

He always takes great pains to be careful and correct. "Nobody can offend me. I always try to see the other person's point of view. I look for excuses for other people. I put up with quite a lot, but sometimes when I have swallowed too much I have to get things off my chest — then I am most certainly right."

He feels comfortable in America although there is much here, too, that disturbs him. He holds himself aloof from Germany and Germans while trying to analyse them and come to a fair judgement of them.

In this case, the following points can be summarized:

1. The predominant way in which he handles his aggression exhibits ambivalent traits. Aggressive impulses are accompanied by inhibitory counter-impulses. As a result he tends to stand aloof from people and intellectualize his problems.

2. This attitude leads to conflict in his work. His inability to devote himself permanently and without restriction to a concrete occupation prevents him from identifying successfully with any sort of work.

3. His contact with other persons is similarly impeded. By trying to "find out what life is really about" he tries to integrate into his social environment.

In conclusion, let us once more enumerate the most important features of the three different success groups.

The persons who are successful in their jobs stand out because of their restless activity. Relaxation, idleness and contemplation are for them not only superfluous but dangerous, because non-activity evokes obsessive memories of the past, namely the time of incarceration. Therefore, these people have to keep running to stop their past from catching up with them and this escape finds at least partial expression in their hectic work activity. Their aggressions are entirely absorbed by the pursuit of this goal. Anything which might disrupt this activity is avoided, especially arguments with other people and conflict with society. In the eyes of those around them, these ex-inmates seem to be socially adapted. And so they are, to the extent that they perform astounding feats of work. However, if one considers their contacts outside the work sphere, such as those with their marital partners, fellowmen and society, it becomes clear that they are almost totally lacking in personal contact, a fact which is only poorly masked by their restless pursuit of their careers. In running away from their concentration camp past, they pass life by.

The persons who are unsuccessful in their work are dynamically almost exactly the opposite. They remain stuck in their concentration camp past, unable to put down any new roots either in their job or in their marriage. They find society without exception rotten and hold it responsible for the fact that their own lives are without meaning or content. They no longer feel obliged to achieve anything or to work. As one ex-inmate puts it "I don't put myself out any more because I suffered unfairly and now the others should look after me". But the less society is able to do to fulfill these demands, the more the persons in question sink into a state of resignation and despair. The aggressions, which in the successful individuals are converted into restless activity, are here channelled into a hostile conflict with the individual's environment. Impotence and rage, exhaustion and aggressive explosions characterize this condition which can be described as one of depression.

In the case of the persons who are partially successful in their occupations, one is struck in the first place by a strong ambivalence. For example, the struggle for occupational success, economic security and social prestige is contrasted with an aversion to the need to work which frequently reminds them of the coercively regimented life in the concentration camp. This is particularly evident in the case of men who were forced to make their first and most memorable contact with the world of work under conditions of persecution. In their case, work has assumed the character of life-threatening exploitation.

This ambivalence is also reflected in their relationship with their fellowmen. On the one hand they seek contact with other people and on the other they turn away from them. They escape from this dilemma by achieving a certain appropriate distance between themselves and other people as well as society in general. Although these people are not given to explosive aggression, the price they have to pay for this is their tendency to intellectualize everything. By holding themselves coolly aloof they feel strange among other people. They do not understand others and yet they only want to comprehend them through their intellect. This group has the most suitable approach to the problem of coping with their concentration camp past. They do not run away from the past, nor do they remain stuck fast in it. They try to achieve gradual inner mastery of their situation. However, what they gain in intellectualization of their problems they at first lose in terms of external success.

6. Interpersonal Relationships

In the foregoing sections some observations have already been made on the connections between adaptation to one's occupation and social contact both inside and outside marriage. We will now examine these connections in greater detail.

a) Social Contact

In the chapter on "Contact with Fellow Humans and Society" (see pages 120 to 125) it is shown that in ex-inmates of concentration camps clear differences can be detected between the direct engagement with the environment and the emotional attitude to one's fellowmen. This characteristic difference is also important in connection with integration into the working world.

Table 65. Ability to cope with society and attitude to fellowmen in the case of (A) successful, (B) partially successful and (C) unsuccessful occupational groups (n=133)

Occupational group	Ability to cope with society		Attitude to fellowmen	
	Integration Number	Isolation Number	Sociability Number	Rejection Number
A successful	30 (66%)	16 (34%)	16 (39%)	23 (61%)
B partially successful	23 (58%)	17 (42%)	15 (35%)	25 (62%)
C unsuccessful	13 (28%)	34 (72%)	11 (23%)	36 (77%)

Table 65 serves to illustrate the differences which are similarly found also for the contact dimensions discussed in the chapter on "Contact with Fellow Humans and Society" (see p. 120):

Persons who are unsuccessful in their work following release from imprisonment are much more frequently socially isolated than persons who achieve good success (0.1% significance) and also are more frequently socially isolated than persons with partial occupational success (1% significance).

There is no statistically significant difference between the persons who are successful in their work and those who are only partially successful.

The three occupational success groups exhibit no statistically significant differences in the dimension "sociability" — "rejection".

Failure in one's occupation and contact disturbances thus usually occur together. Unsuccessful persons frequently live in lonely isolation without continuous relationships with other persons.

In contrast to the sharp discrimination on the basis of the actual contact behaviour, an assessment of the attitude to other people does not reveal any differences between the 3 occupational success groups or, if there is a difference, it is only a statistically insignificant trend.

It can be stated, therefore, that the occupational success of ex-inmates is closely connected with their external ability to make contact but hardly at all with their inner attitude towards other people. The successful mastery of their environment as expressed in good occupational success and in the ability to make contact with other people is not necessarily dependent in our sample on a positive attitude to others. The characteristic of the occupationally successful persons is their greater ability to function on a social plane and not necessarily their more successful mastery of their concentration camp past which expresses itself, among other ways, in renewed and prejudice-free seeking of contact with other people.

The externally adapted persons are usually just as mistrustful of others, and deep down reject other people just as much as persons who are less adapted to work and society. The difference between the occupational groups is that some people, despite their disturbed relationship with their fellowmen remain able to function well in their jobs (or perhaps even use their job as a compensation for their disturbed relationship with other people) while others, together with their inability to make social contact, are also lacking in achievement and cannot relate to their work or occupation.

b) Marriage and Family

The generally good external ability to adapt and make contact, as exhibited by persons with successful job records, also goes together with greater ability to make contact in the intimate sphere of marriage and family.

As Table 66 (page 170) shows, persons who are successful in their work nowadays more frequently lead a satisfactory and harmonious married life than men who are unsuccessful in their work.

The differences demonstrated here can also be proved to be statistically significant on the basis of the factor of family relationships following release, which is discussed on pages 182–183.

Table 66. Family life (n=133)

Occupational group	Harmonious family life Number	Disharmonious family life Number
A successful	29 (63%)	17 (37%)
B partially successful	20 (50%)	20 (50%)
C unsuccessful	10 (21%)	37 (79%)

Persons who are totally unsuccessful in their work following their release more frequently lead a disharmonious family and married life than persons who are successful or partially successful in their occupations (5% significance in each case).

Successful and partially successful persons do not differ from each other as regards family life.

This finding can be seen in connection with the varying degree of adaptability of the ex-inmates. In the case of the occupationally successful persons, this feature is more strongly developed in the areas of achievement and social contact and therefore probably also makes itself felt in a positive manner in family life. In the case of the persons who are unsuccessful in their jobs, we find, on the other hand, not only the greatest number of conflicts in family relationships but also a much higher percentage of men who did not marry after their release from imprisonment (26%). Of the occupationally successful persons only 9% and of the partially successful persons only as few as 7% are single nowadays. This fact could of course, be connected with the somewhat higher average age of the unsuccessful persons, but this is not the full explanation because the unmarried persons in this group include just as many young as old individuals. It is more likely that the higher percentage of unmarried persons among the occupationally unsuccessful types is indicative of an avoidance of marital partnership and family stress or also of the total inability of these persons to find a marital partner.

This assumption is also supported by the observation that the married, occupationally unsuccessful men seldom have any children, and when they do have any then the relationship with them is in 80% of the cases disturbed and lacking

Table 67. Attitudes displayed in bringing up their children by (A) successful, (B) partially successful and (C) unsuccessful occupational groups (n=133)

Occupational group	Cooperative Easy to get on with Approachable Number	Tolerant Lenient Number	Authoritarian Unapproachable Too strict Number	Changeable Indecisive Number	No children Number
A successful	4 (18%)	8 (36%)	5 (23%)	5 (23%)	24
B partially successful	3 (35%)	5 (72%)	4 (17%)	6 (26%)	17
C unsuccessful	4 (18%)	5 (23%)	4 (18%)	9 (41%)	25

in warmth. In this regard, they differ very significantly (1%) significance) from the two other occupational groups.

With regard to their relationship with their own children, the differences — trends only — can be distinguished in the 3 occupational success groups listed in Table 67.

Table 67 shows that the occupationally unsuccessful men tend to adopt an indecisive, changeable, authoritarian-style approach while the successful persons, in contrast, incline towards a more permissive, spoiling attitude. Only in the partially successful occupational group do we find any accent on an adequate cooperative attitude towards the child.

III. Influence of Earlier Phases in the Inmates' Lives

1. Persecution Stress

It seems logical to proceed from the hypothesis that occupational failure following release from imprisonment is directly related to the severity of stress in the concentration camp.

The following stress variables are uncorrelated with occupational success:

> Camp severity,
> Duration of incarceration,
> Loss of parents,
> Loss of marital partner,
> Loss of children.

However, a series of significant differences are discovered when the working conditions in the concentration camps are analysed. It has already been pointed out on p. 16 what great differences in work stress existed for the inmates in almost every camp and how significant the type and duration of the work stress were for the survival of the inmates.

The varying work stress to which the three occupational success groups were exposed in the camps was checked in the case of the following stress characteristics:

> Average work severity;
> Frequency of extremely harsh work;
> Work severity at the start and at the end of incarceration.

More or less significant differences can be distinguished for all the characteristics. The findings show that occupationally unsuccessful men were exposed to the most severe work situation in the concentration camp. The detailed results were as follows:

Persons who were unsuccessful in their work following release from imprisonment

were on average exposed to more severe work stress during incarceration than successful and partially successful persons (5% significance in each case);

in addition, they more frequently had to perform extremely severe work (quarry work, etc.) than representatives of the two comparison groups (5% significance in each case).

Persons with good and partial occupational success do *not* differ as regards work severity.

These findings show that of all the characteristics according to which the severity of the persecution period was determined, only the work stress in the concentration camp exhibits a statistical correlation with the present degree of occupational success.

Several points must be borne in mind when interpreting this connection. It would seem logical to assume that the two phenomena are causally related. It would then have to be assumed that extreme physical stress in the concentration camp leads to an inability to find an occupation following release. The duration of the extreme stress is less important in this connection. A more significant fact would seem to be that the inmates were driven to the limits of resistance and achievement. It should also be considered that an excess of forced labour under conditions which were extremely hostile to life might have caused a fundamental and insuperable aversion to work, the performance principle and associated coercive factors.

This attempted explanation, which takes account of both the physical and psychological aspects, seems to us to come closer to the phenomenon of persecution-induced job failure than the one-sided accentuation of physical causes as put forward in particular by early Danish authors (HELLWIG-LARSEN et al., 1952). These authors also observed that ex-inmates suffered from job problems, but they related these chiefly to hunger dystrophy.

At various points in this study we have referred to the fact that psychologically interpretable personality traits are responsible for the degree of adaptation achieved in the concentration camp and also for the severity of the stress that had to be endured. This relationship also applies in the case of the occupational problems.

On pages 33–37 a description was given of the differences in interpersonal behaviour during incarceration. By means of a factor analysis we were able to define a dimension which we called "adaptation to concentration camp conditions" and which is characterized by the poles "successful adaptation" and "unsuccessful adaptation". From this dimension it is possible to derive characteristic differences for the 3 occupational success groups in the post-incarceration period:

Persons who were unsuccessful in their work following release from imprisonment were also much more frequently disturbed and passive in their socio-communicative behaviour even during incarceration than persons who are nowadays successfully employed (1% significance) and also more frequently than persons who are only partially successful in their post-incarceration occupations (5% significance).

There is *no* difference in this respect between successful and partially successful persons.

This finding indicates that men who managed to establish themselves with good or partial success following their release from the camps were more frequently capable of successful interpersonal contact and possessed good adaptability even under the conditions of incarceration. Conversely, the men who were unable to reintegrate properly into the working world displayed poor contact behaviour with significant frequency under the conditions of persecution.

In view of the conditions prevailing in the camps, it is probable that the contact ability detectable even during imprisonment was also in part responsible for the lesser work stress. This is because, in contrast to the other types of stress (duration of incarceration, type of camp, loss of relatives), work stress was the easiest to influence and shape through one's own activity. This is evident from the following remarks made by ex-inmates:

"I used to work in the evenings as a hairdresser for the camp guards and the administrative staff. In this way I was able to earn myself some extra food on the side. Even in Auschwitz, I soon managed to get myself employed again as a hairdresser thanks to my spruce appearance. I have always placed great importance on that."

"When I arrived in Dachau I got myself some material and started painting and making things. As a result, I managed to get myself a special position. I made a model of an old sailing ship and copied paintings by Rubens. The camp commandant often used to sit beside me and watch me work."

"You know, connections, connections, connections — that's all that mattered in the camp (Auschwitz). To start with I made friends with the older Jewish prisoners, and they helped me. Later on, the political prisoners helped me and protected me. Thanks to my connections I always had easy jobs to do. Most of the time I worked in the depot at Auschwitz-Suna. Better than that you couldn't get. The inmates detailed off for this duty were given kid-glove treatment by the SS, who all wanted to get something or other from the store. Later, some political prisoners with whom I was on very good terms, had me transferred to the camp kitchen."

"Far and away the worst thing in the camp (Auschwitz-Birkenau) was the beatings. I was particularly badly off because my size and Jewish nose attracted attention. I was therefore always the first to get the rough treatment. But then one of my pals helped me learn to become a roofer. That made life easier for me."

"The doctor said he would carry out the selection parade in the prison yard. The emaciated prisoners had to stand on the left and the others, who were in better shape, on the right. I was all skin and bones at that time and had almost reached the point where I didn't care any more. The doctor asked me: 'What do you do?' I lied, and said 'I'm a bricklayer.' The doctor said 'Don't worry. Nothing will happen to you'."

The type of work performed during incarceration, as a significant factor in terms of social reintegration, may have been fortuitous in certain cases, but as a statistical parameter it depended — if not exclusively — on the ability to make active contact in the stress situation.

The question that now needs to be asked is whether this ability is correlated with any particular factors from the time preceding persecution, as far as these can be identified in our material and with our methods.

2. Developmental Influences of Childhood and Adolescence

To start with, let us mention the variables which do *not* exhibit any statistically significant differences in the groups studied. The following variables fall into this category:

> Standard of living in parental family;
> General conditions of existence during adolescence;
> Level of education;
> Level of occupational training.

This finding is particularly remarkable in view of the variously expressed assumption that materially tough conditions during childhood are a better preparation for surviving the horrors of concentration camp life than less severe conditions. According to our findings, neither the standard of living of the family nor severe material conditions of existence had any significant role to play in determining the degree of occupational success achieved after release from imprisonment. Education and occupational training likewise had no decisive influence. Higher education or further occupational training neither helped nor hindered the ex-inmate in his attempts to build up a new occupation following the severe stress of incarceration.

The characteristics that typify the emotional relationship of the interviewees with their parents also seem to be irrelevant as regards the ability to adapt to working life again following release from imprisonment. Thus, the following categories do *not* permit any distinction to be made between the 3 occupational success groups in the post-incarceration period:

Emotional relationship to father or mother (good as against bad emotional relationship);

Attitude of father or mother in bringing up their children (cooperative as opposed to authoritarian method of upbringing).

This finding indicates that the ability to adapt and assert oneself later in life does not necessarily depend on the positive or negative emotional relationship between parents and children. The performance dimensions, as covered in the various occupational success groups, thus seem to be dependent on other developmental factors. The variables which proved to be relevant in the present analysis have been listed in Table 68.

The first statistically significant (chi-square test) factor would appear to be the degree of harmony in the original, parental family:

Persecutees who were unsuccessful in their occupations following release

much more frequently had disharmonious family backgrounds than occupationally successful persons (1% significance).

The term "harmonious family conditions" in our group of interviewees designates above all a functioning family with close bonds between the individual members. Therefore, even a patriarchally oriented family in which all its members have strictly prescribed roles to play, but roles they accept, can be harmonious. On the other hand disharmonious families are those whose coherence is threatened or destroyed by the departure or failure of individual members.

The result reported above can also be understood within the terms of this definition. Harmony, stability and order, as exemplified by the family, usually tend to favour success-oriented behaviour more than family disharmony, instability and disorder. An intact family structure seems to promote social adaptability because this is a feature of the normal standard of behaviour in a well ordered family. It is therefore learned early on and not forgotten.

This explanation is supported by the observation that the men who were successful or partially successful in their occupations in the post-incarceration period tended more frequently to come from families with "strong" father personalities.

Persons who were unsuccessful in their occupations following release from incarceration

come more frequently from families on which the father did not exert a very strong influence. In this respect they tend to differ from the two comparison groups (10% significance in each case).

The extent to which he unequivocally and consciously influences all aspects of family life has been evaluated as the criterion for the strength or weakness of the father personality. The strong father is "strong" to the extent that he guarantees order and stability in the family. The emotional side of intrafamily relationships is again ignored here.

Table 68. Personality traits during the developmental period of (A) successful, (B) partially successful and (C) unsuccessful occupational groups (n=133)

Characteristics of personality development	A Successful	B Partially successful	C Unsuccessful
Life in parental family prior to persecution	on the whole harmonious	neutral	on the whole disharmonious
Influence of father on family	strong	strong	weak
Sibling constellation	frequently the eldest child	various	more frequently the youngest of a large number of siblings, next eldest being a sister
Parent's feeling of belonging to society	neutral	frequently fluctuating between minority and majority orientation	neutral
Relationship to authority figures outside the family	usually no authority problems	frequently authority problems	neutral
Relationship to partners of the opposite sex	frequently poor contact	frequently ability to make contact	neutral
Break with parental home	frequently successful	neutral	frequently unsuccessful
Own standard of living prior to persecution	frequently well off materially	neutral	frequently needy

An examination of the external structure of the family reveals some further clues about the dependence of later achievement on early family influences:

Persecutees who are successful in their jobs following release from imprisonment

were more frequently the eldest children in their respective families. In this regard they tend to differ from the persons of the two comparison groups (10% significance in each case).

Persecutees who were not successful in their jobs following release from imprisonment

were more frequently than persons of the two comparison groups the youngest children in their respective families (10% significance in each case). More frequently than the persons of the two comparison groups, the next eldest sibling in their cases was a sister (5% significance in each case).

These findings suggest the following interpretations:

The willingness to adapt and make an effort in extremely severe situations is found most frequently in eldest sons. In conjunction with the stable family structure and the "strong" father personality, which are characteristic for this group, it seems reasonable to assume that eldest sons are particularly ready to assume and perpetuate parental and especially paternal behaviour patterns. This identification would then form the basis for particularly good adaptability and self-assertion which would stand these individuals in good stead, even in externally severe situations, although it would not necessarily be able to prevent intrapsychic problems of adaptation (see p. 167).

There is a clear gap between this sibling constellation and the one characteristic of persons who are unsuccessful in their occupations. The ability to cope with extremely difficult adaptation situations does not seem to be optimally developed in the younger brother of a large group of siblings. Dependence on others and the tendency to allow oneself to become discouraged are presumably more frequently encountered in this particular constellation than self-assuredness and an achievement-oriented sense of responsibility.

In the case of the partially successful group it is striking that they frequently come from families which had an ambivalent relationship with the society in which they lived before the onset of persecution.

Persecutees who were partially successful in their jobs after release from imprisonment more frequently than persons in the other two comparison groups come from families which were in part minority-oriented (10% significance in each case).

Where the families in question were Jewish, they were just in the process of breaking away from the orthodox belief and behaviour patterns of their forefathers and adapting themselves to the prevailing life patterns and Weltanschauung of the majority. In the case of the parents of political persecutees, on the other hand, it is possible to detect a vacillation between majority orientation and orientation around a party or family ideology. It seems reasonable to correlate these initial family conditions with the poor adaptability observed in the individuals in question following their release. The onset of persecution, which was after all carried on in the name of the majority, interrupted the trend towards assimilation and established the ambivalent conflict vis à vis society in a way which is typical for socially non-integrated persons. In the case of the nowadays partially successful individuals, this ambivalent conflict manifests itself in the contradiction between an accepting and rejecting attitude towards society and its representatives (see p. 168).

Together with these findings, which point to the importance of early family influences on later occupational success, it is possible to detect personality characteristics that become manifest only in the later developmental period. The occupationally successful persons and those without success differ in the following respects:

Persecutees who are successful in their jobs following release broke away from the parental home sooner than the persons who are unsuccessful in their jobs (5% significance);
already before the start of persecution were more successful in their work than persons who are nowadays unsuccessful (5% significance);
had a better self-made standard of living than the present-day occupational failures (10% significance).

These findings lead us to suppose that basic work attitudes as they exist today in ex-inmates were already observable as trends before persecution started. Interviewees who were successful in their occupations following release from the concentration camps also tended to be success-oriented in their work even prior to persecution. In this connection it is important to note that men who had early on with parental protection gained independence to lead a life of their own, proved adaptable and capable of asserting themselves even under extreme conditions. In contrast, men who did not succeed until relatively late in life in breaking away from the parental home tended to be less self-assertive both during incarceration and after their release.

Here we have an indication of a personality characteristic which seems to some extent to be constant throughout the entire life history of the individual and which can be detected even in extreme situations such as that represented by persecution. In general terms this characteristic can be designated as a tendency to gain independence and become achievement-oriented. Where this tendency is missing in our sample, we find a corresponding trend towards dependence on others, passiveness and poor achievement-orientation.

Hints of these two divergent attitudes can be detected in the interviewees in the developmental period before the onset of persecution. They then come clearly to the fore under the influence of persecution and incarceration and play a large part in determining the adaptation after release and the present life of the persons in question.

Summary

1. The occupational problems of former persecutees have not been discussed in detail in the literature published to date on concentration camps. The initial scientific conclusions on the occupational damage caused by concentration camp conditions were arrived at to a large extent under the impression of the catastrophic physical state of the persecutees.

Nowadays it can no longer be claimed that these earlier observations are exclusively valid. A comprehensive picture is not obtained until the job situation of ex-persecutees is seen in conjunction with the overall problem of social reintegration.

2. In purely descriptive terms, the following features of the present occupational situation can be stressed:

After release, ex-persecutees tend not to return to a manual job or trade which they pursued earlier.

About half (49%) of the male persecutees exhibit typical disturbances in the course of reintegrating into the working world.

More than one third (38%) of ex-persecutees now live in economic circumstances which can be described as a state of "material need".

Relatively few persecutees (14%) make use of the opportunity to take an early pension.

More characteristic than the avoidance of a work situation is the attempt to achieve social reintegration in and through one's occupation. Consequently, ex-inmates do not typically exhibit a neurotic desire to be awarded a pension.

3. According to a factor analysis, it is possible to distinguish between three forms of occupational reintegration following release.

Persecutees who are now self-assertive and successful in their work.

Persecutees who now have problems with regard to work and who are only partially successful in their occupations.

Persecutees who proved unable to settle down to a job after release and who therefore remained unsuccessful.

These three occupational groups are distributed uniformly among persecutees who were born in Poland or Germany; those who now live in Germany or abroad (Israel, New York); those who were persecuted on racial or political grounds.

4. It is not possible to detect any clear correlations between occupational success and late physical injury. There is no distinction between the three occupational groups, even on the basis of the persecution-dependent disability ratings. However, the occupationally unsuccessful persons lodged significantly more appeals against the established pension assessment.

The purely psychological impairment of the ability to work, which resulted from the stress of incarceration, does not always seem to have been fully recognized or compensated by the various diagnosing doctors and pension agencies.

5. There are characteristic correlations between age and occupational success following release from imprisonment.

Particularly successful as well as particularly unsuccessful men are on average older than men who were only partially successful in their jobs. This finding can be further differentiated on the basis of individual case analyses.

Older interviewees who are now successfully engaged in an occupation were for the most part success- and achievement-oriented even prior to persecution and during incarceration. Younger interviewees who are nowadays successful in their work stand out because of their extreme restlessness and compulsive drive.

Older persons who now have no success in their jobs were usually strongly identified with their occupation prior to persecution. After release from the camps they lacked the courage to establish a new occupational existence. Younger interviewees who are now unsuccessful in their work are characterized by an unrealistic assessment of their own worth and ability and also by lack of activity and initiative.

Ex-persecutees who are only partially successful in their work are nowadays generally at odds with their occupation. This state of conflict expresses their difficulties in relating to society. This attitude is particularly frequent in younger interviewees.

6. The more severe psychic impairment suffered by the persons who are unsuccessful in their occupations is demonstrated by the average high frequency of symptoms. In addition, it is found that these persons are more severely affected by all three basic forms of psychic disturbance. The partially successful group is least impaired in this respect.

7. The activity developed in coming to terms with the environment following release from imprisonment varies within the three occupational groups in a characteristic way. In the initial adaptation phase (up to 1946) there is still no difference between the three occupational groups in this respect. But already around 1949/50 men with an unsuccessful job record were significantly less active in their attempts to adapt to their environment than persons who are successful or partially successful in their occupations. The occupationally successful persons are the only ones to sustain this active adaptation to the environment during the following 10 years (up to 1960).

There are interesting differences in the direct form taken by this engagement with the environment:

Persons who are successful in their work tend to adopt a more inhibited and controlled manner of getting rid of their aggression.

Persons who are partially successful in their jobs more frequently exhibit signs of a stable and balanced manner of handling aggression.

On the other hand, persons who have no success in their jobs tend to be explosive, uncontrolled or entirely repress their aggressiveness.

8. Occupational failure and disturbances of interpersonal contact as a rule occur together. The people who have no success in their jobs are very frequently also socially isolated. On the other hand, it is not possible to detect any significant correlations between occupational success and the emotional attitude towards other people. Trust and mistrust are approximately uniformly distributed in persons with or without occupational success.

9. Occupational failure frequently occurs in ex-persecutees in conjunction with disturbances in the sphere of family life. These manifest themselves in the form of an unsatisfactory relationship with one's marital partner or in an inadequate, usually authoritarian attitude toward one's children.

10. In order to find out what causes the differences in the ability to adapt to the working world after release from imprisonment, we examined the correlation with various types of stress during incarceration. It was found that neither the duration of the incarceration nor the severity of the camp, or the extent to which members of the family were lost, provide any clue to the work behaviour following release. The only significant correlation was between the work stress in the concentration camp and the occupational success following release: Men who had to perform severe and extremely severe work during the period of persecution usually failed to adapt to an occupation following release.

This finding must be considered together with the observation that the men who remained unsuccessful in their occupations following release were more frequently characterized even during incarceration by a passive adaptation to the camp conditions.

It seems logical to assume that the underlying cause here is to be sought in personality traits which had already developed during childhood and youth and which are responsible for the success or failure achieved in social adaptation.

11. The most striking differences between the persons who are nowadays successfully employed and the two comparison groups can be summarized as follows: Family life in the parental home was mostly harmonious; the father exerted a strong influence on the family. These persons were usually the eldest children. They quite frequently had problems in their ability to get on with girls. On the other hand, their relationship with persons of authority was usually problem-free. As a rule they managed to break away early on and successfully from their families and soon attained a high standard of living of their own.

Persons who managed to attain only a partial measure of success in their occupations following release are characterized by the following data from the developmental period: They come from families which frequently fluctuated between affinity to a social minority group or a social majority group. Quite frequently they display critical attitudes towards person in authority, but in their associations with partners of the opposite sex they are able to make contact and have no problems.

Persons who are nowadays unsuccessful in their occupations are distinguished from the others by the following conspicuous features in the developmental period: They more frequently come from a disharmonious family background. The father played a subordinate role in the family. Frequently they were the youngest of a large number of children and were directly preceded in the order of siblings by a sister. They were either late in managing to break away from the parental home or did not achieve this step at all. For the most part they are unable to look after their own material well-being.

CHAPTER 8

Marriage and Family

Outline of Problem

In the two preceding chapters we described various aspects of the problem of social reintegration. We deliberately refrained from analysing the marriage and family life of former concentration camp inmates because this highly personal sphere of interpersonal contact needs to be studied separately. This area of human relations can be important in that, under certain circumstances, it may be possible through marriage to make contact with society or at least to recover from the destructive experiences of incarceration more easily within the marital partnership. Therefore, this problem will be examined in more detail in a chapter to itself. We are concerned chiefly with the two following questions: What effect does incarceration have on the marital partnership and on the relationships with a person's own children?

In this connection it is above all necessary to clarify the typical manifestations and the special conditions of the family life of former concentration camp inmates.

Should it be found that there are any specific marital and family problems associated with former persecutees, the next question to ask is: What stress criteria are responsible for these? In addition, it is necessary to clarify the role played in present-day family life by pre-persecution developmental influences.

The examination of these problems is based on a special random sample of 165 interviewees who were married at the time of the study. This group comprises 75.4% of the total random sample; 19 ex-inmates (8.7%) are widowed, 15 (6.8%) divorced, and 11 (5.0%) were single before persecution started and remained single after release from imprisonment — none of these have been considered here.

Nine Catholic priests (4.1%) have also been left out, for obvious reasons.

A factor analysis was made for the 165 persons using 45 personality characteristics that seemed relevant for this purpose. The characteristics (see Appendix) include data on marital and family life as well as on the psychic and social spheres. The factors which are revealed by this analysis to some extent repeat constellations of characteristics which have already been discovered in connection with the analysis of the psychic state and the forms of contact of ex-persecutees. They will not be discussed again in this context. On the other hand "family relationships following release" constitutes a new and psychologically important factor. It will be discussed in detail below. The interdependence between this factor and other psychological data is tested with the aid of individual correlations.

In addition to the results of this factor analysis, the family problems are investigated on the basis of certain concentration-camp-specific marital groups. The following groupings are used:

1. Marriages that survived the persecution period intact.
2. Second marriages following release.
3. First marriages following release.

The analysis of these groups is illustrated by descriptions of typical individual case histories.

I. Family Relationships of Ex-Persecutees

1. Harmony of Family Life

The dimension of "family relationships following release from imprisonment", which was obtained by factor analysis and which is relevant for the inmates' present marital and family life, is constituted by the following characteristics (Table 69):

Table 69. Factor of "family relationships following release from imprisonment"

Characteristic	"harmonious family life" (Pole A)	"disharmonious family life" (Pole B)	Loading
Relationship with own children	undisturbed	disturbed	0.63
Relationship of marital partners with each other	good	bad	0.62
Family life	on the whole harmonious	on the whole disharmonious	0.62
Attitude towards bringing up children	cooperative	authoritarian	0.60
Role behaviour in the family	determining role	subordinate role	0.54
Number of children after release	marriages mainly with children	mainly childless marriages	0.45

This factor with the pole "harmonious family life" contrasted with "disharmonious family life" characterizes several fundamental relationships and behavioural attitudes in the marital and family lives of former persecutees.

"Harmonious family life" (Pole A) is revealed above all by a relatively undisturbed relationship of the interviewees with their children. This guiding variable indicates the great importance of children in the present family life of former persecutees. It is not merely that the harmonious families have more children than the disharmonious ones, but also that they are much better able to adjust to their children, and this only seems to be possible if the two marital partners enjoy a harmonious relationship with each other. The children thus constitute an important criterion of marital harmony. In addition, they characterize an attitude to life in which the future — all faith in which was destroyed during incarceration — once more has a role to play.

The positive pole of the dimension "family relationships" denotes the positive attempt of ex-inmates to give new meaning to life, within and through the family, despite all the stressful experiences.

"Disharmonious family life" (Pole B), on the other hand, is determined by features which are typical of an unsuccessful marital partnership and a family life which is prone to trouble and disruption. The persecutees who fall into this category for the most part do not have any children. Any children that may be present cannot be adequately included in the already conflict-ridden partnership. Often they directly reflect the disturbed relationship between the marital partners. Within the families these persons tend to be passive and evasive. They do not live up to their role-specific obligations and duties.

The presence of children, for example, in a marriage very definitely provides new goals to aim for in life and forces one to look ahead to the future, but all this is missing in the disharmonious marriage, and for this reason it is very much more difficult for the persons involved to cope with the memories of their concentration camp past.

Of course, between these extremes there are a large number of individual ways of shaping marital and family life, and these will be discussed in detail further below.

The distribution of the 6 characteristics among the 165 interviewees yields the following pattern:

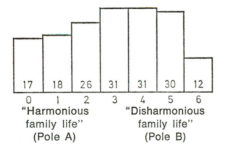

Fig. 18. Distribution of 165 persons over the 6 characteristics of the factor "family relationships following release from imprisonment"

A completely harmonious family life (all 6 characteristics of Pole A) is exhibited by 17 (10.3%) of the married persons. In contrast, the family life of 12 (7.3%) of the interviewees is completely disharmonious. When the scale is dichotomized, 92 of those interviewed (55.7%) tended towards the pole of "harmonious family life" and 73 (44.3%) towards the pole of "disharmonious family life". However, the concept of marital harmony cannot be regarded as an "absolute criterion". This category also, of course, includes marriages in which more or less obvious tensions exist. Nevertheless, it seems justified to regard all marital partnerships as "harmonious" in which there is an active exchange of views between the marital partners and where it is thus possible for conflicts to be settled out in the open.

2. Differences between the Groups of Persecutees

Marital and family problems are examined in our sample group of married persecutees according to 5 sociological characteristics.

As regards sex, age, reason for persecution, origin and present country of residence, *no* statistically significant differences can be found in the "family relationships following release".

This means that for the success of persecutees' marriages in the post-incarceration period, the sex of the persecutees, their age, the reasons why they were persecuted and where they now live are irrelevant factors.

This finding is all the more significant since the sociological characteristics in themselves imply differing stress indices (see the chapter on the stress of incarceration p. 25 et seq.), although these are likewise not decisively important for the harmony of the marital partnership.

In discussing what external characteristics are important for the persecutees' marriages, we should mention at this point the date on which the marriage was concluded. Usually the date of the marriage is discussed in the literature (Trautmann, 1961; Klein, Zellermayer and Shanan, 1963; v. Baeyer, Häfner and Kisker, 1964) in the light of the phenomenon known as the "premature marriage", i.e. the precipitous entry into marriage by the persecutees following their release from the camps. It was mainly Trautmann (1961) who regarded the speed with which these marriages were concluded as a negative condition for their success. The marriages which came about as a "reaction to a catastrophe", as a result of the "feeling of panic engendered by being lost and hopelessly alone in the world", often turn out later to be conflict-ridden unsatisfactory partnerships according to Trautmann. V. Baeyer, Häfner and Kisker (1964) describe this state of affairs as a "perpetuation of disturbances in interpersonal relations in the form of an institutionalized permanent conflict".

Our material also confirms the phenomenon of the early marriage, but it does not reveal any definite correlation with marital harmony. Even marriages which were concluded very soon after the inmates' release from imprisonment can turn out to be harmonious partnerships.

It is remarkable, however, that there are differences between the sexes with regard to the date of marriage in the post-incarceration period. Women tend more frequently than men to marry early. Of the 36 female persecutees who married after their release, 23 (64%) did so within the first two years. On the other hand, in the same period, only 40 (39%) out of 102 men married. This finding can be interpreted in conjunction with the results given in the preceding chapters ("Late-appearing damage to health", "Fundamental forms of psychic disturbance", "Contact with fellow humans and society"). In these chapters it has already been established that women were much more affected in every aspect of their being by the events of persecution than were the male persecutees. Their rapid marriage soon after their release can be seen as an attempt to attain a certain degree of stability by taking a husband and establishing a family. While the men chiefly sought reintegration into society via their work, the women attempted to achieve this by assuming marital and family responsibilities. However, the stronger family orientation of women, which is responsible among other things for the "premature marriages", cannot be taken as a criterion for the success or failure of the partnership. Other conditions must be sought to explain the differences in marital behaviour.

3. Contact Outside the Family

If the marital problems are considered in connection with other interpersonal relationships going beyond the close ties of the family, then we find a series of significant clues. We will start by examining the social contact behaviour outside the family as it was described in the preceding chapter in the dimensions "ability to cope with society" and "attitude to fellowmen". The following correlations are found:

Persecutees who nowadays enjoy a "harmonious family life"
are more frequently "socially integrated";
are more frequently active in seeking contact with others.

Correspondingly, persecutees whose family life is nowadays "disharmonious"
are more frequently "socially isolated" (1% significance);
more frequently "reject" their fellowmen (5% significance).

Happy family relationships thus go together more frequently with successful contact with the outside world.

This finding emphasizes the already mentioned importance of the general ability to make social contact. This not only permits satisfactory relationships to be established outside the family, but also guarantees largely stress-free marital and family life.

Contrasted with this, we find a central impairment of all social functions which does not permit satisfactory marital life nor successful contact with the outside world. However, persecutees who were predominantly sociable and readily made contact prior to incarceration exhibit a special variant in the process of encapsulation from the outside world. This particular behavioural pattern can best be described as "shared loneliness". In this case, all social needs are directed towards the marital partner and must be fulfilled by him or her. The ability to seek social contact with other persons is by and large impaired but an attempt is made to maintain this ability through one single link. The following case description will serve to exemplify this situation:

A German Jew, who is now living with a non-Jewish wife in Germany, believes that he became a hermit because of the experience of incarceration. He is nowadays completely isolated from the outside world and has no social contact at all. For example, he almost never talks with his neighbours: "We exchange greetings, but not much more." For him his marriage is all that there is to help him overcome the concentration camp past. His wife quietly and tenderly looks after him and helps him regain his self-confidence. He says of her: "She is my life."

This is an example of a harmonious marital relationship in which the wife actually satisfies the communicative needs of the persecuted husband. But, there are also cases in which the marital partnership is unsatisfactory and therefore cannot span the unbridgeable gap between the persecutee and the outside world.

However, family relationships are not only correlated with interpersonal contact in the broader sense but also with job success, particularly in the case of the male persecutees. For these, reintegration into society is essentially determined by the degree of success achieved in their respective occupations. It is found that successful marriage is coupled with a certain degree of occupational success, i.e. here too, a general willingness and ability to adapt are positive conditions for a successful working life (see chapter on "Occupational reintegration").

Successful social reintegration and a moderate amount of occupational success are usually reflected in a good standard of living. Of course, the material situation plays an important role in marital life as well. It is a better guarantee for the stability of marital and family relationships if the family enjoys material security. Financial worries about the basic needs for existence can impose severe strain on a marriage, bring latent conflicts to the surface or intensify any existing problems.

4. Psychic Condition

Family and marital relationships can be differentiated further still when the correlations with the present psychic condition of the inmates are examined.

As expected, the symptoms described in the chapter on "Basic forms of psychic disturbance" (see p. 101 et seq.) which were found to be concentration-camp-specific, are also particularly important for the failure of marital and family relationships.

Persecutees whose family life is nowadays "disharmonious" are more frequently
resigned and despairing (1% significance);
apathetic-inhibited (1% significance);
aggressive-irritable (5% significance).

These correlations indicate the interaction between the psychic condition and the course of family life. Psychically ill persons more frequently have unsettled marriages.

Conversely, of course, problems and misunderstandings within the family must also be seen as factors that intensify existing psychological disturbances.

Individual cases can be used to show that the three above-mentioned basic psychic disturbances manifest themselves in different ways within the life of the family.

The following remark, made by a female Polish Jew who is now married and living in Germany, can be regarded as typical for representatives of the factor "resignation and despair":

"When you've been through an experience like that, nothing makes sense any more. My husband can't understand me, but I don't even have the strength to argue with him."

The specific effect of an "apathetic-inhibited" attitude on family life is characterized by the following statement made by a political persecutee of German birth.

"Now that I am out of the camp, I find that sex no longer plays a role in our marriage — perhaps because I have become generally more listless. Often I can't even get on with myself. So I let my wife go out by herself if she wants to."

In contrast to these last two examples, the basic "aggressive-irritable" disturbance tends to be revealed in the open tension between the members of the family. The following remark by a female Polish Jew typifies this situation:

"My husband often complains about my outbursts of rage. So then I make an effort to control myself again. Even the children have to suffer when I blow up. I can't even go over their homework with them because this means continuous arguing."

The examples quoted not only bring out clearly the interaction between psychic disturbances and family life, they also touch on the importance of sexuality. The following finding bears out this correlation:

Persecutees whose family life is nowadays "disharmonious"
more frequently suffer sexual disturbances (5% significance).

But it is no longer possible to establish unequivocally to what extent the present sexual problems (disturbed potency, frigidity, sexual fear, menstrual problems, etc.) are the direct results of the incarceration in a concentration camp, as is assumed by a number of authors (TARGOWLA, 1955; TRAUTMANN, 1961; v. BAEYER, HÄFNER and KISKER, 1964; HERMANN and THYGESEN, 1964, etc.). If this is the case, the sexual problems of the persecutees would be a poor condition for a satisfactory married life. In addition, there is the danger that the disturbances would not be removed in a conflict-ridden marriage, but would merely be intensified.

However, one cannot exclude the possibility that the sexual problems nowadays described by the persecutees merely reflect an already troubled marital situation.

It is interesting to note that purely somatic illnesses (see chapter on "Late-Appearing Damage to Health", p. 48) do not correlate with marital and family harmony. The marriages of persecutees can still be very harmonious even if serious illness is present.

5. Persecution Stress

Having described marriage and family life in relation to contact outside the family and also to the psychic state of the former persecutees, we must now examine in particular what conditions may have caused or at least co-determined the family relationships. We will start by examining the stress characteristics of the period of incarceration. No statistically significant differences in family relationships are caused by work severity, camp severity, duration of incarceration and loss of family (father, mother and siblings).

These findings are surprising, since the degree of harshness of camp conditions and even more so the severity of the work situation have played an important role in almost all the areas discussed so far.

Nevertheless, these stress criteria are in no way detectably correlated with the later success or failure of a marital partnership.

There is, however, a clear difference between the two married groups on the basis of their behaviour during incarceration. This difference is revealed by the factor of "adaptation to concentration camp conditions" (see chapter on "Stresses Imposed by Concentration Camp Incarceration", p. 34).

Persecutees whose family life is nowadays "harmonious"
more frequently achieved "successful adaptation to concentration camp conditions".

Correspondingly, persecutees whose family life is nowadays "disharmonious"
more frequently failed to achieve "adaptation to concentration camp conditions" (0.1% significance).

This finding makes it clear that persons who manage to cope with extreme stress situations are also better able to handle the problems of family life after release from imprisonment. There is obviously a certain amount of constancy in certain social behaviour patterns. This is also borne out by the clear correlations which have been found between "adaptation to the concentration camp" and the relationships with other people following release (see chapter on "Contact with Fellow Humans and Society", p. 139).

It seems reasonable to seek the origins of these different ways of tackling the environment in earlier stages of the inmates' personality development. The following finding indicates this possible interpretation:

Persecutees whose family life is nowadays "harmonious"
more frequently held fast to acquired standards of behaviour during incarceration (5%
significance).

This means to say that persons who now lead a more or less satisfactory family life managed, in the concentration camp, to oppose the destructive influences of camp life and to orient themselves according to criteria which had played a determining role in their lives even before the onset of persecution. This also indicates that the attitude which we have called adaptation to concentration camp conditions by no means involves an "inner" adaptation in the sense that acquired behavioural standards are dropped. On the contrary, the people who achieved external adaptation, the clever ones and the active ones, were only able to attain all this under conditions of extreme stress because some form of inner support (political or religious) existed from an earlier time in their lives.

This continuity of behavioural patterns throughout the entire life history is even more clearly revealed by a study of early developmental influences.

6. Developmental Influences of Childhood and Adolescence

A series of significant findings can be listed concerning the correlation between the present family situation and the experience of life in the parental family:

Persecutees who nowadays enjoy "harmonious family life"
more frequently lived in harmonious parental families before persecution (1% significance),
more frequently got on well with siblings (1% significance),
more frequently came from families which stuck together with even more determination in difficult situations (5% significance).

The parental family is thus found to be a relatively stable entity in the case of persons who later themselves led happy married lives. Even under stressful environmental influences (e.g. unemployment, death of a member of the family) the family bonds are strengthened. This situation seems to be an important condition for the later orientation of family life. The mother plays an extremely important role here:

In the case of persecutees who now enjoy "harmonious family life"
the mother more frequently had a strong influence on the family (5% significance);
the emotional relationship with the mother was more frequently good (5% significance);
the attitude of the mother to bringing up children was more frequently cooperative (5%
significance);
the attitude of the father to bringing up children was more frequently cooperative (10%
significance).

In agreement with corresponding remarks made in other chapters, the influence exerted by the mother is the main factor affecting later development. In keeping with her role within the family community, which includes bringing up the children and satisfying their emotional needs, the maternal example serves as a model for later family behaviour. Since it is the primary function of a mother to maintain and integrate the family, it is understandable that the importance of the father recedes into the background here.

Already in childhood and during adolescence there seems to be a correlation between contact outside the family and a positive attitude towards family life:

Persecutees whose family life is now "harmonious"
more frequently enjoyed undisturbed contact with persons of the same age and sex (1%
significance).

It is found that persons who later managed to lead a harmonious family life not only had good relationships with siblings but were also more successful in making contact with persons in their own age group. These early forms of contact are to be seen as a preliminary stage leading up to partnership with a person of the opposite sex. It must be remembered here that these early contacts did not prove relevant for later relationships outside the family (see chapter on "Contact with Fellow Humans and Society", p. 140).

The following finding rounds off the foregoing remarks:

In the case of persecutees who now lead a "harmonious family life"
the psychic and social development was harmonious (5% significance).

The harmony of the parental family guarantees an undisturbed childhood and adolescence; this has a decisive effect on the formation of personality and provides a person with a healthy opportunity to find his own identity. A clear understanding of one's identity in turn seems to be one of the most important conditions for a mature partnership.

II. Types of Marriage of Former Persecutees

The dimension "family relationships" described in the preceding section referred to all persons who are now married. If one takes a closer look at this group it is found that it constitutes what is in formal terms a very heterogeneous random sample. We can differentiate between three groups of marriages which are defined by the date of the marriage in regard to the period of persecution:

A) Intact marriages:
   Persons who were married before incarceration and whose marriage was still intact at the time of the study (n=27).

B) Second marriages:
   Persons whose first marriage (concluded before incarceration) was terminated by the death of their marital partner in a concentration camp and who entered into a second marriage following their release (n=37).

C) First marriages:
   Persons who were single before incarceration and who married after their release (n=101).

To start with, in this second section, we will stress some of the fundamental differences in this group which failed to stand out when all the married persons were considered together. A short characterization of the individual marriage groups according to their sociological structure is followed, by way of illustration, by the description of several case histories. Table 70 provides an initial overview of the sociological characteristics of the three groups:

Table 70. Sociological distribution of the three marriage groups

Characteristics	A (n=27)	B (n=37)	C (n=101)
Sex:			
male	21 (77.8%)	28 (75.7%)	74 (73.3%)
female	6 (22.2%)	9 (24.3%)	27 (26.7%)
Age in 1960:			
up to 50	3 (11.1%)	16 (43.2%)	77 (76.2%)
51 and over	24 (88.9%)	21 (56.8%)	24 (23.8%)
Reasons for persecution and origin:			
German Jews	10 (37%)	6 (16.2%)	30 (29.7%)
Eastern European Jews (Poland)	6 (22.3%)	30 (81.1%)	52 (51.5%)
Political persecutees	11 (40.7%)	1 (2.7%)	19 (18.8%)
Contry of residence			
Germany	23 (85.2%)	22 (59.5%)	62 (61.4%)
Israel & USA	4 (14.8%)	15 (40.5%)	39 (68.8%)

In our description of the marriage groups, only the characteristic features have been stressed in each case. As regards methodology, it should further be noted that the differences in sex constitute the only feature which does not differentiate the marriage groups because the distribution corresponds approximately to that of the overall study sample. The differences are quoted for the sake of completeness.

1. Marriages that Remained Intact

Out of a total of 84 marriages concluded before persecution started, 27 (31%) were still intact after the inmates' release. As Table 70 shows, the people in question here are predominantly in the older age bracket (over 50) and had reached the stage, before the start of persecution, where they could marry and have a family.

The majority of the persons who managed to keep their marriages intact are political and racial persecutees of German origin. The main reason for this composition is probably to be seen in the different stress conditions encountered by the various groups of persecutees during incarceration.

In the chapter on "Stresses Imposed by Concentration Camp Incarceration" (see p. 26) we have already mentioned that although the political and racial persecutees of German origin had to tolerate longer overall periods of persecution, they faced easier conditions in the concentration camps than the Polish Jews. The first group of persecutees was, furthermore, less affected by the loss of members of their families.

In addition, in the case of the political persecutees, it was usually the case that only one of the marital partners suffered persecution. As a result, these persons had a much better chance of returning to an intact family and this had a very great influence on the subjective experience of persecution.

A further characteristic of this group is the present country of residence. The majority of the persons represented here are now living in Germany. This observation is not all that surprising considering that the political persecutees usually did not think of emigrating and the racial persecutees, because of their advanced average age, were less willing to contemplate starting all over again in a strange country.

An examination of the correlations of this group of marriages with the factor of "family relationships" which has been described above revealed that in each case 50% of the persons represent the positive pole "harmonious" or the negative pole "disharmonious" family life.

An additional comparison made between the state of the marital partnership at the time of the study and in the period preceding persecution did not reveal any significant differences. This shows that the marital harmony or disharmony did not undergo any specific change as a result of the incarceration but instead, despite the long separation, remained as it had been before the start of persecution.

This is remarkable in the light of two assumptions that one might make. On the one hand, it would seem reasonable to assume that the extreme suffering which incarceration caused, not only for the inmate but also for the non-incarcerated partner, would have brought the married couple even closer together. According to this interpretation, each day following the incarcerated partner's liberation would be regarded as a gift and would give each partner the ability to cope with minor and trivial everyday differences after both had survived the "big test". On the other hand, one could equally well assume — and this view is hinted at by the poets and writers (CAYROL, 1959) among the former inmates of concentration camps — that the brutal reality of concentration camp life would have killed all intimate interpersonal relationships, especially the ability for marital love and affection.

Both assumptions are at variance with the statistical facts as measured in accordance with our criteria of marital harmony. In other words, the married persons got on with each other and loved each other in just the same way after the concentration camp experience as before.

In this connection, the children born after the inmates' release can be regarded as a final important aspect of the marital partnerships.

In 18 (67%) of the intact marriages no more children were born. In the remaining 9 marriages (33%), at the most only one more child was born in the post-concentration-camp period. The low number of children is understandable because the average age of the interviewees at the time of the study was 52. Since, naturally, it is hardly likely that any more children will be born to persons of this age, it is not possible to determine the effects of incarceration on the birth rate in this group.

The special problems of the intact marriage can probably best be demonstrated by considering the example of the political persecutees. In retrospect these regarded their persecution and incarceration as a consistent consequence of their resistance to the Nazis. In those cases where the political activity was to a large extent co-determined by the peculiarities of an ideological personality (see the chapter on "Weltanschauung and Concentration Camp Incarceration", p. 211), these persons plunged hectically into politics again after their release with the feeling that they were fulfilling an historic commitment. Thus the successes achieved by these persons remained exclusively restricted to the area outside the family. Again, the marriage had to take second place, as it had done before persecution started. In fact, the marriages were actually concluded on condition that the political work would take precedence over personal needs. Or to put it more precisely, with the ideologists in mind: the pursuit of ideologically motivated political activity is the most personal need that one could have and, in comparison, all normal "personal" needs are of secondary importance.

The following case of a politically persecuted married couple will serve to illustrate these remarks:

Mr. M. was one of a large family living in extremely straitened circumstances. The father, who was himself politically active, was hardly able to earn enough for the bare necessities of life from his job as a factory worker. "Hard-up is not the word for it" said Mr. M., "most of the time we starved."

Looking back, Mr. M. remembers his childhood as a drab and joyless period in his life. The only thing he had to hold on to was his political motivation and the goal of stamping out class conflicts, with which he was confronted even as a young child. In 1919 he joined the youth organisation of the Independent Social Democratic Party. It was in this group that he got to know his wife. It was very important to him that she was the daughter of an old party comrade. This not only guaranteed that they would both share the same views; it also gave him his sole chance of establishing a relationship with his wife without having to give up a life which was almost exclusively devoted to the party.

After spending a short time in custody for being a Communist youth leader, he devoted himself even more intensely to politics. He did not allow himself any time for his private life and gave every free minute to the party. At the same time he prevailed upon his future wife, who had up until then evaded any decision, to marry him. Even the birth of a daughter did nothing to alter his intense devotion to the party and this, according to Mr. M., was accepted by his wife.

However, Mrs. M. admits that she herself did not really have any particular political beliefs, but instead merely espoused her husband's ideas. She found it difficult to do without her husband's company in their free time. According to her she accepted this more out of love for her husband than out of love for any political concept. She admired her husband's consistency, his purposiveness and his courage. However, after two years of marriage the pedagogic manner in which her husband always tried to force his views on her became a threat for Frau M. She started to have arguments with her husband, mostly over trivial matters, which he usually won because he had a greater facility with words. Finally, she felt her personality was being so suppressed by her husband that she got him to agree to a provisional separation for a trial period. When her husband wrote about one year later and told her that he had found another woman, the separation became unbearable for her and she decided to go back to her husband even though she was far from certain that the marriage would work out.

Mr. M. achieved his first successes after he had been on a political training course in Russia. He was elected to the provincial parliament (Landtag) as a representative of the German communist party and he took over the editorship of a workers' newspaper.

In January 1933 he was arrested for the first time by the Nazis. Although he had been warned and his wife had made preparations for his escape, he felt he could not leave "his workers" in the lurch at a time like that. In February 1933 he was arrested. Shortly afterwards his wife was also taken away and was given 4 months in jail. After her release she immediately got in touch with a number of influential people to try and get her husband released as well. When he was set free Mr. M. stated that, even outside prison, he would do everything in his power to help his imprisoned comrades. He was immediately re-arrested and spent the next few years until January 1940 behind bars. Again, as a result of his wife's intervention, he was released and drafted into the army (Wehrmacht). After spending two years as a PoW in Russia he finally returned to his family.

A short while after his return he set himself up in business as a carpenter; but when his firm grew so large that he would have had to take on workers from outside, he gave up his independence saying that he did not wish to exploit anyone. Up until the time that he became unable to work, he was employed in someone else's firm as a cabinet-maker. When he had to stop working, Mr. M. became chairman of several concentration camp organisations to which he now devotes all his time. Even today he still remains true to his earlier political convictions.

Mrs. M. describes her present marital and family situation as a "small harmonious unit in which one is protected and can forget the past". On her relationship with her husband she said: "There is a strong comradely link between my husband and myself and it does not exclude a marital relationship." Nevertheless, she now asks herself the question: "Did we let life pass us by? Wasn't our marriage really just a working partnership? Wasn't it always: work for the party instead of relaxing, work for the party instead of taking a Sunday walk, work for the party instead of . . . to be honest, really living?"

This marriage is a good example of a marital partnership sustained by the common views held by the two partners. From the beginning, the husband regarded his political activity as of paramount importance and for him his marriage and family were peripheral matters. The marriage was concluded at a time when Mr. M. stepped up the intensity of his political work under pressure and was therefore hardly in a position to consider the personal needs of his wife. She is primarily a discussion partner with equal rights and, at least during the first years of the marriage, she co-operated in an extremely active manner with her husband in fighting for political ideals. However, this "working partnership" could only come about because the wife was very ready to adapt and because she subordinated herself completely to the wishes of her husband "less out of love for the ideals than out of love for him". Here is already evidence of the decisive break in the intimate relationship of the partners with each other. To a large extent Mrs. M. had to forego fulfilment of her wishes and needs inside the marriage while her husband was completely absorbed in his outward-oriented activity and did not feel that this ideological one-sidedness was in any way a fault. This marriage was kept intact above all by the links of comradeship between the two marital partners. The emotional personal relationship of the partners receded into the background.

However, our sample group did not just include political inmates whose attitude was marked by the characteristics of an ideological personality, which will be discussed in the following chapter. Alienation of the marital partners can also occur for other, e.g. occupational reasons, without any signs of this ideological attitude. The following example illustrates this state of affairs:

Mr. C. was born in 1907, the eldest of 4 siblings. In his family, in his home village and later at high school he was always regarded as someone "special". His superiority and his intelligence made him an independent and sought-after "outsider" in his class. He knew how to assert his leadership abilities not only intellectually but also physically. As an adolescent and later as an adult, he placed great value on being able to think and act freely without being influenced. When the village priest, who was impressed with his talents, arranged for him to study theology, he accepted. One year later, however, he decided to become a lawyer. He says he never regretted this decision.

After completing his studies Mr. C. became a lawyer and took a job in a National Socialist ministry. However, he soon came into conflict with the religious policy pursued by the regime. After serious arguments in which he did not mince his words, he was dismissed from the staff of the ministry in 1934. He was only expelled from the party after he had made deliberately anti-Nazi remarks. Despite threats and promises he never again put his knowledge at the service of the Nazis' policies of violence. On the contrary, he made use of his position as an independent lawyer and appeared for the defence in various political trials in order to show the regime how totally impotent and incompetent it was. He knew all the time that his life was at stake if he displayed even the slightest weakness.

After several short periods of imprisonment, Mr. C. was interned for five months in Dachau in 1942/43. Because of his alertness, he was skillfully able to avoid being sentenced during any of these periods of detention. He developed a sixth sense for what was going to happen like some sly old fox. Looking back, he regards the period he spent in detention as the "school of life". He used this time to give inmates legal training in how to behave in life-threatening situations. Mr. C. cannot remember any time during which his initiative and self-assurance deserted him. His religious faith, his almost incessant activity and his adapt-ability enabled him to survive in the camps. Sometimes his behaviour and attitude even earned him the liking of his enemies. On his release from Dachau he asked an SS man how he should behave outside. Mr. C. is now convinced that the SS man saved his life, although he certainly did not intend to do so. On the advice of this man Mr. C. closed down his office and went underground for the remaining 3 years of the war as a medical student. He waited until the Nazi regime had collapsed before re-opening his lawyer's office and he devoted himself mainly to indemnification proceedings.

During his imprisonment he came to realize that a person can survive anything provided he has the right psychological characteristics. "I am glad that I had the experience of Dachau. It was an important and valuable part of my life. It made me more aware and more self-critical."

Alongside the description of Mr. C's occupational success, the description of his married life looks rather feeble. Mr. C. only mentions his wife in passing. According to his state-ments, he showed her consideration, care and sympathy once his persecution was over, in order to compensate her for the stress that the persecution had imposed on her and for the sacrifices which his present work involves for her. But, even this considerate attitude which Mr. C. displays appears tyrannical. Mr. C. believes that he must now adopt the role of the ever-understanding, considerate husband towards his wife because she is the one who actually suffered as a result of the persecution. She suffered more from his incarceration than he did. The extreme uncertainty endured over a long period of time has made her very distrustful and she persists in the stubborn belief that everyone is against him. Nowadays, she also worries that he could overwork and damage his health.

He first met his wife at the age of 26 in a neighbouring village and he married her soon afterwards. It was "love at first sight". After one year of marriage, a daughter was born. She was the opposite of his wife and reminded him in appearance very much of his mother with whom he always got on very well "without having to say very much". He realizes that he badly spoils his daughter for this reason. Because she is very like him in character, he right from the start took over the task of bringing her up entirely by himself. At his sug-gestion his daughter studied law at university but, much to her father's dismay, she failed in her first attempt to get her degree. However, she did manage to pass the second time. He plans that she will one day take over his flourishing lawyer's business.

In his profession, his preferred sphere of existence, Mr. C. nowadays consciously gets away from the influence of his wife. As in the case described above, the marital relationships of Mr. C. are little more than a sentimental reminiscence of the past. In the description that he gives of his life one is struck by the emphasis placed on his work, with which he still identifies to a great extent, even today. His relationship with his wife is kept quite separate from the everyday conflicts of the working world.

Following the period of persecution, Mr. C. left his marriage far behind him and gradually and carefully moved away from his wife. However, he still feels responsible when it comes to the education of his daughter. For example, he decisively influenced her choice of profession because as a trained lawyer she might one day be his suc-cessor.

2. Second Marriages after the Inmates' Release from the Camps

Of the 84 persons married before the onset of persecution, 45 (54%) lost their marital partners in the camps. Of these, 37 (82%) remarried following their release.

Compared with the first group, the second marriages are characterized by the larger number of younger persons.

Here again, the reasons for persecution or the origin of the inmates are typical. 50% of these persons are racially persecuted Polish Jews. They were worst affected not only by the loss of their marital partners and their own children but also by the loss of their parental family (see chapter on "Stresses Imposed by Concentration Camp Incarceration", p. 26).

The horrifying extent of the destruction is most apparent in this group. The fact that, nevertheless, the majority of these people decided to remarry probably has something to do with the function of the second marriage — it was frequently a substitute for the destroyed family relationships and it satisfied the inmates' strong desire for protection and security. In these marriages the choice of marital partner was clearly influenced by the persecution fate.

In contrast to racially persecuted persons of German origin, Polish Jews more frequently married a partner who had also been persecuted (0.1% significance).

The common fate suffered by the two partners becomes a basis for marital ties. The persecuted partner, who lost home and family in the same way, is expected to show the greatest understanding for the other person's problems. This is expressed in the following statement:

"Someone who spent time in a concentration camp can only tolerate another camp inmate as a partner. No one else can understand what happened."

A further characteristic of this group is the much higher percentage of emigrants compared with the marriages that remained intact. For Polish Jews, many of whom belonged to a Zionist organisation even before the start of persecution, Israel was the preferred country to which to emigrate (see chapter on "Reasons for Emigration and Ability to Cope with Life", p. 226).

The problems which arise from the conflict with a new sociocultural environment are also effective in motivating a person to conclude a second marriage. One does not wish to be completely alone in a foreign country, but would rather create the basis for a new start with a partner sharing the same views. Although memories of the first marriage impose quite a severe stress on the second marriages of the persecutees, 57% of these persons nevertheless represent the pole "harmonious family life" and 43% represent the pole "disharmonious family life". There is no significant difference between these second marriages and the marriages which remained intact from before the start of persecution. It can be said therefore that, as regards the success or failure of a marriage, it makes little difference whether the marriage survived the period of incarceration intact or whether it was destroyed by the persecution and a second marriage was concluded.

Because of the lower average age of the interviewees who remarried, the percentage of childless couples in the post-incarceration period is lower at 18 (49%) than in the first group: 19 (51%) of the persecutees have one child or more. The marriages of Polish Jews, who themselves mostly came from large families, produced most children (on average two offspring).

The following example of a racially persecuted German Jew is typical of a second marriage in which the memory of the first wife and the concentration camp past had an important influence on the choice of the second marital partner:

Mr. B. was born in Germany in 1897. Today he is comfortably off and lives with his wife in the USA.

Mr. B. met his first wife — a German Jew — in 1935. In order to be able to marry her he gave up the plans which he had at that time of emigrating and remained in Germany. He had an extremely happy relationship with his wife whom he described as being sensitive and possessing striking intellectual abilities.

In 1943 the family was torn apart by the persecution and the members were deported to various camps. After his release from the camp he at first tried to trace his family again and he learned that all his relatives had been killed. A distant female acquaintance, whom he had briefly got to know many years prior to persecution, informed him of the death of his wife. This acquaintance had been imprisoned with his wife and was able to give a first-hand account of how she had died in the camp. Mr. B. married this friend in 1946. He said she was the closest person to him "because she had gone through everything and was a friend of my wife during imprisonment".

Mr. B. has a relatively harmonious marriage with his second wife, too. However, he also admits that occasionally he vents his anger at other people on her. His wife is able to overlook this in a very understanding manner. He is grateful that he can talk to her whenever he wants about the past and especially about his first wife.

It was important for Mr. B. concluding this second marriage, not only that he and his new wife shared a common fate, but also that through the friendship of the two women he was able to forge a new link with his earlier marriage. The chief feature of the marriage is that it keeps alive the memory of Mr. B.'s first wife and she "lives on" so to speak in the present union.

Another typical variant of the second marriage is centred around the loss of a person's own children in concentration camps.

The following case history of a Polish Jew now living in Israel illustrates this situation.

The persecutee, who was 47 years old in 1960, got to know his first wife when he was studying to become a pharmacist in Warsaw. In the same year that his daughter was born, the Germans occupied Warsaw and Mr. F. was put in a ghetto with his wife; but before this happened, he had managed to give his daughter to a priest to look after.

In the ghetto Mr. F. was detailed off wih some other men to poison all small children. This was his first confrontation with the gruesome reality of the persecution of the Jews. When the ghetto was closed down, all the people who had been living in it were transported to Auschwitz. His own child was returned to him and, although he suffered inhuman torture, he managed to take the child along with him and hide her in the camp. Shortly afterwards he was separated from his wife and child and he learned later that both of them had been gassed.

Following this experience, in order to preserve his inner equilibrium he took an interest in the welfare of the children in the camp and protected them as best he could.

After he was liberated from the camp, Mr. F. emigrated to Israel and to start with worked as a teacher in a kibbutz. It was there that he met his second wife, who was also a teacher.

Now, together with his wife, he is running a religious children's home. A number of children who had been in the camps lived in this home in the years after the war. Mr. F.

sees it as his life's task to bring up these children and adolescents. His private life as well as his relationship with his second wife and his own two children take second place to his work in the children's home.

This case demonstrates the attempt by a persecutee to overcome his fixation on the traumatic loss of his child, a loss for which he feels partly responsible, by actively caring for and bringing up other children in need of assistance. The marital relationship is sustained almost solely by the partners' common interests in education. To the outside world the marriage appears relatively harmonious, but a true person-related partnership is replaced by devotion to a group.

3. First Marriages Following Release from Incarceration

Out of 115 persons who were single prior to persecution, 101 (87.8%) married after their liberation. This numerically largest group of first marriages includes the persecutees who were too young to get married before they were imprisoned. Most of these persecutees, who were on average 20 years old at the time of their incarceration, had still been living with their parents and had not yet completed the process of moving away from the parental home and gaining independence. Some of the persecutees had been torn away from their occupational training; those who had completed such training usually had not had any opportunity to gather practical experience or to prove their skills in the job world.

When they emerged from the camps, the male persecutees in particular faced the problem of having to reintegrate into the working world in order to create the material basis for establishing a family. As a result, these persons usually married only after a long phase of orientation and reconstruction.

This group is characterized by the high percentage of racial persecutees (Polish Jews 51%, German Jews 29.8%). In this group, too, the Polish Jews, as already mentioned, frequently married partners who had also been the victims of persecution. In the case of young persecutees, there was a further difference as regards the choice of partner:

In contrast to old persecutees, young persecutees seek their marital partners more frequently in certain reference groups (0.1% significance).

After their release from incarceration, these persecutees at first sought to orient themselves in groups with similar world views or which had suffered similar fates — for example in displaced persons camps, emigrant communities or in kibbutzes — and it was here that they met their later marital partners. This close association with partners in suffering is understandable when one remembers that 62% of the persons had lost some or all of their parental families in concentration camps.

The distribution of the first marriages over the factor "family relationships" is 57% "harmonious" and 42% "disharmonious" families, and this corresponds exactly to the result of the second marriages. The 3 groups of marriages do not differ significantly from each other as regards the success or failure of the marriage. Each group contains about the same number of harmonious and disharmonious families. This is perhaps further evidence to disprove the view that former concentration camp inmates, particularly if they were relatively young when arrested, are no longer capable of love or marriage. In 72 (71%) of the marriages, on average two children

were born, in 29 (29%) there were no children. The reason for the lack of children in
19 of these latter cases (66%) was not that the persecutees were sterile or too old,
but that they were very much against producing any children of their own. If one
enquires into the reasons for this rejection of children, it is tempting to assume that
these persecutees were clearly suffering from physical or mental disturbances or from
impaired social contact. However, this assumption cannot be confirmed statistically.

These persecuted persons constitute a small, special group which should be more
closely observed by studying individual cases. It must be borne in mind here that
the stated reasons are almost certainly not the only decisive ones, since the interviewees were not always ready or able to answer this question frankly. Nevertheless,
it is possible to detect two basic motives here. On the one hand, particularly in the
case of the racial persecutees, we find strong resentment against society predominat-
ing, because these people feel that the process of persecution may repeat itself and
they wish to spare their children this fate.

The following remarks will illustrate this point:

A Polish Jew who is nowadays married to a gentile wife is afraid that his children will
be regarded as "filthy Jews by the Germans but as Germans by the Jews".

A female Polish Jew stated: "We do not want any Jewish children who might have to go
through that sort of thing again."

On the other hand, the reasons for the rejection of children are to be seen in the
needs and desires of the persecutees themselves and, here, having children would
impede the attainment of these desires. This is expressed clearly in the following
quotations:

"I do not want any children because I don't want to share my wife with anyone else. She
looks after me like a child and that is just what I want."

"Children would get on my nerves and hamper me in my work as a travelling preacher."

In the group of first marriages, two aspects of the marital relationships of persecutees stand out as particularly typical:

1. Female persecutees tend more frequently to marry soon.
2. Male persecutees tend to marry only after they have tried to achieve job stability.

This confirms the findings hinted at above according to which panicky, i.e. over-
hasty, marriages are mainly concluded by women while men behave in the customary
and generally accepted manner, i.e. they usually wait until they have completed their
occupational training before getting married.

However, it would be wrong to refer the early marriages of female inmates solely
back to the stress of the endured incarceration. Personality-specific factors are also
important, as is apparent from the findings reported on pp. 188 and 189 on the
significance of the family situation for a harmonious married life. The following
case also illustrates this:

Mrs. R., who was 34 years old in 1960, comes from a rich Polish-Jewish family.

She describes her relationship with her mother as particularly intimate and loving. Even
today she somewhat exaggeratedly idolizes her mother, who died in a concentration camp.
The only thing that Mrs. R. can find to reproach her mother for is that she did not prepare
her daughter for the world and did not explain the sexual facts of life to her.

The seven children enjoyed a traditional orthodox religious upbringing. The girls were
looked after at home by governesses. Mrs. R., in particular, was very spoiled by her parents

and brothers. Since she did well in school, the parents planned to send her to a university. At the age of 14 her schooling was interrupted by the start of persecution.

During incarceration all the members of her family lost their lives. She herself was shot in the head while trying to escape and was then put into a concentration camp. A fellow prisoner saved her from being put to death.

After being liberated from the camp, she immediately joined a kibbutz which was organised from Israel. In 1949 she met her future husband here and married him soon after, before they both emigrated together to Israel. Mrs. R. herself describes this over-hasty decision as "seeking refuge in marriage". Her main motive at that time was her sexual uncertainty and her fear that she would be abused by the men in the displaced person's camp. Her husband was handsome and adored her. However, she never loved him, so she now says.

Despite their common fate — the husband is a Polish Jew, was brought up in an orthodox religious manner like herself and also spent several years in a concentration camp — she never managed to establish a good relationship with her husband. She feels socially degraded by his humble origins as the son of a working-class family and by his present job as a factory worker. As the daughter of a rich and distinguished family, she feels that this marriage is far below her cultural and material rank. If her mother had been alive and if she had not been so "green" and unprepared for life, this unhappy union would never have come about.

She describes her husband as intellectually far inferior to herself, coarse, hot-tempered, inconsiderate and impatient. He does not help her run the house, a job which gets her down, nor does he allow her any kind of change. Mrs. R. says that he lacked maternal warmth and care during his childhood, but she does not feel capable of supplying this warmth now. In addition, she suspects that her husband is mentally ill and that he suffers from depressions. She cannot even discuss everyday matters with him. He retires completely within himself and only wants to be left in peace. He, for his part, criticizes her for her occasional epileptoid attacks and thinks she is "mad".

Her first child, a girl, whom she loved very much, died under tragic circumstances at the age of 9, allegedly as a result of medical incompetence. The death of this child was a decisive caesura in her life. She bitterly reproaches herself and her husband for being partly responsible for the girl's death. As a result of this event, the mutual relationship of the couple took a turn for the worse. Mrs. R. began to rebel against her husband and not to accept everything he said or did uncomplainingly, as in the past. She herself says that around this time she became frigid, although her sex life had been completely normal up to then.

In the meantime, four more children were born. These are healthy and intelligent, and Mrs. R. has a warm and patient relationship with them. She undertakes to bring her children up by herself because her husband does not show any interest in this. Even when a dispute involving the children flares up with a malicious neighbour, he never defends his wife or children but always sides with the other person. He even beats the children without finding out whether this is really warranted.

Mrs. R. finds her present marital situation almost unbearable. Life only seems worth living to her because of the children. She is seriously considering a divorce but so far she has done nothing because of the children.

This case history shows that the failure of the marriage is connected on the one hand with certain personality traits of the ex-inmate and on the other hand with certain external conditions. The very motives for the marriage show that the marital partner is expected to fulfil certain substitute functions. He is not chosen for his own character but initially is selected to satisfy a very strong need for protection. In this special case of a sexually inexperienced and insecure woman, the husband is expected to provide protection from other men who are regarded as dangerous. The reasons for choosing precisely this husband are to be found in more external conditions, such as the common fate and the same ideological-religious attitude. However, these conditions prove incapable of sustaining the marriage. In this case, the different social backgrounds of the partners are particularly unfortunate because the spoiled and intellectually demanding wife is unable to overcome the social gap between herself and her husband. In the final analysis, the failure of the marriage is due to the uncertainty and inexperience in the choice of partner. Of course, the limited possibilities of choice within the small group living on the kibbutz or in other communities played a role here.

The second case history is typical of younger male persecutees whose occupational training was interrupted by persecution and was resumed or completed following release from imprisonment. Here there is no evidence of an anxious search for a partner who is primarily needed to provide protection. The main aim is that of occupational reintegration and this forms the basis for marriage.

Mr. Z. was born in 1928 in Berlin, the second child of Jewish parents. The mother was the focal point of the family. It is thanks to her sacrifices and her optimism that all members of the family were able to survive the severe persecution.

Upon being freed, Mr. Z. first spent several months in hospital. When he was fully recovered, he began to study intensively in order to make up the lost time. According to his description, he worked "like a lunatic" in those days, far harder than at any time later in his life. Nevertheless, he has never been able to get rid of the feeling that the lost time simply cannot be made up.

Before he emigrated to the USA, Mr. Z. took his school-leaving examination. After successfully completing his studies in economics at a college in the USA he was sent all over the world as an export salesman for various firms. After a long stay in India he suddenly became fed up with living alone. The desire to put down roots somewhere grew more and more intense. During a holiday he met his present wife and they became engaged a few weeks later.

Mrs. Z. is a distant relation from Germany and comes from the "same background". She had emigrated to the USA with her parents before the persecutions started.

Mr. Z. says that in his wife he has found a partner whose calm equilibrium complements his own character. Mr. Z. finds her steadfastness acts as a counterweight to the inner agitation which sometimes comes over him when he is under stress at work. At such times he loses control of himself, but it is then that his wife comes into her own. She helps him take important decisions, balancing out his agitation with her considered opinion.

He is deliberately bringing up his children in a very liberal manner, although this is at variance with the way in which he was raised and which he feels is still common in Germany. He has done no more than is customary as regards their religious education because he believes that the children will have to decide later for themselves what they wish to believe in.

This case illustrates a development leading to a harmonious marriage via a positive relationship to the mother and a successful career. One of the reasons for getting married is to achieve a certain stability, not previously attainable through career activity alone. In this case, the training period and the stabilization of the career must be regarded as a positive precondition for a successful and mature choice of partner.

Thus, this case shows how an ex-inmate of a concentration camp, who deep down retained his mental and physical health, was able to pursue a successful career. This is not an escape from himself but constitutes a development of personality in keeping with a masculine existence and it leads, of course, at the right time to marriage with the right partner.

Summary

1. A major factor analysis of the data that appear relevant to us as regards marital and family life revealed a factor designated as "family relationships following release". The poles of this factor are "harmonious" or "disharmonious" family life. Harmonious family life is primarily characterized by the presence of children and by good relationships of the marital partners with each other and also with their own children. Disharmonious family life on the other hand is characterized by a lack of children and poor relationships between the partners.

2. No correlation was found between this factor and age, sex, country of origin and country of residence. The most surprising, and for our investigation most important fact is that the severity of the concentration camp stress is not detectably correlated with the harmony or disharmony of the marriage. On the other hand, there are clear correlations between marital harmony and conditions in the parental family, particularly the emotional devotion to the mother, who is experienced as someone to emulate.

3. Three groups of marriages can be differentiated in relation to the period of incarceration:

a) Marriages that survived the period of incarceration (marriages that remained intact)

b) Marriages that were concluded following liberation from the camp and following the death of a first partner during incarceration (second marriages)

c) Marriages that were concluded for the first time following liberation (first marriages).

The characteristics of these three groups of marriages are described. It is significant that in the case of marriages that remained intact there is no indication that the marriages were affected by the incarceration. The marriages are generally just as good or bad as they were before.

In the group of second marriages, to which mainly political persecutees belong, the concentration camp period plays a role to the extent that the memory of the first partner or of deceased children overshadows the second marriage and makes it difficult to establish a relationship with a new partner.

In the case of the first marriages, which are mainly represented by young racial persecutees, only women show a detectable tendency to panic into concluding early marriages.

CHAPTER 9

Weltanschauung and Concentration Camp Incarceration

Outline of Problem

So far we have made no mention of a phenomenon whose importance is constantly stressed in the literature on concentration camp problems, namely that of the inmates' personal Weltanschauung. Many authors regard this factor as decisively important with regard to the inmates' ability to survive and cope with the stress of concentration camp incarceration. FRANKL (1959), who was able to observe this phenomenon first-hand, stresses that the "will to find some ultimately transcendental sense in events" played an important role in the survival of the individual.

The will to see some sense in the experience of persecution has already been dealt with both directly and indirectly in the preceding chapters. One can argue that the political and religious persecutees were victimized because of some personally selected "rational" activity while the Jews were incarcerated and made the target of an extermination campaign on the basis of some irrational and obscure racial theory. The political and religious persecutees thus had a better chance of finding some sense in their persecution than the racial persecutees.

It is therefore not surprising thay many Jews, as BONDY (1963) noted in the light of his own experience in concentration camps, took issue with fate for having been born Jewish. According to BONDY the only persons who demonstrated great courage in the persecution situation were those "who had strong religious ties or in some way espoused the idea of Zionism". KOGON (1954) also mentions that "strength of character and religious, political or humanitarian goals" were decisive in enabling a person to tolerate the suffering of concentration camp incarceration and that "the straitjacket of social mores was immediately cast aside".

But how can one tell whether such goals had any effect on a person's survival capability? Wherever this problem was investigated the answer pointed back to the group ideal of a particular Weltanschauung. We have also followed a similar course in so far as we enquired into the fate of racial, religious or political persecutees. The personal attitude, as it comes to the fore in FRANKL's formula (1959), was not considered here.

In the German Democratic Republic (East Germany) MÜLLER-HEGEMANN and SPITZNER (1963) investigated 91 active members of the KPD (German Communist Party) and the SPD (German Socialist Party), most of whom had been held for questioning, imprisoned in jail and incarcerated in a concentration camp. They found that these active members of the resistance stood up better than other people to "the effects of solitary confinement and the usually inhuman cross-examinations and other stresses with extreme political perseverance and by developing great personal activity". "Through regular gymnastics and intellectual self-discipline and by striking up contact with other detainees, they were able to overcome the social isolation and to

compensate to a large extent for the very damaging effects on the nervous system."
HUK (1955), in a study of 400 ex-inmates in Austria, found that after their release
from the camps Jews were mainly depressed while the resistance fighters were consistently "active and glad to be alive". HUK (1955) sees the reason for this in "an
ethically unimpeachable morale which provides an enormous source of strength on
which the body can draw and which creates greater powers of resistance even in
situations of extreme stress".

Admittedly, it is necessary to ask what constitutes an "ethically unimpeachable
morale". Usually no attempt is made to answer this question, understandably so,
because there are no clear criteria for such a quality.

Generally, therefore, investigators content themselves with measuring the individual ethos in terms of the "degree of identification with an ideology". V. BAEYER,
HÄFNER and KISKER (1964) also stress that "social identification, for example in the
form of a common ideology" can cushion the ego-damaging effects of the stress
situation.

But, no matter how much the identification with a common ideology strengthens
the morale in a situation like that of the concentration camp, such tendencies are
very different as regards their ethical relevance. Not all Communists, Christians or
Jehovah's Witnesses who espouse their particular Weltanschauung and are able to
derive strength and comfort from it in extreme situations have the same intrapsychic
attitude towards this Weltanschauung.

A rough differentiation of the various "uses" to which a person's Weltanschauung
can be put can be made on the basis of what psychoanalysts call the ideological
attitude. This means that a person can use his particular Weltanschauung to prevent
immature impulses from being consciously perceived and to abreact them under
"ideal" aspects. Without doubt, this mechanism may mean that the person in question
subjectively experiences a stabilisation of his ego structure, but the "ethically unimpeachable attitude" to which HUK (1955) refers and which, last but not least,
manifests itself in the relationship with interpersonal reality can get short shrift.

ERIKSON (1966) regards the phenomenon of an ideological attitude as typical of
puberty; this attitude is then replaced in mature adulthood by the attitude of a
personal ethos. One can therefore say that in the case of the ideological personality
— in older psychiatry only the extreme variant of this personality type, namely the
fanatical psychopath, is mentioned; in modern social psychology we talk here of a
"dogmatic personality" — the transition to the ethos is not successful. If one con-
centrates less on the moral aspect and more on the aspect of faith in a Weltanschauung, then it is possible to talk of a believing attitude during this period. This
would then have to be differentiated from an ideological attitude to one's own Weltanschauung. MATUSSEK (1968) has gone into these differences in more detail elsewhere. In making this distinction it is assumed that the attitudes of representatives
of different Weltanschauungen can be alike in certain respects. Accordingly, it is not
only necessary to enquire into the different beliefs, e.g. in the case of Jews,
Christians or Communists, in connection with a particular behaviour pattern, but
also the inner attitude to the belief should always be established. Seen from this
point of view it is possible for representatives of two different Weltanschauungen to
resemble each other more closely than two people of the same Weltanschauung.
ROKEACH (1960) therefore correctly, and in contrast to the studies made by ADORNO

et al. (1950) on the fascist personality, refers to the fact that dogmatic representatives (we would talk of ideological representatives) of divergent Weltanschauungen can have significantly similar personality traits. On the other hand, two representatives of the same Weltanschauung can integrate their world view in quite different ways into their personality.

Two examples will now be quoted to illustrate the foregoing remarks. These examples strike us as particularly suitable because the persons in question are Catholic priests, i.e. two men who not only share the same Weltanschauung but also have the same profession.

I. Ideology and Faith

1. An Ideological Priest

Father Siegel was born in 1902 in a village, the son of a postman. At home the family life was without any frills and everyone had to "slog hard". When the father was called up to fight in the First World War the mother and her four children, two of whom later entered the church, had to get by alone. The father was a choleric person who kept control of himself at work but at home had "outbursts of violent temper". The mother was the calm, balancing influence in the family. She also knew how to "keep the father in check". Father Siegel feels that he resembles his mother very closely, whereas he believes that he could have managed without his father. "My mother was the corner to which I could escape. She it is who nowadays preaches through me." His mother suffered a lot and worked hard. She was a deeply emotional person with a keen appreciation of beauty, including religious beauty. His mother sparked his interest in entering the priesthood, but he kept his actual plan to do so "a secret".

When he was due to leave elementary school he informed his surprised parents that he wished to become a priest and he took private coaching from a parson. It was during this period in his life that he experienced "severe psychic disturbances" for the first time. He was filled with fear that he would fail and disappoint his father. "However, I worked my way up and was regarded even then as an accomplished speaker." His father was also known for his speaking ability after he had drunk a glas or two of bear. He himself delivered the valedictory address on behalf of his schoolmates. After "a terrible feeling of panic during the opening sentences I suddenly felt as free as an astronaut". He saw that his speech had affected those present because many of them were crying. He was in his element. Toward the end of his time in secondary school he set himself the choice between "either becoming an officer or entering an order". He chose the latter and entered an order in 1923. Wearing his priest's garb gave him the feeling that his fellow students took him seriously. Whenever he was surprised by unexpected situations, such as checks carried out in the seminary, his attacks of fear returned. Even today he still gives a jump when there is a knock at the door. In his 24th to 25th year of life, when he was studying for his "Philosophikum" [4], he started to build up his "own world". At that time he led an isolated and withdrawn existence. He escaped into a world of prayer and enjoyed reading mystical writings. His colleagues were unaware of "the sort of world that existed inside me", although he attracted other people's attention because of his special achievements and his zeal. He sympathized with the Nazi ideals of order and discipline, to such an extent in fact that his superiors regarded him as susceptible to Nazi ideology and transferred him. In his new surroundings he also lived withdrawn because this time it was his turn to find his colleagues too kindly disposed

---

[4] An intermediate examination in a secondary subject (e.g. philosophy or educational science) taken as part of the degree course at a German university by candidates ultimately wishing to teach at "Gymnasien" (high schools or grammar schools).

towards the Nazis. At the urging of his superiors, who wanted him to start work as soon as possible, he concluded his studies extremely quickly with a good examination mark. He did not have any doubts about his faith.

In 1935 he was ordained a priest and was sent to work in a church school. He came into conflict with the principal of the school, who was a convinced Nazi. He himself instructed his pupils along two lines. On the one hand he passed on objective knowledge to them and on the other he gave them tips on what to say in the presence of the SS. His classes had the best marks in examinations supervised by the SS. When he was about to be called up for military service he informed his superiors that he would refuse to serve in the forces. He was then given a position in which he was classified as irreplaceable. In the weeks following the attempted putsch of July 20th, 1944 he was on holiday in the Alps, where he met a well-known member of the group of conspirators who was trying to get away. This person asked Siegel for help and Siegel hid him in the house of one of his former pupils.

The SS found out about this and arrested the Father in October 1944. Up until the time that the hidden conspirator was found in January 1945, Father Siegel was constantly subjected to cross-examinations during which he was not tortured, but was merely supposed to be "demoralized and intimidated". However, he did not betray anything and felt he had "won". The only really unpleasant part of his incarceration was being together with the other prisoners. He was mistreated by them, despised and abused as a "papist". Things did not improve for him until he was given the single cell he had requested.

As late as in January 1945 he was transported to Dachau with 8 other clergymen and was put in the charge of a kapo who was a known murderer and robber. This kapo worked off the beatings which he himself received on his fellow prisoners. The Father found it hard to adjust to the lack of food. He had the impression that the power of hunger was forcing him into servility. Even more of a stress than the hunger during incarceration was for him the fact that he could never be completely alone for a single moment. "There was no corner in which I could say 'here I am by myself'. The detainees were forced into the mass and there was no way anyone could escape this process. However, I was completely isolated and alone." He felt abandoned by his fellow prisoners, his fellow priests and also by the Pope. Prayer protected him from being "entangled with the masses". Through prayer he managed to "split himself off from the world" in which he "ceased to exist physically but only spiritually". For example, he spent hour after hour during imprisonment reading mass and he built up "layer upon layer" around himself so that he was entirely alone and isolated. By maintaining contact with persons who possessed a "glimmer of conscience", he felt in a position to "avoid the masses". As far as possible he kept clear of other clergymen. After spending three months in the concentration camp he was liberated in April 1945. He went by bicycle from Dachau to Straubing where he collapsed with exhaustion. He was taken in by the brothers of his order but he felt completely isolated among them. During his first two nights there he was overcome by crying fits because he felt "You won' get back in. They won't understand you". "They all knuckled under to the Nazis, some even sympathised with them." He felt even more abandoned by his environment than before. When he received a letter from his superior telling him that he should return to work after bis 4 weeks of "leave" he again had the impression that no one understood him. He found that many other inmates of concentration camps suffered from the same feeling. "We are a group to ourselves." The only way he can still find satisfactory contact with other people is through his pastoral activity. Only by applying his experience to restore contact between human beings can he gain "salvation".

After a holiday to rest and recover his strength he taught at a monastery school, but he felt completely miserable there and got into difficulties. Again, he regarded his superior as a Nazi sympathizer who had "hibernated" in Rome during the worst crisis. Father Siegel simply ran away from the school and the monastery. He was then given a position where he could do a lot of preaching and instructing. His preaching abilities were so higly estimated that he was transferred to a large city. He was bluntness personified in the pulpit. On one occasion he railed against a particular film that was being shown in the city, because he found it obscene. In his opinion society was sick mainly because of the general trend towards excessive permissiveness. His remarks triggered a big scandal in the press. Even his superiors criticized him for his irrelevant polemics. He protected himself against these reproaches and against the importunate manner of other people by throwing up an impregnable armour-plated barrier of prayer. He totally rejected any medical assistance, although he really urgently needed attention for an ulcer which had developed soon after he was incarcerated in Dachau and also for various other complaints which continued to give him trouble in the years after his release. He gave the following reasons for this action:

"We concentration camp inmates need a world all to ourselves because our environment cannot tolerate us. We are rejected as asocial." Father Siegel follows a strictly vegetarian diet. He spends his vacations fasting and then mountaineering. His stomach troubles have disappeared. Occasionally, however, he suffers periods of "depressive self-pity" during which he feels incapable of making any decision and cannot work. For the past 8 years he has been practising yoga, which he finds a "most valuable and effective way to achieve inner freedom, detachment and above all superiority over the pressures of the mediocrity of the environment". He has recurring dreams, some of which make him happy while others are painful. In his happy dreams he imagines himself blissfully soaring in a weightless state over the heads of the masses, invisible to normal persons and only certain "specially selected" people are allowed to see him. They spur him on to soar even higher. In his painful anxiety dreams he is unable to keep to deadlines, cannot cope with mathematics in school, or feels stripped naked and persecuted.

He refuses to accept any financial compensation for his persecution. There is "no way that money can make up for the suffering, not even if it were handed over with great ceremony". To accept money would be "a false and hollow act". Many of the changes that have taken place in him he related back to his time in the concentration camp. He is above all more isolated now. He finds other human beings are alien. The time he spent in the camp is regarded by him as a "sort of blemish". The concentration camp is also to blame, so he feels, for his sensitive stomach and his physical weakness. He feels that the public are not concerned enough about the events that occurred in those days. He has nothing but hate for those directly involved in his persecution and he would like to see them "mercilessly punished". His predictions for the future are pessimistic. "Evil and falsity will conquer the world." A positive aspect of his concentration camp experience is that he now feels even more independent and his conscience has become more personal. As regards his attitude to celibacy, he would have nothing against it being abolished as an institution, but for himself he could never enter into any intimate relationship with a woman because this would mean "giving away too much of oneself". "It is no longer possible for me to become one with another person." There have been no major changes in his attitude to the church ever since his childhood days, although he is in disagreement with it on many points, particularly the authority that it wields.

It is apparent from the life history of this priest that the ideological attitude survived unchanged beyond the period of incarceration. If any change has occurred, then it is that the militant-aggressive side of his Weltanschauung has become even more intense and goes hand in hand with growing isolation.

In his parental family, which was characterized not only by financial but also general insecurity, the prevalent idea seems to have been that a secure existence was to be had by entering a religious order. Two of Father Siegel's four siblings took the cloth.

As a child Father Siegel was filled with anxious insecurity and was unable to relate to his father as a result of the latter's choleric and unapproachable character. In his eyes, his father became a problematical figure of authority. He felt that the only way to gain a firm footing in life was to enter holy orders. This was his way of trying to prove himself to his father. On the other hand, his mother was a "safe corner to which he could escape". In his youth, and with the support of his mother, he entered a seminary which then took over the protective role that she had played. This change brought him face to face with his insecurity and feeling of inferiority as a student and as he approached manhood. Reality, particularly when it makes authoritarian demands, still continues to trigger violent fits of panic in him. His description of the way in which he overcame his fear of making his valedictory speech reveals a basic structural element of his character. He rose up like an astronaut above the heads of his listeners and thus freed himself from direct contact with those present. In this way he was able to rid himself of his fear and to face the auditorium. Under the pressure of taking his "Philosophikum" he went into isolation, retreating into a world of prayer and mysticism. In the clash between Church and National Socialism, he refused to go along with the policy of adaptation which was desired by the leaders on both sides and as a result came into conflict with the regime.

A single chance action finally led to his arrest. While he was imprisoned, the greatest problem that he faced was that "one lost one's individuality and became one of the masses" in the camp. He had been unable to make contact with his fellow students at the seminary and now in the camp he had no contact with his fellow prisoners. He used prayer as a means of putting "layer upon protective layer" around himself. Finally, Father Siegel even went so far as to request a single cell for himself in order to escape all contact with his fellow prisoners. Upon his release from the concentration camp the hollowness and isolation of his existence struck home. He complains that nobody cares about him. The only thing that gives him any support is the thought that "as an ex-concentration camp inmate, I am something special", although the duration and severity of his incarceration were far below average. Father Siegel clearly defines his communicative role as a priest when he states that, as a man of the church, he has an institutionally established line of contact at his disposal, particularly when he preaches, which enables him to make contact with his fellow men. This statement is based on a specific understanding of his occupational function which means that both before and after concentration camp incarceration he held himself aloof from other people. He protects himself against criticism, which wounds him deeply, by retiring behind a shield of arrogance, snobbishness and dogmatism. If anyone is guilty, then it is automatically the others.

As he grows older, Father Siegel finds less and less adequate protection in religiosity, which is his main defensive barrier. He counters his stomach trouble by adopting a meditative and vegetarian ideology. More and more keenly he craves to be able to enter into a dialogue with another human being, but this wish is denied him. The persecution is of importance to this priest to the extent that it offers him a role which socially sanctions his desired aloofness and isolation. His ideological attitude protects him from having to come to grips with reality.

This case of a persecuted ideological priest does not exemplify to the fullest extent all facets of the ideological personality and the consequences of persecution. The case contains individual as well as typical features. Contrasting this priest with a believing priest, who was incarcerated for a longer time and who was better able to cope with concentration camp conditions, brings out very clearly the different ways in which ideology and faith worked for the persecutees.

2. A Believing Priest

Father Gast was born in a medium-sized town. His parents owned a small farm and a cabinet-making business. They were both fully occupied in these activities and the mother devoted little attention to the household and her son. These tasks were left to the two sisters.

Father Gast always had the company of neighbours' children on the small farm his parents owned and he used to play the most outrageous pranks with them. At the age of 12 he fell in love with a girl for the first and last time. But it was love from a distance. Later on he followed the girl's life with benevolent interest from afar. When he finished secondary school (Realschule) he wanted to become an electrical engineer. However, at the time — 1921 — it was difficult for him to find a suitable job where he could start his training. His uncle put him in touch with an electrical company that might have an opening for him. While waiting for the firm to make up its mind he promised himself that if he were rejected, he would take this as an indication to become a priest. But, when the rejection did finally come, he did not have the courage to tell anyone of his decision. His sisters, however, had also had the idea that he should enter the church and they urged him to make up his mind. His parents shook their heads in disbelief that this mischievous prankster should want to take up such a profession. Then his uncle intervened, discussed the matter with his parents and also bore the cost of his training to become a priest. Following his ordination he was active in educating young people.

Father Gast was summoned to appear before the Gestapo for the first time in 1937. The reason was that he had delivered a sermon in which he had spoken of the Jews as the chosen people. The Gestapo man leafed through a thick dossier on Father Gast and described him as "a bad type". He had already attracted attention as a poor patriot and an enemy of Germany as far back as 1933. In 1939 he was called before the Gestapo again. In one of his sermons he had questioned whether bombing attacks were such heroic deeds and he had "railed against the war". Father Gast escaped from both cross-examinations unscathed. He was finally arrested because in a conversation with a protestant teacher of religion he had criticized the newly concluded treaty between Germany and Russia because it constituted an increased risk of war. He was initially remanded in custody for 4 months, but then it was arranged that he would be sent to Sachsenhausen. Anything could happen in Sachsenhausen; the treatment given the prisoners was quite arbitrary. Sometimes the SS staggered into the barracks drunk and shot blindly into the prisoners' beds. It was impossible to defend oneself and one's life was always in danger. At that time he still felt young and strong and, so he says, did not allow himself to be impressed by events around him, although this was the start of a difficult period in his life. The group of priests with whom he was imprisoned in the camp was supervised by a professional criminal. He made the priests perform the heaviest type of labour — clearing rubble, loading tree trunks and removing dead bodies from the barracks. Every prisoner who performed heavy work of this type was entitled to extra food rations, but in the case of the priests the kapo kept the extra food for himself. Father Gast lodged a protest in the camp office and was sentenced to be given 25 strokes with a heavy stick. He took the beating without screaming and this impressed both his guards and fellow prisoners. They gave him the task of keeping watch at night in the barracks to prevent people committing suicide. In December 1940 he was transferred to Dachau, which was the collecting point for all interned clergymen from all the camps in Germany. For him Dachau was a "paradise" compared with Sachsenhausen. In Dachau he worked as a medical orderly in the camp hospital up until 1944. Finally, until the time of his release in April 1945, he worked in a market garden where he illegally set up a watch-repair business. He was paid for his work with food. He was given a large number of repair jobs because people believed that a man of the church would not be likely to steal their watches. In addition, his work enabled him to hold the SS in check because they permitted him to go on doing something which was strictly speaking forbidden.

When asked what had helped him survive even the worst experiences, he replied confidently: "You know, I always quite unashamedly trusted in God and His will. I felt that, whatever happened to me, it was what God wanted." He cited two episodes the considered typical of the way in which he survived the experience of incarceration. On one occasion an SS man threatened him with a pistol which was cocked and ready to fire. The SS man put the pistol to Father Gast's temple and observed his reaction. Father Gast, however, remained completely cool and unaffected and thought to himself: "You poor fool. If you shoot me you will only be carrying out God's will, and if it is not God's wish that I should die, then you can't harm me anyway." On another occasion a priest was asked by an SS man what he thought of oral sex. The priest, with his "blindly confessional mentality" practically gave the SS man a sermon explaining why this was a mortal sin. The SS man then turned to Father Gast and asked him for his opinion. The latter replied: "It is certainly not a sin, but merely a question of taste." The answer won him the SS man's respect.

Father Gast refuses to look back on his concentration camp days as a period of intolerable suffering. He also refrains from making any sweeping condemnation of the SS. While he was incarcerated he saw that even one's best comrade could turn into a beast as soon as he became a kapo. He believes that there is good and evil in everyone of us and it merely depends on the situation whether one incurs moral guilt. One should really ask: "What is guilt?" or "Who is the guilty party?"

Following his release, he obtained a motor cycle from the Americans and drove to K. There was a lot of work for him to do there. He had practical tasks to perform everywhere and there was no time for pastoral activity. In 1946 he was transferred to a village parish. In 1951 he took up teaching at a vocational school in a large city. The teaching work gives him much pleasure. In this environment he can use "blunt, but clear language", "you can get something across here". He particularly likes the fact that he can speak more freely than as a clergyman. He is ready to advise and assist the fellow brothers of his order in all practical questions of life.

He did receive compensation for his imprisonment, but he never applied for compensation for a health problem brought on by incarceration. The doctors diagnosed a slight loss of hearing in his case, which was not serious enough to warrant compensation. He attaches no importance to compensation and says that he has all he needs; other people can make better use of the money than he can. Nor does he believe that his prospects in life were in any way impaired by the time he spent in the camps. He even believes that it was a useful experience for him. He believes that he now has a firmer grip on life, that he knows his fellowmen better and is also able to understand people with weak characters. Prior to his incarceration he had been much less tolerant and not so much in tune with life. Consequently, the time that he spent in the camps is of particular use to him in his pastoral work. He refuses to see any heroism in his experience as a concentration camp inmate and he does not even harbour any hatred for his ex-persecutors. He also got on well with the Jehovah's Witnesses in the camps, although he regards them as religious fanatics. His worst experiences were with professional criminals. He has no illusions that atrocities and acts of terror will always be committed, and he also believes that something similar to the horror of National Socialism is possible at any time as soon as people get their hands on too much power. Nevertheless he is optimistic about the future. He feels that the good people outweigh the bad, even if they are somewhat cowardly. It should not be interpreted as resignation on his part if he believes that this world is in God's hands and that one cannot change the course of the world by excessive worry.

The period of persecution does not strike this Catholic priest as a time in which his life was impaired, but as a period which gave him the opportunity to find his way back to life and to become more mature. He seems to have grown up as a normal boy, although he had to become self-reliant at a rather early age. Without any apparent "negative identity" (ERIKSON, 1966), he decided to train for the priesthood. Right from the start he was a courageous critic of the Nazi regime. During incarceration, several dramatically tense situations revealed his unshakeable faith in himself and in God. He is understanding, tolerant, free of prejudice and yet realistic in his assessment of his fellow inmates and the guards. He impressed his fellow inmates and the guards through his strong character and his courageous, realistic behaviour, which was based on a believing attitude. In a case where one of his fellow inmates, a priest with a "blindly confessional mentality", felt compelled to preach and pontificate against an imagined infringement of moral principles, Father Gast saw no fundamental moral problem, but merely one of personal taste. After five years of inprisonment under severe conditions, he left the concentration camp unbroken in body and spirit and immediately provided practical assistance for the persons in need in the years after the war. Within his order he was able to attain both inner and external independence without coming into serious conflict with his superiors. He feels no hatred for his persecutors or for groups with opposite ideologies. Nor does he think of himself as anything special from or better than other people. He believes that there is evil in all of us. He has no rosy illusions about his own future or that of the world, but with his genuine faith in God he is nevertheless optimistic.

3. Differentiating Characteristics

If we compare both cases in the light of their relationships to their own Weltanschauungen, it becomes clear that in the case of Father Siegel religion serves to keep him aloof from his fellowmen, while for Father Gast it brings about an understanding, loving relationship with his fellowmen, even when these represent different moral or religious viewpoints. Thus, one of these priests lives in a permanent and ultimately insoluble state of conflict with his Weltanschauung which teaches one above all to "love thy neighbour as thyself", while the second priest has been able to integrate this commandment into his life as his innermost guide.

The following specific features can be cited to characterize the differences that are apparent here between ideology and faith:

Ideology	Faith
1. Weltanschauung pursued with missionary zeal — tendency to preach and be didactic.	Weltanschauung not obtrusive.
2. Intolerance towards other Weltanschauungen	Tolerance of other Weltanschauungen.
3. Other Weltanschauungen are automatically denigrated.	Readiness to see good in other Weltanschauungen and even to learn from them.
4. External laws and regulations rigidly followed — authoritarian outlook.	Flexible attitude to external commandments based on spiritualized conscience.
5. Narrow moral consciousness. Tendency to be rigoristic.	Broader moral consciousness. Tendency to be broadminded.
6. Feeling of superiority over other people, particularly people with other beliefs.	Feeling of equality with other people, including those with other beliefs.
7. Tendency to be overbearing and dogmatic.	Ability to listen to others and to learn from them.
8. Sensitive to criticisms of self.	Willingness to acknowledge own guilt.
9. Tendency to clash with superiors.	Despite their faults, superiors can be accepted.
10. Aloof attitude towards fellowmen. Tendency to be a "loner".	Sensitive, sympathetic attitude towards fellowmen. Good ability to make contact with others.
11. Contact with others established mainly via the common Weltanschauung. Can be very strong.	Contact mainly established through concrete situations.
12. Difficulties in sphere of intimate contact (especially in marriage).	Satisfactory intimate contact (especially in marriage).

This list of characteristics does not claim to be complete. Nor is it intended to denote that all "ideologists" represent all the characteristics in the same way and to the fullest extent. The degree to which an ideological attitude manifests itself depends on many individual factors, so deviations from the stated characteristics must be expected. In this list of characteristics we have concentrated mainly on those behavioural patterns which express the attitude towards other Weltanschauungen. The list thus indicates a certain type of contact behaviour (see items 7–12).

This contact behaviour embodies an important criterion for judging the ideological attitude — representatives of the extreme variants of such attitudes are referred to as (fanatical) psychopaths in classical psychiatric terms. Psychopaths drop out of society because of their deficient contact with other people. Clearly, the fanatical psychopaths among the ideologists constitute only an extreme minority. However, their striking and obvious contact behaviour can also be detected in less pronounced forms of the ideological attitude.

By stressing the contact disturbances in ideological personalities we can perhaps counter a widespread unscientific belief that such persons are chiefly people who are particularly strongly identified with their Weltanschauung. This assumption would imply that the non-ideological person is less committed to and less strongly engaged with his Weltanschauung.

This is a false conception, as is shown by the examples of the two priests that have been cited. Father Gast was no less committed to his faith than was Father Siegel. On the contrary, one can regard his commitment as even more far-reaching because he was more effectively able than Father Siegel to translate into reality the most fundamental tenet of his faith, love of his fellowmen. The latter was quite unable to give himself body and soul to another person ("It is no longer possible for me to become one with another person"). The unscientific view all too easily overlooks nuances and mistakes fanaticism for commitment, inconsiderateness for devotion, and rigorism and dogmatism for strength and conviction.

II. Peculiarities of Ideological Personalities

It would be logical, on the basis of the characteristics listed, to form two groups of ex-inmates — an ideological group and a believing group — in order to make a statistical comparison of the two. We were unable to do this with the material at our disposal. The group which could definitely have been classified as strongly ideological on the basis of our criteria proved to be too small. It comprises only 20 out of 219 inmates, i.e. barely 10%. It would have been possible to eliminate this deficiency by contrasting the ideological group with a control group of 20 believers selected according to sociological criteria. However, the documentary data available to us were insufficient to permit this. This is understandable if one considers that the behaviour patterns characterized by us as indicative of a believing attitude are relatively neutral and are therefore more difficult to explore with sufficient certainty. In addition, one should not overlook the fact that ideological and believing attitudes are not mutually exclusive, alternative characteristics. Instead, they represent the extremes of a continuum of characteristics in which there are several gradual, difficult-to-identify stages.

Although we were unable to carry out a statistical comparison, we felt it sensible to stress the points which, from a clinical standpoint, are striking in the group of strongly ideological personalities. This group includes:

8 Jehovah's Witnesses (out of a total of 9)
3 Catholic priests (out of a total of 9)
8 political persecutees (out of a total of 36)
1 female Jew (out of a total of 154).

The most strongly integrated group of ideological personalities with the same Weltanschauung is formed by the Jehovah's Witnesses. But even in this group which, because of its sectarian character, attracts or develops mainly ideological personalities, we found one individual who according to our definition belongs more to the "believers" than to the "ideologists". The other members of the ideological group comprise religious ideologists (3 Catholic priests, 1 female orthodox Jew) and political ideologists (Communists, Social Democrats and persons not affiliated to an established party). This distribution already indicates that the percentage of ideological personalities is greatest in dogmatic sects but that ideologists also occur in the "established" Weltanschauungen. The reason for this is that every idea, every value and thus every Weltanschauung can be ideologically "abused".

It does not need to be specially stressed that these "quantitative" selections are not very representative. It is our aim, using the methods of clinical psychology, to determine what peculiarities stand out in particular in the time preceding, during and following incarceration.

1. Pre-Incarceration Period

It was striking that the ideologists consistently complained about disharmonious family conditions in the period preceding incarceration. The constantly recurring characterization of the father as "one-sided, narrow-minded, taciturn, strict and authoritarian" is particularly conspicuous. The mother was described less frequently in such problematical terms, although even here remarks such as "mother was unapproachable or cold" are also recorded. Altogether, the ideologists describe their mood during childhood as depressed, or at best changeable. Since in all 20 cases the ideologists came from needy families, it is possible to assume that the unfavourable material background of these persons in conjunction with an unapproachable father played a certain role in forming the ideological attitude.

This is also confirmed by other investigations. LANGER and MICHAEL (1963) found a clear predominance of authoritarian-ideological attitudes in representatives of the lowest social strata. The studies conducted by ADORNO (1950), FRENKEL-BRUNSWICK (1950), FROMM (1960), ROKEACH (1960) and others revealed that ideological persons received a strict and emotionally cold upbringing from their parents. The affectionless and authoritarian-intolerant child-rearing practices of the parents result in indecision, insincerity in social relationships and recognition of irrational authorities. In the case of men it is the restrictive attitude of the father, and in the case of women that of the mother that seems to play the most decisive role.

In the period of puberty these persons try to break out of the inner predicament of their own family by making contact with groups that are strongly committed to particular Weltanschauungen. In these groups they are able to escape from the oppressive family atmosphere and search for an identity with strongly ideological traits. According to ERIKSON (1961) puberty is characterized by the tendency to adopt an ideological attitude, therefore the behaviour of the ideological persons studied by us would not at first stand out as a particularly striking finding. However, the cases investigated by us are special in that these persons, who still possessed very strong ideological traits even as adults, were very strongly identified with a common Weltanschauung.

They lived in a religiously or politically oriented youth group and, among people with the same beliefs, they stood out through their special commitment to the common idea. Private friendships and heterosexual contact were eschewed, either because the Weltanschauung did not permit them, for example in the case of priests, or because the persons in question were entirely absorbed in the battle for the idea. Thus, the isolation which is detectable in Father Siegel even during his student days, despite his commitment to a cause shared by his entire order, occurs in similar even if usually less pronounced form in the other members of the ideological group. This can be seen from the following remarks:

"I was more strongly committed than the others."

"I despised the others who were still interested in girls or films."

"I think I was regarded as a particularly good Socialist and was quietly envied by the others."

In the case of the ideological persons who had just reached the age of puberty at the time when the Nazi regime came to power, the militant phase described above turned directly into a struggle against National Socialism. While the religious persecutees had more room to manoeuvre in avoiding persecution — after all they were primarily concerned with maintaining their religious identity — the political persecutees clashed with the regime much earlier and were thus thrown into concentration camps sooner. For these people, National Socialism meant not just a Weltanschauung which did not tolerate minorities, but also a political reality which was dangerous for society as a whole and therefore had to be eliminated.

For the political ideologists the fight against Nazism was more consistent but not entirely free from conflict with the authorities in their own group, because the latter often accused them of unwise or naive behaviour. The ideological militant was not always whole-heartedly approved of by his fellow combatants, particularly not by his superiors. These often criticized his behaviour as recklessness or a desire to become a martyr. It is not surprising, therefore, that political ideologists often ended up in concentration camps through their own acts without agreeing on joint tactics, as was characteristically the procedure followed, for example, by the Communists. In other words, despite the "rightness of the idea" and the need to be committed to it, the ideological persecutees exhibited varying degrees of difficulty in the sphere of interpersonal contact, which were founded not least in their clashes with authority.

The disturbance in the socio-communicative sphere does not always have to result from clashes with authority. In particular, this did not happen if the persons' identification with their own particular group was strong enough to confirm their feeling that they were something special. This certainly is apparent mainly in small groups of ideologically oriented persons such as the Jehovah's Witnesses. The quantitative minority offers sufficient justification for regarding oneself as something special because one espouses an "exceptional Weltanschauung". This dynamism also ensures that one believes consistently and without any doubts in the superiority and correctness of one's own world view. This raises one above the mass of "false prophets".

2. Period of Incarceration

In the preceding chapters we have described how experience and behaviour during incarceration were dependent both on external factors and on a series of personality factors which were apparent in some way or another even before incarceration. It is therefore correct to assume that ideological personalities exhibited peculiar traits not only during their development period but also during the time that they spent in the concentration camps.

The literature available on this phenomenon usually stresses the fact that faith in an idea can give moral support in an extreme stress situation. We also found this confirmed in our studies to the extent that some of those interviewed by us mentioned their religious faith as a reason for their survival (see also Table 12). However, this impression needs to be more closely examined because in most of the inmates, for example, it was not possible to detect any explicit faith in an idea or a Weltanschauung as the foundation for a greater ability to withstand suffering. In addition, we can see from the descriptions of the two priests, Father Siegel and Father Gast, that not only members of one and the same faith but also of the same profession experienced their faith in quite different ways during incarceration. For Father Siegel, religion meant a means of keeping the reality of other people away from him during his time in the camp, while for Father Gast it represented a conviction which brought other people closer to him. One priest dug himself in behind a barricade of ritual customs while the other used these in his efforts to serve his fellowmen, no matter how alien and brutal these may have appeared to him in the concentration camp situation.

The different significance of the Weltanschauung for ideologists and believers, as made clear by this example, is also brought out by the group of ideologists on whom this clinical study is based. In general, one can state that in the case of the ideologists the "armour-plate" of the ideology acts in particular as a screen against the reality of other people.

The only orthodox female Jew in our group of ideologists attempted to strengthen her moral defence mechanisms by strictly fulfilling the laws of her religion. For example, she fished all the pieces of pork out of what was to start with a low-calorie soup in order not to infringe the ritual teachings. However, the thought that she had fulfilled the laws even in such an inhuman situation gave her the strength to hold out and to remain convinced that she would survive incarceration. "Nothing that went on around me managed to penetrate my consciousness."

One Jehovah's Witness recited Biblical quotations to himself when other people got too much for him.

Another Jehovah's Witness stated: "I adopted the Biblical image of an armoured warrior who has faith as a shield, the Bible as a sword and a helmet on his head. All wrongs and injustices bounced off me automatically. Emotions were held strictly at a distance. I disconnected all the wires and cables leading to my heart and linking me with the evil in the world. ... Even today I still regard the events going on outside as a theatre show. I always know how things will turn out. I can always predict the end."

Such reports of their experience are by no means exceptional among the ideologically oriented persons; in particular, they confessed that by clinging to ritual thoughts and actions they were trying to ward off suffering. The clear restriction of interpersonal contact which is brought out by these reports was also frequently apparent from the fact that the ideologically oriented persons only associated with members of their own Weltanschauung. The strong identification with their own group, which could be detected as early as the development period, was intensified even more here.

This holds particularly true for the political ideologists. The solidarity within this group was very pronounced. Their high estimation of themselves from the time preceding incarceration was continued into the period of incarceration. Pride and self-respect were maintained through their links with the group. But, this at the same time intensified their antagonism towards other Weltanschauung groups. We can say, then, that for the ideologists, the extreme stress situation widened the gap between them and the other systems of faith while the believers, on the other and, were able under the same severe stress to discover or better understand the fact that all men are equal. The ideologists displayed a certain collective egoism in the camps. KOGON (1954) described this in the case of the Communists who nearly killed him when they thought — wrongly — that he represented a threat to them. BONDY (1943) describes a group of young Jews whom he prepared for emigration and who, thanks to the total commitment of their group, were able to survive the concentration camp experience unscathed. An ex-inmate gave the following account of the Jehovah's Witnesses:

"They stuck together in exemplary fashion, but they were not on very comradely terms with the other prisoners." He reported, outraged, how as the result of an administrative error, the Jehovah's Witnesses for some time were given far too generous food rations. But they were not ready to share any of this with the other prisoners. Compared with this group, the professional criminals were much more comradely. Another unpleasant thing about the Jehovah's Witnesses was that they were always trying to talk people into "buying" their faith.

In view of this finding, which stresses the close association with one's own group and the strong dissociation from all other groups, it is surprising that the ideologists examined by us complained less frequently about a bad relationship with the guards than the others. Many even described their relationships with the SS as good. The following remark was made by a Jehovah's Witness:

"I was the Hauptsturmführer's favourite."

Another Jehovah's Witness stated: "Strangely enough I discovered that the SS were quite receptive to the gospel."

A Communist declared: "I got on quite well with the SS."

These reports do not mean that the abrupt demarcation between one's own Weltanschauung and that of the Nazis was less clear than the demarcation between one's views and the various Weltanschauungen of one's fellow prisoners. None of the ideologists interviewed by us was in any way corrupted in his view of the world. On the contrary, they were all proud that they had come through the period of incarceration with their beliefs not only intact, but even strengthened.

It is possible either to evaluate these relatively good relationships with the guards as a random finding not worth any further attention, or to interpret them in the following terms. Firstly, with the exception of one female Jew, all the ideologically oriented prisoners were Germans who had been persecuted on religious or political grounds. Thus, as already pointed out, the fact that they spoke the same language made it easier for them to establish contact with the SS guards. A more profound interpretation can also be advanced: The incarceration of political and religious opponents was more rational and made the SS feel less guilty towards the ideological inmates. Despite all the overpowering propaganda put out by the Nazi regime, the tortures inflicted on the non-ideological, mostly Jewish persecutees must have engendered a feeling of guilt in the people directly charged with putting the brutal policies into practice. The ideological persecutees were "not on the same side" but at least could be regarded somehow as worthy partners, whereas on the other hand by kicking and abusing the Jews the SS constantly sought to confirm that these people were trash only fit to be persecuted. This gave rise to unconscious feelings of guilt, which in turn had to be worked off precisely on the victims who were being persecuted for no good rational reason.

A further consideration links up here with what has already been said about the relationships of ideological persons with authority. In their childhood the ideological persons had had to adapt themselves to a cold, hard and unapproachable father. This ability stood them in good stead in the concentration camps where they had to conform to an irrational and inscrutable authority. They were able to subordinate themselves to this force. This assumption is confirmed by the fact that ideological persons exhibited the more or less unconscious tendency to deliver themselves up to a rigid, brutal authority. This provoked a certain admiration on the part of the guards, as expressed by Höss, the former commandant of Auschwitz (1963). "The Jehovah's Witnesses willingly accepted all the unbearable stress imposed on them. It was touching to see how they cared for each other with brotherly love and helped each other out where necessary." According to Höss, Himmler is supposed to have remarked: "If the SS had believed so fanatically in their political ideals, Hitler's State would have been guaranteed a long life."

3. The Post-Incarceration Period

The ability to come to terms with one's concentration camp past is a factor which depends not only on one's personal life history and suffering but also on the environment into which one emerges from imprisonment. In Father Siegel's case it is quite apparent that he did not feel understood by his fellow priests. In the first few nights following his liberation and after his return to the familiar environment of his religious order, he suffered several crying fits. "You won't be let in. They don't understand you here." In his eyes, persons who had not lived through the experience of concentration camp incarceration were somehow alien.

As Matussek (1963) has pointed out, the feeling that as an ex-inmate of a concentration camp one cannot hope to be understood by one's environment relates to a more general plane, namely that of society. In the group of ideologists investigated by us, the Jehovah's Witnesses were best able to tolerate society because, in any case, they expected nothing positive from it. For them, the world will only be an acceptable place to live in when the Messiah comes.

Therefore they feel equally comfortable or uncomfortable in society: "Persecution and rejection don't affect us. We need persecution just as we need the wind that blows in our faces."

The members of the established religions and the political ideologists were much more dependent on the social institutions with which they came in contact. This can be clearly seen in the case of Father Siegel. Not only did he fall out with his fellow priests and his superiors, he also complained bitterly about society, which showed too little concern for ex-inmates and instead pursued its own pleasures. Most serious of all in his opinion is the moral, i.e. sexual, decline of society. He feels that the authorities should take much stricter action against immoral films and theatre performances.

Shortly after their release the mood of political ideologists was one of optimism because they hoped that they would be called upon to build a new society to replace the crushed Nazi regime. Initially they did not feel confronted with the "old society" in the same way that Father Siegel experienced this within the framework of his unchanged religious order. While the non-ideological political inmates could accept that the "new society" was not made up solely of tried and proven anti-fascists, many ideologists found this very hard to swallow. In contrast to ex-persecutees who had a more realistic view of the world, they were far less able to tolerate a democratic state with its large number of interest groups and bureaucratic decision paths, and above all they objected to the fact that ex-Nazis had either gone underground or re-emerged unpunished. Therefore, for Communist ideologists it was easier to reintegrate into a socialist country, as MÜLLER-HEGEMANN and SPITZNER (1963) pointed out:

"For the ex-persecutees of the Nazi regime now resident in the German Democratic Republic it is fundamentally important to know that they are no longer exposed to the danger of anti-semitic and neo-fascist meetings and that their past struggles and sufferings have not been in vain. Given these circumstances and all the medical and social aid measures implemented on their behalf, it was easier for these people to seize the opportunity for full (occupational and other) re-integration into life than it is in countries where the persecutees of the Nazi regime are exposed to the suspicion and insults of neo-fascist elements, or where they may even suffer fresh persecution."

"Almost all the inmates released in 1945 reported that despite great physical weakness (they weighed between 40 and 50 kg) they immediately engaged in political-administrative work. Basically what they said was: 'We were needed and we had no time to be ill'. Often they had to work 14–16 hours a day and yet they gradually recovered their strength. It should be stressed that 91 of the interviewees (out of a total of 96) rose significantly in society in the years after 1945. Following release from imprisonment they became mayors, chiefs of police, senior executives, school principals, editors, a commercial counsellor in the diplomatic service, and leading scientists." "With a few exceptions, they have been able to carry a large work load right up to the present day."

MÜLLER-HEGEMANN and SPITZNER (1963) are therefore of the opinion that the call for pensions as a "psychological aid" is justifiable for ex-persecutees now living in capitalist countries but not for those in Communist countries.

These studies make no mention of the fate of non-Communists, particularly the Jews. Thus the interpretation advanced by the cited authors that the ex-resistance fighters found a favourable climate for existence only in Communist countries is really an ideological justification of their own results, because they paid no attention to the fate of non-Communist persecutees.

In addition, on the basis of past scientific studies, it seems unlikely that almost 100% of 96 former concentration camp inmates were able to handle a large work load (often as much as 14–16 hours per day). The literature from the Eastern Bloc countries refers to the fact that many ex-inmates suffered severe work disturbances.

Despite the scientific doubts raised by these and similar studies, which attempt to distort the examination of ex-concentration camp detainees for ideological purposes, they do indirectly highlight one characteristic which is typical for the ideological person in the post-incarceration period. Such a person needs as far as possible a homogeneous group which interprets the world from the same standpoint as himself. The ideologist has no time for other conceptions of society, in contrast to the non-ideological prisoners, whose sufferings helped them gain greater understanding of people who subscribed to other beliefs. Thus, the following remarks are typical of the ideological person:

"The world is full of injustice."
"The Nazis are back at the controls of society."
"The public does not show enough interest in what happened in the concentration camps."

As a result, because of the limitations imposed by society, the opportunities to find their views confirmed, to give their lives some drive and also to discover some sense in life were limited to their own ideological reference group. The positive view of themselves which this engendered ("we are something special") nevertheless needed to be constantly backed up by a feeling of contempt for "others". This fact is not founded in the social conditions alone but also in the history of the persecuted person's personality. FRENKEL-BRUNSWICK (1950) was able to show that it is a personality trait of authoritarian-ideological persons to regard their environment as hostile and life as unpleasant. In a similar manner, TAUSCH (1965) found that there is a correlation between authoritarian and pessimistic attitudes.

On the other hand, non-ideological Communists and priests see in their concentration camp experiences evidence of the true humanity that can be detected behind such social labels as "Jehovah's Witness", "Socialist", "Priest", "Criminal", "SS man". Their present egalitarian attitude towards other people, which permits them to engage in a genuine dialogue with others, is frequently the result of the experience of introversion and the contemplation of the true values of mankind through which they went while incarcerated. The pessimistic expectations of ideological persecutees (a striking example is the prospect of doom continuously preached by the Jehovah's Witnesses) stand in contrast to the hopes cherished by the believing persecutees who expect more from life than calamity.

The extreme group identification of the ideological persons, which hampered the development of a personal and intensely experienced ethos typical of adulthood, manifests itself in the way in which these people accuse society. MATUSSEK (1961) in an earlier study has already drawn attention to the existential prosecutor role of ex-concentration camp inmates, and this does not need to be repeated here. In the present connection, all that need concern us is the type of accusation made by ideologists and non-ideologists, respectively. The accusations levelled by ideological persecutees are frequently formulated in extreme terms, as the following quotations illustrate:

"Whenever I met a guard, I never knew if I might perhaps beat him up" (Aggression against persecutors).

"The Nazis are back in all the positions of power" (Aggression against authorities and institutions).

"There was no comradeship in the concentration camp. Most of the inmates were absolute swine" (Aggression against persecutees).

"Most people are full of hatred. Whenever they get a chance they vent their hatred on others. You can't trust anyone" (Aggression against fellowmen).

These expressions of aggression are qualitatively specific for ideological persecutees insofar as they are general in character rather than personal and concrete. This is also evidenced by the fact that they tend to attack anonymous wielders of power or the system as a whole, while non-ideological persecutees tend to concentrate more on actual individuals as the targets of their hostile comments. This again expresses the attitude of ideological persons: They ignore empirical, concrete and verifiable conditions in favour of abstract, non-verifiable wholes. They themselves justify this attitude saying that they do not wish to lose their "overall view".

Furthermore, this characteristic of hating everything and everyone "in general" makes it possible to understand why these people frequently expressed dissatisfaction with their fate. In particular, ideological priests and Jehovah's Witnesses complain that they have a hard time in this world, as the following remarks make clear:

"I have always had to struggle" (Priest).

"We are hounded by the whole world" (Jehovah's Witness).

"It is the power of evil, not people, that rules the world. Evil governs through people" (Communist).

We must also see these forms of aggression on the part of religious-ideological persecutees as the result of the enduring obligation imposed on them by their faith to love their fellowmen at all costs. However, deep down they are not truly and genuinely able to live up to this imperative, therefore they complain more frequently than the non-ideological persecutees that fate, circumstances or unsatisfactory conditions are responsible for their lives not having followed the course that they would have wished. If we accept that ideological personalities can sense how strongly their lives are determined right from the start and are thus aware that they cannot freely shape their lives as they wish, it is possible to understand their hatred for their fate. Their frequent complaints against authorities, institutions and humanity in general emphasize the already mentioned contact modalities, which are characterized by a loss of confidence in the environment and encapsulation from society as a whole.

It is not surprising therefore that these persons in fact take a less active part in life around them than one would have expected from their declared commitment. They find a great many things which they feel need to be improved, but their effective contribution frequently remains limited merely to pointing out the "good" and "bad" in the world. Nowadays, in many cases, their political or religious activity has been replaced by reading about and contemplating ideological problems.

Finally, we wish to present a last clinical impression of the ideologists in the post-incarceration period. We mentioned at the beginning that, in the case of the ideologists, commitment to the idea was more important during their developmental period than close interpersonal contact. The average age at which the 20 ideologists studied by us got married was relatively high (31 years). The emotional alienation of the ideologists was also manifest in their marriages in the post-incarceration period. In his devotion to the cause of proclaiming salvation or improving the world, a Jehovah's Witness or a Communist can easily neglect the persons closest to him. Frequently he is unable to imagine and accept his marital partner except as a companion in the struggle to attain the goals of the "movement". The attention he pays to his marital partner is dependent on the condition that he can regard his partner as part of an ideological community, for example, which is committed to greater recognition of Nazi victims, which is against the revival of fascism, campaigns for social justice, or works for the future of mankind as a whole.

However, in cases where the ex-persecutee has lost interest in these goals, or where the goals are not regarded as important by the marital partner, the bond of marital communication also breaks down. The marital partners go on living together, each either indifferent to or even in conflict with the other. Their children are deprived of the chance of modelling themselves on the affectionate conjugal union of their parents.

Summary

1. The literature constantly stresses the importance of a personal Weltanschauung for an inmate's ability to survive the suffering of concentration camp incarceration. In the preceding chapter we have attempted to differentiate this phenomenon, focussing our attention not on the type of Weltanschauung nor on the degree of identification with a religious or political idea but, instead, on the person's inner attitude towards this Weltanschauung.

2. For example, it was possible to demonstrate that two representatives of the same Weltanschauung and of the same profession (Catholic priests) had two different attitudes to their Weltanschauung. We termed the one attitude "ideological" and the other "believing" and attempted to illustrate the behavioural patterns which distinguish these two attitudes.

Although both the believers and the ideologists found an important source of strength in their Weltanschauung during their period of incarceration, the ideologists were only able to draw on this force by restricting their interpersonal contacts, while in contrast the believers maintained much more concrete and comprehensive contact with other people. We can conclude from this that the moral support which the ideologist derives from his belief is achieved at the expense of an open and responsive attitude towards his fellowmen.

3. This phenomenon was illustrated by two case histories, but it was not possible to check it statistically because the interview documentation was not sufficient to permit proper classification of 20 believers. Instead, we took 20 interviewees who exhibited clear characteristics of an ideological personality and also described certain peculiarities from their pre-concentration-camp period, the period of incarceration, and the post-incarceration period, to the extent that these features could be regarded as clinically relevant on the basis of our material. As in the preceding chapters, here, too, we discovered a continuous thread running through from the pre-persecution

period to the present, even though this could not be confirmed statistically, for the reasons stated.

In summary, we might interpret this continuity in the following terms: The sometimes indigent family circumstances caused the father or mother to adopt a cold, aloof manner and gave rise to a feeling of inferiority in the child which the latter then balanced out in puberty by associating himself with a strongly ideologically oriented group. Here the child was able to belong to a community that was better than the others. The aggressions that were inadequately processed during childhood were socialized, even idealized, in the rejection of or struggle against other Weltanschauungen. It was the belief in the superiority of one's own group during the period of incarceration that in turn gave rise to the feeling of strength and security which contributed a great deal to the remarkable capacity for suffering exhibited by the ideologists.

After liberation from the concentration camp, the world remained divided into good and bad, friend and foe. The ideologists felt safe and secure only in an environment that corresponded to their own Weltanschauung. In extreme cases, e.g. Father Siegel, however, the association with a particular group was not adequate to overcome the feeling of isolation. For him contact was only possible through preaching, didacticism and frequently also through a hatred directed against anonymous forces. It can be concluded, therefore, that no matter how much strength could be derived in a stress situation from identification with a particular ideology, this nevertheless made it difficult for the individual to find his way to a mature ethos or to a mature belief which embodied a greater open-mindedness and responsiveness in intimate personal relationships. Close interpersonal contact could be achieved more readily by the believing representatives of a religious or political Weltanschauung than by the ideological personalities.

CHAPTER 10

Reasons for Emigration and Ability to Cope with Life in the Case of Jewish Persecutees

Outline of Problem

The preceding chapter was devoted to a study of the peculiarities of political and religious persecutees. It is now time, in conclusion, to analyse the Jewish interviewees separately.

There are two reasons why this is necessary. Firstly, the composition of the group of Jewish interviewees raises questions which have so far not been answered. Secondly, a large number of the findings already reported indicate the special situation of racial persecutees. To start with, therefore, we will briefly summarize some of the findings that characterize the specific aspects of the persecution and of the present psychic and social condition of Jewish interviewees:

1. The Jews were persecuted because of their so-called "race", i.e. for a characteristic that had nothing to do with a particular attitude or activity concerning the National Socialist regime.

2. The aim of the Jewish persecution programme was the complete extermination of the Jews as a people, religion and culture. For each individual Jew this threat represented a degree of stress that was not matched in any of the other groups of persecutees.

3. Within our group of interviewees it can be shown that racial persecutees were more frequently imprisoned in the harshest concentration camps, were exposed to the most severe work stress in these camps and, as a group, were most frequently affected by the loss of relatives.

4. It was more difficult for them than for other former inmates to reintegrate into society following their release. The persecution left the Jews more "homeless" than any of the other groups and in the first few years after the war there was no country in the world that was willing to accept them.

5. With regard to their physical condition, racial persecutees nowadays suffer more frequently from exhaustion states ("psychophysical syndrome") than other groups of persecutees.

6. In Jews the psychic state is more frequently characterized by Factor IV, "Resignation and despair", than in the other groups of persecutees.

Within the group of Jewish persecutees, people of Polish origin suffered more severe persecution stress and also sustained greater physical and psychological damage than persons of German origin. These differences draw attention to the fact that even the Jewish interviewees do not constitute a completely uniform sample. We must now ask what other differences will be revealed by a separate study of the racial persecutees, because it is possible that in selecting the method of comparing groups we obliterated important differences existing within the groups of Polish or German Jews.

The random sample nature of the group of Jewish persecutees provides further reasons for treating them separately. The reasons may be briefly summarized as follows:

1. The Jewish interviewees constitute by far the most numerous unit within the overall group. It is therefore justifiable to analyse them separately.

2. In contrast to the political and religious persecutees, the racial persecutees constitute a by and large representative random sample from the countries of their birth (Germany and Poland). This permits us to claim general validity for the observations and findings made on this group of interviewees.

3. Within our sample, only racial persecutees are nowadays resident outside Germany (in Israel and New York); therefore this random sample can be used to enquire into the reasons for emigrating and for the choice of the new country of residence.

These special characteristics of the group of racial persecutees thus pose the two sets of problems which are dealt with in this chapter.

First, it is necessary to clarify what reasons led the Jews after their release to choose the particular country of residence that they did; second, we wish to learn how the Jewish interviewees in particular "coped with life" following their release. In this connection, it is also of prime importance to study the differences within this group of interviewees. In addition, we must check to see whether this separate analysis of the Jewish interviewees necessitates any corrections or additions to the findings reported so far.

I. Reasons for the Choice of Country of Residence

It is not possible to study the circumstances and motives that have led to the scattering of concentration camp survivors over the entire world without at least briefly reminding ourselves of the political, economic, social and psychological situation of the world, particularly Europe and the Middle East, in the first few years after the war.

At the end of the Second World War, the whole world heaved a sigh of relief. However, this feeling of relief did not last long for the survivors of the concentration camps. Saved from certain death in the camps, they were now faced with a new danger — the catastrophic aftermath of the last war. They were brought painfully face to face with the fact that the world in which they had grown up, their homes, neighbourhoods, friends and families, everything which they had possessed and the places they had occupied in society, had all been lost or destroyed. Everything familiar and well-known to them had disappeared. They were no longer prisoners. The world had invented a new name for them, they were "displaced persons". The survivors were sick, confused and lonely. The terrors of the concentration camps had been replaced by the new horrors of uncertainty and fear — uncertainty about where the survivors should go and what they should do and fear that all other members of their families might have been killed.

The governments in Europe were confronted with an enormous human problem which they were unable to solve because they did not possess the right institutions. The world powers wanted to strengthen their positions in Europe; the "cold war" started; Communist revolutions were planned and carried out; masses of people moved back and forth across Europe, either returning to their homelands or fleeing new and threatening persecutions. The racial persecutee was only one of many displaced persons and was among the last to be helped. Prior to 1948 it was almost impossible to emigrate to the country now known as Israel. The British stood by their pre-war policy of preventing the Jews from entering Israel. Anyone who tried to emigrate illegally was risking his life. Refugees were interned for three years behind barbed wire in so-called "transit camps" on the island of Cyprus. The USA did not relax its immigration restrictions, which had been in force from before the war, and continued to refuse entry to all who were sick or without money or who had no relatives living in the USA, and of course, this eliminated almost all the persecutees.

A number of anti-semitic campaigns were conducted in Poland both by the civilian population and the government. Germany had been destroyed. Housing was practically non-existent and unemployment was widespread. Millions of people of German descent poured out of Czechoslovakia, Poland, Rumania and the eastern parts of the former German Reich into the western zones. They wanted to escape the wrath of the populations of these countries which was directed against all "ethnic Germans", and they were also fleeing before the advancing Russian troops. In this politico-economic and social climate the Jews were made to feel over and over again that they were unwanted. They were unwanted when they tried to return home, unwanted when they tried to emigrate to a new country, and they were not permitted to enter Israel.

In 1948 the state of Israel was proclaimed by the United Nations. The new state accepted with open arms everyone who wanted to make it his new home. Nevertheless, emigration to Israel was not an attractive solution for many refugees because the climate was very hot and the country poor and underdeveloped. Although Israel offered the displaced persons a place to live, it soon turned out that the survivors of the concentration camps faced a new threat here. Life in Israel was going to be tough. Would they be strong enough to put up with all the hardships? Israel did not possess any industry. There was no housing. Where were they going to live? But, above all, the neighbouring Arab countries had declared war on Israel on the very day that it was given its independence. Had the persecutees survived the concentration camps merely to be massacred in another part of the world, and in Israel at that? The Jewish refugees faced a tremendous dilemma. Many were able to establish themselves in Germany in the first few years after the war. Others returned to their homelands in Poland, Rumania or Czechoslovakia in order to seek out their families, friends or the traces of their earlier lives. Many remained there. We can only guess at their reasons because this study does not contain any material on this subject. Others left their old homeland again at a later date, partly because they failed to find any of their family or friends there, partly because of new waves of anti-semitism and partly because of the takeover of the government by the Communists.

In order to examine the reasons that lay behind the choice of country to which to emigrate, the breakdown of the Jewish persecutees according to present country of residence was adopted from the previous chapters, i.e. Israel (n=42), USA (n=26) and Germany (n=97). For the purpose of studying the emigration motivation, interviewees who initially emigrated to Israel or to the USA but then returned to Germany were included in the Israeli or American subgroup. The Israel group therefore contains 47 persons instead of 42, and the USA group 29 persons instead of 26. For the sake of simplicity, the 12 interviewees who chose countries other than Israel or the USA as their first country of residence and who only came to Munich later were included in the German subgroup. A total of 10 categories were used to classify the main reasons for the choice of country made by these displaced persons. In forming these categories we took account of the reasons which the interviewees themselves gave for their choice. Where such data were lacking, we used information on the external conditions under which the choice was made. In some cases more than one reason was apparent for the choice of country. Such cases were classified under the category which obviously had the most decisive influence on the choice.

Table 71 shows the 10 motivation categories and the frequency with which they are represented. In 146 cases (89%) the interview material was considered adequate to answer the question of motivation. The remaining 19 (11%) cases were classified under the category "uncertain".

Table 71. Categories of motivation for the choice of country of residence following release (n=165)

Category	Number
1. Zionism	32 (20%)
2. Interconfessional marriages	31 (19%)
3. Traumatic uprooting	19 (12%)
4. Return to family	18 (11%)
5. Christians	12 (7%)
6. Rejection of Germans	12 (7%)
7. Illness	11 (6%)
8. Occupational-economic reasons	8 (5%)
9. Reparation	3 (2%)
10. Uncertain	19 (11%)
Total	165 (100%)

In the following, each category will be discussed with the choice of country of residence and some other data.

a) Zionism

The 32 interviewees in this category belonged either before, during or after incarceration to Zionist organisations. All had spent at least several years in Israel and the majority (27) still live there. For these interviewees, Zionism was the only real motivation behind their choice of Israel as the country in which to settle.

Only 5 Zionists chose either Munich (4) or New York (1) as their place of residence after spending a few years in Israel. Their reasons for their choices were that they expected to find better job opportunities in these two places. They still support Zionism.

Even before the start of the Jewish persecution programme during the Third Reich, the cohesion of Jewish communities and of Jewish cultural life had declined. The Jews had split up in different ideological directions. According to BLOCH (1966) the following tendencies can be observed in the period preceding the onset of persecution: participation in socialist movements; participation in conservative-nationalist movements; adherence to traditional Jewish habits; Zionist orientation and plans to emigrate to Israel.

In view of the many ideological attitudes represented by European Jews, it is not surprising to find that most of the persecutees who emigrated to Israel were either actively engaged in Zionist movements or were in touch with them. The persecution deprived the Jews in Europe of their homes and thus in a tragic way facilitated and accelerated the emigration to Israel.

It is not just the persons living in Israel who participate in Zionist movements. Several interviewees who were living in Munich at the time of the investigation reported that they had earlier been active in Zionist organisations. They are still interested in such organisations even today. Some of them, as well as some interviewees in the USA, were planning to emigrate later to Israel. It is clear that contact with Zionist organisations did not necessarily result in emigration. We were unable to determine clearly what tipped the scales in favour of emigration in each case. It is probable that other factors, such as surviving members of the family, illness and the rebuilding of an economic existence in the first years after the war in Europe could have prevented a Zionistically motivated emigration.

b) Interconfessional Marriages

The 31 representatives of this group are now all residing in Munich. This choice of location was probably determined by their marriage to a non-Jewish German. Interconfessional marriage frequently goes together with a more or less clear dissociation from Judaism.

None of the representatives of this group show any interest in Judaism, in Israel or in Zionism. Although in several cases marriages were concluded with German Christians in the post-incarceration period, apparently because both parties felt lonely, these marriages only continued a process of cultural and religious assimilation that had begun even before persecution started. This was particularly evident in the life histories of 10 German Jews who married German Christians before persecution commenced. Admittedly, none of them made the change to Christianity for their first marriage, but all of them go to great lengths to stress their Germanity, even the 5 persons (4 women and 1 man) whose non-Jewish spouses separated from them during the Third Reich. None of them displayed even a passing interest in Judaism. Before persecution started they regarded themselves as Germans and they still do. They have finished with Judaism and no longer wish to discuss it.

The remaining 22 representatives of this group married German Christians after the war. In no case did either marital partner adopt the faith of the other one. Of these people, 11 came from Germany, 10 from Poland and one from Hungary.

The 11 German Jews came from semi-assimilated families and showed little interest in Judaism. None of them were Zionists either before or after the Second World War. The Christian partner is the dominant partner in the marriages. The few children of these marriages have all been baptized. The persons who have retained a private interest in Judaism or who describe themselves as "convinced Jews" stress that they are first and foremost Germans.

All 10 Polish Jews — 8 of them were men — had married for a second time. In their first marriages they had all had Jewish partners and had lost these as well as their children in the concentration camps. Most of them regard themselves as too old and sick to consider emigration. They live in social isolation in Germany and are emotionally dependent on their marital partners. Many of these interviewees are financially dependent on their wives. A few have managed to establish a small business in Munich and this brings them in enough to live on. The Polish Jews do not regard themselves as Germans at all because they came to Germany as emigrants.

The German Jews who are married to Christians do not regard themselves as "Jews". This designation goes against their personal feelings and their identification. On the other hand, the Polish Jews who are married to Christians maintain a certain degree of Jewish identity. Admittedly, they do not attend the synagogue, nor do they celebrate Jewish festivals or take part in Jewish community life, but they always describe themselves, when asked, as Jews.

c) Traumatic Uprooting

The psychological state we found in the 19 interviewees in this category can be described as "traumatic uprooting". These persons do not know why they are alive. Apathy and loneliness, sickness and disorientation are their most prominent features as revealed by the interviews. Their "choice" of country (14 in Munich, 4 in New York and 1 in Israel) has to be seen against this background.

Of the Munich subgroup, 9 interviewees were born and grew up in Poland, 3 in Czechoslovakia, one in Rumania and 2 in Germany. After liberation from the camps they first returned to their home districts to look for friends and relatives. Only 2 interviewees were able to find any surviving members of their families. One of them found a brother in Poland, the other learned of the existence of a distant relative in Israel. Most of the representatives of this group did not feel able to live in their old communities following the destruction and death of their families. Many reported that the people in their old home towns and villages had been hostile towards them. During their search for their relatives all these people came to Munich. This was probably because Munich had become a centre for all the aid and refugee organisations. Most of the interviewees married Jewish partners in Munich and became small businessmen, office workers or housewives. Although they grew up in religious families, they never practised their religion and have no contact with the Jewish community in Munich. None of them could say exactly why they had remained in Munich. Occasionally, when a friend or a wife visits Israel, they have a strong desire to emigrate there, but this enthusiasm rapidly evaporates. None of the group belonged to Zionist or Socialist groups, either before or after the period of persecution, nor did they have any interest in such organisations. They have no real roots in any country and they regard their lives as completely devoid of meaning, although some of them are successful doctors, businessmen or housewives.

The 5 persons living in the USA or in Israel do not differ psychologically from the interviewees living in Munich. They are just as much at a loss to explain why they emigrated to Israel or the USA. Their lives are just as empty.

d) Return to the Family

In the case of 18 representatives of this group, the main reason for choosing the country of residence was the desire to join relatives in that country.

USA: 5 of the 8 emigrants presently living in the USA were born in Germany and 3 in Eastern Europe. The 5 Jews of German extraction come from families which did not belong to any particular group in the society within which they lived. Their family life was not religious, nor did they show any interest in Judaism. On the other hand, the families had not become fully assimilated into German society. Before the war they had all tried in vain to emigrate to the USA. After the war relatives and friends helped them with their emigration. The word "Judaism" never cropped up in the reports of these five interviewees except in a social context and usually in connection with anti-semitism. Although it is perhaps a simplification, we can say that people emigrated to the USA because they were not wanted in Germany. For them, their Jewishness was a social stigma.

The 3 Jews from Eastern Europe who belong to this group grew up in religious families in which the celebration of Jewish religious rites was an everyday part of their lives. They lost their entire families, with the exception of a sister or a brother who had been able to escape to New York. At the end of the war these survivors joined up with each other in New York after they had learned of the death of all the other members of their families.

Of the 10 interviewees who emigrated to relatives in Israel, 8 came from Poland and 2 from Germany. The family background varied from religious or semi-religious to assimilated. Some had been loosely associated with a Jewish organisation before the war but did not belong to any Zionist, Communist or Socialist organisation. Their main reason for emigrating to Israel was that they had relatives there or that shortly after or before the war they married someone who was on his or her way to Israel. The representatives of this group do not seem to have any particularly strong beliefs and are not all that happy with life in Israel. Since their choice of country was primarily motivated by family reasons, they left Israel and the USA for Munich as soon as the family ties became weaker.

e) Christians

Our study group of "racial persecutees" includes 12 persons with a Christian family background. All of them were baptized and raised in the Christian faith. They never had any interest in Judaism as a religion, culture or nation. The only link between them and Judaism is their Jewish forefathers. To avoid being regarded as "Jews" by the persons around them, they made every effort to keep their "Jewish descent" secret. All were living in Munich at the time when they were investigated. None of them has any intention of emigrating to another country. It is one of the historic tragedies of the Third Reich that these people were persecuted because they were allegedly Jews. These bitterly ironic events are the result, among other things, of the tendency of many people even today to misuse anthropological and biological concepts to classify nations as well as religious, cultural and ethnic groups.

f) Rejection of the Germans

The 12 representatives of this group are nowadays living in New York. They state that they left Germany because they did not wish to be in daily contact with Germans. Typical remarks were: "I can see the murderer of my family in each of them" or "Who knows who murdered my sister and my aunt?"

A former lawyer and judge from Berlin put it as follows: "In 1945 I returned to Berlin and campaigned for the return of the Berlin Jews to Berlin. The resistance which this proposal encountered in official quarters and similar events resulted in my decision to emigrate. There is no room for Jews in Germany. There are certain elements in the administrative and political system that have not grasped how much the Jews suffered under the Nazis. I therefore believe that it is no longer possible for Jews to live in Germany."

One of the Poles comes from Poznan. He said his family always felt German. After the war he studied at Erlangen University and complained about anti-semitism there. He then completed his studies in the USA and is now a professor at a well-known American university.

Nine of the 12 interviewees were born in Germany and 3 in Poland. Most of the representatives of this group have relatives in England, Sweden, the USA and Israel. They describe their family background as religious but, with the exception of the American professor, they did not mention any Zionist or Socialist experience. It is striking that despite the reasons given for their emigration, the people in this group exhibit a clear leaning towards Germany.

g) Sickness

All 11 persons in this group live in Munich. They remained in Germany mainly because of the poor state of their health. Nine of them come from Poland, 2 from Germany. They all grew up in religious families and were religious even before the war. For the most part they are active members of the present Jewish community in Munich. All wanted to emigrate after the war, most of them to Israel and only 2 to the USA. The poor state of their health and the immigration quotas defeated these plans. It is not possible to establish satisfactorily how far this reason is put forward as an excuse and how far it is genuine. Since these people did not have any relatives abroad, it is tempting to assume that they did not feel capable of accepting the challenge of emigration.

h) Occupational-Economic Reasons

Eight interviewees, all living in Munich, gave financial factors and their occupations as the reasons for living in Germany. Six of these persons come from Poland, one from Germany and one from Hungary. One of these interviewees is a doctor with his own practice, another is the owner of a flourishing textile plant, others are simple employees. Five of the people in this group are women whose husbands are businessmen. This group also contains the greatest number of interviewees from religious families who associate only with Jews in Munich. Some of them complain about anti-semitism and are considering the possibility of emigrating to Israel at a later date.

i) Indemnification

This category comprises 3 male persecutees. As children they all attended Jewish schools, 2 in Hungary and 1 in Poland. They emigrated to Israel in 1948–1949. When they became ill there, they returned to Munich because they felt they could more actively pursue their pension applications from that city.

j) Not Clear

In 19 cases the interview material was inadequate to explain why a particular country of residence was chosen. Of these interviewees 13 were born in Poland, 3 in Germany and one each in Russia, Greece and Czechoslovakia. Five are living in the USA, 10 in Germany and 4 in Israel. The great majority of them came from religious families. All those born in Poland attended Jewish schools. None of them mentioned having any relatives in the countries in which they chose to live and none stated that they cooperated with Zionist groups or had come into contact with similar ideas. None of them experienced any anti-semitism after 1945. Almost all of them are the sole survivors of their respective families.

Table 72 summarizes the reasons for emigration grouped according to the 3 countries of residence.

The Table shows that there are clear differences between the 3 emigration groups. Different motives are characteristic for each of the three countries. We have summarized these differences in the following and added data on the sociological structure of the emigration groups.

Israel: The Israeli interviewees emigrated from Europe to Israel between 1945 and 1954. The majority of them live and work in towns and cities. Some of them live on kibbutzim, which are agricultural and industrial communities with a socialistic work and wage structure — membership in a kibbutz is voluntary.

Most of the persons who emigrated to Israel had come into contact with Zionist ideas before or during persecution. Zionism as a reason for emigration is linked exclusively with Israel and no other country. In terms of content this particular motivation can be described as positive and future-oriented. It is associated with hope for a new life in a new country, a life that will also re-unite the immigrant with the thousands of years of Jewish culture and history. The Israeli group contains on average the youngest interviewees. At the time of the interview, 75% of them were under 50. In this respect they differ distinctly from the group of persons who emigrated to America. The lower average age also goes together with the fact that the Israeli group included the greatest number of people who married for the first time after their release from the concentration camps. Also, the number of children is on average higher in the case of the Israeli emigrants than in the other groups. In Israel the number of children per family is 1.8, in Germany it is 0.9 and in the USA 0.7.

An analysis of the occupational structure reveals that the Israelis relatively frequently have jobs involving manual labour:

Table 72. Main motives for the choice of country of residence following liberation from the concentration camps (n=165)

Israel	Number	USA	Number	Germany	Number
Zionism	32 (68%)	Rejection of Germans	12 (41%)	Interconfessional marriages	31 (34%)
Return to family	10 (21%)	Return to family	8 (28%)	Traumatic uprooting	14 (16%)
Traumatic uprooting	1 (2%)	Traumatic uprooting	4 (14%)	Christians	12 (14%)
Unclear	4 (9%)	Unclear	5 (17%)	Illness	3 (4%)
				Occupational-economic reasons	8 (9%)
				Indemnification	3 (4%)
				Unclear	10 (11%)
Total	47 (100%)	Total	29 (100%)	Total	89 (100%)

In Israel 57% of the interviewees performed some sort of manual labour, in the USA the figure was 27% and in Germany only 6%. On the other hand, our random sample of Israelis does not include any businessmen. In addition, in relative terms the highest percentage of former persecutees with a good standard of living are resident in Israel.

USA: The American interviewees also emigrated from Europe in the period between 1945 and 1954. They are all residents of New York City, which is the largest aggregation of Jewish communities in the world with a population of almost 3 million Jews accounting for about 22% of the city's total population. Rejection of the Germans is the characteristic reason given for emigrating to the USA. This rejection is, in part, the expression of a deep disappointment. The interviewees had previously felt strongly attached to Germany but had been forced to realize after their release from the concentration camps that they could never again feel at home in Germany. The fact that America and not Israel was chosen as the new country in which to live seems also to be connected with the rooting of these persons in the German and European culture. These interviewees believed the USA would be more like Europe than was Israel. Furthermore, America, with its large Jewish minority, seemed best able to satisfy these persons' desire for peace and security. The sociological structure of the people who emigrated to the USA is very similar to that of the persons now living in Germany. On average they are older than the Israelis, more frequently unmarried or married without children and they are nowadays divided equally between the upper and lower middle class strata of society.

Germany: Some of the ex-concentration camp inmates now living in Germany were interned in refugee camps in the Munich area in the first few years after the war. As soon as they were able to leave these camps they came to Munich and settled there. Other members of this group were released from concentration camps in various European countries and subsequently lived for several years outside Germany.

In the years 1947 to 1956 they then came to Munich to live and work. Most of them do not originate from Germany. According to their statements their stay in Munich is not intended to be permanent. They are planning to emigrate later on to Israel or the USA.

The largest group of ex-concentration camp inmates who remained in Germany is made up of persons married to non-Jewish partners. In the case of those interviewees who were also born in Germany, this choice of partner corresponds to a tendency toward assimilation that was apparent even before persecution started. In the case of the Jews born in Poland, the choice of a non-Jewish partner and the resulting dissociation of these persons from Judaism must instead be interpreted as a specific consequence of incarceration. This form of persecution damage can be described as a "cultural loss of identity". The element of resignation that is implied in this concept is found to a greater or lesser extent in the majority of persons in this group.

The range of ages in the group of Jews living in Germany is greater than in the other two groups. On average, they are older than the persons now living in Israel. They have the highest percentage of second marriages. Frequently these marriages do not produce children.

In contrast to the persons who emigrated to Israel or to the USA, the persons living in Germany include a higher percentage of businessmen and pensioners. The businessmen as a rule are Jews of Polish descent. On the other hand, Jews of German descent who nowadays also reside in Germany frequently work as salaried employees or are self-employed.

II. General Mastery of Life

1. Different Ways of Coping with Life

Having examined the reasons for the choice of country in which to live we can now study how the Jewish concentration camp inmates came to terms with their fate.

This study is intended to answer the question raised at the beginning of this chapter: "What significant differences can be detected within the group of Jewish persecutees which may have been levelled out by the procedure adopted so far?" We developed for this purpose a complex category labelled "general mastery of life". This category takes account of data from the following areas of life: interpersonal contact, occupation, marriage and family, and reaction to the experience of incarceration. Details on the way in which the category "general mastery of life" was developed are given in the Appendix (see p. 259).

Table 73 lists the correlations between the individual areas of life and the summarizing category "general mastery of life".

All the correlations are statistically significant or very significant. The closest correlation exists between the areas of interpersonal contact and the ability to cope intellectually and emotionally with the experience of incarceration. The weakest correlation exists between the areas of marriage-family and occupation. We will not interpret the magnitude and differences of the individual correlation coefficients in detail. It is merely important here to note that each individual area exhibits the strongest correlation with the overall category "general mastery of life". This overall

Table 73. Intercorrelations of 4 areas of life and the overall category "general mastery of life" (n=165)

	Marriage and family	Contact	Occupation	Reaction to incarceration	Overall category
Marriage and family	—	0.38	0.19	0.36	0.53
Contact		—	0.29	0.50	0.66
Occupation			—	0.19	0.60
Reaction to incarceration				—	0.66
Overall category					—

category can thus be seen as the best possible representation of all sub-categories, therefore this is the category that we will use in the following. With the aid of the characteristics that make up the category "general mastery of life" we can distinguish between three different groups of persons (see also Appendix, p. 259):

A: Persons who are able to cope successfully with life
B: Persons who are partially able to cope with life
C: Persons who are unable to cope with life.

In the further course of this investigation we will restrict ourselves mainly to the extreme groups A and C. These two groups will be described in detail below.

Persons able to cope successfully with life (A):

Of course, the fact that an ex-inmate is successful in coping with life does not mean that he leads an ideal existence, devoid of problems or conflict. As it relates to the present group under study, the concept of successful mastery of life means that a number of conditions must be satisfied in certain individual areas:

Interpersonal contact: The interviewee has personal acquaintances. He is interested in the persons in his particular environment and if necessary can establish contact with them. He keeps up with socio-political affairs in the world around him.

Occupation (men only): The interviewee is able to support himself and his family through his work. From the time of his release his career has continued to develop successfully more or less without interruption. Job changes are made at his own wish and always with the aim of improving himself and his job skills. By and large the interviewee is satisfied with his occupation.

Marriage: The marital partners make an effort to show respect and understanding for each other. They feel affection for each other. Their marital life is a source of satisfaction to them. The bonds are relatively stable. Conflicts that occur can usually be handled by the partners either acting separately or together.

Reaction to incarceration: The interviewee is no longer prevented by resurgent memories of his incarceration from devoting himself to his family, his friends and his job. He is not completely "paralysed" by his concentration camp experience, but he does not repress it either.

Persons unable to cope successfully with life (C):

Like group A, this group also presents a uniform picture, although it is the picture of a largely ruined life.

Interpersonal contact: The interviewee is lonely and socially completely isolated. He has no friends and no confidants. At best he may know a few former fellow sufferers who were also incarcerated in concentration camps. These are the only people with whom he can hold any conversation. He is not involved or interested in a broader social environment. Frequently he emphatically refuses to have anything to do with problems that go beyond his own realm of existence.

Occupation (men only): The interviewee here either drops out of the working world early on or makes repeated unsuccessful attempts to pursue a career. Whenever he does get a job he is dissatisfied with what he is doing, changes jobs frequently and does not earn very much money.

Marriage: Family life is disharmonious. The marital relationship is conflict-ridden. As a rule, the marital partners are alienated from each other and live together without any emotional attachment.

Reaction to concentration camp experience: The interviewee has not been able to overcome mentally the events of his persecution. His memories and his dreams confront him over and over again with the terrors and fears of those days. Although the external conditions of his life have changed since his liberation, he is unable to come to terms mentally with his concentration camp past.

Persons partially able to cope with life (B):

It is characteristic of former inmates in this group that their methods of coping with life vary considerably. Some, for example, have a relatively harmonious marriage but fail completely when it comes to reintegrating into a job. Others have managed to achieve a certain amount of success in their work and can even establish contact with their social environment but at the same time they are completely inhibited by the resurgent memories of their concentration camp days. Within this group of persons there is a wide range of combinations of successful and unsuccessful attempts to cope with the various aspects of life.

It is important to note that this middle group is closer, overall, to the group of persons who are unsuccessful in coping with life. In purely quantitative terms, it was established that the evaluation "unsuccessful" occurred twice as frequently in Group B as the evaluation "successful".

The quantitative distribution of the 165 Jewish interviewees among the 3 "mastery of life" groups is given in the following Figure:

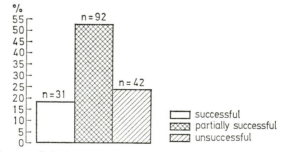

Fig. 19. Distribution of the interviewees among the 3 "mastery of life" groups (n=165)

This distribution shows clearly that most Jewish persecutees were totally (25%) or partially (57%) unable to come to terms with life after their liberation. Out of the whole group, 31 persons (18%) show clear signs of being able to cope successfully with life.

Thus we find that even within the group of Jewish interviewees there are very definite differences as regards the way in which they handle their fate. Despite a strong tendency to be unable to cope with life, the Jewish interviewees cannot be regarded as a homogeneous group in this respect.

In order to determine the reasons for the differences in the ability to cope with life, we first examined the influence of some sociological group characteristics. *No statistically significant relationships were found to exist for the following characteristics:*

sex,
age,
country of origin,
country of residence.

This finding tells us that all the sub-groups of Jewish persecutees contain approximately equal numbers of persons who are successful or unsuccessful in their attempts to master life. Thus, as regards the overall assessment of the mastery of life, we cannot confirm the observation, made at several points in this study, that Jews of Polish descent suffer more persecution damage than those of German descent. Even among the Polish Jews there are a number of people who have managed to cope successfully with their concentration camp past in such a way that they can nowadays lead a relatively successful and happy life.

As regards the psychological state of health, there are clear differences between persons of Group A and those of Group C. These differences are highly significant for all three basic forms of psychic disturbance (see p. 100).

Persons unable to master life more frequently display characteristics of "resignation and despair", "apathy and inhibition" and "aggressive-irritable moodiness" than do persons who can cope successfully with life (0.1% significance in each case).

This confirms that the close connection between the external structure of a person's life and the inner psychological state, a connection to which we have referred repeatedly in this study, is also found when extreme groups of Jewish persecutees are compared. The failure in the spheres of interpersonal contact, job and marriage, as well as the still upsetting memories of concentration camp experience, go together with a large number of psychic symptoms. There seems little point in examining the causal interaction of these disturbances because they merge together to form the complex picture of a ruined, unhappy life. On the other hand, it is important to look for characteristics of childhood development and persecution stress which might elucidate differences in the ability to master life.

2. Influences of Childhood and Adolescence

None of the Jewish interviewees in the two extreme groups said much about their childhood, but what they said was mainly positive. According to their statements their family life was as a rule harmonious and the economic conditions in the parental family were solidly based. Both extreme groups are characterized by the fact that both parents were equally active in moulding the life of the family. The relationships of the interviewees with their fathers and siblings did not display any disturbances.

Nor did any conflicts worth mentioning arise from the minority status of the parents in a predominantly non-Jewish environment.

The only significant difference between the two extreme groups refers to the relationship of the interviewees with their mothers:

Persecutees who were unsuccessful in coping with life report more frequently than persons who coped successfully that they had a poor relationship with their mothers (5⁰/o significance).

This finding means that the interviewees of Group A described their relationship with their mother mainly in terms of respect, affection and recognition, sometimes also with reverence, while the relationship with the mother in the case of Group C interviewees was not infrequently characterized by conflict as well as by feelings of rejection and alienation.

Apart from these differences, neither extreme group revealed any childhood clues which might have indicated a particularly difficult or problematical development. The childhood development of the Jewish interviewees was in the great majority of cases relatively harmonious and sheltered.

This situation differs considerably from the results of the analysis of the childhood of "ideological personalities" (see p. 212). The childhood characteristics particularly typical of this group — namely, emotional coolness and aloofness of the parents towards their children, the strictness and narrow outlook of the father, and the authority problems associated therewith — were not detected in any of the interviewees in either of the extreme Jewish groups.

When problems crop up in Jewish families — and this is the case with a large number of the representatives of Group C — they are centred around the person of the mother. Note, however, that these difficulties were not as severe in extent and intensity as the problems centred around the father in the case of the ideological persons.

Summarizing, we can contrast the childhood influences of Jewish and ideological persons as follows:

The family life of the ideological persons was dominated by a strict and authoritarian father. All conflicts and tensions within the family centred around him. In contrast, the mother receded into the background. She plays a secondary role in the memories of the interviewees in question.

In the case of the Jewish representatives of the two extreme groups discussed here the family relationships of early childhood tended to be different. These interviewees talk of a harmonious parental home. Both parents cooperated in running the family. If any conflict situations arose, they centred around the mother. Within the Jewish group, these conflicts are found more frequently in the case of persons unable to master life (Group C). Apart from this problem in the relationship with the mother, it was not possible to determine any other factors of early childhood that might have helped to explain the differences in the later ability of Jewish interviewees to cope with life. We shall therefore now consider the influences of adolescence.

When we compare the psychic development during adolescence of the two extreme Jewish groups, we must above all pay attention to the aspect of social relationships. It is repeatedly found that a number of characteristics are the same in both groups of interviewees. Thus, no statistically significant differences are found for the following variables:

Mood during adolescence
Relationship with persons of the same age and sex
Interest in the world around one.

In both extreme groups about 85% of the interviewees in each case mentioned that they felt confident, satisfied and cheerful during their adolescence. The same number of persons demonstrated an ability to establish contact with persons of the same age and sex and to take a more or less active part in the world around them.

Although there are no statistically significant differences between the two extreme groups as regards the following characteristics, there are at least traces of qualitative differences. The two characteristics in question are those of:

Contact with persons of the opposite sex
Move away from the parental home.

Persons of Group A, i.e. persons who were able to cope with life following their liberation, were more frequently able to establish contact with partners of the opposite sex during their adolescence. Usually, in their search for a suitable partner, they took the initiative themselves and they rarely found the partner in a formally organised youth group. In contrast, persons in Group C rarely had contact with partners of the opposite sex. When they looked for a partner they were almost always dependent on organised groups. As regards their separation from the parental home, it is again apparent that persons from Group A were more determined and more active in taking the initiative. They were more frequently successful than persons of Group C in establishing an independent working existence and also in moving physically away from the parental home. However, since this observation is not statistically significant, we will not go into it any further.

The differences between the two groups are even more obvious when we consider the overall psycho-social situation of adolescent development.

Persons unable to cope with life more frequently mention anomalies in their psychological and social development than persons who can successfully cope with life's problems (5% significance).

In order to gain a better understanding of these characteristics, we list the problems that occurred most frequently in this connection:

Difficulties in adapting in school,
Uncertainty in choosing an occupation and occupational training,
Tendency to be a "loner",
Anxiety-ridden relationships with other people,
Lack of spontaneity in experience and action,
Hypochondriac complaints.

The following finding must also be considered in conjunction with these problems.

Persons unable to cope with life more frequently had bad relationships with authority figures outside the family than interviewees who were able to cope with life (1% significance).

This finding indicates that persons in Group C more frequently had difficulties in their dealings with teachers, superiors and representatives of the State than persons in Group A. It is striking that this problem with authority cannot be detected in the conflict with the father. This contradiction can perhaps be understood in terms of a shift of conflict — the stable family situation, above all the harmony between father and mother, did not permit persons of Group C to have a direct conflict with their fathers. The bottled-up conflicts were then discharged to some extent in quarrels with the mother and to some extent on father-like figures of authority outside the family. It must be assumed for Group A that — given an otherwise similar family structure — no important and remembered conflict situations occurred in the relationship with the father.

It must be stressed at this point that the psychological and social problems which were detected in the childhood and adolescence of the interviewees of Group C are quite often encountered during puberty in general. However, in the persons studied by us they are found in this frequency only in representatives of Group C.

3. Persecution Stress and Behaviour during Incarceration

In our search for further factors responsible for the later success in coping with life, we should first examine the influence of objectively comparable stress characteristics. The following two characteristics do *not* differentiate the two groups:

Duration of incarceration
Loss of relatives.

The duration of incarceration and the loss of parents, marital partners or children cannot therefore be used to explain the differences in the later ability to cope with life. The representatives of the two extreme groups are affected in approximately the same way by these two forms of stress. However, differences are found for two other stress characteristics:

Persecutees who are unable to cope with life were more frequently exposed to severe work stress in the concentration camps (1% significance); on the other hand, they were more frequently incarcerated in less harsh camps than interviewees who successfully managed to cope with life (5% significance).

This is the first time that we have encountered this combination of a particular group being exposed to severe work stress while on the other hand being housed in less harsh camps. In most other cases in which the influence of stress was determined, severe work stress or the harsh camp conditions either featured together or independently of each other. This finding and its correlation with the ex-inmate's ability to master life may be interpreted as follows:

Extremely severe work conditions during incarceration were in large part responsible for the failure of the persons in question to re-integrate into society following their liberation. On the other hand, interviewees who suffered less psychological and physical stress in the camps had better opportunities to make a new start in life following their release. This interpretation ties in with the correlations that exist with almost all other late injuries that have been discussed in this book.

The fact that persons unable to cope with life are at the same time characterized by severe work stress and relatively low incarceration stress probably indicates that Jews who were exposed simultaneously to both types of stress in extreme form did *not* as a rule survive the concentration camp.

However, this interpretation does not explain how the personality of the perse-cutee himself played a part in shaping his fate.

In the course of the study, we discovered over and over again in various connec-tions that the inmates themselves were able to exert a certain influence on the type of work they were expected to perform. They were thus able to influence their physical and psychic state and thereby also to affect their chances of survival. These connections will now be examined for both extreme groups of Jewish persecutees discussed here. For this purpose we compare the behaviour variables of Groups A and C in the concentration camp. In order to gain a differentiated view, we will not use the factor "adaptation to concentration camp conditions" (see p. 34) but instead we will take all four variables that go to make up this factor. We can then draw the following picture:

Persecutees unable to cope with life are more frequently characterized by passive survival than persecutees who are able to cope (0.1% significance);

they were more frequently unable to establish contact with their fellow prisoners (0.1% significance);

their attitude to fellow prisoners was more frequently characterized by lack of interest (1% significance);

they more frequently failed to adapt to the guards (5% significance).

This view is complete in itself and contains no contradictions. For the sake of completeness, we briefly outline the contrasting picture of Group A persons:

Persecutees who are able to master life are more frequently characterized by active survival than persons unable to cope;

they more frequently took the initiative in making contact with fellow prisoners;

their attitude to fellow prisoners was more frequently characterized by comradeliness;

they more frequently managed to adapt to the guards.

This contrast highlights the extremely different forms of reaction to concentration camp incarceration displayed by the representatives of Groups A and C. It should be remembered, of course, that the stress effects in these two groups were also differ-ent. While all the interviewees developed behavioural attitudes which saved them from annihilation, the type of behavioural pattern and the concentration camp ex-periences to which it gave rise are very different.

Persons who are successful in coping with life following their liberation are characterized by their readiness for action and their wealth of initiative, not only during the entire period of persecution but also in all spheres of their existence. In the concentration camps they forged escape plans or at least thought up ways to improve their situation. They engaged the help of fellow prisoners in carrying out these plans or themselves offered to help others. They frequently even risked their lives to improve their lot or that of a comrade. In contrast, the persons who failed to come to grips with life in the post-incarceration period tried to survive the terror of the camps by adopting a passive and conformist attitude. They usually faithfully obeyed all the orders issued by the guards in order to avoid attracting attention. They blended in with the broad mass of inmates and sought safety and protection in complete anonymity.

This attitude made it completely impossible for them to feel responsible for the welfare of their fellow inmates as well. Persons of Group C quite frequently exhibited distinctly hostile and rejective traits in their attitude to fellow sufferers. They almost never had any firm friends and some of them were complete outsiders with no personal contact even among the prisoners.

The persons in Group A on the other hand were emotionally receptive and ready to cooperate with their fellow inmates. They were fully able to appreciate and responds to other people's needs. In some cases friendships formed in the concentration camp survived after liberation and are still going strong today.

The differences that can be detected in the attitude to the guards are particularly important. In order to understand this problem we must remind ourselves of the following: The majority of the concentration camp guards remained completely unmoved by the suffering of the inmates. They took sadistic pleasure in causing other people pain and watching them suffer. Among other things they were responsible for allocating the work, and this alone gave them the chance either to crush an individual inmate or to give him a job that was less punishing and less dangerous. In addition, the guards determined how often and in what way an inmate was punished.

On the other hand, even the SS guards were open to bribes. In return for some service or other they were able to get an inmate better job opportunities, protect him from the gas chambers, get him extra rations, or arrange for him to go into the camp hospital. These examples are intended to demonstrate that to a large extent the lives of the inmates were in the hands of the guards. The ability to adapt to the mentality and methods of the guards was therefore important for survival. Our comparison of the extreme groups has shown that not all Jewish inmates were able to achieve this adaptation.

Persons in Group A report more frequently that they had better contact with the guards. These contacts, which in no case lasted for the entire period of incarceration, but which were always dependent on the particular situation, must be seen in connection with the better ability of these persons to make contact with fellow inmates as well. The ability to get on with others and to adapt to their needs and peculiarities must be regarded as a very important factor in determining how someone survived concentration camp incarceration.

In addition, it is necessary to point out the fundamental importance of the ability to remain active in threatening and stressful situations. In all persecution situations, persons in Group A actively tried to influence their environment. For example, right at the start of persecution they reacted in an active way to the imminent danger. They tried to escape, to emigrate or to hide, and some directly resisted arrest. This attitude was maintained throughout their imprisonment in the camps. They tried to defend themselves or improve their situation with the means at their disposal. They refused to accept passively and without resistance the situation that was forced on them.

It is precisely this passive, inactive attitude that is typical of persons in Group C, i.e. the persecutees who did not manage to cope with incarceration. Right at the start of persecution they exhibited an attitude which they retained throughout the entire period that they spent in the camps: passivity, evasion, submergence in the anonymous mass of their fellow sufferers. They voluntarily renounced any active attempt to play a part in shaping their terrible fate.

It seems sensible to compare the findings discussed here with those of other chapters:

a) As with the overall group of interviewees, so in the case of the two extreme groups of Jewish inmates, activity on the part of the individual frequently resulted in a lesser work stress.

b) In contrast to the trend in the overall group, a positive correlation was found in the case of the extreme groups of Jewish interviewees between less severe work stress, comradeliness and initiative in making interpersonal contact. It was the comradely and sociable Jewish inmates in Group A who were able to avoid severe work stress.

c) The extreme groups of Jewish interviewees also deviate from the overall trend as regards the connection between comradeliness and camp stress. In the overall group, comradeliness and low camp stress are correlated. Interviewees of Group A, on the other hand, were more comradely although as a rule they were incarcerated in more severe camps. In contrast, interviewees in Group C were less comradely although they spent their time in less harsh camps. In order to interpret this difference, we must remember that the Jewish interviewees of Group A had more interpersonal contact and were more comradely before persecution started than the Group C persons. Presumably, in both Groups, these were abilities or characteristics that the inmates brought with them into the camp situation and which they did not develop during incarceration.

a) The most frequently mentioned reasons for survival were, for the overall group:

Discipline and self control
Chance or luck
Comradeliness with fellow inmates.

These reasons for survival are not mentioned with the same frequency by Jewish interviewees. For example, they only rarely cite "discipline and self-control". "Comradely relations with fellow inmates" is mentioned above all by Jewish interviewees of Group A.

The fact that Jewish inmates rarely mention "discipline and self-control" may be because they were much more helplessly exposed to the concentration camp stresses than for example the political or religious persecutees. The totality and overwhelming power of the persecution apparatus was so crushingly experienced by the Jews that they can hardly ascribe their survival to their own attitude and their personal resistance. On the other hand, it seems to be typical of Jewish interviewees that they regard their survival as due to luck or chance (particularly Group C). In contrast, a comradely attitude towards fellow inmates, mentioned chiefly by Group A persons, in itself constitutes a high degree of independence in attempting to modify the incarceration situation.

4. Reasons for the Differences in Ability to Master Life

One important result to which we have referred in this chapter is the continuity of behaviour at various stages in an inmate's life. A comparison of extreme groups of Jews showed the general tendency for attitudes and behaviour already manifested in childhood and adolescence to play an important role in determining the attitudes and behaviour during incarceration and also to influence the present forms of coping with life.

These facts can be presented as follows for persons who are nowadays unable to cope with life:

The childhood and adolescence of these persons were characterized by a conflict-ridden relationship with the mother and by a state of dependence on the family. Many of them experienced tensions in their dealings with authority figures outside the parental home. In addition, there were disturbances in the area of contact with persons of the opposite sex. The mainly "good" relationships with persons of the same age and sex, which these interviewees report, must be critically examined against this background.

It can be assumed that the parental family was no longer willing or able, as the interviewees grew older, to satisfy all the emotional and social needs of the adolescent. Thus, these persons were faced with the necessity of looking after themselves. The loosening of family ties made it necessary to look for contacts outside the family. As it turned out, the persons in question were frequently unable to establish stable relationships with teachers or supervisors, etc. Many of them were also unable to make any contact with persons of the opposite sex. The easiest course for them to follow was to join a group of persons of the same age in a religious, political or sports association. In the long run, however, contact with people of the same age and sex was disappointing because not all of the strong emotional and social needs which the persons in question brought with them could be satisfied. This frustration gave rise to intense concern with one's own problems and an almost total lack of interest in those of other people. It is precisely this constellation that was characteristic of the attitude and behaviour of these particular persons in the concentration camp.

The onset of persecution usually severed the last ties that still existed between them and their family. As a result, the interviewees were left to fend entirely for themselves in an extremely difficult and stressful period. In this situation, the only source of support and aid was to be found in the other prisoners. But the persons in question were unable to make use of this opportunity because they had not learned the necessary cooperative attitudes and behaviour patterns. We showed that these unsatisfactory conditions were in turn the basis for a considerable amount of additional stress during the period of incarceration. The extreme stresses during incarceration were responsible for the fact that these persons did not succeed in building a new and successful life following their release. We cannot hold puberty problems responsible for the failure of these persons to cope with life. Instead, it can be assumed that these puberty problems were intensified under severe stress and that these not very resistant persons broke down completely under the much tougher stress and were unable to recover.

In clear contrast to this is the continuity of attitude and behaviour of the persons who succeeded in mastering their lives. The interviewees in this group were already active before persecution started. This attitude was manifest in their dealings with figures of authority outside the parental home and also in their relationships with persons of the opposite sex. These positive abilities of adaptation and self-assertion were retained even under the extreme stress of persecution. The ability to establish contact with others quickly and easily and also the conscious attempt to play an active role in moulding one's environment were the most important means of keeping the unbearable aspects of concentration camp incarceration at bay.

Bearing in mind the large number of symptoms associated with the reaction to incarceration (see p. 235), it can be assumed that the active interviewees of Group A survived the period of persecution with less physical and mental damage. On their release they possessed adequately functioning behavioural patterns which permitted them to make a new start in life. In the subsequent period they were in fact able to attain a minimum degree of success and harmony in the sphere of interpersonal contact, occupation and marriage. In addition, they also succeeded in coping better with the cruel experience of persecution.

Summary

1. Since the racial persecutees differ both quantitatively (percentage of our random sample) and qualitatively (special findings) from the political and religious persecutees in our sample, these persons were made the subject of a special analysis. The aim was to clarify what factors determined the choice of the present country of residence and whether and in what different ways they were able to master life in the post-persecution period.

2. The motivation for choosing the present country of residence was broken down into 9 categories. However, these categories were not always strictly distinct from each other. Frequently several motives were decisive. "Zionism" was the reason most frequently stated for the choice of Israel as the country of residence. In addition to this reason the only other important motive in this group was the desire to "return to one's family". The main reasons for emigration given by the Jews now living in New York were "rejection of the Germans" and also "return to one's family". For the persecutees who remained in Germany the main motives were "interconfessional marriages", "traumatic uprootings", "sickness". Twelve of these interviewees were "Christians" who, despite their persecution on "racial" grounds, were not identified with Judaism.

3. On the basis of a large number of individual characteristics covering the areas of interpersonal contact, occupation, marriage and family and reaction to incarceration, we were able to construct a complex category labelled "General Mastery of Life" for the group of Jewish interviewees. This category breaks down into 3 subgroups:

Persecutees who successfully coped with life.
Persecutees who were partially successful in coping with life.
Persecutees who failed to cope with life.

By far the greatest number of Jewish interviewees (62%) showed signs of being only partially successful or even totally unsuccessful in handling their present lives. The proportion of Jewish interviewees who were relatively successful in coping with life is very small (18%).

4. A comparison of the two extreme groups shows that sociological characteristics such as sex, age, country of origin or present country of residence contributed little or nothing to explaining the differences in ability to cope with life. On the other hand, there were very strong correlations with the basic forms of psychic disturbances.

According to these findings, interviewees now unable to master life's problems are more frequently resigned and despairing, apathetic and inhibited, aggressive and irritable.

5. Persons unable to cope with life reported some striking features from their childhood and adolescence which could not be found in the comparison group. For example, they more frequently had poor emotional relationships with their mothers and during puberty they had difficulty in making contact with persons of the opposite sex in their age group; they also had conflict-ridden relationships with figures of authority outside the family.

Persons who have managed to master life, on the other hand, have in general fewer problems and are more decisive and active in facing up to their environment.

6. As regards persecution stress, there is no difference between the two groups with respect to duration of incarceration and loss of relatives. On the other hand, the persons who were unable to cope with life were more frequently incarcerated in the less harsh type of camp but were exposed to a much more severe work stress.

7. The more severe work stress suffered during incarceration must be correlated with the chiefly passive adaptation and survival tactics of these persons. In contrast to the persons who nowadays are successfully in command of their lives, they more frequently showed no interest in their fellow prisoners. They were rarely able to adapt in a sensible manner to the mentality and methods of the guards. They themselves frequently ascribed their survival to chance or luck.

8. The group who were able to cope successfully with life more frequently regarded their comradeship with fellow inmates as the reason for their survival. This group made far more use of active techniques to change their situation. They more frequently took the initiative in establishing contact with other prisoners. They had a comradely attitude towards their fellow inmates. In addition, they were much more skilled in the way they handled the guards. This active and adaptable attitude did much to reduce the work stress to which they were exposed.

9. This analysis showed that the behavioural patterns and attitudes which had already been learned in early childhood contributed to determining the type and degree of concentration camp stress. Failure to master the present-day problems of life is to a large extent the result of the greater amount of stress suffered during incarceration.

Conclusion

In conclusion, we wish to summarize some of the most important issues, findings and theoretical implications of this study.

1. From a methodological standpoint there are three characteristics that distinguish this investigation from most previous works on the subject:

a) The samples used in earlier investigations were obtained primarily through referrals from doctors and are therefore restricted to patients who consulted a doctor about their health or who were examined by a doctor in connection with indemnification procedures. In the present study a random sample technique was used. This made it possible to include many people who had made no claim for indemnification. We were thus able to compare the complaints cited by persons who had submitted claims for indemnification with those of the people who had made no such claims.

b) In collecting the data we took account of more than just the clinically relevant complaints and diagnoses. By conducting extensive interviews we were able to examine the developmental history of the ex-inmates up to the time of their incarceration, the various kinds of stress that they endured in the concentration camps, as well as the onset of psychological disturbances during the post-war period in the areas of interpersonal relationships, marital life, occupation and "Weltanschauung". Separate investigation of each of the above-mentioned areas revealed both the variability and depth of the psychological disturbances of ex-concentration-camp prisoners independently of the question of their clinical relevance.

c) In order to progress beyond merely recording a list of clinical symptoms, the individual variables were subjected to a factor analysis. With the aid of this statistical technique it was possible to determine the interconnectedness of a large number of specific data. The resulting factors can be viewed as an independent illness (complaint, attitude, etc.), dimensions which mark, as it were, the points at which the concentration stress intrudes into the personality of the inmate.

2. The percentage of psychologically "healthy" survivors is very small in our sample. Since these people on the whole enjoyed relatively easy conditions in the camps, it seems fair to assume that disturbance-free survival was possible only after exposure to mild stress.

3. In contrast to the widely held view that there is one specific type of late injury resulting from incarceration in a concentration camp, our subjects displayed a broad spectrum of somatic and psychological complaints occurring long after the date of liberation. However, it is important to note that not one of these complaints was significantly correlated with the stress of incarceration. It was only when the factor analysis was performed that we discovered complaint dimensions that are clearly related to the concentration camp experience.

Of the four factors, the one we have called the "psychophysical syndrome" proved to be particularly significant. This factor combines both psychological and somatic complaints and can be interpreted as indicating a general state of exhaustion. It corresponds roughly to the frequently cited and variously described "concentration camp syndrome" which some researchers regard as an "obligatory" manifestation in all former inmates of concentration camps. Our data show this condition to be only one of several frequently appearing reactions to the stress of incarceration.

In addition to the two purely somatic illness dimensions ("Internal disorders" and "Gynaecological disorders") a third, purely psychological illness dimension was found. It includes such characteristics as mistrust, a feeling of social isolation and paranoid ideation. We see this dimension as representing a "social illness", not greatly different from the modern concept of anomie. This social illness dimension is of central importance for the theory of concentration camp stress and its consequence. It shows that, even when clinically relevant somatic complaints are not present or have begun to dissipate, the socio-communicative sphere can still be disturbed. So far this disturbance has received little attention from doctors studying the condition of ex-inmates.

The lack of clarity in both the diagnosis and compensation of these psycho-social disturbances is reflected in the relatively undifferentiated manner in which they have been recorded and named by doctors. The psychiatric diagnoses made for those of our interviewees who were seen by psychiatrists, either in connection with claims for compensation or on a private basis, are confusing and inconsistent and as a result they cannot be regarded as definitive. It follows that these diagnoses do not provide an adequate base on which to build theories about the consequences of concentration camp incarceration. For these reasons, the psychic and socio-communicative late injuries were analysed independently of the clinical diagnoses.

4. The psychological condition of former concentration camp inmates can be characterized by three basic disturbance factors.

The most serious of these we termed "Resignation and Despair". This factor denotes a condition in which the individual regards his life as meaningless and senseless and sees no future goals worth striving for. This condition resembles the "deep depression" described in the clinical literature.

The reaction we have called "Apathy and Inhibition" is characterized by a feeling of personal failure, personal worthlessness and general passivity. This factor most closely resembles the condition of "asthenic failure" described in the literature.

The third factor, which we have called "Aggressive-Irritable Moodiness", is a psychological condition that has frequently been overlooked in the literature on concentration camps. It manifests itself above all in outbursts of aggression which the individual has failed to master. Uncontrolled hostility is directed against the environment or hypochondriacally against the person's own body.

As one might have expected, the basic psychic disturbances are also coupled with obvious socio-communicative problems. For example, marital life is in part determined by the psychic condition of the partners. This does not mean that the marital lives of psychologically disturbed persons always centre around the same problems, but rather that the marital situation of a person characterized by "resignation and despair" is recognizably different in general character from that of a person suffering from "aggressive-irritable moodiness". Moreover, it is also possible to observe forms of marital life which have drawn a certain degree of internal and external stability from the psychic suffering of one or even both of the partners.

Similarly, there is also a relationship between the psychic disturbance of ex-inmates and their ability to reintegrate successfully into the working world. Again, it is fundamentally true to say that the greater the psychic disturbance, the poorer the chance the person has of achieving occupational success. There are also cases, however, in which severe psychological disturbances are masked by increased work activity and the external trappings of success. Despite his hopeless psychological condition, an ex-inmate can, through his work, keep open at least a few channels of communication with the world around him.

5. It proved rewarding, in connection with the socio-communicative disturbances, to examine the ex-inmate's external ability to function and his internal psychic condition, which is largely independent of the former ability. A separate factor analysis revealed two different modes of current social contact. One mode we labelled "Ability to Cope with Society" and the other "Sociability". All former inmates of concentration camps have problems of one sort or another in their social lives. Paradoxically these problems are most apparent and intense in those persecutees who strictly avoid any active contact with their environment. For them the interpersonal world has ceased to exist. They live in social isolation which steadily intensifies as time passes. To some extent, however, their environment has contributed to their plight. Society's attitude toward and treatment of ex-inmates vary considerably as a result of hidden guilt and secret aggression. Not infrequently, we find that exaggerated concern is contrasted with cool disinterest and over-estimation is juxtaposed with disdain. Some persecutees react in a typical manner to these situations by attempting to hush up or deny their past sufferings or, at the other extreme, by consciously playing the "role" of an ex-inmate in order to establish contact with other people.

Another social injury resulting from incarceration is the disturbed or shattered ability to turn toward and be concerned about one's fellowmen. As a result of the persecution experience, the "other person" has become an enemy or a potential murderer in the eyes of many former concentration camp inmates.

6. The type and intensity of the stress experienced during incarceration are of central importance for the etiology of the above-mentioned somatic, psychic and socio-communicative disturbances. The more narrative descriptions of concentration camp life, which have been written mainly by people who experienced the camps in person, give a clear picture of the hellish conditions in all their tragic and terrible detail. There have so far been only a few, for the most part inadequate attempts in the scientific literature to define the specific stress factors and to identify their precise effect. This omission is due to the view of many authors that it is both morally and scientifically questionable and hence objectionable to use rational quantitative methods to assess the torture of human beings.

Our view was that it is necessary and desirable to break down the complex concept of stress into its component parts and to distinguish the various levels of intensity. This was done in order to investigate empirically the postulate that incarceration is responsible for the injuries suffered by the survivors. Using this procedure, we were able to demonstrate over and over again in the course of our study that it is not the duration of incarceration nor the type of camp but rather the kind of work to which the inmate was exposed which is primarily responsible for the late injuries discussed above. The work situation, more than any other single variable, most clearly expresses the stress conditions that each person had to endure. Once the work stress became more than the inmate could bear, whether this situation lasted for a long while or not, no other factor had many major influence on the development of the later injuries. It made no difference whether the inmate was incarcerated in a harsh or mild camp or whether he spent a short or long time in a concentration camp.

In order to understand the eminent importance of the work stress in determining not only the inmate's chances of survival but also the severity of the incarceration-specific damage, it is necessary to remember that the type of work that a person had to perform in a concentration camp was linked with a large number of stress-intensifying or stress-relieving conditions. Much as in normal life, the work one actually had to perform in a concentration camp identified one's social position. In the final analysis, the social status of the inmate in the cruel hierarchy of the concentration camp determined on the one hand the degree of hunger, sickness, mistreatment and degradation to which he was exposed and on the other the amount of support, help, security and protection that he was given. For these reasons, the work stress may be viewed as the most reliable index for assessing the extent to which the survivors of the camps have lost their ability to identify with the human world and its values.

7. Discrimination and quantification of the individual stress characteristics in order to calculate their correlations with each other as well as with other data from the pre- and post incarceration periods provided an additional important insight. We were able to show that the inmate's personality also played a role in determining the nature and intensity of the stress he endured.

In this connection, using the method of factor analysis, we identified a personality dimension which we labelled "ability to make contact". The active pole is characterized by active, comradely and contact-initiating behaviour, and persons representing this pole were even able to adapt to the methods and mentality of the concentration camp guards; they were also in a position to exert a certain amount of influence on their situation in the camps and thus, indirectly, to determine their chances of survival. In contrast, passive inmates who lacked the ability to make contact allowed themselves to be subjected to the worst possible conditions.

There is a strong and clear correlation between the above behavioural dimension and work stress. Inmates with a highly developed ability to make contact had lighter work to perform than those who exhibited disturbed contact behaviour. Corresponding correlations exist between the ability to adapt to camp conditions and the extent of the present injuries brought on by the experience of incarceration.

These different modes of interpersonal contact, which were of such great importance in determining a person's survival and also the course of his life after liberation, had for the most part already been formed by the time the prisoners entered the concentration camps. It was as a rule not possible to go through the long and wearisome process of acquiring positive forms of contact and adaptation techniques once one was incarcerated. These personality characteristics had started to form in early childhood, and it was rarely possible to modify them even slightly.

8. In reconstructing the life history of the inmates during their childhood and adolescence, we were forced to rely on the facts they could still remember and were willing to divulge. It seems appropriate therefore to emphasize only those results which were repeatedly confirmed in different contexts.

One remarkable and relatively well-substantiated phenomenon is the continuity of behaviour and attitude through to the present time. Particular forms of activity and of the ability to make contact that were already apparent in late childhood, or at least in puberty, were subsequently maintained, without major change, throughout the years of persecution and incarceration and in the post-liberation period.

The mother played a central role in the learning histories of the survivors and she was particularly influential in determining their ability to establish interpersonal relations and to feel socially comfortable. In our material, a disturbed mother-child relationship is correlated with a subsequent passive behavioural pattern, which in turn is reflected in the following findings — passive reaction to the onset of persecution, uncomradely attitude during incarceration, more severe stress during incarceration and, as a result, unsuccessful readjustment following liberation.

The personality characteristics formed during childhood seem to be particularly deeply anchored and able to resist the pressures of incarceration. This observation was confirmed in the case of two additional behavioural patterns, namely the manner and choice of marital partner and the inmate's "Weltanschauung". The ability to find a suitable marital partner and to lead an harmonious married life appears to depend to a great degree on the way in which the persons in question experienced their parental home and the marriage of their parents. The stress of incarceration has little effect on this ability.

The same may be said for the "Weltanschauung", at least in those cases in which the "Weltanschauung" was consciously and intensely perceived at an early age. As a rule, identification with a particular "Weltanschauung" occurs early on in a person's development, and it frequently reflects the positive or negative outcome of the child's attitude to the parental figures of authority. This is particularly apparent where the "Weltanschauung" is ideologically experienced. The ideological posture almost always hides an unresolved conflict with the father. The ideology serves the person as a crutch and as an ego-fortification in the struggle with a hostile and all-powerful environment. Such an ego-fortification often provides the "ideologist" with an amazing amount of inner strength and external resistance to survive the severest stress situations seemingly unscathed. But this method of reinforcing the ego is almost always accompanied by deficiencies, inhibitions and restrictions in the person's ability to communicate with others.

9. The special position of the "racial persecutee" in contrast to the religious and political persecutee was noted at several points in our study. For this reason, this group was analysed separately. We developed a complex category which we called "General Mastery of Life" as an index of their present condition. This category is made up of individual variables representing the relative success achieved in occupation, marriage, social contact and also in coping with the experience of incarceration. Measured in this way, the overwhelming majority of Jewish survivors appear moderately or severely injured. Only a small number were able to survive the camps relatively uninjured but in these cases it was not just the lighter stress but also certain developmental characteristics that were responsible for the lack of damage. The quantitative distribution between successful and unsuccessful mastery of life confirmed the relationship between late injury and the degree of stress as detected in the individual chapters. Personality development, which is responsible for the evolution of certain "adaptation characteristics", plays only a secondary role in the causation

of late injury. The "double uprooting" the Jewish survivors suffered was a factor of considerable importance. Not only were they exposed to the severest types of stress during incarceration, but following their liberation they were unable to return to their old and familiar environments. Even in those cases where family members also survived and would gladly have received the liberated inmates, both internal and external problems made a return impossible. These people had to search for another country in which to live. The motives for the choice of a particular country in which to settle are very heterogeneous and reflect the diversity of the individual fates and personalities. This result also reconfirms a striking finding that we encountered throughout our study, namely that, just as incarceration in a concentration camp does not constitute a uniform stress variable, so the reaction to this stress differs. The internal and external life histories of the inmates, their individual dispositions and also social factors are all inextricably linked in determing the various ways in which these people overcame the horrors of life in a concentration camp.

Appendix

The Appendix starts with a list of the characteristics that were used in the factor analyses; next, the procedure for establishing the three forms of "coping with life" is described; this is followed by a list of the Rorschach categories used and, finally, the representativeness of the special samples in relation to the overall sample is presented in tabular form. Our main intention in listing the characteristics is to clarify the qualitative basis of the factor analyses. We have already described and discussed in the text the different frequencies of the characteristics in various groups, and we have shown how the intercorrelation between relevant characteristics is calculated. The factor loadings of the characteristics are also given in each case in the text. There would not have been much point in giving the agreements and variances except for the overall factor matrices, and even this would have provided too much irrelevant and uninterpretable material. Although the phi-correlations on which the factor analyses are based are generally very low, we only interpreted those factors which clarified statistically relevant areas of the total variance. Finally, it should be noted that the definitions of the characteristics sometimes meant that the degree of correlation was artificially high. However, such instances were discussed in the text or taken into account when arriving at our interpretations.

We have had to forego presenting and commenting on all the numerical data, nor was it possible to give a detailed description of the process of categorization. This would have made the book one third longer than it is now. However, the documentation can be examined at the Forschungsstelle für Psychopathologie und Psychotherapie in der Max-Planck-Gesellschaft, 8 Munich 23, Montsalvatstrasse 19, West Germany.

I. The 23 characteristics used in the factor analysis for the chapter "Stresses Imposed by Concentration Camp Incarceration":

1. Reaction at onset of persecution   Active reactions
   Passivity

2. Protective reaction at onset of persecution   Protect self first
   Protect community first

3. Effects of persecution on the sphere of family contact prior to incarceration   Severe
   Slight

4. Effects of persecution on the occupational-material sphere prior to incarceration   Severe
   Slight

5. Development of activity during incarceration   Active posture
   Passive posture

6. Attitude towards fellow prisoners   Comradely
   Disinterested

7. Contact behaviour towards fellow prisoners   Took initiative in making contact
   Difficulty in making contact

8. Relationships with guards	Adapted to guards
	Did not adapt to guards
9. Threat to life during incarceration	Threat experienced
	No threat experienced
10. Severity of camp	Long time spent in moderately severe camps
	Long time spent in severe camps
11. Duration of incarceration	Between 3 and 48 months
	Between 49 and 96 months
12. Pre-incarceration stress	Yes
	No
13. Work stress in concentration camp	Performed light or moderately heavy work for long time
	Performed heavy or extremely heavy work for long time
14. Sex	Male
	Female
15. Country of origin	Germany
	Eastern Europe
16. Reasons for persecution	Race
	Politics, religion
17. Age at start of persecution	Up to 30
	Over 30
18. Overall duration of persecution	Between 3 and 72 months
	Between 73 and 144 months
19. Marital status prior to incarceration	Single, widowed or divorced
	Married
20. Present marital status	Single, widowed or divorced
	Married
21. Present country of residence	Germany
	USA and Israel
22. Loss of parents, loss of siblings	Yes — No
23. Loss of marital partner, loss of children	Yes — No

II. The 28 characteristics used in the factor analysis for the chapter "Damage to Health" (in each case the listed complaint is to be understood as being "present" or "absent"):

1. Age at start of persecution
2. Sex
3. Vegetative complaints
4. Rheumatic complaints
5. Head complaints
6. Hearing and sight defects
7. Dental complaints
8. Pulmonary-bronchial complaints
9. Cardiovascular complaints
10. Stomach complaints
11. Intestinal disorders
12. Hepatic/bilious complaints
13. Gynaecological complaints
14. Urological complaints
15. Spinal column complaints
16. Complaints resulting from injuries to limbs
17. Anxiety dreams
18. Depressive moods
19. Inner agitation, irritability
20. Disturbances of memory and concentration
21. Sleep disturbances
22. Mistrust
23. Anxiety states
24. Tiredness
25. Feeling of isolation
26. Paranoid ideation
27. Feelings of hatred
28. Impaired vitality (lack of appetite, feeling of pressure in head and chest, upset bowel movements)

III. The 13 characteristics used in the factor analysis for the chapter "Psychiatric Diagnoses" (in each case the listed complaint is to be understood as being "present" or "absent"):

1. Anxiety dreams
2. Anxiety states
3. Paranoid ideation
4. Feelings of hatred
5. Inner agitation, irritability
6. Disturbances of memory and concentration
7. Mistrust
8. Feeling of isolation
9. Depressive moods
10. Sleep disturbances
11. Impaired vitality
12. Tiredness
13. Thoughts of suicide

(Characteristics 1 to 12 are identical with the characteristics used in the factor analysis for the chapter on "Late-Appearing Damage to Health".)

IV. The 35 characteristics used in the factor analysis for the chapter "Basic Forms of Psychic Disturbance":

1. Depressive states — pronounced / not pronounced

2. Agitation — pronounced / not pronounced

3. Distractibility — pronounced / not pronounced

4. Tendency to tire easily — pronounced / not pronounced

5. Irritability — pronounced / not pronounced

6. Hostility — pronounced / not pronounced

7. Sexual disturbances — detectable / not detectable

8. Incarceration has "maturing" effect — apparent / not apparent

9. Incarceration produces feeling of despair — apparent / not apparent

10. Overemphasis on own incarceration — apparent / not apparent

11. Present mood — on the whole cheerful / on the whole depressed

12. Present attitude to period of incarceration — positive aspects also seen / seen as senseless and a threat to life

13. Plaintiveness — present / absent

14. Affective instability — present / absent

15. Hypochondriac complaints — pronounced / not pronounced

16. Feeling of guilt — pronounced / not pronounced

17. Self-pity — pronounced / not pronounced

18. Dissatisfaction — pronounced / not pronounced

19. Sleep disturbances	present
	absent
20. Drive	present
	absent
21. Despondency	pronounced
	not pronounced
22. Eccentricity	present
	absent
23. Aloofness	pronounced
	not pronounced
24. Emotional responsiveness	present
	absent
25. Pattern of symptoms	diffuse
	unequivocal
26. Stability of symptoms	unstable
	stable
27. Repressive tendency	pronounced
	not pronounced
28. Anxiety dreams	present
	absent
29. Disavowal (of concentration camp past)	apparent
	not apparent
30. Ideological processing of incarceration experiences	apparent
	not apparent
31. Sex	male
	female
32. Age at start of persecution	up to 30
	over 30
33. Reason for persecution	race
	politics and religion
34. Country of origin	Germany
	Eastern Europe
35. Country of residence	Germany
	USA and Israel

V. The 25 characteristics used in the first factor analysis for the chapter "Contact with Fellow Humans and Society":

1. Reproach and accusation	apparent
	not apparent
2. Superficial adaptation	apparent
	not apparent
3. Isolation and rejection	apparent
	not apparent
4. Present personal contacts	contacts also outside family
	chiefly isolated
5. Present participation in the life of society	participation in social activities
	no interest in social activities
6. Present attitude towards fellowmen	mainly trust
	mainly mistrust
7. Present standard of living	materially well-off
	materially needy

8. Present Weltanschauung	has a Weltanschauung
	has no Weltanschauung
9. Present influence of Weltanschauung on lifestyle	has an effect
	has no effect
10. Present interest in environment	open-minded, responsive
	narrow-minded, reserved
11. Adaptation to environment up to 1949/50	effort made to adapt
	poor adaptation
12. Present capability for self-assertion outside family	active, expansive behaviour
	passive, evasive behaviour
13. First reactions following liberation	attempted orientation
	collapse
14. Attempt to understand and forgive others	apparent
	not apparent
15. Behaviour during liberation	activity
	passivity
16. Occupational patterns following liberation	steady upward trend
	fluctuating up and down or no rise at all
17. Changes of location following liberation	settled down quickly
	settled down late
18. Present form of aggression	aggressiveness openly expressed
	aggression inhibited
19. Hostility	pronounced
	not pronounced
20. Prejudices towards fellowmen	pronounced
	not pronounced
21. Sex	male
	female
22. Age at start of persecution	up to 30
	over 30
23. Reason for persecution	race
	politics, religion
24. Country of origin	Germany
	Eastern Europe
25. Country of residence	Germany
	USA and Israel

The following 7 Rorschach ratings (1–7) and 19 questionnaire items (8–26) were used in the second factor analysis for the chapter "Contact with Fellow Humans and Society":

1. Affective adaptation
2. Affective instability
3. Ability to make contact
4. Desire to make contact
5. Inwardly directed aggression
6. Explosive, outwardly directed aggression
7. Inhibition or suppression of aggression
8. As an ex-concentration-camp inmate are you respected by your fellowmen?
9. Do you believe that in view of your sufferings in a concentration camp you are entitled to more respect from your fellowmen?
10. Do you feel that you are now different from other people as a result of incarceration?
11. Have you become alienated from your fellowmen as a result of incarceration?

12. Do you think that you are in any way better off than most other people?
13. Do you nowadays feel at a disadvantage compared with other people?
14. Do you think that the world is run by evil persons?
15. Do you think that what you have been through makes it difficult for you to establish contact with other people?
16. Can one rely on the friendliness of other people?
17. Do you also sometimes take the initiative in striking up acquaintance?
18. As a result of what you have been through, are you more reserved in your dealings with others?
19. Do you sometimes set the tone in a particular group?
20. Is there anyone with whom you can discuss absolutely anything that matters to you?
21. Do you prefer to remain within the circle of your family (friends) or do you rather go out?
22. Are there any people who matter to you so much that you would miss them if they were not around?
23. What do you do if someone annoys you?
24. What do you do if someone insults you?
25. You are waiting in a queue. Suddenly someone pushes in front of you. How do you behave and what are your thoughts?
26. If you have a reason to be angry with someone, do you let them know it? Do you regret doing so later?

Characteristics 8–22 are questionnaire items which were used as simple characteristics involving a yes-no answer.

Characteristics 23–26 are questionnaire items the answers to which were rated according to the type and frequency of the aggression expressed by the interviewees.

VI. The 16 characteristics used in the factor analysis for the chapter "Occupational Reintegration Following Release":

1. Education prior to persecution	elementary school, intermediate school, high school
2. Occupational patterns following liberation	constant upward trend fluctuation up or down, or no rise at all
3. Return to work	at latest one year after release later than one year after release
4. Occupational activity during incarceration	mainly active in own occupation mainly active in other than own occupation
5. Work situation in camp given as reason for survival	yes no
6. Work stress in camp(s)	performed light or moderately severe work for long time performed heavy or extremely heavy work for long time
7. Standard of living of parental family	materially well off materially needy
8. Occupational training prior to persecution	training completed training not completed
9. Occupational success prior to persecution	successful in occupation unsuccessful in occupation
10. Occupational reintegration following release	successfully reintegrated difficulties in reintegrating
11. Present occupational level compared with pre-persecution period	same or higher level lower level

12. Present standard of living	materially well-off
	materially needy
13. Country of origin	Germany
	Eastern Europe
14. Country of residence	Germany
	USA and Israel
15. Reason for persecution	race
	politics and religion
16. Age at start of persecution	up to 30
	over 30

VII. The 42 characteristics used in the factor analysis for the chapter "Marriage and Family":

1. Depressive moods	pronounced
	not pronounced
2. Inner agitation	pronounced
	not pronounced
3. Distractibility	pronounced
	not pronounced
4. Tendency to tire easily	pronounced
	not pronounced
5. Irritability	pronounced
	not pronounced
6. Hostility	pronounced
	not pronounced
7. Sexual disturbances	detectable
	not detectable
8. Incarceration has "maturing" effect	apparent
	not apparent
9. Incarceration causes attitude of despair	apparent
	not apparent
10. Overemphasis on own incarceration	apparent
	not apparent
11. Present mood	on the whole cheerful
	on the whole depressed
12. Present attitude to incarceration	positive aspects also seen
	seen as senseless and a threat to life
13. Reproach and accusation	apparent
	not apparent
14. Superficial adaptation	apparent
	not apparent
15. Isolation and rejection	apparent
	not apparent
16. Present personal contacts	contacts also outside family
	chiefly isolated
17. Present participation in the life of society	participation in social activities
	no interest in social activities
18. Present attitude to fellowmen	mainly trust
	mainly mistrust

19. Present standard of living   materially well-off
                                                materially needy

20. Present Weltanschauung   has a Weltanschauung
                                                has no Weltanschauung

21. Present influence of Weltanschauung on   has an effect
    lifestyle   has no effect

22. Present interest in environment   open-minded, responsive
                                                narrow-minded, reserved

23. Adaptation to environment up to 1949/50   effort made to adapt
                                                poor adaptation

24. Present capability for self-assertion   active, expansive behaviour
    outside the family   passive, evasive behaviour

25. First reactions following liberation   attempted orientation
                                                collapse

26. Mistrust   present
                                                absent

27. Sex   male
                                                female

28. Reason for persecution   race
                                                politics and religion

29. Total duration of persecution   between 3 and 72 months
                                                between 73 and 144 months

30. Loss of parents   yes
                                                no

31. Choice of partner following liberation   persecutee
                                                non-persecutee

32. Mood prior to persecution   generally cheerful
                                                generally depressed

33. Present relationship of marital partners   good
    with each other   bad

34. Search for marital partner following   discreet
    liberation   overt

35. Choice of first marital partner prior to   chosen within a reference group
    persecution   chosen independently of a reference group

36. Degree to which present family life is   mainly oriented to present and future
    past- or future-oriented   mainly oriented to past

37. Present family life   on the whole harmonious
                                                on the whole disharmonious

38. Number of children following liberation   marriages usually produce children
                                                marriages mainly childless

39. Present relationship with own children   good
                                                bad

40. Present attitude to raising children   authoritarian
                                                cooperative

41. How cared for following liberation   took care of self
                                                institutionalized care needed

42. Present role behaviour in family   determining role
                                                subordinate role

(Characteristics 1–12 are identical with characteristics 1–12 of the factor analysis "Basic forms of psychic disturbance". Characteristics 13–25 are identical with characteristics 1–13 of the factor analysis "Contact with Fellow Humans and Society".

VIII. The 17 characteristics used to define the "General Mastery of Life" exhibited by former persecutees. The characteristics are broken down according to four areas of life:

Marriage and family

1. Present relationship of marital partners with each other	good bad
2. Degree to which present family life is past- or future-oriented	mainly oriented towards present and future mainly oriented towards past
3. Present family life	on the whole harmonious on the whole disharmonious

Interpersonal contact

4. Present personal contacts	apparent not apparent
5. Present participation in the life of society	participation in social activities no interest in social activities
6. Present attitude to fellowmen	mainly trust mainly mistrust
7. Present form of aggression	aggressiveness openly expressed aggression inhibited
8. Present capability for self-assertion outside family	active, expansive behaviour passive, evasive behaviour

Occupation

9. Occupational patterns following liberation	steady upward trend fluctuating up or down or no rise at all
10. Occupational reintegration following release	successfully reintegrated difficulties in reintegrating
11. Present occupational level compared with pre-persecution period	same or higher level lower level
12. Present standard of living	materially well-off materially needy

Reaction to incarceration

13. Present attitude to incarceration	positive aspects also seen seen as senseless and a threat to life
14. Incarceration has "maturing" effect	apparent not apparent
15. Attempt to understand and forgive others	apparent not apparent
16. Incarceration causes attitude of despair	apparent not apparent
17. Reproach and accusation	apparent not apparent

The three forms of coping with life, namely:

A: successful coping with life
B: partially successful coping with life
C: unsuccessful coping with life

were assessed by summating the scores in the four areas of "marriage", "occupation", "interpersonal contact", "reaction to incarceration". Each area of life, and the characteristics contained in it, was rated equal in arriving at the final value for "General Mastery of Life".

The final scores were calculated in three steps. First, each person was given a rating for each characteristic within each of the 4 areas of life. These ratings were 0 = successful, 1 = partially successful, 2 = unsuccessful. Since each area of life contained 3 to 5 characteristics the individual scores were summated in step II and the resulting distribution again broken down into three categories. This gave each person a general rating of 0, 1 or 2 in each area of life. In the third step these ratings were again summated and the resulting distribution was broken down into three categories. The persons who obtained an overall rating of 0–2 were designated as category A: "successful in coping with life", persons with an overall rating of 3–6 were designated category B: "partially successful in coping with life" and persons with an overall rating of 7–8 were put in category C: "unsuccessful in coping with life".

IX. The ratings obtained from the Rorschach test correspond to the following interpretations and responses (after Bohm and Holtzmann):

1. Affective adaptation

   Sharp perception of shape; colour perception mainly determined by shape; sharp perception of outlines of bodies and objects. (High $F+\%$ — left colour type — high blocking $\%$ — good reality index.)

2. Affective instability

   Few animal figure responses; few stereotyped responses; frequently diffuse overall impression of shading values; colour perception takes no account of shape. (Low $T\%$ — low $V\%$ — high $Hd\%$ — right colour type.)

3. Ability to make contact

   Many human movement responses; original interpretations more frequently sharply seen rather than blurred; sharp perception of shape; sharp perception of outlines of bodies and objects. (High $B\%$ — $O_+ > 0$ — high $F+\%$ — high blocking $\%$ — good reality index.)

4. Desire for contact

   Many human figure responses; above-average response frequency; colour perceptions take no account of shape. (High $M\%$ — high response $\%$ — right colour type.)

5. Inwardly directed aggression

   Responses such as "explosion", "cloudburst", "volcanic eruption"; signs of irritation at red or chromatic colour blots; many human figure responses; many human movement responses; background stimuli responses instead of foreground figures together with human movement responses; criticism of own response. (High $Dyn\%$ — many red and colour shocks — high $M\%$ — high hostility content — relatively high $B\%$ — $Dzw+B$ — subjective criticism.)

6. Explosive outwardly directed aggression

   Translucent outlines of bodies and objects seen; many colour responses; many original responses; perception of shape not very sharp. (High penetration $\%$ — high colour $\%$ — high $O\%$ — low $F+\%$ — short reaction time.)

7. Inhibited aggression

   Colour perception primarily determined by shape; signs of irritation at red or chromatic colour blots; signs of irritation at very dark colour blots. (Left colour type — many red and colour shocks — many dark shocks.)

8. Anxiety in interpersonal contact

   More human detail responses than total human figure responses; perception of colour takes no account of shape; irritation at red or chromatic colour blots. (Md > M — right colour type — many red and colour shocks.)

9. Rational adaptation

Many stereotyped responses; average response frequency ; colour perception primarily determined by shape. (High V% — medium response % — left colour type.)

10. Rational control

Many shape responses; few colour responses; more detail rather than whole responses. (High F% — low Fb — High D%.)

11. Capability for intellectualization and introversion

Many human movement responses; more sharply perceived forms in the original responses than blurred forms; good agreement between form and colour determinants in the responses. (High B% — $O_+ > 0$ — middle colour type.)

X. Representativeness of the special samples in relation to the total sample (figures in %).
(Chapters "Late-Appearing Damage to Health" (A), "Contact with Fellow Humans and Society" (B), "Marriage and Family" (C), "Reasons for Emigration and Mastery of Life in the case of Jewish Persecutees" (D)).

		Total sample (n=219) %	A (n=144) %	B (n=82) %	C (n=165) %	D (n=165) %
Sex	male	71	74	71	74	63
	female	29	26	29	26	37
Age in 1960	below 50	51	44	53	58	65
	50 and over	49	56	47	42	35
Reason for persecution	race	76	72	68	81	—
	politics and religion	24	28	32	19	—
Country of origin	Germany	53	51	70	47	52
	Eastern Europe	47	49	30	53	48
Country of residence	Germany	69	82	62	65	46
	USA and Israel	31	18	38	35	54

References

ADORNO, T. W., FRENKEL-BRUNSWIK, E., LEVINSON, D. J., SANFORD, R. N.: The authoritarian personality. New York 1950.

BAYER, W. v.: Erschöpfung und Erschöpftsein. Nervenarzt **32**, 193 (1961).

— Erlebnisbedingte Verfolgungsschäden. Nervenarzt **32**, 534 (1961).

— HÄFNER, H., KISKER, K. P.: Psychiatrie der Verfolgten. Berlin-Göttingen-Heidelberg 1964.

BASTIAANS, J.: Psychosomatische gevolgen von onderdrukking en verzet. Amsterdam 1957.

BENSHEIM, H.: Die KZ-Neurose rassisch Verfolgter. Nervenarzt **31**, 462 (1960).

BETTELHEIM, B.: The informed heart; autonomy in mass age. New York 1960.

BLOCH, J.: Judentum in der Krise. Göttingen 1966.

BOHM, E.: Lehrbuch der Rorschach-Psychodiagnostik. Bern-Stuttgart 1957.

BONDY, C.: Problems of internment camps. J. abnorm. soc. Psychol. **38**, 453 (1943).

BONHOEFFER, K.: Über die Bedeutung der Kriegserfahrungen für die allgemeine Psychopathologie und Ätiologie der Geisteskrankheiten. In: Hdb. d. ärztl. Erfahrungen im Weltkriege 1914/18, Bd. 4. Leipzig 1922.

— Vergleichende psychopathologische Erfahrungen aus den beiden Weltkriegen. Nervenarzt **18**, 1 (1947).

BRADY, J. V.: Ulcers in "executive" monkeys. Scient. Amer. **199**, 4 (1958).

BÜRGER-PRINZ, H.: Probleme der Psychiatrie und Umwelt. Stud. Gen. **4**, 227 (1951).

CAYROL, J.: Lazarus unter uns. Stuttgart 1959.

CHODOFF, P.: Late effects of the concentration camp syndrome. Arch. gen. Psychiat. **8**, 323 (1963).

DÖRING, G. K.: Spezifische Spätschäden der weiblichen Psyche durch die politische Verfolgung. In: Psychische Spätschäden nach politischer Verfolgung. Hrsg.: H. PAUL und H.-J. HERBERG. Basel 1963.

DOLLARD, J., DOOB, L. W., MILLER, N. E., MOWRER, O. H., SEARS, R. R.: Frustration and aggression. New Haven 1939.

EISENSTADT, S. N.: The process of absorption of new immigrants in Israel. Hum. Relat. **5**, 223 (1952).

EITINGER, L.: Pathology of the concentration camp syndrome, Preliminary report. Arch. gen. Psychiat. **5**, 371 (1961).

— Examination of Norwegian ex-concentration-camp prisoners II. Psychiatric post-conditions in former concentration camp inmates. Congr. The Hague 1961.

— Concentration Camp Survivors in Norway and Israel. London 1964.

ENGESET, A.: Examination of Norwegian ex-concentration-camp prisoners IV.: Pneumo-encephalographic findings in ex-concentration-camp inmates. Congr. The Hague 1961.

ERIKSON, E. H.: Identität und Lebenszyklus. Frankfurt 1966.

— Kindheit und Gesellschaft. Stuttgart 1961.

FICHEZ, L., KLOTZ, A.: Die vorzeitige Vergreisung und ihre Behandlung. (An Hand von Beobachtungen an ehemaligen Deportierten und KZ-Häftlingen). Wien 1961.

FRANKL, V. E.: Psychohygienische Erfahrungen im Konzentrationslager. In: Hdb. d. Psychother. u. Neurosenlehre, Bd. 4. München-Berlin 1959.

— Psychologie und Psychiatrie des Konzentrationslagers. In: Psychiatrie der Gegenwart, Bd. III. Berlin-Göttingen-Heidelberg 1961.

FRENKEL-BRUNSWIK, E.: In: The authoritarian personality. Hrsg.: T. W. ADORNO, E. FRENKEL-BRUNSWIK, D. J. LEVINSON and R. N. SANFORD. New York 1950.

FREUD, S.: Über den psychischen Mechanismus hysterischer Phänomene. Wien 1892.

FROMM, E.: Die Furcht vor der Freiheit. Frankfurt 1966.

GRÖNVIK, O., LÖNNUM, A.: Examination of Norwegian ex-concentration-camp prisoners III. The neurological condition of ex-prisoners from concentration camps. Congr. The Hague 1961.

HARMAN, H. H.: Modern Factor Analysis, Chicago 1960.

HELWEG-LARSEN, P., HOFFMEYER, H., KIELER, J., HESS THAYSEN, E., HESS THAYSEN, J., THYGESEN, P., HERTEL WULF, M.: Famine disease in German concentration camps. Copenhagen 1952.

— — — — — — — Die Hungerkrankheit in den deutschen Konzentrationslagern. In: Gesundheitsschäden durch Verfolgung und Gefangenschaft und ihre Spätfolgen. Hrsg.: M. MICHEL. Frankfurt 1955.

HERMANN, K.: Die psychischen Symptome des KZ-Syndroms. In: Gesundheitsschäden durch Verfolgung und Gefangenschaft und ihre Spätfolgen. Hrsg.: M. MICHEL. Frankfurt 1955.

— THYGESEN, P.: KZ-syndromet. Kopenhagen 1954.

— — Die Wirkungen des KZ-Syndroms 19 Jahre danach — eine medico-soziale Analyse. Kongr. Bukarest 1964.

HOCHREIN, M., SCHLEICHER, J.: Die vegetative Dystonie beim Spätheimkehrer. Med. Klin. 50, 2017 u. 2057 (1955).

HÖSS, R.: Kommandant in Auschwitz. München 1963.

HOLTZMAN, W. H. et al.: Inkblot Perception and personality. Austin 1961.

HOPPE, K. D.: Verfolgung, Aggression und Depression. Psyche 16, 521 (1962).

HUK, B.: Reihenuntersuchung ehemaliger KZler. In: Gesundheitsschäden durch Verfolgung und Gefangenschaft und ihre Spätfolgen. Hrsg.: M. MICHEL. Frankfurt 1955.

KLEIN, H., ZELLERMAYER, J., SHANAN, J.: Former concentration camp inmates on a psychiatric ward. Arch. gen. Psychiat. 8, 334 (1963).

KLIMKOVA-DEUTSCHOVA, E.: Neurologische Beiträge zur Diagnostik und Therapie der Folgezustände des Krieges. Kongr. Lüttich 1961.

KOGON, E.: Der SS-Staat — Das System der deutschen Konzentrationslager. 5. Aufl. Berlin 1955.

KOLLE, K.: Die Opfer der nationalsozialistischen Verfolgung in psychiatrischer Sicht. Nervenarzt 29, 148 (1958).

KRAL, V. A.: Psychiatric observations under severe chronic stress. Amer. J. Psychiat. 108, 185 (1951).

KRYSTAL, H., NIEDERLAND, W. G.: Psychic sequelae in concentration camp survivors. Kongr. New York 1965, quoted from PAUL, H.: „Neuere Studien zum Thema." In: Psychische Spätschäden nach politischer Verfolgung. Hrsg.: H. PAUL und H.-J. HERBERG. 2. Aufl. Basel 1967.

LANGNER, F. S., MICHAEL, S. T.: Life Stress and Mental Health. London 1963.

LESNIAK, R., ORWID, M., SZYMUSIK, A., TEUTSCH, A.: Psychiatric studies of former prisoners of the Auschwitz concentration camp. International Congress of social Psychiatric. London 1964.

LEVINGER, L.: Psychiatrische Untersuchungen in Israel an 800 Fällen mit Gesundheitsschaden-Forderungen wegen Nazi-Verfolgung. Nervenarzt 33, 75 (1962).

LIENERT, G. A.: Verteilungsfreie Methoden in der Biostatistik. Meisenheim 1962.

LÖNNUM, A.: An analytical survey of the literature published on delayed effects of internment in concentration camps and their possible relation to the nervous system. Congr. Oslo 1960.

MATUSSEK, P.: Die Konzentrationslagerhaft als Belastungssituation. Nervenarzt 32, 538 (1961).

— Die Rückgliederung von Verfolgten — die Bewältigung ihres Schicksals. Therapiewoche, Bd. 13, Heft 22, 1109 (1963).

— Ideologie als Faktor der Persönlichkeit. Mitteilungen aus der Max-Planck-Gesellschaft z. F. d. W. Heft 2, 93 (1968).

MICHEL, M.: Gesundheitsschäden durch Verfolgung und Gefangenschaft und ihre Spätfolgen. Frankfurt 1955.

MINKOWSKI, E.: L'anaesthésie affective. Ann. méd.-psychol. 104, 80 (1946).

MÜLLER-HEGEMANN, D., SPITZNER, G.: Reihenuntersuchungen bei Verfolgten des Naziregimes — mit besonderer Berücksichtigung von Einzelhaftfolgen. Dtsch. Gesundh.-Wes. 18, 107 (1963).

PAUL, H.: Psychologische Untersuchungsergebnisse 15 Jahre nach der Verfolgung. In: Psychische Spätschäden nach politischer Verfolgung. Hrsg.: H. PAUL und H.-J. HERBERG. Basel 1963.

— HERBERG, H.-J.: Psychische Spätschäden nach politischer Verfolgung. Basel 1963.

PFISTER-AMENDE, M.: Zur Psychopathologie der Entwurzelung. Bull. schweiz. Akad. med. Wiss. **8**, 338 (1952).

RAUSCHNING, H.: Gespräche mit Hitler. Zürich-Wien-New York 1940.

RICHET, CH., DREYFUS, G., FICHEZ, L.-F., UZAN, H.: Die Folgeerscheinungen des physiologischen Elendszustandes. In: Gesundheitsschäden durch Verfolgung und Gefangenschaft und ihre Spätfolgen. Hrsg.: M. MICHEL. Frankfurt 1955.

— MANS, A.: Pathologie de la Déportation. Cannes 1958.

ROKEACH, M.: The open and closed mind. New York 1960.

ROSEN, B. C.: Race, ethnicity, and the achievement syndrome. Amer. soc. Rev. **24**, 47 (1959), quoted in HECKHAUSEN, H.: Hoffnung und Furcht in der Leistungsmotivation. Meisenheim 1963.

SEGELLE, P., ELLENBOGEN, R.: Fréquence et gravité des differentes affections et infirmités rencontrés chez les survivants des camps de concentration. Kopenhagen 1954.

SELYE, H.: Einführung in die Lehre vom Adaptationssyndrom. Stuttgart 1953.

SHUVAL, J. T.: Some persistent effects of Trauma: Five years after the Nazi Concentration Camps. Social Problems **5**, 230 (1957/58).

SPITZ, R.: Die Entstehung der ersten Objektbeziehungen. Stuttgart 1960.

Statist. Jahrbuch f. d. Bundesrepublik Deutschland.

STRAUS, E.: Diskussionsbemerkungen zu vorstehenden Beiträgen von W. v. BAEYER, P. MATUSSEK u. W. JACOB. Nervenarzt **32**, 551 (1961).

STRAUSS, H.: Besonderheiten der nichtpsychotischen Störungen bei Opfern der nationalsozialistischen Verfolgung und ihre Bedeutung bei der Begutachtung. Nervenarzt **28**, 344 (1957).

— Psychiatric disturbances in victims of racial persecution. In: Proc. of the Third World Congr. of Psychiatry. Montreal 1961.

STRÖM, A., EITINGER, L., GRÖNVIK, O., LÖNNUM, A., ENGESET, A., OSVIK, K., ROGAN, B.: Untersuchungen an norwegischen ehemaligen Konzentrationslagergefangenen. T. norske Lœgeform 13 (1961).

TANNER, J. M., MAXWELL, J.: The psychological symptoms and the physiological response to exercise of repatriated prisoners of war with neurosis. J. Neurol. Neurosurg. Psychiat. **2**, 233 (1948).

TARGOWLA, R.: Syndrom der Asthenie der Deportierten. In: Gesundheitsschäden durch Verfolgung und Gefangenschaft und ihre Spätschäden. Hrsg.: M. MICHEL. Frankfurt 1955.

TAUSCH, R., TAUSCH, A.: Pädagogische Psychologie. Göttingen 1965.

THAYSEN, E. H., THAYSEN, J. H.: Medizinische Probleme bei ehemaligen Gefangenen deutscher Konzentrationslager. In: Gesundheitsschäden durch Verfolgung und Gefangenschaft und ihre Spätschäden. Hrsg.: M. MICHEL. Frankfurt 1955.

TRAUTMANN, E. C.: Psychiatrische Untersuchungen an Überlebenden der nationalsozialistischen Vernichtungslager 15 Jahre nach der Befreiung. Nervenarzt **32**, 545 (1961).

UTITZ, E.: Psychologie des Lebens im Konzentrationslager Theresienstadt. Wien 1948.

VENZLAFF, U.: Die psychoreaktiven Störungen nach entschädigungspflichtigen Ereignissen. (D. sog. Unfallneurosen.) Berlin-Göttingen-Heidelberg 1958.

— Grundsätzliche Betrachtungen über die Begutachtung erlebnisbedingter seelischer Störungen nach rassischer und politischer Verfolgung. Wiedergutm. Beil. d. allg. Wochenzeitung der Juden in Deutschland (1960).

VEROFF, J., FELD, SH. C., GURIN, G.: Achievement motivation and religious background. Amer. sociol. Rev. **27**, 205 (1962).

VIC DUPONT, FICHEZ, L.-F., WEINSTEIN, S.: Die Tuberkulose bei den Deportierten. In: Gesundheitsschäden durch Verfolgung und Gefangenschaft und ihre Spätschäden. Hrsg.: M. MICHEL. Frankfurt 1955.

ZERBIN-RÜDIN, E.: Endogene Psychosen. In: Hdb. d. Humangenetik, Bd. V. Hrsg.: P. E. BECKER. Stuttgart 1967.

Subject Index

Uprooting and After

Editors: C. Zwingmann,
M. Pfister-Ammende

42 tables, 16 figures. XI, 361 pages.
1973
ISBN 3-540-05516-9 Cloth DM 60,80
ISBN 0-387-05516-9 (North America)
Cloth US $22.50

The present volume summarizes research
in the areas of uprooting and resettlement. This is followed by carefully
chosen examples of sociopsychological
filed work with resettlement groups in
the various nations. This form of presentation provides an inner continuity in
a field of study and research which by
its nature is multidisciplinary and
transcultural.

To Life and To Die:
When, Why, and How

Editor: R.H. Williams

20 figures. XIX, 346 pages. 1973
ISBN 3-540-06220-3 Cloth DM 35,—
ISBN 0-387-06220-3 (North America)
Cloth US $12.95
Soft cover edition:
ISBN 0-387-90097-7 (North America)
US $5.90

In this book distinguished contributors
address themselves to the problem of
living and dying in our advanced techno-
logical society. Developments in science
and medicine, population density, new
lifestyles and the erosion of criminal
justice have called traditional standards
of morality into question and led many
to seek new value systems for a rapidly
changing society. A number of concepts
discussed in this book run counter to
religious tenets and existing laws and
are the subject of heated debate among
laymen, as well as within professional
communities.

Scientists in Search
of Their Conscience

Proceedings of a Symposium on "The
Impact of Science on Society",
organized by The European Committee
of The Weizmann Institute of Science,
Brussels, June 28 - 29, 1971
Editors: A.R. Michaelis, H. Harvey
With contributions by numerous experts.

18 figures. XIII, 230 pages. 1973
ISBN 3-540-06026-X Cloth DM 46,—
ISBN 0-387-06026-X (North America)
Cloth US $18.90

This symposium, organized by the
European Committee of the Weizmann
Institute of Israel, debates the responsibility of scientists for the uses to
which society puts their findings.

Sir J.C. Eccles
Facing Reality

Philosophical Adventures by a Brain
Scientist

36 figures. XI, 210 pages. 1970
(Heidelberg Science Library, Vol. 13)
ISBN 3-540-90014-4 DM 25,—
ISBN 0-387-90014-4 (North America)
US $6.70

Distribution rights for U.K., Great
Britain, and the Traditional British
Market: English Universities Press Ltd.,
London

The title of the book refers to personal
reality and the book is concerned with
the attempt of each person to face up
to his own personal existence as a
unique conscious self, recognizing at
the same time how dependent this is
upon the functioning of his brain and
on his evolutionary origin.

Prices are subject to change without
notice

Springer-Verlag
Berlin Heidelberg New York

E.W. Straus, M. Natanson, H. Ey
Psychiatry and Philosophy
Editor: M. Natanson
XII, 161 pages. 1969
Contributions are taken from
"Psychiatrie der Gegenwart" 1/2.
Translator: E. Eng, S.C. Kennedy
ISBN 3-540-04726-3
Cloth DM 36,–
ISBN 0-387-04726-3
(North America) Cloth US $14.60

The main objective of the book
is to present theoretical analyses
of psychiatric themes (the concept
of disease and especially of
psychosis, communication between
fellow-men, and the larger hori-
zons of therapy and understanding)
from a broad phenomenological
standpoint.

Brain and Human Behavior
Editors: A.G. Karczmar,
J.C. Eccles
162 figures. XI, 475 pages. 1972
ISBN 3-540-05331-X
Cloth DM 98,–
ISBN 0-387-05331-X
(North America) Cloth US $32.10

The neuromolecules, the neurons,
the neuronal systems, the
organism and its social and genetic
interplays — these are the various
levels that this book deals with.
The pertinent discussion by
20 authorities, including three
Nobel Prize winners, leads on to
the challenging query of the philosophical implications of the subject.

Progress in Behaviour Therapy
Volume 1
Chief Editor: J.C. Brengelmann
Editors Volume 1:
J.T. Quinn, P.J. Graham,
J.J.M. Harbison, H. McAllister
In preparation

Social Psychiatry /
Sozialpsychiatrie /
Psychiatrie Sociale
Editors: S. Fleck, H. Häfner,
N. Kreitman (Editor-in-Chief),
C. Müller

Sample copies as well as
subscription and back-volume
information available upon
request

Please address:

Springer-Verlag
Werbeabteilung 4021
D 1000 Berlin 33
Heidelberger Platz 3

or

Springer-Verlag
Promotion Department
175 Fifth Avenue
New York, N.Y. 10010

Prices are subject to change
without notice

Springer-Verlag
Berlin
Heidelberg
New York